Deductive Databases and Logic Programming

SUBRATA KUMAR DAS

Queen Mary and Westfield College, University of London

ADDISON-WESLEY PUBLISHING COMPANY

Wokingham, England · Reading, Massachusetts · Menlo Park, California · New York · Don Mills, Ontario · Amsterdam · Bonn · Sydney · Singapore · Tokyo · Madrid · San Juan · Milan · Paris · Mexico City · Seoul · Taipei

Cover designed by Hybert Design & Type, Maidenhead
and printed by The Riverside Printing Co. (Reading) Ltd.
Camera-ready copy prepared by the author
Printed in Great Britain at the University Press, Cambridge

First printed 1992.

ISBN 0-201-56897-7

British Library Cataloguing in Publication Data
A catalogue record for this book is available from the British Library

Library of Congress Cataloguing in Publication Data available

In memory of my sister KABITA

International Series in Logic Programming

Other Titles in the Series

Parallel Logic Programming in PARLOG: The Language and its Implementation Steve Gregory

Programming in PARLOG Tom Conlon

Advanced Prolog: Techniques and Examples Peter Ross

Logic Programming: Systematic Program Development
Yves Deville

Preface

The book

In the past two decades enormous growth has been observed in the fields of logic programming and deductive databases. These fields are closely related and in many respects their study can be made from a single point of view. The principal objectives of this book are two-fold. The first is to cover in a systematic and intensive manner the theoretical foundations common to both logic programming and deductive databases and the second is to focus more specifically on selected theoretical and practical aspects of deductive databases. This book is self-contained, providing a comprehensive presentation of the background material in the early chapters with definitions, theorems and their proofs, algorithms and program code are included wherever they are relevant.

Readership

This book may be used as a textbook for graduate courses and as a reference book for researchers in universities. The interested reader in academic computer science may also read it to his/her advantage while computer professionals in commerce and industries will find the book useful as a vehicle for moving towards a new generation of databases and programming concepts.

Contents

The book is divided into five parts: the Introduction (Chapter 1), Background Material (Chapters 2–4), Logic Programming (Chapters 5–9), Deductive Databases (Chapters 10–16) and the Conclusion (Chapter 17).

PART I – Introduction
Chapter 1 presents the history of the development of logic programming and deductive databases. It also provides an informal overview of the main areas covered in the rest of the book. This overview will help beginners to use the book in a systematic fashion.

PART II – Background Material

Chapters 2, 3 and 4 provide a comprehensive presentation of background material.

Chapter 2 introduces some mathematical concepts including, sets, relations, functions, graphs, trees and fixpoint.

Chapter 3 presents different aspects of mathematical logic including propositional and first-order predicate logic, Skolemization, prenex normal form, first-order theory with equality, the soundness and completeness theorem, the compactness theorem, the Löwenheim and Skolem theorem and Herbrand's theorem. This chapter provides the major theoretical foundation of the main material in the book.

Chapter 4 covers resolution theorem proving which is the immediate predecessor of both logic programming and deductive databases. The concept of unification, the unification algorithm, unification theorem and the resolution theorem are discussed in detail. Some of the well-known refinements of the resolution method are presented including set of support, unit resolution, input resolution, linear resolution and SL-resolution.

PART III – Logic Programming

This part presents the common theoretical foundations of logic programming and deductive databases using logic programming terminology. The logic programming language Prolog is also presented.

Chapter 5 introduces the concepts of logic programming and declarative programming. Clauses and programs are categorized and the concepts of the three common semantics of logic programs (declarative, procedural and fixpoint) are described in detail. The concepts of the semantics for negation are also described.

Chapter 6 deals with different aspects of definite logic programs. This chapter includes a description of minimal model and fixpoint semantics of definite programs and then investigates SLD-resolution and its soundness and completeness results. The closed world assumption and the negation as failure rule are introduced in this chapter and their use in inferring negative information from definite programs is explained.

Chapter 7 is about normal programs. The declarative semantics of normal programs is studied by means of several proposals including completed program semantics, perfect model semantics and well-founded model semantics. Particular attention is given to stratified normal programs. Several procedural semantics for normal programs are discussed including SLDNF-resolution. The soundness and completeness results of the SLDNF-resolution with respect to completed program semantics are also provided in this chapter. Extended normal programs are described to enhance the expressive power of normal programs.

Chapter 8 focuses on disjunctive as well as general programs. A generalized fixpoint operator is defined for disjunctive programs. The minimal model semantics and SLI-resolution are introduced to study declarative and procedural semantics respectively for disjunctive programs. A number of rules for inferring negative information are studied. These include the disjunctive database rule and the generalized closed world assumption and its extensions. Perfect model semantics and semantics by possible forms are studied to handle the class of general programs. Finally, circumscription is presented to give semantics for negative information in an arbitrary set of first-order formulae as a program.

Chapter 9 presents Prolog which is the most widely known logic programming language. Prolog's theoretical background is established in connection with resolution theorem proving. Different Prolog programming techniques are discussed by means of a number of examples. The extralogical features of Prolog and meta-programming in Prolog are also discussed.

PART IV – Deductive Databases

This part focuses specifically on selected theoretical and practical aspects of deductive databases.

Chapter 10 introduces the deductive database model and its model-theoretic and proof-theoretic views. A number of differences are observed between deductive database systems and logic programming systems and a connection is established to allow deductive databases to be viewed as logic programs. This facilitates theoretical studies on deductive databases by treating them as logic programs.

Chapter 11 concerns query evaluation in deductive database systems, currently an active area of research. A number of basic characteristics of the process of query evaluation is established. Techniques are introduced based on both top-down resolution based techniques (such as SLD-AL resolution) and bottom-up techniques (such as magic sets).

Chapter 12 is about integrity constraints in deductive databases. Various aspects of integrity constraints including definition, classification, formal representation, verification and satisfiability are discussed in this chapter.

Chapter 13 deals with some methods for checking integrity constraints in deductive databases. The efficient handling of integrity constraints in deductive databases is an important issue and a number of methods have been proposed in the past few years to serve this purpose. Some of the well-known methods for checking the static non-aggregate kind of integrity constraints in normal deductive databases are described and a comparative evaluation of these approaches is given.

Chapter 14 presents different architectures for deductive database systems including loose coupling, tight coupling and integration. By constructing a prototype deductive database system on top of a Prolog interpreter a practical demonstration of the closeness of logic programming and deductive databases is given. The core Prolog code of a prototype capable of evaluating queries using the magic sets technique and SLDNF-resolution and with the ability to impose and verify integrity constraints is presented and discussed.

Chapter 15 covers the aspects of parallelism relevant to deductive databases. The efficient processing of queries in deductive databases is now an active area of research and the exploitation of parallelism is one way to achieve this goal. The two main parallel architectures, shared nothing and shared everything, are presented and a technique for evaluating queries on shared nothing architectures is described.

Chapter 16 returns to the topic of integrity constraints and formalizes both aggregate and transitional constraints. Aggregate constraints are represented by a number of aggregate predicates. It is shown that transitional constraints can be handled in the same way as static ones.

PART V – Conclusion

Chapter 17 provides additional references for the areas covered in the text and brief introductions to some other important areas of research in the fields of logic programming and deductive databases. The areas discussed include typed, meta-level and higher order extension of logic programming and deductive databases.

Guide to reading this book

Readers who are new to the subjects of logic programming and deductive databases are advised not to skip the first chapter which includes an informal overview. The beginner should not be dismayed by the use of some unfamiliar terminologies in this chapter as these will be introduced in later chapters. However, an overall understanding of this chapter will prevent the reader from becoming lost later in reading the book.

Readers who have been reasonably exposed to the subjects of mathematical logic and theorem proving may omit the background part of the book. The chapters relevant to deductive databases deal mainly with their definite forms. Therefore, those who intend to emphasize deductive databases for this class of databases can skip Chapter 8 and most of Chapter 7. Readers without prior knowledge of the theory of logic programming should study carefully Chapter 9.

The last section of each chapter is a collection of exercises. Few of these exercises establish any new results. Instead they verify established results and allow the reader to work through various procedures. Most readers will find the majority straightforward. Note that some exercises required to establish other results are contained within the main text at appropriate places (in the form of lemmas, theorems, and so on) to maintain the flow of reading.

Conventions

In general, the following conventions are followed for symbols representing terms, clauses, sets, and so on:

- Variables: italicized lower case letters x, y, z, ..., x_1, y_1, z_1, ...
- Constant symbols: italicized lower case letters a, b, c, ..., a_1, b_1, c_1, ... or an italicized string starting with an upper case letter, for example, *Daniel*, *Mathematics*.
- Function symbols: italicized lower case letters f, g, h,..., f_1, g_1,... or an italicized string starting with an upper case letter, for example, *Succ*.
- Predicate symbols: italicized upper case letters P, Q, R, P_1, Q_1, R_1, ... or an italicized string starting with an upper case letter, for example, *Even*, *Employee*.
- Atoms or literals: italicized upper case letters A, B, L, M, ..., A_1, B_1, L_1, M_1, ...
- Formulae or goals or clauses: roman upper case letters A, C, F, G, ..., A_1, C_1, F_1, G_1, ...
- Sets: bold roman upper case letters **A**, **P**, **S**, ..., $\mathbf{A}_1$, $\mathbf{P}_1$, $\mathbf{S}_1$, ...
- Special sets: Zapf Chancery typeface string starting with an upper case letter, for example, *Pos*, *Comp*(**P**), *HB*(**P**), *GCWA*(**P**), ...
- Prolog program code: Courier typeface, for example,

```
append([], L, L).
append([X|L1], L2, [X|L3]):-append(L1, L2, L3).
```

New terminology is highlighted on its first use through the use of italics. Lemmas, theorems, figures are numbered by chapter.

Acknowledgements

I wholeheartedly thank my wife Janique for her love, patience and inspiration throughout the preparation of this book. My sincere thanks go to Steven Salvini, Heriot-Watt University, Edinburgh for his careful reading of the first draft. I would also like to thank my colleagues and supervisor at the Heriot-Watt University for providing me with a good environment during my doctoral as well as postdoctoral research which inspired me to write this book. Thanks to Addison-Wesley, especially Simon Plumtree, Stephen Bishop, Susan Keany and Lynne Balfe, for their help in producing the book from the beginning. Special thanks are due to the two anonymous reviewers who made a number of technical as well as stylistic suggestions. Finally, I thank my parents, brothers, sisters and other family members back home in my village of Patuli in Burdwan, WB, India for patiently accepting my absence and showing their encouragement through their many letters.

This book is largely based on the work of several researchers and I express my gratitude to those who have directly or indirectly contributed so much to the fields of logic programming and deductive databases. I have made my best effort to make this book informative, readable and free from mistakes and I would welcome any criticism or suggestions for improvements.

Subrata Kumar Das
Edinburgh
May 1992

Contents

PART I

Introduction

1

History and overview

This chapter presents a brief history of the development of logic programming and deductive databases and examines their roots in mathematical logic. This is followed by an informal overview of the main areas covered in the remainder of the text.

1.1 History

Mathematical logic has a history (Church *et al.*, 1978; Jørgensen, 1931; Nidditch, 1962) of more than two thousand years. Aristotle's (384–322 BC) theory of *syllogistic* reasoning in ancient times was the foundation and the early growth of mathematical logic (Church, 1952; Hodges, 1988; Kleene, 1967). Syllogism (Keynes, 1928) is a theory of particular kind of implication with two conditions and one outcome. The work of Megarian, Stoic and Philo on the *logic of statement connection* (particularly on if–then type connections), at about the same period as Aristotle, also influenced the development of modern mathematical logic. From then until the seventeenth century little of any real significance happened in the field of mathematical logic.

Modern mathematical logic then began with the work of Descartes (1596–1650) and Leibniz (1646–1716) on what was called a *universal language*, a general calculus for reasoning. Two hundred years later, Boole's (1815–1864) work on the *mathematical analysis of logic* (Boole, 1948) was an important step towards changing Aristotle's syllogistic reasoning. This involved the development of a logic based on algebra. This body of work forms the basis of one of the two main aspects of mathematical logic, namely the *mathematics of logic*. Boole's algebra was subsequently modified and enriched by the work of several logicians and mathematicians. This included Jevon's (1835–1882) *deductive theory*, Peirce's (1839–1914) *quantifier theory*, Schroeder's (1841–1902) *algebra of logic*,

Whitehead's (1861–1947) *universal algebra* and Huntington's (1874–1952) *second-order theory*.

Turning to the other side of mathematical logic, the *logic of mathematics* is based mainly on work on the axiom systems and arithmetic by Frege (1848–1925), Cantor (1845–1914) and Peano (1858–1932). The three-volume *Principia Mathematica* (1910, 1912, 1913) by Whitehead and Russell (1925–1927) united these two aspects of logic and formed an important landmark in the history of mathematical logic.

After *Principia Mathematica*, important developments in the 1920s and 1930s were the works of Post, Hilbert, Ackerman and Gödel on the consistency and completeness of the *Principia Mathematica* axiom system, followed by contributions from Brourer and Gödel in proving the incompleteness of arithmetic. The *theory of computability* (Boolos and Jeffrey, 1988; Cohen, 1989) arose from an important branch of mathematical logic called *recursive function theory* (Goodstein, 1971; Kleene, 1967), together with its relation to machines and *mechanical* or *automated theorem proving* (Chang and Lee, 1973; Gallier, 1987; Loveland, 1978; Prawitz, 1969). The development of machines and mechanical theorem proving started in the 1930s and was largely due to the work of Gödel, Skolem, Church, Kleene, Turing, Herbrand and Löwenheim. Herbrand proposed a very important mechanical method (Herbrand, 1930, 1931) to prove theorems and this was to provide the basis for most modern automated theorem proving procedures.

The *resolution theorem proving* method was developed by Robinson (1965b). This approach avoided the major combinatorial obstacle to efficiency inherent in earlier theorem proving procedures (Davis and Putnam, 1960; Gilmore, 1960) based on Herbrand's fundamental theorem concerning first-order logic. Robinson's theorem proving scheme was based on a sole inference rule called the *resolution principle*. The basic idea of the resolution principle is to derive a new sentence from two parent sentences using the concept of *unification*. The resolution theorem proving method is a *refutation* method and is *complete* in the sense that given an unsatisfiable set of sentences, it will always arrive at a contradiction. Many variants of the resolution method have been proposed (Blausius *et al.*, 1981; Chang, 1970; Chang and Lee, 1973; Kowalski, 1975; Kowalski and Kuehner, 1971; Loveland, 1969; Robinson, 1965a, 1979; Stickel, 1988) to improve its efficiency by reducing the search space for the refutation. Many of these variants have been adopted in the field of logic programming.

Logic programming (Deville, 1990; Elcock, 1988; Gallaire, 1986; Hogger, 1984; Kowalski, 1979a, 1979b, 1985; Lloyd, 1987; Tarnlund, 1977; Thayse, 1988) is an offshoot of earlier work in mechanical theorem proving. In fact, resolution theorem proving forms the basis of most current logic programming systems. The principal idea behind logic programming is the use of mathematical logic as a programming language. This was introduced by Kowalski (1974) in the early 1970s and was made practical by Colmerauer through the implementation (Roussel, 1975) of the first logic programming language, PROLOG (PROgramming in LOGic) (Colmerauer *et al.*, 1973). For his formalization Kowalski considered a subset of first-order logic called *Horn clause logic.* A clause or sentence in this logic may have multiple positive conditions but only one or no positive conclusion.

In the procedural interpretation of logic programming (Kowalski, 1974; van Emden and Kowalski, 1976) each Horn sentence with one positive conclusion is considered as a procedure declaration for the conclusion and a set of such procedure declarations forms a program. Computation starts from an initial goal statement which is a Horn sentence with a null conclusion. It then proceeds to derive a sequence of goal statements until a halt statement (an empty clause) is reached. Each goal statement is derived by applying the resolution principle to the previous goal and any other procedure. Given a single goal statement several procedure declarations can have a name which matches the selected procedure call from the goal and hence this use of predicate logic as a programming language is *non-deterministic.*

The restriction of using Horn logic as a programming language naturally reduces the complexity of finding solutions through refutation. Extensive research has been carried out in a number of different branches of logic programming including handling sentences with negative premises (Apt *et al.*, 1988; Barbuti and Martelli, 1986; Cavedon and Lloyd, 1989; Clark, 1978; Fitting and Ben-Jacob, 1988; Ross, 1989; Chan, 1988; Gabby and Sergot, 1986; Reiter, 1978b; Shepherdson, 1984), declarative and procedural (or operational or proof procedure) semantics (Gelfond and Lifschitz, 1988; Jaffar *et al.*, 1983; Kunen, 1991; Przymusinski, 1988b; Ross, 1989; Van Emden and Kowalski, 1976; van Gelder *et al.*, 1988), extension to full first-order logic (Lobo *et al.*, 1988; Minker, 1988a; Ross and Topor, 1988), extension to higher order logics (Miller and Nadathur, 1986), study of mathematical properties (Maher, 1986; Mancarella and Pedreschi, 1988) and different applications of logic programs.

According to Kowalski (1979b), an algorithm can be regarded as consisting of a *logic component* which defines the logic of the algorithm, and a *control component* which specifies the manner in which the logic component is used to solve the problem. The logic component determines the meaning of the algorithm and the control component affects only the efficiency. An ideal logic programming language is purely *declarative.* In a declarative programming environment a programmer need specify only the logic component of an algorithm, leaving the control component of the algorithm to the system itself. Substantial effort is being spent in making present-day logic programming more declarative in nature.

The *deductive database* concept (Gallaire, 1983; Gallaire *et al.*, 1978, 1981a, 1981b, 1983, 1984; Gallaire and Minker, 1978; Minker, 1988b; Thayse, 1989) is an extension of work by Green (1969a, 1969b) for his question–answer system. From the theoretical point of view, deductive databases can be regarded as logic programs which generalize the concept of *relational databases* (Brodie and Manola, 1989; Codd, 1970; Date, 1986; Gardarin and Valduriez, 1989; Ullman, 1984). However, for all practical purposes, deductive database systems deal with sentences which are less complex than those generally dealt with by logic programming systems. Also, the number of *rules* (sentences with non-empty conditions) in a typical deductive database system is much less than the number of *facts* (sentences with empty condition). Another point of contrast is that logic programming systems emphasize functionalities while deductive database systems emphasise efficiency. Consequently, inference mechanisms used in deductive database systems to compute answers are less general than those in logic programming systems.

In addition to expressing databases sentences using logic, *queries* and *integrity constraints* may also be so expressed. Queries are equivalent to goals in the context of logic programming, while integrity constraints (Das, 1990; Date, 1985 Eswaran and Chamberlin, 1975; Fernandez *et al.*, 1981; Nicolas and Yazdanian 1978; Reiter, 1981; Ullman, 1984) are properties that the data of a database is required to satisfy. Query evaluation (Bancilhon and Ramakrishnan, 1989; Ceri *et al.*, 1990; Chandra, 1988; Chang, 1981) and integrity constraints' maintenance are two major aspects of deductive databases. Many query evaluation techniques (Bancilhon *et al.*, 1986; Lozinski, 1985; Vieille, 1986) and a number of integrity constraint verification algorithms (Asirelli *et al.*, 1985; Das and Williams, 1989a; Decker, 1986; Kowalski *et al.*, 1987; Lloyd and Topor, 1985) have been developed in deductive database contexts. Algorithms are also being developed for processing deductive database queries on parallel architectures (Das, 1991c; Ganguly *et al.*, 1990; Hulin, 1989; Kanellakis, 1986; van Gelder, 1986; Wolfson and Ozeri, 1990; Wolfson and Silberschatz, 1988).

Figure 1.1 illustrates some of the important landmarks in the development of logic programming and deductive databases.

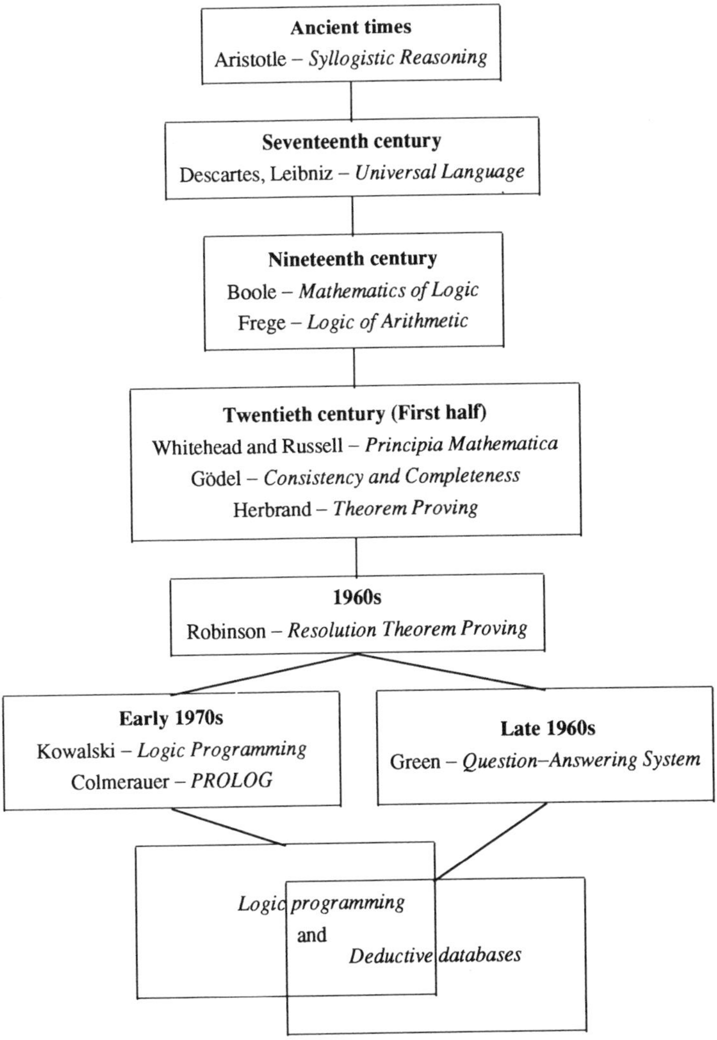

Figure 1.1 Important landmarks in the development of logic programming and deductive databases.

1.2 An informal overview

Mathematical logic is a systematic study of valid arguments using the notions of mathematics. An *argument* consists of certain statements (or propositions or sentences), called *premises*, from which another statement, called the *conclusion*, follows. Consider the following example of an argument.

Argument 1.1

Every undergraduate student sat the final examination. (Premise)
Daniel is an undergraduate student. (Premise)
Therefore, Daniel sat the final examination. (Conclusion)

In the above argument, the first two statements are premises, respectively *conditional* and *assertional*, and the third statement is the conclusion. 'Therefore' is a sign of argument. The above argument is a valid argument. Often arguments are advanced without stating all the premises as is evident from the following example.

Argument 1.2

Daniel has failed the final examination twice.
Therefore, Daniel will be sent down.

The above is not a valid argument as the premise does not imply that if a student fails the final examination twice, the particular student will be sent down. Again, consider the following example which has an incomplete premise.

Argument 1.3

Daniel is either an undergraduate or a postgraduate student.
Christelle is a postgraduate student.
Therefore, Daniel is a postgraduate student.

The premise of the above argument does not definitely say that Daniel is a postgraduate student. Hence it is an invalid argument.

A *valid argument* has the property that the conclusion must be true whenever the premise(s) is (are) true. Consider the following example of a valid argument.

Argument 1.4

Every research student stays on the university campus.
Daniel does not stay on the university campus.
Therefore, Daniel is not a research student.

Although the above argument is valid, it is not known if Daniel is staying on the university campus. Therefore the validity of an argument is neither concerned with the subject matter nor with the truth or falsehood of the premises and conclusion.

Mathematical logic does not study the truth or falsehood of the statements in the premises and conclusion but rather studies whether or not the truth of the premises implies the truth of the conclusion.

Valid arguments are studied independently of the fields from which arguments are drawn. This is achieved by expressing valid arguments in their *logical form* or *symbolized form*. The second premise of Argument 1.1, which is a (*positive*) *assertional premise*, is symbolized as

$$Undergraduate\,(Daniel) \tag{1.1}$$

where the expression $Undergraduate\,(x)$ is used to represent 'x is an undergraduate student'. The first premise of Argument 1.1, which is a *conditional premise*, is symbolized as

$$\forall x\ (Undergraduate\,(x) \rightarrow Examination\,(x)) \tag{1.2}$$

where the expression $Examination\,(x)$ denotes 'x sat the final examination' and the symbols '$\forall$' and '$\rightarrow$' are read as 'for all' (or 'for every') and 'implies' respectively. The expression $Undergraduate\,(x)$ which appears on the left of the symbol '$\rightarrow$' in the above conditional premise is treated as the *antecedent* of the premise. The expression following the symbol is the *consequent*. With the help of (1.1) and (1.2), Argument 1.1 is symbolized as

$$\forall x\ (Undergraduate\,(x) \rightarrow Examination\,(x)),\ Undergraduate\,(Daniel) \vdash Examination\,(Daniel) \tag{1.3}$$

where '$\vdash$' means 'therefore'. The symbolized premises appear on the left of the symbol '$\vdash$' and are separated by commas.

The above symbolization is within the framework of *first-order logic* and using the premises of (1.3), an *axiomatic deduction* of the conclusion of the Argument 1.1 is as follows.

Derivation 1.1

Step 1: $\forall x\ (Undergraduate\,(x) \rightarrow Examination\,(x))$	(Premise or axiom)
Step 2: $Undergraduate\,(Daniel)$	(Premise or axiom)
Step 3: $Undergraduate\,(Daniel) \rightarrow Examination\,(Daniel)$	(Step 1, particularization)
Step 4: $Examination\,(Daniel)$	(Steps 2 and 3, modus ponens)

The premises in steps 1 and 2 are considered as *proper axioms*. The above deduction is a *proof* of the conclusion *Examination* (*Daniel*) and hence a *theorem* follows from the first-order system with the two proper axioms. Step 3 is derived from step 1 by particularization of the first premise. If the first premise is true for all students, then it is also true for the student Daniel. Step 4 is arrived at by the application of an *inference rule* of first-order logic, called *modus ponens*. Modus ponens states that given $A \rightarrow B$ and A are true then it follows that B is true, where A and B are arbitrary sentences. This demonstrates the theorem proving approach.

In contrast to the theorem proving approach, resolution theorem proving is based on the refutation principle. This states that if a set of premises is inconsistent then there must be a refutation. Based on this principle, in the context of Argument 1.1, it must be assumed that the negation of the conclusion

Daniel did not sit in the final examination

is also as a premise. The symbolized form of this premise is

$$\neg\, Examination\,(Daniel) \tag{1.4}$$

where '¬' is read as 'not'. As this assumption is inconsistent with the other two premises, a refutation will result. To do this, first the symbolized premises are converted to their equivalent *clausal form*. In this example the assertional premises are already in clausal form while the first premise can be converted to clausal form to give

$$\forall x\,(\neg\, Undergraduate\,(x) \vee Examination\,(x)) \tag{1.5}$$

where '∨' is read as 'or'. A sentences in clausal form is normally written by removing $\forall x$-type signs from its front and these are assumed by default. Following this convention, clausal form (1.5) can be rewritten as

$$\neg\, Undergraduate\,(x) \vee Examination\,(x) \tag{1.6}$$

According to (1.6), the first premise of Argument 1.1 can now be read as

Every student is either not an undergraduate student or else sat the final examination

which is the same as the original form of the first premise in Argument 1.1. The steps of the refutation of Argument 1.1 are given below.

Derivation 1.2

Step 1: $\neg$ *Undergraduate* $(x) \vee$ *Examination* (x)	(Premise)
Step 2: *Undergraduate* (*Daniel*)	(Premise)
Step 3: $\neg$ *Examination* (*Daniel*)	(Daniel did not sit the examination)
Step 4: $\neg$ *Undergraduate* (*Daniel*)	(Steps 1 and 3, resolution principle)
Step 5: □	(Steps 2 and 4, resolution principle)

The complement *Examination* (*Daniel*) of the atomic premise in step 3 of Derivation 1.2 and a subexpression *Examination* (x) of the premise in step 1 can be made equal by a *most general unification* $\{x/Daniel\}$, that is, by substituting *Daniel* in place of x. The expression $\neg$ *Undergraduate* (*Daniel*) is then obtained by applying the *resolution principle* to steps 1 and 3. This means applying most general unifiers to both expressions and then merging and cancelling the complementary expressions. To complete Derivation 1.2, the resolution principle can be applied again to steps 2 and 4. After cancelling the complementary atomic expressions the resultant expression is empty and hence a refutation of the argument has been arrived at ('□' denotes a refutation). This shows that the assumption in step 3 is wrong and therefore its complement is true, that is, Daniel sat the final examination.

Let us now look at how resolution theorem proving applies to logic programming. A *logic program* is a set of premises (conditional or assertional) called the *procedures* (or *statement*) of the program. The premises of Argument 1.1 in the form of a logic program are given in Program 1.1.

Program 1.1

Examination $(x) \leftarrow$ *Undergraduate* (x)
Undergraduate (*Daniel*)

where the symbol '$\leftarrow$' is just a notational variance of '$\rightarrow$' and has been adopted in logic programming for the sake of readability. Again, '$\forall x$' is assumed by default at the front of the conditional premise in Program 1.1. The expression on the right of the symbol '$\leftarrow$' in a conditional assertion is its *antecedent* or *body* and the expression on the left is its *consequent* or *head*. The head is therefore the name of a procedure with a set of input and output parameters.

Computation in a logic program starts from a negative premise, called the *goal*, and proceeds to derive a sequence of intermediate goals before reaching a halt statement. Each goal statement is derived by applying the resolution principle to the previous goal and a procedure. The fact that Daniel sat the final examination is an implicit assertion in the program and if the goal is to prove this assertion then its *SLD-derivation* is as follows.

Derivation 1.3

Step 1: $Examination(x) \leftarrow Undergraduate(x)$	(Conditional premise)
Step 2: $Undergraduate(Daniel)$	(Assertional premise)
Step 3: $\leftarrow Examination(Daniel)$	(Goal)
Step 4: $\leftarrow Undergraduate(Daniel)$	(Resolving goal with the conditional premise)
Step 5: $\Box$	(Resolving step 4 with the assertional premise)

The goal from step 4 is the resolvent of the original goal from step 3 and the only conditional premise in the program. The halt statement (empty goal) in step 5 is the resolvent of the goal from step 4 and the only assertion in the program. Steps 3, 4 and 5 of the above procedure correspond to steps 3, 4 and 5 respectively of the resolution theorem proving method in Derivation 1.2.

More complex forms of conditional assertions are allowed in a logic program. For example, the conditional assertion

A student who is not a research student sat the final examination

can be symbolized as

$$Examination(x) \leftarrow Student(x) \wedge \neg Research(x) \tag{1.7}$$

where the expression $Research(x)$ is used to mean 'x is a research student'. Even more complex forms of conditional assertion with multiple conclusions may arise, for example,

A student who is not a research student is either an undergraduate or a postgraduate student

This can be symbolized as

$$Undergraduate(x) \vee Postgraduate(x) \leftarrow Student(x) \wedge \neg Research(x) \quad (1.8)$$

These more complex conditional statements allow negation in their bodies unlike those in Program 1.1. The logic programming language PROLOG cannot cope directly with the more complex statements such as (1.8).

Negative assertions are not normally stored explicitly in a logic program. Instead they are deduced by proving the absence of their complementary positive assertions from the program. For example, a symbolized representation of the conditional premise of Argument 1.4, together with the second premise of the argument in the form of a logic program is given in Program 1.2.

Program 1.2

$Campus(x) \leftarrow Research(x)$
$Undergraduate(Daniel)$

where $Campus(x)$ means 'x is staying in the campus'. Failure to prove implicit or explicit presence of the assertional premises $Campus(Daniel)$ and $Research(Daniel)$ in the program will imply that Daniel is neither a research student nor does he stay on the university campus.

Presence or absence of an assertion in a logic program is inferred by studying the meaning or *declarative semantics* of the program. The only assertional premise which has been explicitly stated is $Undergraduate(Daniel)$. Although the assertional premise $Examination(Daniel)$ has not been stated explicitly, its presence can be assumed due the presence of $Undergraduate(Daniel)$ and the conditional premise $Examination(x) \leftarrow Undergraduate(x)$. No other assertional premise can be assumed, therefore, the semantics of Program 1.1 can be given by the set

$$\{Undergraduate(Daniel), Examination(Daniel)\}$$

which is its *minimal model*. The semantics explains that except for Daniel, there are no other undergraduate students and also that no other students sat the final examination. Consider another student, Christelle, who is staying on the university campus. The corresponding assertion $Campus(Christelle)$ is added to Program 1.1 resulting in Program 1.3.

Program 1.3

$$Examination\,(x) \leftarrow Undergraduate\,(x)$$
$$Undergraduate\,(Daniel)$$
$$Campus\,(Christelle)$$

The semantics of Program 1.3 is given by its minimal model $\{Undergraduate\,(Daniel),\ Examination\,(Daniel),\ Campus\,(Christelle)\}$. From this it can be seen that Daniel does not stay on the university campus and that Christelle is neither an undergraduate student nor did she appear in the examination. The applicability of this kind of semantics to statements such as (1.7) or (1.8) is unclear. Consider the following symbolization of Argument 1.3 as a logic program.

Program 1.4

$$Undergraduate\,(Daniel) \lor Postgraduate\,(Daniel)$$
$$Postgraduate\,(Christelle)$$

Here one can assume neither that 'Daniel is not an undergraduate student' nor that 'Daniel is not a postgraduate student'. However, one can assume that 'Christelle is not an undergraduate student'. For this reason, it seems there are two minimal models, $\{Undergraduate\,(Daniel),\ Postgraduate\,(Christelle)\}$ and $\{Postgraduate\,(Daniel),\ Postgraduate\,(Christelle)\}$ for Program 1.4. Consider the following logic program.

Program 1.5

$$Graduate\,(x) \leftarrow Student\,(x) \land \neg Research\,(x)$$
$$Student\,(Daniel)$$

where $Graduate\,(x)$ means 'x is a graduate student'. The first statement can be stated as

A student is either a graduate student or a research student

hence Daniel is either a graduate or a research student. The problem of finding the semantics of a program like (1.5) is the same as in Program 1.4 except that their *intended* meanings are different. By putting $\neg Research\,(x)$ in the antecedent of the first statement of Program 1.5, it says that students are, in general, graduate students unless it is either explicitly or implicitly stated that they are research students. Since Daniel is a student and neither explicitly nor implicitly stated as a research student, Daniel will be considered as a graduate student and hence the semantics is given by the model {*Student* (*Daniel*), *Graduate* (*Daniel*)}, and not by the model {*Graduate* (*Daniel*), *Research* (*Daniel*)}.

An important alternative treatment of logic programs is to consider them as *deductive databases*. These are considered to be the most promising successor to *relational databases*. From a theoretical point of view a deductive database can be considered as a logic program. However, in a typical deductive database, the number of *rules* (conditional premises) is much lower than the number of *facts* (assertions). Such databases are called deductive database (also called *logic databases*) because, by following the nature of logic programming, they are able to make deductions from known facts and rules at the time of answering queries. Programs 1.1–1.5 are typical example premises from a student database. The information about each student is stored in the form of assertions; several thousands assertions may be expected for a given institution. As a non-database example consider the following set of statements describing the odd–even property of non-negative integers.

Program 1.6

$Even(0)$
$Even(s(s(x))) \leftarrow Even(x)$
$Odd(x) \leftarrow \neg Even(x)$

where s is a function symbol representing the successor function. The above set of statements is more like a logic program than a deductive database.

A *query* in a deductive database can be regarded as a logic programming goal and query evaluation in deductive databases can be regarded as derivations in logic programming. To give an example of query evaluation, consider the following deductive database in the form of a logic program.

Program 1.7

$Student(x) \leftarrow Undergraduate(x)$
$Student(x) \leftarrow Postgraduate(x)$
$Undergraduate(Daniel)$
$Postgraduate(Janique)$

Also consider the query $\leftarrow Student(x)$ to find all students in the context of the above database. Following a logic programming style of execution, the resolvent of the goal and the first premise of the database produce $\leftarrow Undergraduate(x)$ as an intermediate goal. This goal resolves with the assertion $Undergraduate(Daniel)$ producing the empty clause and a substitution $\{x/Daniel\}$ as an answer to the original query. Upon *backtracking*, an alternative substitution $\{x/Janique\}$ can be found when the original goal is resolved with the second clause of the database.

Efficient processing of queries in deductive databases is an important issue and *parallelism* is one of the ways to achieve efficiency. To demonstrate how parallelism can improve the performance of query processing, consider the Program 1.7 and the query $\leftarrow Student(x)$. The problem of searching all facts about students in the database is reduced to the problem of searching all undergraduate students and all postgraduate students. These two searches can be performed independently (or in parallel) in a distributed environment. That is to say, the resolution of the original goal with each of the two conditional assertions of Program 1.7 can be carried out concurrently on two different processors. This gives a significant reduction of the total processing time over sequential execution of the query based on backtracking, that is, performing two searches one after another.

Another important aspect of deductive databases is the maintenance of integrity constraints. These are properties that the statements of a database must satisfy. Integrity constraints must be symbolized in a more general way than is allowed by the clausal form of first-order logic. For example, the integrity constraint

Every research student should have a supervisor

is symbolized as

$$\forall x\,(Research(x) \rightarrow \exists y\ Supervisor(y, x)) \tag{1.9}$$

where the symbol '$\exists$' stands for 'there exists' and the assertion 'y is a supervisor of x' has been symbolized as $Supervisor(y, x)$. Suppose this constraint is imposed on the following database.

Program 1.8

$$Examination\,(x) \leftarrow Undergraduate\,(x)$$
$$Student\,(Daniel)$$
$$Research\,(Janique)$$
$$Research\,(Christelle)$$
$$Supervisor\,(Robert, Janique)$$

The database will not satisfy the constraint as Christelle is a research student and does not have a supervisor in the database.

Exercise

1.1 Associate one or more topics/publications from the right-hand column to each of the logicians/mathematicians/philosophers/scientists on the left according to their contribution:

Ackerman	Algebra of logic
Aristotle	Automated theorem proving
Boole	Consistency and completeness
Cantor	Deductive database
Church	Deductive theory
Colmerauer	Incompleteness of arithmetic
Descartes	Logic of mathematics
De Morgan	Logic of statement connection
Freege	Logic programming
Gödel	Mathematical analysis of logic
Green	Mathematics of logic
Herbrand	*Principia Mathematica*
Hilbert	Quantifier theory
Huntington	Recursive function theory
Jevon	Resolution theorem proving
Kleene	Second-order theory
Kowalski	Syllogism
Leibniz	Theory of computability
Löwenheim	Unification
Peano	Universal algebra
Peirce	Universal language
Philo	
Post	
Robinson	
Schoeder	
Skolem	
Turing	
Whitehead	

PART II

Background Material

2

Mathematical preliminaries

This chapter provides the preliminary mathematical concepts which will be used throughout the book.

2.1 Sets

The set is a very fundamental idea and it can be used to achieve most of the formalizations. This section introduces the concepts.

Definition 2.1: A well-defined collection of distinct elements is called a *set* (Fraenkel and Bar-Hillel, 1984; Halmos, 1974; Stoll, 1963).

Given a set $\mathbf{S}$, $a \in \mathbf{S}$ means 'a is an element of $\mathbf{S}$' or 'a belongs to $\mathbf{S}$' or 'a is a member of $\mathbf{S}$'. In a similar way the notion $a \notin \mathbf{S}$ will be used to mean 'a is not an element of $\mathbf{S}$'. A shorthand notation for a set $\mathbf{S}$ is

$$\mathbf{S} = \{x | P(x)\}$$

which is read as '$\mathbf{S}$ is the set of all elements x such that the property P holds'. When it is possible to list all the elements, or at least to list sufficiently many to make clear just what the elements of a set $\mathbf{S}$ are, then $\mathbf{S}$ is written as $\{a, b, c, ...\}$.

Definition 2.2: An *empty set* has no elements and is denoted as { } or $\emptyset$.

Definition 2.3: A set $\mathbf{A}$ is a *subset* of a set $\mathbf{S}$ (or $\mathbf{A}$ is included in $\mathbf{S}$ or $\mathbf{A}$ is contained in $\mathbf{S}$ or $\mathbf{S}$ contains $\mathbf{A}$), denoted as $\mathbf{A} \subseteq \mathbf{S}$, if every element of $\mathbf{A}$ is an element of $\mathbf{S}$, that is, $a \in \mathbf{A}$ implies $a \in \mathbf{S}$.

By definition a set is a subset of itself and an empty set is a subset of every set. If two sets $\mathbf{A}$ and $\mathbf{B}$ are same (or *equal*), then it is denoted as $\mathbf{A} = \mathbf{B}$.

Definition 2.4: If $\mathbf{A} \subseteq \mathbf{S}$ and $\mathbf{A} \neq \mathbf{S}$, then $\mathbf{A}$ is a *proper subset* of $\mathbf{S}$ and is denoted as $\mathbf{A} \subset \mathbf{S}$. In other words, if $\mathbf{A} \subset \mathbf{S}$ then there exists at least one $a \in \mathbf{S}$ such that $a \notin \mathbf{A}$.

EXAMPLE 2.1

{1, 4, 7, 9}, {{a,b}, c, d}, {0, 1, 2, ...} are examples of sets. Let $\mathbf{N}$ be the set {1, 2, 3, ...} of all natural numbers. Then $\{x \in \mathbf{N} | x \text{ is odd}\}$ is the set {1, 3, 5, ...}. The set {4, 7} is a proper subset of {1, 4, 7, 9}.

Definition 2.5: The *union* (or *join*) of two sets $\mathbf{A}$ and $\mathbf{B}$, written as $\mathbf{A} \cup \mathbf{B}$, is the set $\{x | x \in \mathbf{A} \text{ or } x \in \mathbf{B}\}$, that is, the set of all elements which are members of either $\mathbf{A}$ or $\mathbf{B}$ (or both). The union of an arbitrary collection of sets is the set of all elements which are members of at least one of the sets in the collection. The *intersection* of two sets $\mathbf{A}$ and $\mathbf{B}$, denoted $\mathbf{A} \cap \mathbf{B}$, is the set $\{x | x \in \mathbf{A} \text{ and } x \in \mathbf{B}\}$, that is, the set of all elements which are members of both $\mathbf{A}$ and $\mathbf{B}$. The intersection of an arbitrary collection of sets is the set of all elements which are members of every set in the collection. The *difference* of two sets $\mathbf{A}$ and $\mathbf{B}$, denoted $\mathbf{A} - \mathbf{B}$, is the set $\{x | x \in \mathbf{A} \text{ and } x \notin \mathbf{B}\}$, that is, the set of all elements which are members of $\mathbf{A}$ but not members of $\mathbf{B}$.

EXAMPLE 2.2

Suppose $\mathbf{A} = \{a, b, c\}$ and $\mathbf{B} = \{a, c, d\}$. Then $\mathbf{A} \cup \mathbf{B} = \{a, b, c, d\}$, $\mathbf{A} \cap \mathbf{B} = \{a, c\}$, $\mathbf{A} - \mathbf{B} = \{b\}$.

Definition 2.6: Suppose $\mathbf{I}$ is an arbitrary set and for each $\alpha \in \mathbf{I}$ consider a set $\mathbf{A}_\alpha$. Then the set of sets $\{\mathbf{A}_\alpha | \alpha \in \mathbf{I}\}$ is denoted as $\{\mathbf{A}_\alpha\}_{\alpha \in \mathbf{I}}$ and $\mathbf{I}$ is called an *index set*.

The join of all sets in the collection $\{\mathbf{A}_\alpha | \alpha \in \mathbf{I}\}$ is denoted as

$$\bigcup_{\alpha \in \mathbf{I}} \mathbf{A}_\alpha$$

and the intersection is denoted as $\bigcap_{\alpha \in \mathbf{I}} \mathbf{A}_\alpha$.

Definition 2.7: Given a set $\mathbf{S}$, the *power set* of $\mathbf{S}$, denoted as $\mathcal{P}(\mathbf{S})$, is the set $\{\mathbf{A} | \mathbf{A} \subseteq \mathbf{S}\}$, that is, the set of all possible subsets of $\mathbf{S}$. If a set $\mathbf{S}$ contains n elements, where n is an integer, then $\mathcal{P}(\mathbf{S})$ contains 2^n elements.

EXAMPLE 2.3

Suppose $\mathbf{A} = \{a, b, c\}$. Then $\mathcal{P}(\mathbf{A}) = \{\varnothing, \{a\}, \{b\}, \{c\}, \{a, b\}, \{a, c\}, \{b, c\}, \{a, b, c\}\}$.

2.2 Relations

A relation (Tarski, 1965) is usually described by a statement which involves elements from a collection of sets. The formal definition of a relation and its properties are given in this section.

Definition 2.8: Given a collection of sets $\mathbf{S}_1, \mathbf{S}_2, ..., \mathbf{S}_n$, the *cartesian product* of these n sets, denoted by $\mathbf{S}_1 \times \mathbf{S}_2 \times \cdots \times \mathbf{S}_n$, is the set of all possible ordered *n-tuples* $<a_1, a_2, ..., a_n>$ such that $a_i \in \mathbf{S}_i$, for $i = 1, 2, ..., n$. When each $\mathbf{S}_i$ is equal to $\mathbf{S}$ then the product is written as $\mathbf{S}^n$.

EXAMPLE 2.4

Suppose $\mathbf{S}_1 = \{a_1, a_2\}, \mathbf{S}_2 = \{b\}, \mathbf{S}_3 = \{c_1, c_2, c_3\}$. Then $\mathbf{S}_1 \times \mathbf{S}_2 \times \mathbf{S}_3 = \{<a_1, b, c_1>, <a_1, b, c_2>, <a_1, b, c_3>, <a_2, b, c_1>, <a_2, b, c_2>, <a_2, b, c_3>\}$.

Definition 2.9: An *n-ary relation* $\mathbf{R}$ on the sets $\mathbf{S}_1, \mathbf{S}_2, ..., \mathbf{S}_n$ is a subset of $\mathbf{S}_1 \times \mathbf{S}_2 \times \cdots \times \mathbf{S}_n$. An n-ary relation $\mathbf{R}$ on a set $\mathbf{S}$ is a subset of $\mathbf{S}^n$. If $\mathbf{R}$ is a binary relation on a set $\mathbf{S}$, then the notation $a\mathbf{R}b$ implies that $<a, b> \in \mathbf{R}$, where $a, b \in \mathbf{S}$.

Definition 2.10: A binary relation $\mathbf{R}$ on a set $\mathbf{A}$ is

(1) *reflexive* if $x\mathbf{R}x$, for all $x \in \mathbf{A}$.

(2) *symmetric* if $x\mathbf{R}y$ implies $y\mathbf{R}x$, for all $x, y \in \mathbf{A}$.

(3) *transitive* if $x\mathbf{R}y$ and $y\mathbf{R}z$ implies $x\mathbf{R}z$, for all $x, y, z \in \mathbf{A}$

(4) *antisymmetric* if $x\mathbf{R}y$ and $y\mathbf{R}x$ implies $x = y$, for all $x, y \in \mathbf{S}$.

An *equivalence relation* $\mathbf{R}$ on a set $\mathbf{A}$ is reflexive, symmetric and transitive. Let $\mathbf{A}$ be a set and $\mathbf{R}$ be an equivalence relation on $\mathbf{A}$. Then the *equivalence class* of $a \in \mathbf{A}$ is the set $\{x \in \mathbf{A} | a\mathbf{R}x\}$ and is denoted by $Eq_{\mathbf{A}}[a, \mathbf{R}]$.

Theorem 2.1 provides an association between an equivalence relation and equivalence classes.

Theorem 2.1: Let $\mathbf{A}$ be a set and $\mathbf{R}$ be an equivalence relation on $\mathbf{A}$. Then $\mathbf{R}$ provides a decomposition of $\mathbf{A}$ as a union of mutually disjoint subsets of $\mathbf{A}$. Conversely, given a decomposition on $\mathbf{A}$ as a union of mutually disjoint subsets of $\mathbf{A}$, an equivalence relation can be defined on $\mathbf{A}$ such that each of these subsets are the distinct equivalence classes.

Proof Since $x\mathbf{R}x$ holds, therefore $x \in Eq_{\mathbf{A}}[x, \mathbf{R}]$. Suppose $Eq_{\mathbf{A}}[a, \mathbf{R}]$ and $Eq_{\mathbf{A}}[b, \mathbf{R}]$ are two equivalent classes and let $x \in Eq_{\mathbf{A}}[a, \mathbf{R}] \cap Eq_{\mathbf{A}}[b, \mathbf{R}]$. Since $x \in Eq_{\mathbf{A}}[a, \mathbf{R}]$, $a\mathbf{R}x$. Since $x \in Eq_{\mathbf{A}}[b, \mathbf{R}]$, $b\mathbf{R}x$, i.e. $x\mathbf{R}b$, since $\mathbf{R}$ is symmetric. Now, $a\mathbf{R}x$ and $x\mathbf{R}b$, and therefore by transitivity of $\mathbf{R}$, $a\mathbf{R}b$. Suppose, $y \in Eq_{\mathbf{A}}[b, \mathbf{R}]$ and thus $b\mathbf{R}y$. Also, $a\mathbf{R}b$ is already proved. Therefore, by transitivity of $\mathbf{R}$, $a\mathbf{R}y$ and hence $y \in Eq_{\mathbf{A}}[a, \mathbf{R}]$. Since y is an arbitrary element chosen from $Eq_{\mathbf{A}}[b, \mathbf{R}]$, $Eq_{\mathbf{A}}[b, \mathbf{R}] \subseteq Eq_{\mathbf{A}}[a, \mathbf{R}]$. In a similar way it can be proved that $Eq_{\mathbf{A}}[a, \mathbf{R}] \subseteq Eq_{\mathbf{A}}[b, \mathbf{R}]$. Thus $Eq_{\mathbf{A}}[a, \mathbf{R}]$ = $Eq_{\mathbf{A}}[b, \mathbf{R}]$ and hence distinct equivalent classes are mutually disjoint.

To prove the converse, suppose $\mathbf{A} = \bigcup_{\alpha \in \mathbf{T}} \mathbf{A}_{\alpha}$, where $\mathbf{T}$ is an index set and $\mathbf{A}_{\alpha} \cap \mathbf{A}_{\beta} = \emptyset$, when $\alpha \neq \beta$ and $\alpha, \beta \in \mathbf{T}$. Define an equivalence relation $\mathbf{R}$ on $\mathbf{A}$ as $x\mathbf{R}y$ if and only if x and y belong to the same $\mathbf{A}_{\alpha}$. It is straightforward to verify that $\mathbf{R}$ is an equivalence relation on $\mathbf{A}$. ■

EXAMPLE 2.5

Let $\mathbf{I}$ be the set of all integers. Define a relation Mod_5 on $\mathbf{I}$ as $xMod_5y$ if and only if $x - y$ is divisible by 5, for $x, y \in \mathbf{I}$. Then

(1) $x - x = 0$ and 0 is divisible 5. Therefore, Mod_5 is reflexive.

(2) If $x - y$ is divisible by 5 then $y - x$ is also divisible by 5. Therefore, Mod_5 is symmetric.

(3) If $x - y$ is divisible by 5 and $y - z$ is divisible by 5, then $x - z$ is also divisible by 5. Therefore, Mod_5 is transitive.

Hence, Mod_5 is an equivalence relation on $\mathbf{I}$. In fact, such an equivalence relation Mod_i exists on $\mathbf{I}$, for every positive integer i. The equivalence class of 3 is $Eq_{\mathbf{A}}[3, \mathbf{R}] = \{..., -12, -7, -2, 3, 8, 13, ...\}$. The mutually disjoint equivalence classes corresponding to Mod_5 are $\{..., -10, -5, 0, 5, 10, ...\}$, $\{..., -9, -4, 1, 6, ...\}$, $\{..., -8, -3, 2, 7, ...\}$, $\{..., -7, -2, 3, 8, ...\}$ and $\{..., -6, -1, 4, 9, ...\}$.

2.3 Functions

Functions provide a way of describing connections between elements of different sets. A formal definition of a function can be given as follows.

Definition 2.11: Let $\mathbf{A}$ and $\mathbf{B}$ be two non-empty sets. Then a *function* f (or *mapping* or *transformation* or *operator* or *correspondence*), denoted as $f : \mathbf{A} \rightarrow \mathbf{B}$, is a subset $\mathbf{C}$ of $\mathbf{A} \times \mathbf{B}$ such that for every $x \in \mathbf{A}$ there exists a unique $y \in \mathbf{B}$ for which $<x, y> \in \mathbf{A} \times \mathbf{B}$.

Clearly, any function $f : \mathbf{A} \rightarrow \mathbf{B}$ is a particular kind of relation on $\mathbf{A}$ and $\mathbf{B}$. The element x is said to have been mapped into y (or y is the image of x or y is the value of f at x) and y is denoted as $f(x)$.

Definition 2.12: The notation $f(\mathbf{A})$ is the set $\{y \in \mathbf{B} |$ for some $x \in \mathbf{A}$, $<x, y> \in \mathbf{A} \times \mathbf{B}\}$ and is called the *image* of f. The set $\mathbf{A}$ is called the *domain* of f and $\mathbf{B}$ is called the *range* (or *co-domain*) of f.

Definition 2.13: A mapping $f : \mathbf{A} \rightarrow \mathbf{A}$ is said to be an *identity mapping* if $f(x) = x$, for all $x \in \mathbf{A}$.

Definition 2.14: Suppose $f : \mathbf{A} \rightarrow \mathbf{B}$ is a mapping. Then f is said to be *onto* (or *surjective*) if given $b \in \mathbf{B}$, there exists an element $a \in \mathbf{A}$ such that $f(a) = b$. The mapping f is said to be *one-to-one* (or *injective*) if for all $x, y \in \mathbf{A}$ and $x \neq y$ implies that $f(x) \neq f(y)$. The mapping f is a *one-to-one correspondence* between two sets $\mathbf{A}$ and $\mathbf{B}$ (or equivalently f is *bijective*) if f is a one-to-one mapping of

$\mathbf{A}$ onto $\mathbf{B}$.

Definition 2.15: Two mappings $f : \mathbf{A} \to \mathbf{B}$ and $g : \mathbf{A} \to \mathbf{B}$ are *equal* if for all $x \in \mathbf{A}$, $f(x) = g(x)$.

Definition 2.16: Suppose $g : \mathbf{A} \to \mathbf{B}$ and $f : \mathbf{B} \to \mathbf{C}$ are two mappings. Then the *composition* of f and g, denoted as fg, is a mapping $fg : \mathbf{A} \to \mathbf{C}$ defined by $(fg)(x) = f(g(x))$, for all $x \in \mathbf{A}$.

Now, $((fg)h)(x) = (fg)(h(x)) = f(g(h(x))) = f((gh)(x)) = (f(gh))(x)$, that is, $(fg)h$ and $f(gh)$ are equal, where f, g and h are mappings with appropriate domains and ranges. Thus the mapping composition operation follows the associative property and hence the positions of parentheses are irrelevant when mappings are composed.

EXAMPLE 2.6

Suppose $\mathbf{I}$, $\mathbf{E}$, $\mathbf{O}$ and $\mathbf{N}$ are respectively the sets of all integers, even integers, odd integers and natural numbers. Let $\mathbf{N}_0$ be $\mathbf{N} \cup \{0\}$. Then the mapping $f : \mathbf{E} \to \mathbf{O}$ defined by $f(x) = x + 1$ is a one-to-one correspondence between $\mathbf{E}$ and $\mathbf{O}$. The mapping $f : \mathbf{I} \to \mathbf{N}_0$ defined by $f(x) = |x|$ is onto but not one-to-one. The mapping $f : \mathbf{I} \to \mathbf{N}_0$ defined by $f(x) = x^2$ is neither one-to-one nor onto.

2.4 Graphs and trees

Some special binary relations on sets, for example, graphs and trees (Bondy and Murty, 1976; Deo, 1974; Doerr and Levasseur, 1986; Harary, 1969; Wilson, 1985) are introduced in this section.

Definition 2.17: A (*simple*) *graph* $\mathcal{G}$ is a pair $(\mathbf{V}(\mathcal{G}), \mathbf{E}(\mathcal{G}))$, where $\mathbf{V}(\mathcal{G})$ is a non-empty set of elements called *vertices* (or *nodes*), and $\mathbf{E}(\mathcal{G})$ is a set of unordered pairs of distinct elements of $\mathbf{V}(\mathcal{G})$ called *edges*.

EXAMPLE 2.7

Figure 2.1 represents the graph $(\{N_0, N_1, N_2, N_3\}, \{N_0N_1, N_1N_2, N_1N_3, N_0N_3\})$.

The definition of a *directed graph* (or *digraph*) is given in the same way as a graph except that the set $\mathbf{E}(\mathcal{G})$ is a set of ordered pairs of elements of $\mathbf{V}(\mathcal{G})$.

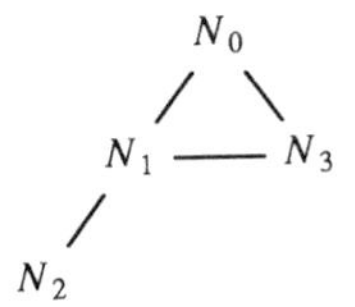

Figure 2.1 A graph.

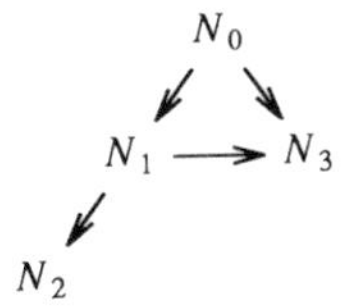

Figure 2.2 A directed graph.

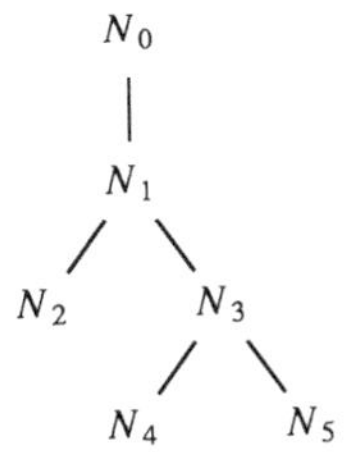

Figure 2.3 A tree.

EXAMPLE 2.8

Figure 2.2 represents the directed graph $(\{N_0, N_1, N_2, N_3\}, \{<N_0, N_1>, <N_1, N_2>, <N_1, N_3>, <N_0, N_3>\})$.

Definition 2.18: A *path* (of length m) in a graph $\mathcal{G}$ is a finite sequence of edges of the form

$$N_0 N_1, N_1 N_2, \ldots, N_{m-1} N_m$$

such that $N_0, N_1, \ldots, N_m$ are distinct (except possibly $N_0 = N_m$).

Definition 2.19: A graph $\mathcal{G}$ is a *tree* if and only if any two vertices of $\mathcal{G}$ are connected by exactly one path.

EXAMPLE 2.9

Figure 2.3 is the tree ({N_0, N_1, N_2, N_3, N_4, N_5}, {N_0N_1, N_1N_2, N_1N_3, N_3N_4, N_3N_5}).

Definition 2.20: A *rooted tree* is a tree which contains a distinguished vertex, called the *root*. Suppose N_0N_1, N_1N_2, ..., $N_{m-1}N_m$ is a path of a tree whose root has been designated as N_0. The vertices occurring in this path are described in genealogical terms as follows:

(1) N_{i+1} is a *child* of N_i, for $0 \le i < m$.

(2) N_i is a *parent* of N_{i+1}, for $0 \le i < m$.

(3) N_i, ..., N_j are *ancestors* of N_{j+1}, for $i \le j, 0 \le i < m, 0 \le j < m$

(4) N_i, ..., N_j are *descendants* of N_{i-1}, for $i \le j, 0 < i \le m, 0 < j \le m$

Unless otherwise stated, each reference of the term 'tree' would be regarded as 'rooted tree'. A *leaf* of a tree is a node without any children. The *level* of a vertex of a tree is the number of edges between the vertex and the root. The *depth* of a tree is the maximum level of the vertices in the tree. The level of the root in a tree is 0.

EXAMPLE 2.10

Consider the tree in Figure 2.3. Vertex N_0 has been designated as the root of the tree. Then N_1 is the only child of N_0; N_2, N_3 are the children of N_1; N_1 is the parent of N_2 and N_3; N_2, N_3, N_4, N_5 are the descendants of N_1; N_1 is an *ancestor* of N_4; N_2, N_4, N_5 are the leaf nodes; and so on. The level of the vertices N_0, N_1, N_2, N_3, N_4 and N_5 are 0, 1, 2, 2, 3 and 3 respectively. Therefore the depth of the tree is 3.

2.5 Ordered sets

A set can be partially or fully ordered by defining special kinds of relations in it. This section introduces different kinds of ordering on a set.

Definition 2.21: A binary relation **R** on a set **A** is called (*partial*) *ordering in* **A** if and only if **R** is reflexive, antisymmetric and transitive. The relation **R** is called a *full* (or *linear* or *total* or *well*) *ordering in* **A** if and only if **R** is a partial order and for any two elements $x, y \in \mathbf{A}$, either $x\mathbf{R}y$ or $y\mathbf{R}x$.

Definition 2.22: A set **A** together with an ordering **R** in **A** constitutes a *partially ordered set* (or *poset*) and is denoted as (**A**, **R**). When the ordering relation **R** is clear from the context, it is simply denoted as **A**. If **R** is a full order in **A**, then (**A**, **R**) is called a *fully* (or *linearly* or *totally* or *well*) *ordered set* or a *chain.*

EXAMPLE 2.11

The set of all integers **I** together with the natural ordering '$\leq$', that is, (**I**, $\leq$) is a fully ordered set.

EXAMPLE 2.12

Any collection $\mathcal{S}$ of sets can be considered a partially ordered set in which the partial ordering ρ can be defined as $\mathbf{A}\,\rho\mathbf{B}$ if and only if $\mathbf{A} \subseteq \mathbf{B}$, for $\mathbf{A}, \mathbf{B} \in \mathcal{S}$.

Ordering relations will sometimes be represented using the symbol '$\leq$' irrespective of the sets on which they are defined. These are not to be confused with the natural ordering of numbers.

Definition 2.23: Let $(\mathbf{S}, \leq)$ be an ordered set and $\mathbf{A} \subseteq \mathbf{S}$.

(1) An element $a \in \mathbf{S}$ is an *upper bound* of **A** if $x \leq a$ for all $x \in \mathbf{A}$.

(2) An element $a \in \mathbf{S}$ is a *lower bound* of **A** if $a \leq x$ for all $x \in \mathbf{A}$.

(3) An element $a \in \mathbf{S}$ is a *least upper bound* (or *lub* or *supremum*) of **A**, denoted as *lub* (**A**), if a is an upper bound of **A** and $a \leq x$ for all upper bounds x of **A**.

(4) An element $a \in \mathbf{S}$ is a *greatest lower bound* (or *glb* or *infimum*) of **A**, denoted as *glb* (**A**), if a is a lower bound of **A** and $x \leq a$ for all lower bounds x of **A**.

Given that $\mathbf{S} \subseteq \mathbf{S}$, if *glb* (**S**) (called the *top element* of **S**) and *lub* (**S**) (called the *bottom element* of **S**) exist, then they are denoted as $\top$ and $\perp$ respectively.

2.6 Lattices

Many important properties of ordered sets are studied using the existence of certain upper and lower bounds of subsets of the given ordered set. One such important class of ordered sets is called a *lattice* (Davey and Priestley, 1990).

Figure 2.4 The lattice (chain) of natural numbers.

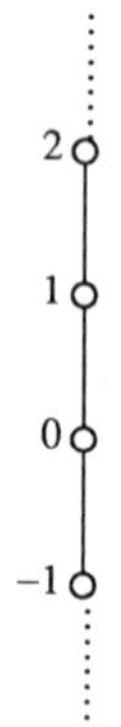

Figure 2.5 The lattice (chain) of integers.

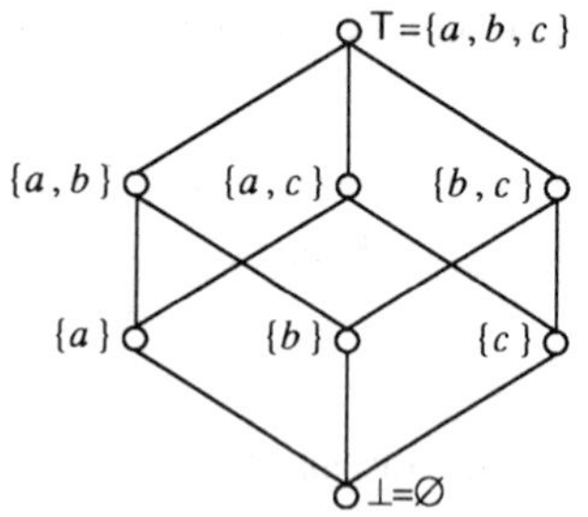

Figure 2.6 A complete lattice.

Definition 2.24: Let $(\mathbf{S}, \leq)$ be an ordered set.

(1) If $glb(\{x, y\})$ and $lub(\{x, y\})$ exist for all $x, y \in \mathbf{S}$ then $(\mathbf{S}, \leq)$ is a *lattice*.

(2) If $glb(\mathbf{A})$ and $lub(\mathbf{A})$ exist for all $\mathbf{A} \subseteq \mathbf{S}$ then $(\mathbf{S}, \leq)$ is a *complete lattice*.

EXAMPLE 2.13

Consider the three sets of real, integer and natural numbers and denote them as **R**, **I** and **N** respectively. Each of these three sets together with the usual ordering '$\leq$' on numbers forms a chain lattice. None of these lattices is a complete lattice as each of **R**, **I** and **N** contains the set **N** whose upper bound does not exist. The lattices $(\mathbf{N}, \leq)$ and $(\mathbf{I}, \leq)$ are diagrammatically represented in Figures 2.4 and 2.5 respectively.

EXAMPLE 2.14

Let $\mathbf{S} = \{a, b, c\}$. The usual ordered set $(\mathcal{P}(\mathbf{S}), \subseteq)$ is a complete lattice and is represented in Figure 2.6.

(1) If $\mathbf{A} = \{\{b\}, \{a, b\}, \{b, c\}\}$, then $glb(\mathbf{A}) = \{b\}$ and $lub(\mathbf{A}) = \top$. The $lub(\mathbf{A})$ does not belong to $\mathbf{A}$.

(2) If $\mathbf{A} = \{\{a\}, \{b\}, \{a, b\}\}$, then $glb(\mathbf{A}) = \bot$ and $lub(\mathbf{A}) = \{a, b\}$. The $glb(\mathbf{A})$ does not belong to $\mathbf{A}$.

(3) If $\mathbf{A} = \{\{b\}, \{c\}\}$, then neither its $glb(\mathbf{A})$ nor its $lub(\mathbf{A})$ is a member of $\mathbf{A}$.

2.7 Ordinals

In this section, the set of natural numbers (including zero) is extended to a set of ordinal numbers (Russell, 1948) by preserving the natural ordering relation.

Definition 2.25: Two sets **A** and **B** are *similar* (denoted as $\mathbf{A} \sim \mathbf{B}$) if and only if there exists a one-to-one correspondence between **A** and **B**.

Suppose **U** is the set of all sets which are relevant to the development. Consider the power set $\mathcal{P}(\mathbf{U})$. Similarity is an equivalence relation on $\mathcal{P}(\mathbf{U})$ and partitions **U** into disjoint classes of sets. Each of these classes is a *cardinal number*. Hence the cardinal number of $\mathbf{A} \in \mathcal{P}(\mathbf{U})$ is the class containing **A**. The cardinal number of a finite set **A** is a *finite cardinal* and is represented by the number of elements in **A**. A non-finite cardinal is an *infinite* or *transfinite cardinal*.

Definition 2.26: A set is *denumerable* if and only if it is one-to-one correspondent with the set of all natural numbers. A set is *countable* if and only if it is either finite or denumerable.

Definition 2.27: Suppose $\leq_1$ and $\leq_2$ are two orderings for the sets **A** and **B** respectively. A function $f : \mathbf{A} \to \mathbf{B}$ is *order preserving* (or *monotonic*) relative to the orderings $\leq_1$ and $\leq_2$ if and only if $x \leq_1 y$ implies $f(x) \leq_2 f(y)$, for all $x, y \in \mathbf{A}$.

Definition 2.28: An *isomorphism* between the two chains $(\mathbf{A}, \leq_1)$ and $(\mathbf{B}, \leq_2)$ is a one-to-one correspondence, say f, between **A** and **B** such that f is order-preserving. Two chains $(\mathbf{A}, \leq_1)$ and $(\mathbf{B}, \leq_2)$ are called *ordinally similar* (denoted as $\mathbf{A} = \mathbf{B}$) if and only if there exists an isomorphism between $(\mathbf{A}, \leq_1)$ and $(\mathbf{B}, \leq_2)$.

Ordinal similarity is an equivalence relation on any class of well-ordered sets and an equivalence class under ordinal similarity is called an *order type*. The order type of a well-ordered set is called an *ordinal number* (or simply an *ordinal*).

Suppose $(\mathbf{A}, \leq_1)$ and $(\mathbf{B}, \leq_2)$ are two well-ordered sets such that **A** and **B** have the same cardinality n which is finite. Suppose the elements of **A** are a_1, ..., a_n with $a_1 \leq_1 \cdots \leq_1 a_n$ and the elements of **B** are b_1, ..., b_n with $b_1 \leq_2 \cdots \leq_2 b_n$. Define a mapping $f : \mathbf{A} \to \mathbf{B}$ such that $f(a_i) = b_i$, $i = 1, ..., n$. It can be easily verified that f is an isomorphism between $(\mathbf{A}, \leq_1)$ and $(\mathbf{B}, \leq_2)$. Hence any two finite sets with the same cardinality belong to the same order type. Furthermore, if two well-ordered sets $(\mathbf{A}, \leq_1)$ and $(\mathbf{B}, \leq_2)$ belong to the same order type, then the cardinality of **A** is equal to the cardinality of **B**. Hence all finite cardinals can be uniquely and equivalently represented by natural numbers.

The ordinals which are not natural numbers are called *transfinite ordinals.* Transfinite ordinals are denoted by ω, $\omega + 1$, $\omega 2$, $\omega 3$, ω^2, etc. If α and β are ordinals, then $\alpha < \beta$ if and only if there exists a representative of α which is ordinally similar to an initial segment of one for β. In such case, α is said to be a *predecessor* of β. Ordinals having a predecessor are *ordinal numbers of the first kind* (or *successor ordinals*) and those having no predecessor are *ordinal numbers of the second kind* (or *limit ordinal*).

EXAMPLE 2.15

The ordinals 7, $\omega + 4$, $\omega 2 + 9$, $\omega^2 + 11$ are successor ordinals while ω, $\omega 2$, $\omega 3$, ω^2 are limit ordinals.

The ordering of the set of all ordinals is as follows. The first transfinite and limit ordinal ω occurs after the set of all finite ordinals 0, 1, 2, ... The successor of ω is $\omega + 1$, the successor of $\omega + 1$ is $\omega + 2$, and so on. The sequence 0, 1, 2, ..., ω, $\omega + 1$, $\omega + 2$, ... has order type $\omega + \omega$ and is represented as $\omega 2$. Thus the next limit ordinal is $\omega 2$. Continuing this way one can derive the well-ordered sequence

$$0, 1, 2, ..., \omega, \omega + 1, \omega + 2, ..., \omega 2, \omega 2 + 1, ..., \omega 3, ..., \omega^2, \omega^2 + 1, ...$$

This well-ordered sequence will be considered as an extension of the natural number sequence.

2.8 Fixpoints

This section studies *fixpoints* of mappings defined on lattices.

Definition 2.29: Let $(\mathbf{S}, \leq)$ be an ordered set and $f : \mathbf{S} \rightarrow \mathbf{S}$ be a mapping. Then $a \in \mathbf{S}$ is a *fixpoint* of f if $f(a) = a$.

Definition 2.30: Let $(\mathbf{S}, \leq)$ be an ordered set and $\mathbf{A} \subseteq \mathbf{S}$. Then $\mathbf{A}$ is said to be *directed* if every finite subset of $\mathbf{A}$ has an upper bound in $\mathbf{A}$.

Definition 2.31: Let $(\mathbf{L}, \leq)$ and $(\mathbf{M}, \leq)$ be two complete lattices. A mapping $f : \mathbf{L} \rightarrow \mathbf{M}$ is *continuous*, if for every directed set $\mathbf{D}$ of $\mathbf{L}$, $f(lub(\mathbf{D})) = lub(f(\mathbf{D}))$.

Theorem 2.2: Let $(\mathbf{L}, \leq)$ be a complete lattice and the mapping $f : \mathbf{L} \rightarrow \mathbf{L}$ is continuous. Then $f : \mathbf{L} \rightarrow \mathbf{L}$ is monotonic.

Proof Left as an exercise. ■

Theorem 2.3: (Knaster–Tarski fixpoint theorem) Let $(\mathbf{L}, \leq)$ be a complete lattice, $f : \mathbf{L} \rightarrow \mathbf{L}$ be monotonic and $\mathbf{F}$ be the set of all fixpoints of f. Then

(1) $lub\ \{x \in \mathbf{L} | x \leq f(x)\} \in \mathbf{F}$ is called the *greatest fixpoint* of f and is denoted as $gfp(f)$.

(2) $glb\ \{x \in \mathbf{L} | x \geq f(x)\} \in \mathbf{F}$ is called the *least fixpoint* of f and is denoted as $lfp(f)$.

Proof (1) Let $\mathbf{S} = \{x \in \mathbf{L} | x \leq f(x)\}$ and $a = lub(\mathbf{S})$. For all $x \in \mathbf{S}$, $x \leq a$ and hence $x \leq f(x) \leq f(a)$ (since f is monotonic). Then $f(a)$ is an upper bound of $\mathbf{S}$. Since a is the least upper bound of $\mathbf{S}$, $a \leq f(a)$. The mapping f is order-preserving and therefore $a \leq f(a)$ gives $f(a) \leq f(f(a))$. This implies that

$f(a) \in \mathbf{S}$ and so $f(a) \leq a$. Thus $a = f(a)$.

Proof (2) Similar to the proof of (1). ■

Definition 2.32: Let $(\mathbf{L}, \leq)$ be a complete lattice and $f : \mathbf{L} \rightarrow \mathbf{L}$ be monotonic. *Ordinal powers* of f are defined as follows:

$f \uparrow 0 = \bot$
$f \uparrow \alpha = f(f \uparrow (\alpha-1))$, if α is a successor ordinal
$f \uparrow \alpha = lub(\{f \uparrow \beta | \beta < \alpha\})$, if α is a limit ordinal
$f \downarrow 0 = \top$
$f \downarrow \alpha = f(f \downarrow (\alpha-1))$, if α is a successor ordinal
$f \downarrow \alpha = glb(\{f \downarrow \beta | \beta < \alpha\})$, if α is a limit ordinal

Proposition 2.1: Let $(\mathbf{L}, \leq)$ be a complete lattice and $f : \mathbf{L} \rightarrow \mathbf{L}$ be monotonic. Then for any ordinal α

(1) $f \uparrow \alpha \leq lfp(f)$
(2) $f \downarrow \alpha \geq gfp(f)$
(3) $lfp(f) = f \uparrow \alpha_1$, for some ordinal α_1
(4) $gfp(f) = f \downarrow \alpha_2$, for some ordinal α_2
(5) $f \uparrow \omega \leq f \downarrow \omega$

Proof

(1) The proof is carried out by the principle of transfinite induction (see Section 2.9). Suppose α is an arbitrary ordinal and assume that $f \uparrow \beta \leq lfp(f)$, for all ordinal $\beta < \alpha$. Consider the following two cases:

(a) α is a limit ordinal: since $f \uparrow \beta \leq lfp(f)$, for all $\beta < \alpha$, therefore $f \uparrow \alpha = lub\{f \uparrow \beta | \beta < \alpha\} \leq lfp(f)$.

(b) α is a successor ordinal:

	$f \uparrow (\alpha-1) \leq lfp(f)$	By induction hypothesis
that is	$f(f(\uparrow(\alpha-1)) \leq f(lfp(f))$	Since f is monotonic
that is	$f \uparrow \alpha \leq f(lfp(f))$	By the definition of f
that is	$f \uparrow \alpha \leq lfp(f)$	Since $lfp(f)$ is a fixpoint

(2) Left as an exercise.

(3) Left as an exercise.

(4) Left as an exercise.

(5) $f \uparrow \omega \leq lfp(f) \leq gfp(f) \leq f \downarrow \omega$ ■

Theorem 2.4: Let $(\mathbf{L}, \leq)$ be a complete lattice and $f : \mathbf{L} \to \mathbf{L}$ be continuous. Then $lfp(f) = f \uparrow \omega$.

Proof The mapping f is continuous and hence monotonic. Hence the set $\{f \uparrow n : n < \omega\}$ is directed. Therefore $f(f \uparrow \omega) = f(lub\{f \uparrow n | n < \omega\}) = lub\{f(f \uparrow n) | n < \omega\} = f \uparrow \omega$. Hence $f \uparrow \omega$ is a fixpoint. Also, by Proposition 2.1(1), $f \uparrow \omega \leq lfp(f)$. Thus $f \uparrow \omega = lfp(f)$. ■

2.9 Induction principles

Most of the proofs in this book will be carried out using the induction principle. The two kinds of induction principle, namely the principle of weak induction and the principle of strong induction, are given in this section.

Definition 2.33: Suppose $P(n)$ stands for 'the natural number n has the property P'. The *principle of weak induction* can be stated as follows. If $P(0)$ (called the *base step*) and, for each natural number m, $P(m)$ implies $P(m+1)$ (called the *induction step*), then $P(n)$, for each natural number n.

EXAMPLE 2.16

Let $\mathbf{N}_0$ be the set $\mathbf{N} \cup \{0\}$ and $s : \mathbf{N}_0 \to \mathbf{N}_0$ be a function. Suppose that for all $p, q, r, n \in \mathbf{N}_0$

$$
\begin{aligned}
0 + p &= p \\
s(1+p) &= 1 + s(p) \\
p + (q + r) &= (p + q) + r
\end{aligned}
$$

Then $s(n+p) = n + s(p)$, for all $p, n \in \mathbf{N}_0$. To prove this by induction hypothesis, consider $P(n)$ as $s(n+p) = n + s(p)$. Since $s(0+p) = s(p) = 0 + s(p)$ (using $0 + p = p$), therefore $P(0)$. Hence the base step of the induction principle is established. Now, assume $P(m)$, that is, $s(m+p) = m + s(p)$. Then

$$\begin{aligned}
s((m+1)+p) &= s(m+(1+p)) && \text{Applying } p+(q+r)=(p+q)+r \\
&= m+s(1+p) && \text{Since } s(m+p)=m+s(p), \text{ for all } n \\
&= m+(1+s(p)) && \text{Applying } s(1+p)=1+s(p) \\
&= (m+1)+s(p) && \text{Applying } p+(q+r)=(p+q)+r
\end{aligned}$$

Hence $s((m+1)+p) = (m+1)+s(p)$, that is, $P(m+1)$. Thus by induction hypothesis, $P(n)$, for all $n \in N$.

The second kind of induction principle, called the *principle of strong induction*, is stated as follows: if for all natural numbers m, $P(r)$ for all $r < m$ implies $P(m)$, then $P(n)$, for each natural number n.

Each of the two principles of induction described as above can be generalized to start with any natural number n_0 rather than 0 only.

The generalized induction principle, called the *principle of transfinite induction*, for the ordinal numbers can be stated as follows: suppose $P(\alpha)$ stands for 'the ordinal number α has the property P'. If for each ordinal β, $P(\gamma)$ for each ordinal $\gamma < \beta$ implies $P(\beta)$, then $P(\alpha)$ for each ordinal α.

Exercises

2.1 Compute $\mathbf{A} \cup \mathbf{B}$, $\mathbf{A} \cap \mathbf{B}$ and $\mathbf{A} - \mathbf{B}$ for the following:

(a) $\mathbf{A} = \{1, 2, 3, 4\}$, $\mathbf{B} = \{2, 4, 5\}$

(b) $\mathbf{A} = \{a, b, c\}$, $\mathbf{B} = \{1, 2\}$

(c) $\mathbf{A} = \{x | x \text{ is an integer and } x \geq 5\}$, $\mathbf{B} = \{x | x \text{ is an integer and } x \leq 5\}$

(d) $\mathbf{A} = \{1, 1/2, 1/3, 1/4, ...\}$, $\mathbf{B} = \{1, 1/3, 1/5, 1/7, ...\}$

2.2 Compute $\mathbf{N} \times \mathbf{A}$ and $\mathbf{N} \times \mathbf{A} \times \mathbf{D}$, where $\mathbf{N}$ = {Robert, Daniel, Didier}, $\mathbf{A}$ = {30, 40, 50} and $\mathbf{D}$ = {Fin, Admin}.

2.3 Compute $\mathcal{P}(\mathbf{A})$ for the following:

(a) $\mathbf{A} = \{a, b, c\}$

(b) $\mathbf{A} = \{x | x \text{ is an integer and } 1 \leq x \leq 5\}$

2.4 Let $\mathbf{I}$ be the set of all integers. Define $f : \mathbf{I} \to \mathbf{I}$ as $f(x) = x + 2$ and $g : \mathbf{I} \to \mathbf{I}$ as $g(x) = x^2$. Compute gf and f^{-1}, g^{-1} (if they exist).

2.5 Let $\mathbf{A} = \{1, 2, 3\}$, $\mathbf{B} = \{a, b, c\}$ and $\mathbf{C} = \{p, q\}$. Define $f : \mathbf{A} \to \mathbf{B}$ as $f(1) = a$, $f(2) = b$, $f(3) = c$, define $g : \mathbf{B} \to \mathbf{C}$ as $g(a) = g(b) = p$, $g(c) = q$. Determine whether each of these mappings is injective, surjective or bijective. Also, compute fg, gf and f^{-1}, g^{-1} (if they exist).

2.6 Let $\mathbf{S} = \{a, b, c\}$ and ρ be a binary relation on $\mathcal{P}(\mathbf{S})$ which is defined by $\mathbf{A} \rho \mathbf{B}$ if and only if $\mathbf{A} \cap \mathbf{B} = \emptyset$, for $\mathbf{A}, \mathbf{B} \in \mathcal{P}(\mathbf{S})$. Compute the whole relation and state the nature of ρ, that is, whether ρ is reflexive, symmetric, antisymmetric or transitive.

2.7 Let $\mathbf{I}$ be the set of all integers. Define a binary relation Mod_4 on $\mathbf{I}$ such that $<i, j> \in Mod_4$ if and only if $i - j$ is divisible by 4, for all $i, j \in \mathbf{I}$. Verify that Mod_4 is an equivalence relation and compute its equivalence classes.

2.8 Let $\mathbf{A} = \{1, 2, 3, 4\}$. Define a ternary relation ρ on $\mathbf{A}$ such that $<i, j, k> \in \rho$ if and only if $i \leq j \leq k$, for all $i, j, k \in \mathbf{I}$. Compute the relation ρ.

2.9 Let $\mathbf{A} = \{1, 2, 3, 4, 6, 12\}$ and define the divisibility relation ρ on $\mathbf{A}$ by $x \rho y$ if and only if x divides y, for all $x, y \in \mathbf{A}$. Prove that $(\mathbf{A}, \rho)$ is a partially ordered set and draw the lattice diagram in this case.

2.10 Let $\mathbf{I}$ be the set of all integers and '$\leq$' be the natural ordering relation on $\mathbf{I}$. Then $(\mathbf{I}, \leq)$ is a partially ordered set. State in which of the following cases is the mapping $f : (\mathbf{I}, \leq) \to (\mathbf{I}, \leq)$ order-preserving:

(a) $f(x) = |x|$
(b) $f(x) = x^2$
(c) $f(x) = x + 5$

2.11 Draw the graph $\mathcal{G}$ whose vertex set is $\{N_i | i = 0, 1, 2, 3, 4, 5, 6, 7\}$ and the edge set is $\{N_0 N_1, N_1 N_2, N_1 N_3, N_3 N_4, N_3 N_5, N_0 N_6, N_6 N_7\}$. State whether $\mathcal{G}$ is a tree or not. If it is then by considering N_0 as the root of the tree derive all the genealogical relations among the nodes of the tree.

3

Mathematical logic

The first half of this chapter studies a rather simple logical system called propositional logic. An extended logical system, known as first-order logic, is introduced in the latter half.

3.1 Propositional logic

A *proposition* (Sinclair, 1937) is a declarative sentence which is either *true* or *false* but not both. Examples of propositions are

Daniel is an undergraduate student
Janique sat the final examination

Propositions will be symbolized as P, Q, R, ... and are called *atoms* or *atomic formulae*. Compound propositions are formed by modifying with the word *not* or by connecting sentences with words *and*, *or*, *if ... then*, *if and only if*. These five are called *logical connectives* (Lemmon, 1977) and will be symbolized as $\neg$, $\wedge$, $\vee$, $\rightarrow$ and $\leftrightarrow$ respectively. Examples of compound propositions are as follows.

> *If Daniel is an undergraduate student then Daniel sat the final examination.*
> *Daniel did not sit the final examination.*
> *Janique is an undergraduate student or Janique is a postgraduate student.*

The above composite propositions are symbolized respectively in the *propositional language* as

$$P \rightarrow Q$$
$$\neg Q$$
$$R \vee S$$

where

> P stands for 'Daniel is an undergraduate student'
> Q stands for 'Daniel sat the final examination'
> R stands for 'Janique is an undergraduate student'
> S stands for 'Janique is a postgraduate student'

These compound propositions are called *well-formed formulae* (*wffs*) as part of the propositional language and the symbols occurring in the formulae are part of the propositional alphabet. Formal definitions of these terms are given below.

Definition 3.1: A *propositional alphabet* consists of the following:

(1) Two parentheses '(' and ')'.
(2) A set of propositional variables P, Q, R, ... as atoms.
(3) A set of logical connectives $\neg$, $\wedge$, $\vee$, $\rightarrow$ and $\leftrightarrow$.

Definition 3.2: *Well-formed formulae* or *formulae* in propositional logic (Copi, 1979; Delong, 1970; Mendelson, 1987; Stoll, 1963) are defined as follows:

(1) An atomic formula is a formula.
(2) If F is a formula then $(\neg F)$ is a formula.
(3) If F and G are formulae then $(F \wedge G)$, $(F \vee G)$, $(F \rightarrow G)$, $(F \leftrightarrow G)$ are formulae.
(4) An expression is a formula only if it can be shown to be a formula by the above three conditions.

A formula of the form (¬ F) is called the *negation* of the formula F. Formulae of the forms (F ∧ G) and (F ∨ G) are called the *conjunction* and *disjunction*, respectively of the formulae F and G. A formula of the form (F → G) is called a *conditional* formula; F is called the *antecedent* and G is called the *consequent*. A formula of the form (F ↔ G) is called a *biconditional* formula.

The following conventions are used to avoid using parentheses in a formula. The connective '¬' is applied to the smallest formula following it, then '∧' is to connect the smallest formulae surrounding it, and so on for the rest of the connectives '∨', '→' and '↔' in order. Thus if parentheses are restored in the formula

$$\neg P \wedge Q \rightarrow R \leftrightarrow Q \vee R \wedge P$$

then the resulting formula would be

$$((((\neg P) \wedge Q) \rightarrow R) \leftrightarrow (Q \vee (R \wedge P))).$$

Definition 3.3: Given a propositional alphabet, the *propositional language* comprises the set of all formulae constructed from the symbols of the alphabet.

Definition 3.4: One of 'truth' (denoted as **T**) or 'falsity' (denoted as **F**) assigned to a formula is its *truth value.*

For every assignment of truth values **T** or **F** to the symbolized atomic propositions that occur in a formula, there corresponds a truth value for the formula. This can be determined using the *truth table* of the formula.

EXAMPLE 3.1

Table 3.1 is the combined truth table for the formulae $\neg P$, $P \wedge Q$, $P \vee Q$, $P \rightarrow Q$ and $P \leftrightarrow Q$. Using this basic truth table, the truth table for the formula

$$(\neg P \leftrightarrow Q) \rightarrow (P \wedge (Q \vee R))$$

is displayed in Table 3.2.

Definition 3.5: Given a formula F, suppose P_1, ..., P_n are all atomic formulae occurring in F. Then an *interpretation* of F is an assignment of truth values to P_1, ..., P_n and no P_i is assigned by both **T** and **F**. Hence every row in a truth table for a formula F is an interpretation of F.

Table 3.1 Truth table in propositional logic.

P	Q	$\neg P$	$P \wedge Q$	$P \vee Q$	$P \rightarrow Q$	$P \leftrightarrow Q$
T	**T**	**F**	**T**	**T**	**T**	**T**
T	**F**	**F**	**F**	**T**	**F**	**F**
F	**T**	**T**	**F**	**T**	**T**	**F**
F	**F**	**T**	**F**	**F**	**T**	**T**

Table 3.2 Truth table for $(\neg P \leftrightarrow Q) \rightarrow (P \wedge (Q \vee R))$.

P	Q	R	$\neg P$	$\neg P \leftrightarrow Q$	$Q \vee R$	$P \wedge (Q \vee R)$	$(\neg P \leftrightarrow Q) \rightarrow$ $(P \wedge (Q \vee R))$
T	**T**	**T**	**F**	**F**	**T**	**T**	**T**
T	**T**	**F**	**F**	**F**	**T**	**T**	**T**
T	**F**	**T**	**F**	**T**	**T**	**T**	**T**
T	**F**	**F**	**F**	**T**	**F**	**F**	**F**
F	**T**	**T**	**T**	**T**	**T**	**F**	**F**
F	**T**	**F**	**T**	**T**	**T**	**F**	**F**
F	**F**	**T**	**T**	**F**	**T**	**F**	**T**
F	**F**	**F**	**T**	**F**	**F**	**F**	**T**

Definition 3.6: A formula F is a *tautology* or is *valid* (denoted as $\models$ F) if its value is **T** under all possible interpretations of F.

EXAMPLE 3.2

The formula $P \rightarrow P \vee Q$ is a tautology according to Table 3.3.

Definition 3.7: A formula F is *false* (or *inconsistent* or a *contradiction*) if and only if its value is **F** under all possible interpretations.

EXAMPLE 3.3

The formula $P \vee Q \leftrightarrow \neg P \wedge \neg Q$ is false by Table 3.4.

Definition 3.8: If a formula F is true under an interpretation I, then I *satisfies* F or F is *satisfied* by I and in such cases, I is a *model* of F.

Table 3.3 A tautology.

P	Q	$P \vee Q$	$P \rightarrow P \vee Q$
T	T	T	T
T	F	T	T
F	T	T	T
F	F	F	T

Table 3.4 A contradiction.

P	Q	$\neg P$	$\neg Q$	$P \vee Q$	$\neg P \wedge \neg Q$	$P \vee Q \leftrightarrow \neg P \wedge \neg Q$
T	T	F	F	T	F	F
T	F	F	T	T	F	F
F	T	T	F	T	F	F
F	F	T	T	F	T	F

Definition 3.9: Two formulae F and G are said to be *equivalent* (or F is *equivalent* to G), denoted as F ≡ G, if and only if the truth values of F and G are the same under every interpretation. In other words if F ↔ G is a tautology then F and G are equivalent.

EXAMPLE 3.4

$P \vee Q \equiv \neg P \rightarrow Q$,
$P \wedge Q \equiv \neg (P \rightarrow \neg Q)$,
$P \leftrightarrow Q \equiv (P \rightarrow Q) \wedge (Q \rightarrow P)$.

Therefore it can be said that a formula F can be transformed to an equivalent formula G (F ≡ G) containing only the connectives '¬' and '→'.

The following two equivalences prove the associative properties of the two connectives '∧' and '∨'.

$$(P \wedge Q) \wedge R \equiv P \wedge (Q \wedge R)$$
$$(P \vee Q) \vee R \equiv P \vee (Q \vee R)$$

Hence the positions of parentheses between subformulae $F_1, ..., F_n$ or their order in a formula $F_1 \vee \cdots \vee F_n$ or $F_1 \wedge \cdots \wedge F_n$ are immaterial.

Definition 3.10: A formula of the form

$$F_1 \vee \cdots \vee F_n$$

is called a *disjunction* of $F_1, ..., F_n$ and a formula of the form

$$F_1 \wedge \cdots \wedge F_n$$

is called a *conjunction* of $F_1, ..., F_n$.

Definition 3.11: A *literal* is either an atom or the negation of an atom.

Definition 3.12: A formula F is in *conjunctive normal form* (*cnf*) if F has the form $F_1 \wedge \cdots \wedge F_n$ $(n \geq 1)$ and each F_i is a disjunction of literals. A formula F is in *disjunctive normal form* (*dnf*) if F has the form $F_1 \vee \cdots \vee F_n$ $(n \geq 1)$ and each F_i is a conjunction of literals.

EXAMPLE 3.5

The formula $(P \vee Q) \wedge (Q \vee \neg R) \wedge (P \vee R \vee S)$ is in cnf and $(P \wedge Q \wedge R) \vee (Q \wedge \neg S)$ is in dnf.

The following distributive laws can easily be verified:

$$F \vee (G \wedge H) \equiv (F \vee G) \wedge (F \vee H)$$
$$F \wedge (G \vee H) \equiv (F \wedge G) \vee (F \wedge H)$$
$$\neg (F \vee G) \equiv \neg F \wedge \neg G$$
$$\neg (F \wedge G) \equiv \neg F \vee \neg G$$

Using the above distributive laws and the negation elimination

$$\neg (\neg F) \equiv F$$

any formula can be transformed to its equivalent disjunctive or conjunctive normal form and the procedure is informally described in the following. Its counterpart for first-order logic will be described more formally later.

Step 1: Eliminate $\rightarrow$ and $\leftrightarrow$ using the equivalences $F \rightarrow G \equiv \neg F \vee G$ and $F \leftrightarrow G \equiv (\neg F \vee G) \wedge (\neg G \vee F)$.

Step 2: Repeatedly use the equivalence $\neg (F \vee G) \equiv \neg F \wedge \neg G$, $\neg (F \wedge G) \equiv \neg F \vee \neg G$ and $\neg (\neg F) \equiv F$ to bring the negation sign immediately before atoms.

Step 3: Repeatedly use the two distributive properties to obtain the required normal form.

The following example illustrates the above algorithm.

EXAMPLE 3.6

$(\neg P \leftrightarrow Q) \rightarrow (P \wedge (Q \vee R))$	Given formula
$(\neg \neg P \vee Q) \wedge (\neg Q \vee \neg P) \rightarrow (P \wedge (Q \vee R))$	By step 1
$\neg((\neg \neg P \vee Q) \wedge (\neg Q \vee \neg P)) \vee (P \wedge (Q \vee R))$	By step 1
$\neg(P \vee Q) \vee \neg(\neg Q \vee \neg P) \vee (P \wedge (Q \vee R))$	By step 2
$(\neg P \wedge \neg Q) \vee (Q \wedge P) \vee (P \wedge (Q \vee R))$	By step 2
$(\neg P \wedge \neg Q) \vee (Q \wedge P) \vee (P \wedge Q) \vee (P \wedge R)$	By step 3

This formula is in disjunctive normal form.

Definition 3.13: A formula G is said to be a *logical consequence* of a set of formulae $F_1, ..., F_n$ (denoted as $F_1, ..., F_n \models G$) if and only if for any interpretation I in which $F_1 \wedge \cdots \wedge F_n$ is true G is also true.

EXAMPLE 3.7
The formula $P \vee R$ is a logical consequence of $P \vee Q$ and $Q \rightarrow R$.

This completes a brief introduction to propositional logic. Now an example is given to demonstrate how propositional logic establishes the conclusion of a valid argument. Consider the following example of a valid argument (Hodges, 1988; Newton-Smith, 1985).

Argument 3.1

If Daniel is an undergraduate student then Daniel sat the final examination.
Daniel did not sit the final examination.
Therefore, Daniel is not an undergraduate student.

Table 3.5 Truth table to establish $P \rightarrow Q, \neg Q \models \neg P$.

P	Q	$P \rightarrow Q$	$\neg Q$	$\neg P$
T	T	T	F	F
T	F	F	T	F
F	T	T	F	T
F	F	T	T	T

A symbolization of the first two premises of Argument 3.1 in propositional logic is $P \rightarrow Q$ and $\neg Q$, where P stands for 'Daniel is an undergraduate student' and Q stands for 'Daniel sat the final examination'. To prove the validity of Argument 3.1, it is necessary to show that $\neg P$ (the symbolization of the last premise of Argument 3.1) is a logical consequence of $P \rightarrow Q$ and $\neg Q$. Table 3.5 establishes the fact that $P \rightarrow Q, \neg Q \models \neg P$.

3.2 Formal axiomatic theory

An alternative approach to truth tables for dealing with more complex problems concerning logical connectives is by means of *formal axiomatic theories.* Such a theory $\mathcal{T}$ consists of the following:

(1) A countable set of *symbols* (also called an *alphabet*). An *expression* is a finite sequence of such symbols.

(2) A set of *formulae* (also called the *language* over the alphabet) which is a subset of the set of all expressions of $\mathcal{T}$.

(3) An effective procedure to determine whether an expression is a formula or not.

(4) A set of *axioms* which is a subset of the set of all formulae of $\mathcal{T}$.

(5) An effective procedure to determine whether a formula is axiom or not.

(6) A finite set of *rules of inference* each of which is a relation among formulae.

(7) Given an $(n+1)$-ary relation **R** as a rule of inference and given an arbitrary set of formulae F_1, ..., F_n, there is an effective procedure to determine whether F, F_1, ..., F_n are in relation **R** to F. If so, the formula F is called a *direct consequence* of F_1, ..., F_n by the application of the rule of inference **R**.

Definition 3.14: A *proof* (or *axiomatic deduction*) in the axiomatic theory $\mathcal{T}$ is a sequence $F_1, ..., F_n$ of formulae such that each F_i is either an axiom or a direct consequence of some of $F_1, ..., F_{i-1}$ by the application of a rule of inference. A proof $F_1, ..., F_n$ is called the *proof of* F_n. A formula F is a *theorem* in an axiomatic theory $\mathcal{T}$, denoted as $\vdash_{\mathcal{T}} F$ or simply $\vdash F$, if there is a proof of F in $\mathcal{T}$.

Suppose **S** is a set of formulae and $\mathcal{T}$ is an axiomatic theory. A formula F is said to be a *theorem* of **S** in $\mathcal{T}$, denoted as $\mathbf{S} \vdash_{\mathcal{T}} F$ or simply $\mathbf{S} \vdash F$, when the theory $\mathcal{T}$ is clear from the context, if and only if there is a sequence $F_1, ..., F_n$ of formulae such that $F_n = F$ and each F_i is either in **S** or a direct consequence of some of $F_1, ..., F_n$ by the application of a rule of inference. Such a sequence is called a *proof* of F from **S**. The members of **S** are called *hypotheses* or *premises*. If **S** is $\{G_1, ..., G_m\}$ then $\{G_1, ..., G_m\} \vdash F$ would be written as $G_1, ..., G_m \vdash F$. If **S** is empty then F is a theorem, that is $\vdash F$.

Definition 3.15: An axiomatic theory $\mathcal{T}$ is *decidable*, if there exists an effective procedure to determine whether an arbitrary formula is a theorem or not. If there is no such procedure, then $\mathcal{T}$ is called *undecidable*.

3.3 Formal axiomatic theory for propositional logic

A formal axiomatic theory $\mathcal{PL}$ for the propositional logic is defined as follows:

(1) The symbols of $\mathcal{PL}$ are a propositional alphabet.

(a) *Parentheses* (,)

(b) *Logical connectives* $\neg, \rightarrow$ (elimination of the other connectives from the alphabet is deliberate as they can be defined by the considered two and hence would be considered as abbreviations rather than part of the alphabet).

(c) *Propositional variables* $P, Q, R, P_1, Q_1, R_1, ...$.

(2) Formulae of $\mathcal{PL}$ (the *propositional language* over the propositional alphabet) are inductively defined as follows:

(a) All propositional variables are formulae.

(b) If F is a formula then $(\neg F)$ is a formula.

(c) If F and G are formulae then $(F \rightarrow G)$ is a formula.

(d) An expression is a formula if and only if it can be shown to be a formula on the basis of the above conditions.

For a particular theory only those symbols that occur in the theory are used to construct formulae. The normal convention is adopted concerning the omission of parentheses in a formula.

(3) If F, G, H are any formulae of $\mathcal{PL}$ then the following are axioms of $\mathcal{PL}$:

A1. $F \rightarrow (G \rightarrow F)$
A2. $(F \rightarrow (G \rightarrow H)) \rightarrow ((F \rightarrow G) \rightarrow (F \rightarrow H))$
A3. $(\neg G \rightarrow \neg F) \rightarrow (F \rightarrow G)$

(4) The rule of inference of $\mathcal{PL}$ is as follows:

Modus Ponens (MP): G is a direct consequence of F and $F \rightarrow G$.

The study of axiomatic theory for propositional language is completed by introducing the other logic connectives '$\wedge$', '$\vee$' and '$\leftrightarrow$' through the following definitions:

(1) $(F \wedge G)$ for $\neg (F \rightarrow \neg G)$
(2) $(F \vee G)$ for $\neg F \rightarrow G$
(3) $(F \leftrightarrow G)$ for $(F \rightarrow G) \wedge (G \rightarrow F)$

3.4 Soundness and completeness theorem for propositional logic

The soundness and completeness theorem for propositional logic provides an equivalence between the two approaches, namely the truth-table approach and the formal axiomatic approach. These two approaches are also called the *model-theoretic approach* and the *proof-theoretic approach.* This section states the theorem along with other important results in propositional logic. Their proofs have not been provided here because more generalized versions exist in first-order logic and they will be established in a subsequent section.

Lemma 3.1: If F and G are formulae in propositional logic, then $\models$ F and $\models$ F $\rightarrow$ G implies $\models$ G.

Proof Left as an exercise. ■

Theorem 3.1: (deduction theorem for propositional logic) If Γ is a set of formulae and F and G are formulae in propositional logic, then Γ, F, $\vdash$ G implies $\Gamma \vdash$ F $\rightarrow$ G.

Proof Left as an exercise. ■

Theorem 3.2: (soundness theorem for propositional logic) If F is a formula in propositional logic then $\vdash$ F implies $\models$ F.

Proof If F is an axiom then $\models$ F. If F is not an axiom then it has come from axioms by one or more uses of MP. Therefore, by Lemma 3.1, $\models$ F. ■

Theorem 3.3: (completeness theorem for propositional logic) If F is a formula in propositional logic then $\models$ F implies $\vdash$ F.

Proof Left as an exercise. ■

Theorem 3.4: (soundness and completeness theorem for propositional logic) A formula F in propositional logic is a theorem if and only if it is a tautology, that is, $\vdash$ F if and only if $\models$ G.

Proof Straightforward from Theorems 3.2 and 3.3. ■

Theorem 3.5: (strong soundness and completeness theorem for propositional logic) If F_1, ..., F_n, F are formulae in propositional logic then $F_1, ..., F_n \vdash$ F if and only if $F_1, ..., F_n \models$ F. In other words, F is a theorem of F_1, ..., F_n if and only if $(F_1 \rightarrow (F_2 \rightarrow (\cdots (F_n \rightarrow F) \cdots)))$ is a tautology.

Proof Left as an exercise. ■

Theorem 3.6: (consistency theorem for propositional logic)
The theory $\mathcal{PL}$ is consistent.

Proof Left as an exercise. ■

Proposition 3.1: Prove that $\vdash F \leftrightarrow \neg\neg F$, for any formula F.

Proof Left as an exercise. ■

Proposition 3.2: Prove that $F_1 \leftrightarrow F_2 \vdash G_1 \leftrightarrow G_2$, where G_2 is obtained from G_1 by simultaneously replacing each occurrence of F_1 in G_1 by F_2.

Proof Left as an exercise. ■

In contrast to the justification of valid Argument 3.1 by the truth-table method, the following is an axiomatic deduction of the conclusion of Argument 3.1:

Step 1:	$P \rightarrow Q$	Hypothesis
Step 2:	$\neg Q$	Hypothesis
Step 3:	$(\neg\neg P \rightarrow \neg\neg Q) \rightarrow (\neg Q \rightarrow \neg P)$	Axiom A3
Step 4:	$(P \rightarrow Q) \rightarrow (\neg Q \rightarrow \neg P)$	From step 3, Props 3.1 and 3.2
Step 5:	$\neg Q \rightarrow \neg P$	MP on steps 1 and 4
Step 6:	$\neg P$	MP on steps 2 and 5

3.5 First-order logic

There are various kinds of arguments which cannot be stated by propositional logic. As an example consider the following argument.

Argument 3.2

Daniel is an undergraduate student.
All undergraduate students sat the final examination.
Therefore, Daniel sat the final examination.

The above argument is a valid argument. However, if the three premises are symbolized as P, Q and R respectively, it is not possible to prove R from P and Q within the framework of propositional logic. The correctness of Argument 3.2 relies upon the meaning of the expression 'all' which has not been considered in the propositional logic. First-order logic (Copi, 1979; Mendelson, 1987; Stoll, 1963) handles this kind of argument and extends propositional logic by incorporating more logical notations, such as terms, predicates and quantifiers. The set of symbols (the *first-order alphabet*) in the case of first-order logic is defined as follows:

Delimiter:	, (comma)
Parentheses:	(,)
Primitive connectives:	$\neg$, $\rightarrow$
Universal quantifier:	$\forall$ (for all)
Individual variables:	$x, y, z, x_1, y_1, z_1, \ldots$
Individual constants:	$a, b, c, a_1, b_1, c_1, \ldots$
For each natural number n,	
n-ary predicate symbols:	$P^n, Q^n, R^n, P_1^n, Q_1^n, R_1^n, \ldots$
For each natural number n,	
n-ary function symbols:	$f^n, g^n, h^n, f_1^n, g_1^n, h_1^n, \ldots$

Definition 3.16: *Terms* are expressions which inductively are defined as follows:

(1) A variable or an individual constant is a term.

(2) If f is an n-ary function symbol and $t_1, \ldots, t_n$ are terms then $f(t_1, \ldots, t_n)$ is a term.

(3) An expression is a term if it can be shown to be so only on the basis of the above two conditions.

Definition 3.17: If P is an n-ary predicate symbol and $t_1, \ldots, t_n$ are terms then $P(t_1, \ldots, t_n)$ is an *atomic formula* or *atom* or *positive literal.* A *negative literal* is a formula of the form $\neg A$, where A is an atom. A *literal* is either positive or negative.

Definition 3.18: Well-formed formulae (wffs) or formulae of first-order logic are defined as follows:

(1) Every atomic formula is a formula.

(2) If F is a formula then $\neg$ F is a formula.

(3) If F is a formula and x is a variable then $\forall x(F)$ is a formula.

(4) If F and G are formulae then $F \rightarrow G$ is a formula.

(5) An expression is a formula only if it can be generated by the above four conditions.

For convenience the other logical connectives $\wedge$, $\vee$ and $\leftrightarrow$, are also introduced and defined in terms of $\neg$ and $\leftarrow$ as in the case of propositional logic. Also an *existential quantifier*, denoted as $\exists$, is introduced and defined as follows:

$\exists x\,(F)$ is defined by $\neg(\forall x\,(\neg F))$.

In the formulae $\exists x\,(F)$ and $\forall y\,(G)$, F and G are called the *scope* of the quantifiers $\exists x$ and $\forall y$ respectively. As in the case of propositional calculus, the same convention is made about the omission of parentheses in a formula. A formula in propositional logic can be considered as a formula in first-order logic without any variables and quantifiers and vice versa. Hence all the results established so far in connection with propositional logic are also applicable to the set of all quantifier and variable-free formulae in first-order logic. Each ground atomic formula occurring in this set is considered as a propositional symbol.

Definition 3.19: Given a first-order alphabet, the *first-order language* comprises the set of all formulae constructed from the symbols of the alphabet.

Using the first-order language, a symbolization of the first two premises of Argument 3.2 is as follows:

$Undergraduate\,(Daniel)$
$\forall x\,(Undergraduate\,(x) \rightarrow Examination\,(x))$

where *Undergraduate* and *Examination* are predicate symbols.

Definition 3.20: An occurrence of a variable x in a formula F is said to be *bound* (or x *is bound in* F) if either $\forall x$ occurs in F or x lies within the scope of a quantifier $\forall x$ in F. If the occurrence of x in F is not bound its occurrence is said to be *free* in F (or simply x *is free in* F). A variable occurrence in a formula may be both free and bound. This case may be avoided by simultaneously renaming the variables in the quantifier and its associated bound occurrences by new variables.

Definition 3.21: A formula without any free variable is called a *closed formula* (or a *sentence* or *statement*). If $x_1, \ldots, x_n$ are all free variables of F then the formula $\forall x_1 \cdots \forall x_n$ F is called the *closure* of F and is abbreviated as $\forall$F.

EXAMPLE 3.8

Suppose F = $\forall x(P(x,y))$ and G = $\forall x(P(x,y) \rightarrow \forall yQ(y))$. The variable x is bound in F and G. The variable y is free in F and both free (the first occurrence) and bound (the second occurrence) in G.

Use of the notation F$[x_1, ..., x_n]$ emphasizes that $x_1, ..., x_n$ are some of the free variables of F. The notation F$[x_1/t_1, ..., x_n/t_n]$ denotes substitution of the terms $t_1, ..., t_n$ for all free occurrences of $x_1, ..., x_n$ respectively in F.

Definition 3.22: A term t is said to be *free for a variable* x in a formula F if no free occurrence of x lies within the scope of any quantifier $\forall y$, where y is a variable occurring in t.

EXAMPLE 3.9

Consider the formula $\forall x(P(x,y)) \rightarrow Q(z)$ and the term $f(a,x)$. The term is free for z in the formula but not free for y in the same formula.

Definition 3.23: An interpretation I of a first-order language consists of the following:

(1) A non-empty set $\mathbf{D}$, called the *domain of interpretation.*

(2) An assignment to each n-ary predicate symbol of an n-ary relation in $\mathbf{D}$.

(3) An assignment to each n-ary function symbol of an n-ary function with domain $\mathbf{D}^n$ and codomain $\mathbf{D}$.

(4) An assignment to each individual constant of a fixed element of $\mathbf{D}$.

In an interpretation logical connectives and quantifiers are given their usual meanings and variables are thought of as ranging over $\mathbf{D}$. If t is a closed term (or function or predicate symbol), then $I(t)$ denotes the corresponding assignment by I. If t is a closed term and has the form $f(t_1, ..., t_n)$ then the corresponding assignment by I is $I(f)(I(t_1), ..., I(t_n))$.

Definition 3.24: Suppose I is an interpretation with domain $\mathbf{D}$ and $t \in \mathbf{D}$. Then $I_{(x_i/t)}$ is an interpretation which is exactly the same as I except that the ith variable x_i always takes the value t rather than ranging over the whole domain.

Let I be an interpretation with domain $\mathbf{D}$. Let Σ be the set of all sequences of elements of $\mathbf{D}$. For a given sequence $S = (s_1, s_2, ...) \in \Sigma$ and for a term t consider the following *term assignment* of t with respect to I and S, denoted as $S^*(t)$, as follows:

(1) If t is a variable x_j then its assignment is s_j.

(2) If t is a constant then its assignment is according to I.

(3) If $r_1, ..., r_n$ are the term assignments of $t_1, ..., t_n$ respectively and f' is the assignment of the n-ary function symbol f, then $f'(r_1, ..., r_n) \in \mathbf{D}$ is the term assignment of $f(t_1, ..., t_n)$.

The definition of *satisfaction of a formula* with respect to a sequence and an interpretation can be inductively defined as follows:

(1) If F is an atomic wff $P(t_1, ..., t_n)$, then the sequence $S = (s_1, s_2, ...)$ satisfies F if and only if $P'(r_1, ..., r_n)$ (that is, the n-tuple $<r_1, ..., r_n>$ is in the relation P'), where P' is the corresponding n-place relation of the interpretation of P.

(2) S satisfies $\neg$ F if and only if S does not satisfy F.

(3) S satisfies $F \wedge G$ if and only if S satisfies F and S satisfies G.

(4) S satisfies $F \vee G$ if and only if S satisfies F or S satisfies G.

(5) S satisfies $F \rightarrow G$ if and only if either S does not satisfy F or S satisfies G.

(6) S satisfies $F \leftrightarrow G$ if and only if S satisfies both F and G or S satisfies neither F nor G.

(7) S satisfies $\exists x_i$(F) if and only if there is a sequence S_1 that differs from S in at most the ith component such that S_1 satisfies F.

(8) S satisfies $\forall x_i$(F) if and only if every sequence that differs from S in at most the ith component satisfies F.

Definition 3.25: A wff F is *true for the interpretation* (alternatively, F can be given the *truth value* $\mathbf{T}$) I (written $\models_I$ F or $I(\mathrm{F}) = \mathbf{T}$) if and only if every sequence in Σ satisfies F; F is said to be *false for the interpretation* I if and only if no sequence of Σ satisfies F.

If a formula is not closed then some sequence may satisfy the formula while the rest of the sequences may not. The truth value of a closed formula does not depend on the sequence of interpretation and in such a situation the satisfaction of the formula is with respect to the interpretation only. The rest of the text mainly deals with closed formulae.

Definition 3.26: Let I be an interpretation of a first-order language $\mathcal{L}$. Then I is said to be a *model* for a closed wff F if F is true with respect to I. I is said to be a *model* for a set Γ of closed wffs of $\mathcal{L}$ if and only if every wff in Γ is true with respect to I.

Definition 3.27: Let Γ be a set of closed wffs of a first-order language $\mathcal{L}$. Then

(1) Γ is *satisfiable* if and only if $\mathcal{L}$ has at least one interpretation which is a model for Γ.

(2) Γ is *valid* if and only if every interpretation of $\mathcal{L}$ is a model for Γ.

(3) Γ is *unsatisfiable* if and only if no interpretation of $\mathcal{L}$ is a model for Γ.

Definition 3.28: Let F be a closed wff of a first-order language $\mathcal{L}$. A closed wff G is said to be *implied by* F (or, equivalently, F *implies* G) if and only if for every interpretation I of $\mathcal{L}$, I is a model for F implies I is a model for G. Two closed wffs F and G are said to be *equivalent* if and only if they imply each other.

Definition 3.29: Let Γ be a set of closed wffs of $\mathcal{L}$. A closed wff F is said to be a *logical consequence* of Γ (written $\Gamma \models$F) if and only if for every interpretation I of $\mathcal{L}$, I is a model for Γ implies that I is a model for F. Therefore, $\Gamma \models$F means every formula in Γ implies F.

EXAMPLE 3.10

Consider the following two formulae in a first-order language $\mathcal{L}$.

$$P(a)$$
$$\forall x (Q(f(x)) \leftarrow P(x))$$

Consider an interpretation of $\mathcal{L}$ as follows (concentrating only on the symbols occurring in the above two clauses):

(1) The domain of interpretation is the set of all natural numbers.

(2) Assign a to 0.

(3) Assign f to the successor function.

(4) Suppose P and Q are assigned to P' and Q' respectively under the interpretation. A natural number x is in relation P' if and only if x is even. A natural number x is in relation Q' if and only if x is odd.

The two formulae are true under the above interpretation. If the function f were to be interpreted as function f' where $f'(x) = x + 2$ then the second formula would have been false.

3.6 Formal axiomatic theory for first-order logic

A formal axiomatic theory $\mathcal{T}$ for first-order logic known as *first-order theory* is defined as follows:

(1) The set of symbols of a first-order theory is a first-order alphabet.

(2) The language of a first-order theory is a first-order language over the alphabet. For a particular first-order theory $\mathcal{T}$, only those symbols that occur in $\mathcal{T}$ are used to construct the language of $\mathcal{T}$.

(3) The axioms of $\mathcal{T}$ are divided into the following two classes:

   (a) *Logical axioms* If F, G, H are formulae, then the following are logical axioms of the theory:

   A1. $F \rightarrow (G \rightarrow F)$
   A2. $(F \rightarrow (G \rightarrow H)) \rightarrow ((F \rightarrow G) \rightarrow (F \rightarrow H))$
   A3. $(\neg G \rightarrow \neg F) \rightarrow (F \rightarrow G)$
   A4. $(\forall x\ F) \rightarrow G$ if G is a wff obtained from F by substituting all free occurrences of x by a term t and t is free for x in F.
   A5. $\forall x (F \rightarrow G) \rightarrow (F \rightarrow \forall x\ G)$ if F is a wff that contains no free occurrences of x.

   (b) *Proper axioms* Proper axioms vary from theory to theory. A first-order theory in which there are no proper axioms is called a *first-order predicate logic*.

(4) *Rules of inference*

   (a) *Modus ponens* (MP): G follows from F and $F \rightarrow G$.
   (b) *Generalization*: $\forall x$ (F) follows from F.

Since the alphabet of a first-order language is considered as denumerable and formulae of the language are strings of primitive symbols, the set of all formulae of the language can be proved to be denumerable.

3.7 Soundness and completeness theorem for first-order logic

Similar to the case of propositional logic, this section provides the equivalence between the model-theoretic and proof-theoretic approaches of first-order logic. To prove this equivalence, some definitions and results must be established.

Definition 3.30: A set of formulae Γ is *inconsistent* if and only if $\Gamma \vdash F$ and $\Gamma \vdash \neg F$, for some formula F. If Γ is not inconsistent then it is *consistent.*

Lemma 3.2: If Γ is inconsistent, then $\Gamma \vdash G \wedge \neg G$, for some formula G.

Proof Straightforward. ■

Definition 3.31: A set of statements $\mathbf{M}$ is *maximally consistent* if $\mathbf{M}$ is consistent, and for any statement F, if $\mathbf{M} \cup \{F\}$ is consistent then $F \in \mathbf{M}$.

Lemma 3.3: If $\mathbf{M}$ is a maximally consistent set then the following two properties hold in $\mathbf{M}$:

(1) $F \in \mathbf{M}$ if and only if $\mathbf{M} \vdash F$.
(2) Exactly one of F and $\neg F$ is a member of $\mathbf{M}$.

Proof (1) Suppose $F \in \mathbf{M}$. Then obviously $\mathbf{M} \vdash F$. Conversely, assume $\mathbf{M} \vdash F$. This means there exists a finite subset $\mathbf{M}_1$ of $\mathbf{M}$ such that $\mathbf{M}_1 \vdash F$. Then $\mathbf{M}_1 \cup \{F\}$ is consistent. If not, there exists a finite subset $\mathbf{M}_2$ of $\mathbf{M}$ and a formula G such that $\mathbf{M}_2, F \vdash G \wedge \neg G$. Since $\mathbf{M}_1 \vdash F$, therefore $\mathbf{M}_2, \mathbf{M}_1 \vdash G \wedge \neg G$, which contradicts the consistency of $\mathbf{M}$. Thus $\mathbf{M}_1 \cup \{F\}$ is consistent. Since $\mathbf{M}$ is a maximally consistent set, $F \in \mathbf{M}$.

(2) Neither F nor $\neg$ F can be a member of $\mathbf{M}$; otherwise the consistency of $\mathbf{M}$ would be contradicted. If neither F nor $\neg$ F is a member of $\mathbf{M}$, then each of $\mathbf{M} \cup \{F\}$ and $\mathbf{M} \cup \{\neg F\}$ is inconsistent. Since $\mathbf{M}$ is consistent and $\mathbf{M} \cup \{F\}$ is consistent, $\mathbf{M} \vdash \neg F$. Similarly, $\mathbf{M} \vdash F$ and hence $\mathbf{M} \vdash F \wedge \neg F$, which again contradicts the consistency of $\mathbf{M}$. ■

Lemma 3.4: If $\models$ F then $\models \forall$F, where $\forall$F is the closure of F.

Proof Left as an exercise. ■

Lemma 3.5: Let F[x] be a formula in which x is free for y. Then

(1) $\models \forall x\, F[x] \rightarrow F[x/y]$, and

(2) $\models F[x/y] \rightarrow \exists x\, F[x]$

Proof Left as an exercise. ■

Lemma 3.6: Suppose F is a formula without any free occurrences of the variable x and G[x] is any formula. Then

(1) If $\models F \rightarrow G[x]$ then $\models F \rightarrow \forall x\, G[x]$.

(2) If $\models G[x] \rightarrow F$ then $\models \exists x\, G[x] \rightarrow F$.

Proof Left as an exercise. ■

Lemma 3.7: If F and G are formulae in first-order logic, then $\models$ F and $\models F \rightarrow G$ imply $\models$ G.

Proof Left as an exercise. ■

Theorem 3.7: (soundness theorem for first-order logic) If F is a formula in first-order logic then $\vdash$ F implies $\models$ F.

Proof Using the soundness theorem for propositional calculus (Theorem 3.2) and Lemma 3.5(1), it can be proved that the theorem is valid for each instance for each axiom schema. Again, using Lemma 3.7 and Lemma 3.6(1), it can be proved that any theorem F is valid which has been obtained by the application of a rule of inference on the previous two theorems. Hence $\vdash$ F implies $\models$ F. ■

Theorem 3.8: (weak deduction theorem for first-order logic) If Γ is a set of formulae and F and G are formulae of first-order logic such that F is closed, then Γ, F $\vdash$ G implies $\Gamma \vdash F \rightarrow G$.

Proof Left as an exercise. ■

Lemma 3.8: If **S** is a set of formulae and F and G are two formulae then $\mathbf{S} \vdash F \to G[x]$ implies $\mathbf{S} \vdash F \to \exists x G[x]$.

Proof Left as an exercise. ■

Lemma 3.9: If **S** is a set of formulae and F a formula such that $\mathbf{S} \vdash F[x/a]$, where a does not occur in any member of $\mathbf{S} \cup \{F[x]\}$, then $\mathbf{S} \vdash F[x/y]$, for some variable y which does not occur in a proof P of $F[x/a]$.

Proof Since the constant a does not occur in any member of $\mathbf{S} \cup \{F[x]\}$, another proof P_1 of $F[x/y]$ can be constructed from P by replacing each occurrence of a in P by y. ■

Lemma 3.10: If **S** is a set of formulae and $F[x]$ a formula such that $\mathbf{S} \vdash F[x]$, then $\mathbf{S} \vdash F[x/y]$, where y does not occur in F.

Proof Similar to Lemma 3.9. ■

Theorem 3.9: Let $\mathbf{S}_c$ be a consistent set of statements of a first-order predicate logic $\mathcal{P}$. Then $\mathbf{S}_c$ is satisfiable in a domain **D** which is countable. Moreover, the domain **D** is a one-to-one correspondent to the cardinality of the set of primitive symbols of $\mathcal{P}$.

Proof Suppose the domain of individual constants of $\mathcal{P}$ is extended by adding a_1, a_2, ... The resulting domain is also denumerable. Let $\mathcal{F}$ be the extended logic and $\exists x F_1[x]$, $\exists x F_2[x]$, ... are all the statements of $\mathcal{F}$ of the form $\exists x F[x]$. Suppose $\mathbf{S}_0 = \mathbf{S}_c$. Let a_{i_1} be the first constant in a_1, a_2, ... that does not occur in $\exists x F_1[x]$, where $i_1 = j$, for some $j = 1, 2, ...$. Consider

$$\mathbf{S}_1 = \mathbf{S}_0 \cup \{\exists x F_1[x] \to F_1[x/a_{i_1}]\}$$

From the set $\mathbf{S}_j$, for $j = 1, 2, ...$, the set $\mathbf{S}_{j+1}$ is defined as follows. Let $a_{i_{j+1}}$ be the first constant in a_1, a_2, ... that does not occur in $F_1[x/a_{i_1}], ..., F_j[x/a_{i_j}]$. Set

$$\mathbf{S}_{j+1} = \mathbf{S}_j \cup \{\exists x F_{j+1}[x] \to F_{j+1}[x/a_{i_{j+1}}]\}$$

Now, consider the set $\mathbf{S}_1$. If $\mathbf{S}_1$ is inconsistent, by Lemma 3.2, for some formula H

	$\mathbf{S}_c, \exists x F_1[x] \rightarrow F_1[x/a_{i_1}] \vdash H \wedge \neg H$	
that is,	$\mathbf{S}_c \vdash (\exists x F_1[x] \rightarrow F_1[x/a_{i_1}]) \rightarrow H \wedge \neg H$	By Theorem 3.8
that is,	$\mathbf{S}_c \vdash (\exists x F_1[x] \rightarrow F_1[x/y]) \rightarrow H \wedge \neg H$	By Lemma 3.9, for some y
that is,	$\mathbf{S}_c \vdash (\exists x F_1[x] \rightarrow \exists y F_1[x/y]) \rightarrow H \wedge \neg H$	By Lemma 3.8
that is,	$\mathbf{S}_c \vdash (\exists x F_1[x] \rightarrow \exists x F_1[x]) \rightarrow H \wedge \neg H$	By Lemma 3.10
but,	$\mathbf{S}_c \vdash (\exists x F_1[x] \rightarrow \exists x F_1[x])$	
hence	$\mathbf{S}_c \vdash H \wedge \neg H$	By applying MP

Hence $\mathbf{S}_c$ is inconsistent, which violates the initial assumption that $\mathbf{S}_c$ is consistent. By applying the induction hypothesis, it can easily be proved that each $\mathbf{S}_j$ is consistent for $j = 1, 2, \ldots$.

Let

$$\mathbf{S} = \bigcup_{j \in \mathbf{N}} \mathbf{S}_j$$

where $\mathbf{N}$ is the set of all natural numbers. Construct a set $\mathbf{M}$ as follows:

(1) $\mathbf{M}_0 = \mathbf{S}$

(2) $\mathbf{M}_{j+1} = \mathbf{M}_j \cup \{A\}$, if $\mathbf{M}_j \cup \{A\}$ is consistent.

(3) $\mathbf{M} = \bigcup_{j \in \mathbf{N}} \mathbf{M}_j$

Thus $\mathbf{S}_c \subseteq \mathbf{S} \subseteq \mathbf{M}$. Clearly $\mathbf{M}$ is a maximally consistent set of $\mathcal{F}$. Let F be any formula such that $\mathbf{M} \cup \{F\}$ is consistent. Suppose F is the $(n+1)$th formula in the chosen enumeration of the formulae of $\mathcal{F}$. Since $\mathbf{M} \cup \{F\}$ is consistent, $\mathbf{M}_n \cup \{F\}$ is consistent. Hence by definition of $\mathbf{M}_{n+1}$, F is a member of $\mathbf{M}_{n+1}$ and then a member of $\mathbf{M}$. Since $\mathbf{M}$ is a maximally consistent set, the two properties in Lemma 3.3 hold. Suppose a formula of the form $\exists x F[x]$ is in $\mathbf{M}$. From the construction of $\mathbf{S} \subseteq \mathbf{M}$, $\exists x F[x] \rightarrow F[x/a_j]$ is in $\mathbf{S}_j$, for some constant a_j. Now

$$F[x/a_j] \in \mathbf{M}\text{ , for some } j \tag{A}$$

If $F[x/a_j] \notin \mathbf{M}$, for all j, then $\exists x F[x] \rightarrow F[x/a_j] \notin \mathbf{M}$, for all j (since $\exists x F[x]$ is in $\mathbf{M}$ and also $\mathbf{M}$ is consistent). Hence $\exists x F[x] \rightarrow F[x/a_j] \notin \mathbf{S}$, for all j, which violates the fact that $\mathbf{S}_0 \subseteq \mathbf{S}$. The next part of the proof is to construct a model for $\mathbf{M}$.

Define an interpretation I of the language of F as follows:

(1) The domain **D** of I is the set of all individual constants of $\mathcal{F}$.

(2) If P is an n-place predicate symbol in the language of F then the corresponding n-ary relation R is defined as $<t_1, ..., t_n> \in R$ if and only if $\mathbf{M} \vdash P(t_1, ..., t_n)$, for all closed terms $t_1, ..., t_n$.

(3) If f is an n-place function symbol in the language of F then the corresponding n-place function f' is defined as $f'(t_1, ..., t_n) = f(t_1, ..., t_n)$, for all closed terms $t_1, ..., t_n$.

To prove that the interpretation I is a model of $\mathbf{M}$, it suffices to show that

F is true in I if and only if $\mathbf{M} \vdash$ F (B)

for each statement F of $\mathcal{F}$, that is, $\models$ F if and only if $\mathbf{M} \vdash$ F. Suppose this is established and G is any formula such that $\vdash$ G. Then by generalization, $\mathbf{M} \vdash \forall$G and thus $\models \forall$ G (by (B)). Therefore $\models$ G (since by Lemma 3.4, for any formula F, $\models \forall$F if and only if $\models$ F). Hence I is a model of $\mathbf{M}$.

The proof of (B) is carried out by induction on the number n of connectives and quantifiers of F. Suppose (B) holds for any closed formulae with fewer than k connectives and quantifiers. Consider the following cases:

(1) Suppose F is a closed atomic formula of the form $P(t_1, ..., t_n)$. Then (B) follows directly from the definition of P.

(2) Suppose F is of the form $\neg$ G. Then the number of connectives in G is one less than that of F. Now assume that F is true in I. Then, by induction hypothesis, it is not the case that $\mathbf{M} \vdash$ G. Hence by Lemma 3.3(1), G is not a member of $\mathbf{M}$. Again, by Lemma 3.3(2), $\neg$ G is a member of $\mathbf{M}$. Hence by Lemma 3.3(1), $\mathbf{M} \vdash \neg$ G, that is, $\mathbf{M} \vdash$ F. To prove the converse, assume that $\mathbf{M} \vdash$ F, that is, $\mathbf{M} \vdash \neg$ G. Since $\mathbf{M}$ is consistent, it is not the case that $\mathbf{M} \vdash$ G. By induction hypothesis, G is not true and hence F is true in I.

(3) Suppose F is G $\rightarrow$ H. Since F is closed, so are G and H. Let $\mathbf{M} \vdash$ F and assume F is false for I. Then G is true and H is false. Each of G and H contains fewer connectives than in F. Hence by induction hypothesis, $\mathbf{M} \vdash$ G and it is not the case that $\mathbf{M} \vdash$ H. Consider the following proof:

Step 1:	$\mathbf{M} \vdash$ G	Given
Step 2:	$\mathbf{M} \vdash \neg$ H	As case (2)
Step 3:	$\mathbf{M} \vdash$ G $\rightarrow (\neg$ H $\rightarrow \neg$ (G $\rightarrow$ H))	Tautology

Step 4:	$\mathbf{M} \vdash \neg H \rightarrow \neg (G \rightarrow H)$	MP on steps 1 and 3
Step 5:	$\mathbf{M} \vdash \neg (G \rightarrow H)$	MP on steps 2 and 4
Step 6:	$\mathbf{M} \vdash \neg F$	Since F is $G \rightarrow H$

Since $\mathbf{M}$ is consistent, it is not the case that $\mathbf{M} \vdash F$. This contradicts the initial assumption and hence F is true for I. On the other hand, assume F is true for I. If it is not the case that $\mathbf{M} \vdash F$, then by the properties of Lemma 3.3, $\mathbf{M} \vdash \neg F$, that is, $\mathbf{M} \vdash G \wedge \neg H$, which means $\mathbf{M} \vdash G$ and $\mathbf{M} \vdash \neg H$. By induction hypothesis, G is true for I. Since $\mathbf{M}$ is consistent, it is not the case that $\mathbf{M} \vdash H$. Therefore H is false for I. Thus F is false for I. This again contradicts the initial assumption. Thus F is true for I.

(4) Suppose F is $\forall G$ and G is a closed formula. By induction hypothesis, $\models G$ if and only if $\mathbf{M} \vdash G$, that is, $\mathbf{M} \vdash G \leftrightarrow \forall x G$, since x is not free in G. Hence $\mathbf{M} \vdash G$ and $\mathbf{M} \vdash \forall x G$. Furthermore, $\mathbf{M} \models G$ if and only if $\mathbf{M} \models \forall x G$, since x is not free in G. Hence $\mathbf{M} \vdash \forall x G$ if and only if $\models \forall x G$, that is, $\mathbf{M} \vdash F$ if and only if $\models F$.

(5) Suppose F is $\forall x G[x]$ and $G[x]$ is not closed. Since F is closed, x is the only free variable in G. Let $\models \forall x G[x]$ and assume it is not the case that $\mathbf{M} \vdash \forall G[x]$. Applying Lemma 3.3, $\mathbf{M} \vdash \neg \forall G[x]$, that is, $\mathbf{M} \vdash \exists x \neg G[x]$. From (A) there exists an individual constant a of $\mathcal{F}$ such that $\mathbf{M} \vdash \neg G[x/a]$. By induction hypothesis, $\models \neg G[x/a]$. Also, $\models F$, that is, $\models \forall x G[x]$. Therefore, $\models \forall x G[x] \rightarrow G[x/a]$, that is, $\models G[x/a]$, which contradicts the consistency of the interpretation I. Therefore, $\mathbf{M} \vdash \forall x G[x]$. Again, let $\mathbf{M} \vdash \forall x G[x]$ and if possible assume it is not the case that $\models \forall x G[x]$. Hence some sequence $\mathcal{S}$ does not satisfy $G[x]$. Let t be the ith component of $\mathcal{S}$ which has been substituted for x in showing the unsatisfiability of $G[x]$ wrt s. Then the sequence $\mathcal{S}$ does not satisfy $G[x/t]$ either, since the closed term t is mapped to itself under $\mathcal{S}^*$. Furthermore, $\mathbf{M} \vdash \forall x G[x]$, that is, $\mathbf{M} \vdash \forall x G[x/t]$. Hence by induction hypothesis, $\models G[x/t]$. Therefore a contradiction arises and $\models \forall x G[x]$, that is, $\models F$.

Thus the interpretation I is a model for $\mathbf{M}$ and hence a model for $\mathbf{S}_c$. The domain of this interpretation is a one-to-one correspondent with the set of all primitive symbols of $\mathcal{P}$. Hence the proof. ■

Theorem 3.10: Every consistent theory has a denumerable model.

Proof Immediate from Theorem 3.9. ■

Theorem 3.11: (Gödel's completeness theorem) For each formula F in first-order logic, if $\models$ F then $\vdash$ F.

Proof Suppose that $\models$ F. Then by Lemma 3.4, $\models \forall$F and hence $\neg \forall$F is not satisfiable. By Theorem 3.9, $\{\neg \forall F\}$ is inconsistent. Therefore by Lemma 3.2

$$\neg \forall F \vdash G \wedge \neg G, \text{ for some formula } F$$

Then by the deduction theorem (Theorem 3.8)

$$\vdash \neg \forall F \rightarrow G \wedge \neg G$$

and thus $\vdash \forall$ F. Suppose $x_1, x_2, ..., x_n$ are free variables of F and thus

$$\vdash \forall x_1 \forall x_2 \cdots \forall x_n F$$

Axiom A4 gives

$$\vdash \forall x_1 \forall x_2 \cdots \forall x_n F \rightarrow \forall x_2 \cdots \forall x_n F$$

By applying MP, $\vdash \forall x_2 \cdots \forall x_n$F. Continuing this way gives $\vdash$ F. ■

Theorem 3.12: (soundness and completeness theorem of first-order logic) For each formula F in first-order logic, $\models$ F if and only if $\vdash$ F.

Proof Immediate from Theorems 3.7 and 3.11. ■

Theorem 3.13: (strong soundness and completeness theorem of first-order logic) Suppose Γ is any set of formulae and F is a formula in first-order logic. Then $\Gamma \models$ F if and only if $\Gamma \vdash$ F. In other words, F is a logical consequence of Γ if and only if F is a theorem of Γ.

Proof Left as an exercise. ■

3.8 Application of soundness and completeness theorem

Some important theorems will be established in this section by using the soundness and completeness theorem of first-order logic.

Definition 3.32: A theory $\mathcal{K}_1$ is said to be an *extension of a theory* $\mathcal{K}$ if every theorem of $\mathcal{K}$ is a theorem of $\mathcal{K}_1$.

Definition 3.33: A theory $\mathcal{K}$ is *complete*, if for any closed formula F of $\mathcal{K}$, either $\vdash$ F or $\vdash \neg$ F.

Lemma 3.11: Suppose $\mathcal{K}$ is a consistent theory. Then $\mathcal{K}$ is complete if and only if $\mathcal{K}$ is maximally consistent.

Proof Left as an exercise. ■

Lemma 3.12: (Lindenbaum's lemma) If $\mathcal{K}$ is a consistent theory then $\mathcal{K}$ has a consistent, complete extension.

Proof Left as an exercise. ■

Theorem 3.14: (compactness) A set of formulae **S** in first-order logic is satisfiable if and only if every finite subset of **S** is satisfiable.

Proof The forward part of the theorem follows easily. To prove the converse, suppose every finite subset of **S** is satisfiable. Then every finite subset of **S** is consistent. If not, there is a finite subset $\mathbf{S}_1$ of **S** which is inconsistent. Then $\mathbf{S}_1 \vdash$ F and $\mathbf{S}_1 \vdash \neg$ F, for some formula F. By the soundness theorem, $\mathbf{S}_1 \models$ F and $\mathbf{S}_1 \models \neg$ F. Hence $\mathbf{S}_1$ cannot be satisfiable, which is a contradiction. Since every finite subset of **S** is consistent, **S** itself is consistent. For, if **S** is inconsistent then some finite subset of **S** is inconsistent which is a contradiction. Since **S** is consistent, by Theorem 3.9, **S** is satisfiable. ■

Theorem 3.15: (Skolem–Löwenheim theorem) Any theory $\mathcal{K}$ that has a model has a denumerable model.

Proof If $\mathcal{K}$ has a model, then $\mathcal{K}$ is consistent. For, if $\mathcal{K}$ is inconsistent, then $\vdash$ F and $\vdash \neg$ F, for some formula F. By the soundness theorem, $\models$ F and $\models \neg$ F. If a formula is both true and false then $\mathcal{K}$ cannot have a model, which is a contradiction. By Theorem 3.10, $\mathcal{K}$ has a denumerable model. ■

3.9 Normal forms of clauses

A procedure for determining whether or not a formula is a theorem of a particular theory $\mathcal{K}$ is called a *theorem proving procedure* or *proof procedure* for the theory $\mathcal{K}$. Theorem proving procedures deal with formulae in standard forms, for example, prenex normal form, Skolem conjunctive normal form and clausal form. This section provides tools for obtaining these forms from given formulae.

Definition 3.34: A formula is said to be in *prenex normal form* if it is of the form

$$Q_1 x_1 \cdots Q_n x_n \mathrm{B} \tag{3.1}$$

where each Q_i is either $\forall$ or $\exists$ and B is quantifier free. The formula B is called the *matrix*.

Definition 3.35: A prenex normal form formula is said to be in *Skolem conjunctive normal form* if it has the form

$$\forall x_1 \cdots \forall x_n \mathrm{B} \tag{3.2}$$

where the matrix B is in conjunctive normal form, that is, a conjunction of disjunction of literals.

Definition 3.36: A Skolem conjunctive normal form formula (3.2) is said to be a *clause* if it has the form

$$\forall x_1 \cdots \forall x_n (L_1 \vee \cdots \vee L_n) \qquad n \geq 0 \tag{3.3}$$

where each L_i is a literal and $x_1, ..., x_n$ are the free variables of the disjunction $L_1 \vee \cdots \vee L_n$. A formula is said to be in *clausal form* if it is a clause.

For the sake of convenience, (3.3) is rewritten as the disjunction $L_1 \vee \cdots \vee L_n$ of literals without its quantifiers or as the set $\{L_1, ..., L_n\}$ of literals. Thus when a disjunction $L_1 \vee \cdots \vee L_n$ or a set $\{L_1, ..., L_n\}$ is given as a clause C, where each L_i is a literal then C is regarded as of the form (3.3) where x_1,

..., x_n are all the free variables occurring in all the L_i s.

Every formula F can be transformed to some formula G in Skolem conjunctive normal form such that F ≡ G by going through the following steps of different transformations.

Step 1: (Elimination of → and ↔)
Applying the following two conversion rules to any subformula within the given formula:

(1) $F \rightarrow G$ to $\neg F \vee G$
(2) $F \leftrightarrow G$ to $(\neg F \vee G) \wedge (F \vee \neg G)$

Step 2: (Moving ¬ inwards)
Applying the following conversion rules repeatedly until all negations are immediately to the left of an atomic formula:

(1) $\neg\neg F$ to F
(2) $\neg (F \wedge G)$ to $\neg F \vee \neg G$
(3) $\neg (F \vee G)$ to $\neg F \wedge \neg G$
(4) $\neg \forall x F$ to $\exists x \neg F$
(5) $\neg \exists x F$ to $\forall x \neg F$

Step 3: (Moving quantifiers inwards)
Apply the following conversion rules to any subformula within the formula until no rule is applicable:

(1) $\forall x (F \wedge G)$ to $\forall x F \wedge \forall x G$
(2) $\exists x (F \vee G)$ to $\exists x F \vee \exists x G$
(3) $\forall x (F \vee G)$ to $\forall x F \vee G$, provided x is not free in G.
(4) $\exists x (F \wedge G)$ to $\exists x F \wedge G$, provided x is not free in G.
(5) $\forall x (F \vee G)$ to $F \vee \forall x G$, provided x is not free in F.
(6) $\exists x (F \wedge G)$ to $F \wedge \exists x G$, provided x is not free in F.
(7) $\forall x F$ to F, provided x is not free in F.
(8) $\exists x F$ to F, provided x is not free in F.

(9) $\forall x \forall y (F \vee G)$ to $\forall y \forall x (F \vee G)$

(10) $\exists x \exists y (F \wedge G)$ to $\exists y \exists x (F \wedge G)$

The last two transformations in this step should be applied in a restricted manner to avoid infinite computation. These two should be applied to a subformula of a given formula provided y is free in both F and G and x is not free in either F or G.

Step 4: (Variable renaming)
Repeat this step until no two quantifiers share the same variable.
When two quantifiers share the same variable, rename simultaneously one of the variables in the quantifier and its associated bound occurrences by a new variable.

Step 5: (Skolemization)
Repeat this step until the formula is free from existential quantifiers.
Suppose the formula contains an existential quantifier $\exists x$. At each occurrence of x other than as quantifier name, replace x by the term $f(x_1, ..., x_m)$, where f is an m-ary function symbol which does not occur in the formula. Each x_i is universally quantified in the formula and this quantifier has $\exists x$ in its scope. If $m = 0$ then $f(x_1, ..., x_m)$ is taken as constant symbol. This process of removing existential quantifiers from a formula is called *Skolemization* and each newly entered $f(x_1, ..., x_m)$ is called a *Skolem function instance.*

Step 6: (Rewrite in prenex normal form)
Remove all universal quantifiers from the formula and place them at the front of the remaining quantifier free formula (which is the matrix). The resulting formula is now in prenex normal form.

Step 7: (Rewrite in Skolem conjunctive normal form)
Apply the following transformations repeatedly to the matrix of the formula until the matrix is transformed to conjunctive normal form:

(1) $F \vee (G \wedge H)$ to $(F \vee G) \wedge (F \vee H)$

(2) $(F \wedge G) \vee H$ to $(F \vee H) \wedge (G \vee H)$

EXAMPLE 3.11
This shows the conversion of a formula to its equivalent Skolem conjunctive normal form. The applicable step from the transformation procedure is given in the right-hand column.

$\forall x(\neg R(x) \to P(a) \wedge \neg \exists z \neg Q(z,a)) \wedge \forall x(P(x) \to \exists y Q(y,x))$	Given
$\forall x(\neg\neg R(x) \vee P(a) \wedge \neg \exists z \neg Q(z,a)) \wedge \forall x(\neg P(x) \vee \exists y Q(y,x))$	By step 1
$\forall x(R(x) \vee P(a) \wedge \forall z \neg\neg Q(z,a)) \wedge \forall x(\neg P(x) \vee \exists y Q(y,x))$	By step 2
$\forall x(R(x) \vee P(a) \wedge \forall z\ Q(z,a)) \wedge \forall x(\neg P(x) \vee \exists y Q(y,x))$	By step 2
$(\forall x R(x) \vee P(a) \wedge \forall z\ Q(z,a)) \wedge \forall x(\neg P(x) \vee \exists y Q(y,x))$	By step 3
$(\forall x R(x) \vee P(a) \wedge \forall z\ Q(z,a)) \wedge \forall t(\neg P(t) \vee \exists y Q(y,t))$	By step 4
$(\forall x R(x) \vee P(a) \wedge \forall z\ Q(z,a)) \wedge \forall t(\neg P(t) \vee Q(f(t),t))$	By step 5
$\forall x \forall z \forall t((R(x) \vee P(a) \wedge Q(z,a)) \wedge (\neg P(t) \vee Q(f(t),t)))$	By step 6
$\forall x \forall z \forall t((R(x) \vee P(a)) \wedge (R(x) \vee Q(z,a)) \wedge (\neg P(t) \vee Q(f(t),t)))$	By step 7

3.10 Herbrand's theorem

By the definition of satisfiability, a formula F is unsatisfiable if and only if it is false under all interpretations over all domains. Therefore it is an enormous and almost impossible task to consider all interpretations over all domains to verify the unsatisfiability of F. Hence it is desirable to have one specified domain such that F is unsatisfiable if and only if F is false under all interpretations over this special domain. Fortunately, this kind of special domain exists: it is the Herbrand universe of F, for a given formula F. The power of the Herbrand universe will now be demonstrated by using it to establish some results.

Definition 3.37: Given a formula F in Skolem conjunctive normal form, the *Herbrand universe* of F, denoted as $\mathcal{HU}(\mathrm{F})$ is inductively defined as follows:

(1) Any constant symbol occurring in F is a member of $\mathcal{HU}(\mathrm{F})$. If F does not contain any constant symbol, then $\mathcal{HU}(\mathrm{F})$ contains the symbol a.

(2) If f is an n-ary function symbol occurring in F and $t_1, ..., t_n$ are in $\mathcal{HU}(\mathrm{F})$ then $f(t_1, ..., t_n)$ is a member of $\mathcal{HU}(\mathrm{F})$.

Definition 3.38: The *Herbrand base* of a formula F, denoted by $\mathcal{HB}(\mathbf{F})$, is the set $\{P(t_1, ..., t_n) | \; P$ is an n-ary predicate symbol occurring in F and $t_1, ..., t_n \in \mathcal{HU}(\mathrm{F})\}$.

Definition 3.39: A *ground instance* of a formula F in Skolem conjunctive normal form is a formula obtained from the matrix of F by replacing its variables by constants.

EXAMPLE 3.12

Suppose F = $\forall x (Q(x) \wedge (\neg P(x) \vee P(f(x))))$. Then $\mathcal{HU}$(F) = $\{a, f(a), f(f(a)), \ldots\}$ and $\mathcal{HB}$(**F**) = $\{Q(a), Q(f(a)), Q(f(f(a))), \ldots, P(a), P(f(a)), P(f(f(a))), \ldots\}$. The formula $Q(f(a)) \wedge (\neg P(f(a)) \vee P(f(f(a))))$ is a ground instance of F.

EXAMPLE 3.13

Suppose F = $\forall x (P(a, b) \wedge (\neg P(x, y) \vee Q(x)))$. Then $\mathcal{HU}$(F) = $\{a, b\}$ and $\mathcal{HB}$(**F**) = $\{P(a, a), P(a, b), P(b, a), P(b, b), Q(a), Q(b)\}$.

Definition 3.40: Given a formula F in prenex normal form, an interpretation $\mathcal{HI}$ over $\mathcal{HU}$(F) is a *Herbrand interpretation* if the following conditions are satisfied:

(1) $\mathcal{HI}$ assigns every constant in $\mathcal{HU}$(F) to itself.

(2) Let f be an n-ary function symbol and $t_1, \ldots, t_n$ be elements of $\mathcal{HU}$(F). Then $\mathcal{HI}$ assigns f to an n-place function that maps the n-tuple $<t_1, \ldots, t_n>$ to $f(t_1, \ldots, t_n)$.

Theorem 3.16: Suppose F = $\forall x_1 \cdots \forall x_p \mathrm{B}[x_1, \ldots, x_p]$, $p \geq 0$, is a formula in prenex normal form, where B is the matrix of F. Then F is unsatisfiable if and only if F is false under all Herbrand interpretations.

Proof If a formula is unsatisfiable then F is false under all interpretations and hence false under all Herbrand interpretations.

Conversely, suppose F is satisfiable. Then there is an interpretation I over a domain **D** such that I(F) = **T**. Construct a Herbrand interpretation $\mathcal{HI}$ as follows. for any n-ary predicate symbol P occurring in F and any $t_1, \ldots, t_n \in \mathcal{HU}$(F), $<t_1, \ldots, t_n> \in P$ if and only if $<I(t_1), \ldots, I(t_n)> \in I(P)$.

For any atomic formula A, $\mathcal{HI}$(A) = I(A). Hence if $p = 0$ in F, that is, if F is a quantifier free formula, $\mathcal{HI}$(F) = I(F) = **T**. If $p > 0$ in F then without any loss of generality one can assume that F has the form $\forall x \mathrm{B}[x]$, where B is the matrix of F. Now, I(F) = $I(\forall x \mathrm{B}[x])$ = **T**. Therefore, $I(\mathrm{B}[x/I(t)])$ = **T**, where t is an arbitrary member of **D**. Now

$$\mathcal{HI}_{(x/t)}(\mathrm{B}([x]))$$
$$= I_{(x/I(t))}(\mathrm{B}[x]), \text{ since } \mathrm{B}[x] \text{ is quantifier free } \mathcal{HI}(\mathrm{B}[x/t]) = I(\mathrm{B}[x/I(t)])$$
$$= I(\mathrm{B}[x/I(t)])$$
$$= \mathbf{T}$$

Therefore, $\mathcal{HI}(\mathrm{F}) = \mathcal{HI}(\forall x\ \mathrm{B}[x]) = \mathbf{T}$.

Thus if a formula F is satisfiable in an interpretation then F is also satisfiable under the Herbrand interpretation. Hence if F is unsatisfiable under all Herbrand interpretations then F is unsatisfiable. ■

Definition 3.41: Suppose $\forall x_1 \cdots \forall x_n \mathrm{B}[x_1, ..., x_n]$ is a formula in prenex normal form. An *instance of matrix* B means a formula of the form $\mathrm{B}[x_1/t_1, ..., x_n/t_n]$ where $t_1, ..., t_n$ are elements of the Herbrand universe of the given formula.

Theorem 3.17: (Herbrand's theorem) Suppose $\mathrm{F} = \forall x_1 \cdots \forall x_n \mathrm{B}[x_1, ..., x_n]$ is a formula in prenex normal form. Then F is unsatisfiable if and only if there are finitely many instances of the matrix $\mathrm{B}[x_1, ..., x_n]$ which are unsatisfiable.

Proof Without any loss of generality, the formula F can be assumed to be of the form $\forall x\, \mathrm{B}[x]$, where B is quantifier free. Suppose $\mathrm{B}[x/t_1], ..., \mathrm{B}[x/t_n]$ are finitely many instances of $\mathrm{B}[x]$. Then

$$\forall x\, \mathrm{B}[x] \vdash \mathrm{B}[x/t_1] \wedge \cdots \wedge \mathrm{B}[x/t_n].$$

Thus the satisfiability of $\forall x\, \mathrm{B}[x]$ implies the satisfiability of the instances $\mathrm{B}[x/t_1]$, ..., $\mathrm{B}[x/t_n]$. Hence if the instances are unsatisfiable, then the formula $\forall x\, \mathrm{B}[x]$ itself is unsatisfiable.

Conversely, suppose $\forall x\, \mathrm{B}[x]$ is unsatisfiable and, if possible, let any finitely many instances of $\mathrm{B}[x]$ be satisfiable. Then by the compactness theorem $\{\mathrm{B}[x/t] \mid t \in \mathcal{HU}(\mathrm{F})\}$ is satisfiable. Accordingly, $\mathcal{HI}(\forall x\, \mathrm{B}[x]) = \mathbf{T}$, contradicting the assumption that $\forall x\, \mathrm{B}[x]$ is unsatisfiable. Hence there exist finitely many instances of $\mathrm{B}[x]$ which are unsatisfiable. ■

Suppose F is an arbitrary formula. With the aid of the transformation procedure described in Section 3.9, one can assume that the formula F has the Skolem conjunctive normal form

$$\forall x_1 \cdots \forall x_n (\mathrm{B}_1 \wedge \cdots \wedge \mathrm{B}_m), \tag{3.4}$$

where each B_i is a disjunction of literals. If $x_1, ..., x_n$ are all the free variables of the conjunction then, for the sake of convenience, the formula (3.4) is rewritten as the set $\{\mathrm{B}_1, ..., \mathrm{B}_m\}$.

Thus when a set $\mathbf{S} = \{B_1, ..., B_m\}$ is given, where each B_i is a disjunction of literals then $\mathbf{S}$ is regarded as the form (3.4) where $x_1, ..., x_n$ are all the free variables occurring in all the B_is. The set $\mathbf{S}$ can also be regarded as the conjunction of clauses $\forall B_1, ..., \forall B_m$.

EXAMPLE 3.14

In the case of Example 3.11, the given formula can equivalently be written as a set $\{\forall x(R(x) \vee P(a)), \forall x \forall z(R(x) \vee Q(z, a)), \forall t(\neg P(t) \vee Q(f(t), t))\}$ of clauses or as a set $\{R(x) \vee P(a), R(x) \vee Q(z, a), \neg P(t) \vee Q(f(t), t)\}$ of clauses when the free variables are assumed to be universally quantified at the front of each clause.

An alternative version of Herbrand's theorem regarding the representation of a formulae as a set of clauses is as follows:

Theorem 3.18: A set $\mathbf{S}$ of clauses is unsatisfiable if and only if there are finitely many ground instances of clauses of $\mathbf{S}$ which are unsatisfiable.

Proof Follows from Theorem 3.17. ■

3.11 Implementation of Herbrand's theorem

Suppose $\mathbf{S}$ is a finite unsatisfiable set of clauses. Then according to Herbrand's theorem, the unsatisfiability of $\mathbf{S}$ can be proved in the following manner. First, enumerate a sequence $\mathbf{S}_1 \subseteq \mathbf{S}_2 \subseteq \cdots$ of finite sets of ground instances from $\mathbf{S}$ and then test the satisfiability of each $\mathbf{S}_i$. One way of enumerating the sequence $\mathbf{S}_1 \subseteq \mathbf{S}_2 \subseteq \cdots$ is that each member of $\mathbf{S}_i$ is of length at most i. Since each member of $\mathbf{S}_i$ is ground, its satisfiability can be checked by a standard method (for example by truth table) of propositional logic.

Gilmore's approach (Gilmore, 1960) was to transform each $\mathbf{S}_i$, as it is generated, to its equivalent disjunctive normal form D and then to remove from D any conjunction in D containing a complementary pair of literals. If D (disjunction equivalent to $\mathbf{S}_i$, for some i) becomes empty at some stage due to this transformation, then $\mathbf{S}_i$ is unsatisfiable and therefore $\mathbf{S}$ is unsatisfiable. Gilmore's idea was combinatorially explosive because, for example, if an $\mathbf{S}_i$ contains 10 three-literal clauses then there will be 3^{10} conjunctions to be tested.

A more efficient approach to test the unsatisfiability for a set of ground clauses was devised by Davis and Putnam (1960). This method consists of a number of rules which are stated below. A discussion on the reasoning behind introducing these rules and their correctness will be described in Chapter 4.

(1) *Tautology rule* Suppose $\mathbf{S}_1$ is obtained from $\mathbf{S}$ by deleting all clauses from $\mathbf{S}$ that are tautologies. Then $\mathbf{S}_1$ is unsatisfiable if and only if $\mathbf{S}$ is satisfiable.

(2) *One-literal rule* Suppose there is a unit clause L in $\mathbf{S}$ and $\mathbf{S}_1$ is obtained from $\mathbf{S}$ by

   (a) deleting all clauses from $\mathbf{S}$ containing an occurrence of L, and then

   (b) replacing each clause C from the rest of $\mathbf{S}$ by a clause obtained from C by removing the occurrence (if any) of the complement of L.

   Then $\mathbf{S}_1$ is unsatisfiable if and only if $\mathbf{S}$ is satisfiable.

(3) *Pure literal rule* If a literal L occurs in some clause in $\mathbf{S}$ but its complement L' does not occur in any clause, then $\mathbf{S}_1$ is obtained from $\mathbf{S}$ by deleting all clauses containing an occurrence of L. Then $\mathbf{S}$ is unsatisfiable if and only if $\mathbf{S}_1$ is unsatisfiable. This literal L in this case is called a *pure literal.*

(4) *Splitting rule* Suppose $\mathbf{S} = \{C_1 \vee A, ..., C_m \vee A, D_1 \vee \neg A, ..., D_n \vee \neg A, E_1, ..., E_p\}$, where A is an atom and each of C_i, D_j and E_k does not contain any occurrence of A or $\neg A$. Suppose $\mathbf{S}_1 = \{C_1, ..., C_m, E_1, ..., E_p\}$ and $\mathbf{S}_2 = \{D_1, ..., D_n, E_1, ..., E_p\}$. Then $\mathbf{S}$ is unsatisfiable if and only if each of $\mathbf{S}_1$ and $\mathbf{S}_2$ is satisfiable.

(5) *Subsumption rule* Suppose $\mathbf{S}_1$ is obtained from $\mathbf{S}$ by deleting every clause D from $\mathbf{S}$ for which there is another clause C in $\mathbf{S}$ such that every literal that occurs in C also occurs in D. Then $\mathbf{S}$ is unsatisfiable if and only if $\mathbf{S}_1$ is unsatisfiable.

The above set of rules is applied repeatedly until no more rules can be applied on the resulting sets. If each of the resulting sets contains the empty clause, then the given set of clauses will be unsatisfiable.

EXAMPLE 3.15

Step 1:	$\{P(a) \vee \neg P(a) \vee Q(b), Q(a), Q(a) \vee P(c),$ $R(a) \vee P(b), \neg Q(a) \vee S(a) \vee R(b),$ $\neg S(b) \vee \neg P(b), S(b)\}$	Given set $\mathbf{S}$

Step 2:	$\{Q(a), Q(a) \vee P(c), R(a) \vee P(b),$ $\neg Q(a) \vee S(a) \vee R(b),$ $\neg S(b) \vee \neg P(b), S(b)\}$	Tautology rule
Step 3:	$\{R(a) \vee P(b), S(a) \vee R(b),$ $\neg S(b) \vee \neg P(b), S(b)\}$	One-literal rule
Step 4.	$\{S(a) \vee R(b), \neg S(b) \vee \neg P(b), S(b)\}$	Pure literal rule
Step 5:	$\{\neg S(b) \vee \neg P(b), S(b)\}$	Pure literal rule
Step 6:	$\mathbf{S}_1 = \{\Box\}$ $\mathbf{S}_2 = \{\neg P(b)\}$	Splitting rule $D_1 = \neg P(b)$ and $C_1 = \varnothing$
Step 7:	$\mathbf{S}_1 = \{\Box\}$ $\mathbf{S}_2 = \{\}$	One-literal rule

The set $\mathbf{S}_1$ is unsatisfiable but $\mathbf{S}_2$ is not. Therefore, $\mathbf{S}$ is satisfiable.

Exercises

3.1 By using the truth-table method determine whether each of the following propositional formulae is a tautology or a contradiction or neither of them:

(a) $P \wedge Q \rightarrow P \vee Q$

(b) $(P \rightarrow Q) \wedge P \wedge \neg Q$

(c) $(P \vee Q) \rightarrow P \wedge \neg Q$

(d) $(P \leftrightarrow Q) \rightarrow (P \rightarrow Q)$

3.2 Formalize the following argument in propositional logic and establish the validity of the argument using the truth-table method:

(a) If I go out for shopping then either I buy clothes or I purchase foods. I spend money only when I buy clothes or I purchase foods. I did not spend any money. Therefore I did not go out for shopping.

3.3 Formalize the following arguments in first-order logic and prove the validity of the arguments:

(a) A person a is an ancestor of b if either a is a father of b or there exists a person c such that a is the father of c and c is an ancestor of b. Maurice is the father of Robert and Robert is the father of Daniel.

Therefore, Maurice is an ancestor of Daniel.

(b) Someone who is a student and not an undergraduate student is a postgraduate student. All undergraduate students sat the final examination. Daniel is a student and did not sit the final examination. Therefore, Daniel is a postgraduate student.

3.4 Determine the status (that is, free or bound or both) of each of the variables occurring in the following formulae and hence determine whether it is closed or not.

(a) $\forall x (P(x) \rightarrow \exists y Q(x, y))$

(b) $\forall x P(x) \rightarrow \exists y Q(x, y)$

(c) $\forall x \forall y (P(x, y) \wedge P(y, z) \rightarrow P(x, z))$

3.5 Show that the sentence $\forall x P(x) \rightarrow \exists x P(x)$ is valid in all domains.

3.6 Show that the sentence $\forall y \exists x P(x, y) \rightarrow \exists x \forall y P(x, y)$ is satisfiable but not valid.

3.7 Prove that $\forall x \exists y (y > x)$ is satisfiable where the domain of interpretation is the set of all natural numbers, and where '>' is interpreted as the strict ordering symbol.

3.8 Prove the sentences $\exists x \forall y P(x, y) \rightarrow \forall y \exists x P(x, y)$.

3.9 Show each of the following:

(a) $P(a), \forall x (P(x) \rightarrow Q(x)) \vdash Q(a)$

(b) $\forall x (P(x) \rightarrow Q(x)) \vdash \forall x \neg Q(x) \rightarrow \forall x \neg P(x)$

(c) $\forall x (P(x) \rightarrow Q(x)), \forall x (\neg R(x) \rightarrow P(x)) \vdash \forall x (Q(x) \vee R(x))$

3.10 Find the Skolem conjunctive normal form for each of the following formulae and hence determine their equivalent sets of clauses:

(a) $\forall x \neg \exists y P(x, y) \rightarrow \neg \forall x (\exists z P(x, y) \rightarrow \forall y P(t, y))$

(b) $\forall x (\exists y P(x, y) \leftrightarrow \exists z Q(z, x))$

(c) $\forall x \forall z (\neg P(x, z) \rightarrow \exists y \neg (\neg Q(x, y) \wedge \neg Q(f(x), y) \rightarrow \neg R(x, y))) \wedge$
$\exists x \forall y \neg P(x, y)$

(d) $\neg (\forall x P(x) \vee \neg \forall y Q(y)) \vee (\forall x P(x) \vee \exists y \neg Q(y))$

3.11 By applying the Davis–Putnam procedure, prove the unsatisfiability for the set of clauses $\{P(a) \vee \neg P(a),\ Q(a),\ Q(a) \vee P(c),\ R(a) \vee P(b),\ \neg Q(a) \vee S(a) \vee R(b),\ \neg S(b) \vee T(b),\ \neg Q(a) \vee S(b),\ \neg T(b) \vee T(a),\ \neg T(a)\}$.

4

Resolution theorem proving

Theorem proving in a system of first-order logic using the *resolution principle* as the sole inference rule is called the *resolution theorem proving*. This style of theorem proving avoids the major combinatorial obstacles to efficiency found in earlier theorem proving methods (Gilmore, 1960; Davis and Putnam, 1960) which used procedures based on Herbrand's fundamental theorem concerning first-order logic. A logic programming system adopts a version of resolution theorem proving as its inference subsystem. Hence it is important to have a clear idea about this kind of theorem proving to understand the internal execution of a logic programming system. This chapter carries out a detailed discussion of the resolution principle, resolution theorem proving and some important relevant topics including unification and refinements of the resolution principle. Most of the results in this chapter (except the last section) are due to Robinson (1965b).

4.1 Resolution principle and unification

The resolution principle is an inference rule of first-order logic which states that from any two clauses C and D, one can infer a *resolvent* of C and D. The principle idea behind the concept of resolvent, and hence behind the resolution principle, is that of unification. *Unification* (Knight, 1989; Martelli and Montanari, 1982; Paterson, 1978; Robinson, 1971) is a process of determining whether two expressions can be made identical by some appropriate substitution for their variables. Some definitions and results must be established before formally introducing the concept of unification.

Definition 4.1: Terms and literals are the only *well-formed expressions* (or simply *expressions*).

Definition 4.2: A *substitution* θ is a finite set of pairs of variables and terms, denoted by $\{x_1/t_1, ..., x_n/t_n\}$, where x_is are distinct and each t_i is different from x_i. The term t_i is called a *binding* for x_i. θ is called a *ground substitution* if each t_i is a ground term. The substitution given by the empty set is called the *empty substitution* (or *identity substitution*) and is denoted by $\{\}$ or ε.

Definition 4.3: In a substitution $\{x_1/t_1, ..., x_n/t_n\}$, $x_1, ..., x_n$ are called the *variables of the substitution* and $t_1, ..., t_n$ are called the *terms of the substitution.*

Definition 4.4: Let $\theta = \{x_1/t_1, ..., x_n/t_n\}$ be a substitution and E be an expression. The *application* of θ to E, denoted by $E\theta$, is the expression obtained by simultaneously replacing each occurrence of the variable x_i in E by the term t_i. In this case $E\theta$ is called the *instance* of E by θ. If $E\theta$ is ground then $E\theta$ is called a *ground instance* of E. Also, E is referred to as a *generalization* of $E\theta$.

EXAMPLE 4.1

Let $E = p(x, f(x), y, g(a))$ and $\theta = \{x/b,\ y/h(x)\}$. Then $E\theta = p(b, f(b), h(x), g(a))$.

Definition 4.5: Let $\theta = \{x_1/t_1, ..., x_m/t_m\}$ and $\phi = \{y_1/s_1, ..., y_n/s_n\}$ be two substitutions. Then the *composition* $\theta\phi$ of θ and ϕ is the substitution obtained from the set

$$\{x_1/t_1\phi, ..., x_m/t_m\phi, y_1/s_1, ..., y_n/s_n\}$$

by deleting any binding $x_i/t_i\phi$ for which $x_i = t_i\phi$ and deleting any binding y_i/s_i for which $y_i \in \{x_1, ..., x_m\}$.

EXAMPLE 4.2

Let $\theta = \{x/b, y/h(z)\}$ and $\sigma = \{z/c\}$. Then $\theta\sigma = \{x/b, y/h(c), z/c\}$.

The following lemmas describe different properties of substitutions and their compositions.

Lemma 4.1: For any substitution θ, $\varepsilon\theta = \theta\varepsilon = \theta$.

Proof Straightforward. ■

Lemma 4.2: Let E be any string and α, β be two arbitrary substitutions. Then $(E\alpha)\beta = E(\alpha\beta)$.

Proof Let $\alpha = \{x_1/e_1, ..., x_n/e_n\}$ and $\beta = \{y_1/s_1, ..., y_m/s_m\}$. The string E can be assumed of the form $E = E_0 x_{i_1} E_1 \cdots x_{i_p} E_p$, ($p \geq 0$), where none of the substring E_j of E contains occurrences of variables $x_1, ..., x_n$, some of E_j are possibly null and $1 \leq i_j \leq n$ for $j = 1, 2, ...,$ p. Therefore, $E\alpha = E_0 e_{i_1} E_1 \cdots e_{i_p} E_p$ and $(E\alpha)\beta = T_0 t_{i_1} T_1 \cdots t_{i_p} T_p$, where each $t_{i_j} = e_{i_j}\beta$ and $T_j = E_j\gamma$, where γ is a substitution whose variables are not among $x_1, ..., x_n$. But each element in the composite substitution $\alpha\beta$ is of the form x_i/t_k whenever t_k is different from x_i. Hence $E(\alpha\beta) = T_0 t_{i_1} T_1 \cdots t_{i_p} T_p$. ■

Lemma 4.3: Let α, β be two arbitrary substitutions. If $E\alpha = E\beta$ for all string E, then $\alpha = \beta$.

Proof Let $x_1, ..., x_n$ be all variables of the two substitutions α and β. Since $E\alpha = E\beta$ for string E and each x_i is also a string, $x_i\alpha = x_i\beta$, $i = 1, 2, ..., n$. Hence the elements of α and β are the same. ■

Lemma 4.4: The composite operation on substitution is associative, that is, for any substitution α, β, γ, $(\alpha\beta)\gamma = \alpha(\beta\gamma)$. Hence in writing a composition of substitutions, parentheses can be omitted.

Proof Let E be a string. Then by Lemma 4.2, $E((\alpha\beta)\gamma) = (E(\alpha\beta))\gamma = ((E\alpha)\beta)\gamma = (E\alpha)(\beta\gamma) = E(\alpha(\beta\gamma))$. Hence by Lemma 4.3, $(\alpha\beta)\gamma = \alpha(\beta\gamma)$. ■

Definition 4.6: Let $\mathbf{S}$ be any set $\{E_1, ..., E_n\}$ of well-formed expressions. Then the *disagreement set* of $\mathbf{S}$, denoted as $\mathcal{D}(\mathbf{S})$, is obtained by locating the first symbol at which not all E_i have exactly the same symbol, and then extracting t_i from each E_i $(1 \leq i \leq n)$ the subexpression that begins with the symbol. The set $\{t_1, ..., t_n\}$ is the disagreement set of $\mathbf{S}$.

EXAMPLE 4.3

Let $\mathbf{S}$ be $\{P(a, b, x, y), P(a, b, f(x, y), z), P(a, b, g(h(x)), y)\}$. The string of the first six symbols in each of the expressions in $\mathbf{S}$ is '$P(a, b,$'. The first symbol position at which not all expressions in $\mathbf{S}$ are exactly the same is the seventh position. The extracted subexpressions from each of the expressions in $\mathbf{S}$ starting from the seventh position are x, $f(x, y)$, $g(h(x))$. Hence $\mathcal{D}(\mathbf{S}) = \{x, f(x, y), g(h(x))\}$.

Definition 4.7: A *unifier* of two expressions E and E' is a substitution θ such that $E\theta$ is syntactically identical to $E'\theta$. If the two atoms do not have a unifier then they are not *unifiable*. A unifier θ is called a *most general unifier* (*mgu*) for the two atoms if for each unifier α of E and E' there exists a substitution β such that $\alpha = \theta\beta$.

EXAMPLE 4.4

An mgu of two expressions $p(x, f(a, y))$ and $p(b, z)$ is $\{x/b, z/f(a, y)\}$. A unifier of these two expression is $\{x/b, y/c, z/f(a, c)\}$.

An mgu is unique up to variable renaming. Because of this property the mgu of two expressions is used quite often. The following algorithm finds an mgu for a set of expressions (if it exists).

Algorithm 4.1 (Unification algorithm)

Input: $\mathbf{S}$, a set of well-formed expressions.

Step 1: Set $i = 0$, $\theta_0 = \varepsilon$.

Step 2: If $\mathbf{S}\theta_i$ is a singleton then set $\theta_{\mathbf{S}} = \theta_i$ and return $\theta_{\mathbf{S}}$ as an mgu for $\mathbf{S}$.

Step 3: If elements x_i and e_i do not exist in $\mathcal{D}(\mathbf{S}\theta_i)$ such that x_i is a variable and x_i does not occur in e_i then stop; $\mathbf{S}$ is not unifiable.

Step 4: Set $\theta_{i+1} = \theta_i\{x_i/e_i\}$.

Step 5: Set $i = i+1$ and go to step 2.

The above unification algorithm always terminates for any finite non-empty set of well-formed expressions; otherwise an infinite sequence $\mathbf{S}\theta_0$, $\mathbf{S}\theta_1$, ... would be generated. Each $\mathbf{S}\theta_i$, for $i = 0, 1, 2, \cdots$, is a finite non-empty set of well-formed expressions and $\mathbf{S}\theta_{i+1}$ contains one less variable than $\mathbf{S}\theta_i$. This is not possible because $\mathbf{S}$ contains only finitely many distinct variables. Theorem 4.1 proves that if $\mathbf{S}$ is unifiable then the algorithm always finds an mgu for $\mathbf{S}$.

EXAMPLE 4.5

Find an mgu for $\mathbf{S} = \{P(x, g(y), f(g(b))), P(a, z, f(z))\}$

1.	$i = 0, \theta_0 = \varepsilon$	By step 1
2.	$\mathbf{S}\theta_0 = \mathbf{S}$ and $\mathbf{S}\theta_0$ is not a singleton.	By step 2
3.	$\mathcal{D}(\mathbf{S}\theta_0) = \{x, a\}, x_0 = x, e_0 = a$.	By step 3
4.	$\theta_1 = \{x/a\}$	By step 4
5.	$i = 1$	By step 5
6.	$\mathbf{S}\theta_1 = \{P(a, g(y), f(g(b))), P(a, z, f(z))\}$	By step 2
7.	$\mathcal{D}(\mathbf{S}\theta_1) = \{g(y), z\}, x_1 = z, e_1 = g(y)$	By step 3
8.	$\theta_2 = \theta_1\{z/g(y)\} = \{x/a\}\{z/g(y)\} = \{x/a, z/g(y)\}$	By step 4
9.	$i = 2$	By step 5
10.	$\mathbf{S}\theta_2 = \{P(a, g(y), f(g(b))), P(a, g(y), g(y))\}$	By step 2
11.	$\mathcal{D}(\mathbf{S}\theta_2) = \{y, b\}, x_2 = y, e_2 = b$	By step 3
12.	$\theta_3 = \theta_2\{y/b\} = \{x/a, z/g(y)\}\{y/b\} = \{x/a, z/g(b), y/b\}$.	By step 4
13.	$i = 3$	By step 5
14.	$\mathbf{S}\theta_3 = \{P(a, g(b), f(g(b)))\}$. $\mathbf{S}\theta_3$ is a singleton and $\theta_{\mathbf{S}} = \theta_3$.	By step 2

The algorithm terminates here.

EXAMPLE 4.6

The set $\mathbf{S} = \{P(x, x), P(f(a), g(a))\}$ does not have an mgu.

Definition 4.8: The check in step 3 of the unification algorithm of whether x_i occurs in e_i or not is called the *occur check.*

Theorem 4.1: Let $\mathbf{S}$ be any finite non-empty set of well-formed expressions. If $\mathbf{S}$ is unifiable then the unification algorithm (Algorithm 4.1) always terminates at step 2, and $\theta_{\mathbf{S}}$ is an mgu of $\mathbf{S}$.

Proof Suppose $\mathbf{S}$ is unifiable. To prove that $\theta_{\mathbf{S}}$ is an mgu of $\mathbf{S}$, then for each $i \geq 0$ (until the algorithm terminates) and for any unifier θ of $\mathbf{S}$, $\theta = \theta_i \beta_i$ must hold at step 2, for some substitution β_i. This is proved by induction on i.

- *Base step* $i = 0, \theta_0 = \varepsilon$ and hence β_i can be taken as θ.

- *Induction step* Assume $\theta = \theta_i \beta_i$ holds for $0 \leq i \leq n$. If $\mathbf{S}\theta_n$ is a singleton, then the unification algorithm stops at step 2. Since $\theta = \theta_n \beta_n$, θ_n is an mgu of $\mathbf{S}$. If $\mathbf{S}\theta_n$ is not a singleton then the unification algorithm will find

$\mathcal{D}(\mathbf{S}\theta_n)$ at step 3. Since $\theta = \theta_n\beta_n$ and θ is a unifier of $\mathbf{S}$, β_n unifies $\mathbf{S}\theta_n$. Therefore β_n also unifies the disagreement set $\mathcal{D}(\mathbf{S}\theta_n)$. Hence x_n and e_n defined in step 3 of the unification algorithm satisfy $x_n\beta_n = e_n\beta_n$. Since $\mathcal{D}(\mathbf{S}\theta_n)$ is a disagreement set, at least one well-formed expression in $\mathcal{D}(\mathbf{S}\theta_n)$ begins with a variable. Since a variable is also a well-formed expression, at least one well-formed expression in $\mathcal{D}(\mathbf{S}\theta_n)$ is a variable. Take this variable as x_n and suppose e_n is any other well-formed expression from $\mathcal{D}(\mathbf{S}\theta_n)$. Since β_n unifies $\mathcal{D}(\mathbf{S}\theta_n)$ and x_n, e_n are members of $\mathcal{D}(\mathbf{S}\theta_n)$, $x_n\beta_n = e_n\beta_n$. Now if x_n occurs in e_n, $x_n\beta_n$ occurs in $e_n\beta_n$. This is impossible because x_n and e_n are distinct well-formed expressions and $x_n\beta_n = e_n\beta_n$. Therefore x_n does not occur in e_n. Hence the algorithm does not stop at step 3. Step 4 will set $\theta_{n+1} = \theta_n\{x_n/e_n\}$. Step 5 will set $i = n+1$ and the control of the algorithm will be back at step 2.

Set	β_{n+1}	$= \beta_n - \{x_n/x_n\beta_n\}$	
	β_n	$= \{x_n/x_n\beta_n\} \cup \beta_{n+1}$	
		$= \{x_n/e_n\beta_n\} \cup \beta_{n+1}$	Since $x_n\beta_n = e_n\beta_n$
		$= \{x_n/e_n(\{x_n/x_n\beta_n\} \cup \beta_{n+1})\cup\beta_{n+1}$	Since $\beta_n = \{x_n/x_n\beta_n\} \cup \beta_{n+1}$
		$= \{x_n/e_n\beta_{n+1}\} \cup \beta_{n+1}$	Since x_n does not occur in e_n
		$= \{x_n/e_n\}\beta_{n+1}$	Definition of composite subst.

Thus $\theta = \theta_n\beta_n = \theta_n\{x_n/e_n\}\beta_{n+1} = \theta_{n+1}\beta_{n+1}$.
Hence $\theta = \theta_i\beta_i$ for $i = 0, 1, \ldots, n+1$.

By the induction principle, for all $i \geq 0$, there is a substitution β_i such that $\theta = \theta_i\beta_i$ until the algorithm terminates in step 2, for some $i = m$. Furthermore, $\theta_\mathbf{S} = \theta_m$ is an mgu for $\mathbf{S}$. ■

Definition 4.9: Suppose a subset of the set of all literals occurring in a clause C has the same sign and has an mgu θ. Then Cθ is called a *factor* of C. If Cθ is a unit clause then it is called a *unit factor* of C.

EXAMPLE 4.7

Suppose $C = P(x,a) \vee P(f(y),z) \vee Q(y,z)$. Then the literals $P(x,a)$ and $P(f(y),z)$ have the same sign and unify with an mgu $\theta = \{x/f(y), z/a\}$. Thus Cθ $= P(f(y),a) \vee Q(y,a)$ is a factor of C. If $C = P(x,a) \vee P(f(y),z) \vee P(f(b),a)$, then $P(f(b),a)$ is a unit factor of C.

Definition 4.10: Suppose C and D are two clauses with no variables in common. Suppose L and M are literals occurring in C and D respectively. The literals L and M are complementary to each other and their atoms unify with an mgu θ. Then the clause $(C\theta - \{L\theta\}) \cup (D\theta - \{M\theta\})$ is called a *binary resolvent* of C and D. The literals L and M are called the *literals resolved upon* and C and D are *parent clauses* of the resolution operation.

EXAMPLE 4.8
Suppose $C = P(x, z) \vee Q(f(a)) \vee Q(z)$ and $D = \neg Q(f(y)) \vee \neg R(y)$. Consider L and M as $Q(f(a))$ and $\neg Q(f(y))$ respectively. Then $\theta = \{y/a\}$ and $(C\theta - \{L\theta\}) \cup (D\theta - \{M\theta\}) = P(x, z) \vee Q(z) \vee \neg R(a)$.

Definition 4.11: A resolvent of clauses C and D is a binary resolvent of C_1 and D_1, where C_1 is either C or a factor of C, and D_1 is either D or a factor of D. Hence a binary resolvent of two clauses C and D is also a resolvent C and D.

EXAMPLE 4.9
Suppose $C = P(x, z) \vee Q(f(a)) \vee Q(z)$ and $D = \neg Q(f(y)) \vee \neg R(y)$. Then the resolvent $P(x, f(a)) \vee \neg R(a)$ of C and D is a binary resolvent between the factor $P(x, f(a)) \vee Q(f(a))$ of C and D.

4.2 Resolution theorem

This section establishes first resolution theorem proving for ground clauses. It is then generalized to establish resolution theorem for first-order clauses.

Definition 4.12: If $\mathbf{S}$ is any set of clauses then the *resolution* of $\mathbf{S}$, denoted by $\mathcal{Res}(\mathbf{S})$, is the set of all clauses consisting of the members of $\mathbf{S}$ together with all the resolvents of all pairs of members of $\mathbf{S}$.

Definition 4.13: If $\mathbf{S}$ is any set of clauses then the nth resolution of $\mathbf{S}$, denoted by $\mathcal{Res}^n(\mathbf{S})$, is defined as follows:

$$\mathcal{Res}^0(\mathbf{S}) = \mathbf{S}$$
$$\mathcal{Res}^{n+1}(\mathbf{S}) = \mathcal{Res}(\mathcal{Res}^n(\mathbf{S})),\ n = 0, 1, \ldots$$

It is clear from the above definition that

$$\mathcal{Res}^0(\mathbf{S}) = \mathbf{S} \subseteq \mathcal{Res}^1(\mathbf{S}) \subseteq \mathcal{Res}^n(\mathbf{S}) \subseteq \cdots \subseteq \mathcal{Res}^n(\mathbf{S}) \subseteq \cdots$$

Lemma 4.5: If $\mathbf{S}$ is a finite set of ground clauses then not all inclusions in the above chain are proper.

Proof Straightforward because resolution does not introduce any new literals in the case of ground clauses. ■

Theorem 4.2: (ground resolution theorem) If $\mathbf{S}$ is any finite set of ground clauses then $\mathbf{S}$ is unsatisfiable if and only if $\mathcal{Res}^n(\mathbf{S})$ contains $\Box$, for some $n \geq 0$.

Proof Suppose $\mathbf{S}$ is unsatisfiable and consider the chain

$$\mathbf{S} \subseteq \mathcal{Res}(\mathbf{S}) \subseteq \mathcal{Res}^n(\mathbf{S}) \subseteq \cdots$$

By Lemma 4.5, this clause terminates. Let $\mathbf{T} = \mathcal{Res}^n(\mathbf{S})$ be the terminating set. The set $\mathbf{T}$ is closed under resolution and $\mathbf{S} \subseteq \mathbf{T}$. Suppose $\mathbf{T}$ does not contain the empty clause $\Box$. Suppose $A_1, ..., A_m$ are all the atoms occurring in $\mathbf{T}$. Let $\mathbf{M}$ be a set constructed as follows:

$\mathbf{M}_0 = \varnothing$

$\mathbf{M}_j = \mathbf{M}_{j-1} \cup \{A_j\}$, if there does not exist a clause $M_1 \vee \cdots \vee M_p$ in $\mathbf{T}$ such that $\{M_1^c, ..., M_p^c\} \subseteq \mathbf{M}_j$, where M_i^c is the complement of M_i.

$= \mathbf{M}_{j-1} \cup \{\neg A_j\}$, otherwise for $j = 1, 2, ..., m$.

$\mathbf{M} = \mathbf{M}_m$

It can now be shown that $\mathbf{M}$ satisfies $\mathbf{T}$. If not, there is a clause C in $\mathbf{T}$ such that the complement of each of the literals occurring in C belongs to $\mathbf{M}_j$, for the least $j, 0 \leq j \leq m$. Hence $\mathbf{M}_j$ is $\mathbf{M}_{j-1} \cup \{\neg A_j\}$. Thus C contains A_j (by the leastness of j). Since $\mathbf{M}_j$ is $\mathbf{M}_{j-1} \cup \{\neg A_j\}$, there exists a clause D in $\mathbf{T}$ such that the complement of each of the literals occurring in D belongs to $\mathbf{M}_{j-1} \cup \{A_j\}$. Thus D contains $\neg A_j$ (by the leastness of j). If the resolvent (C-$\{A_j\}$)∪(D-$\{\neg A_j\}$) is non-empty then the complement of each of the literals occurring in this resolvent is in the set $\mathbf{M}_{j-1}$. By the definition of construction of $\mathbf{T}$, (C-$\{A_j\}$)∪(D-$\{\neg A_j\}$) is a member of $\mathbf{T}$ and cannot be empty. This contradicts the leastness of j. Hence $\mathbf{M}$ satisfies $\mathbf{T}$. Since $\mathbf{T}$ is satisfiable and $\mathbf{S} \subseteq \mathbf{T}$, $\mathbf{S}$ is also satisfiable, therefore, it is a contradiction. Thus the original assumption, that $\mathbf{T}$ does not contain empty clause, is false. Hence $\mathbf{T}$ contains $\Box$.

To prove the converse of the theorem, suppose $\mathcal{Res}^n(\mathbf{S})$ contains $\square$ and hence $\mathcal{Res}^n(\mathbf{S})$ is unsatisfiable. Therefore $\mathcal{Res}^n(\mathbf{S})$ does not have any model. If C and D are two ground clauses then any model of {C, D} is also a model of {C, D, (C-$\{L\}$)∪(D-$\{L'\}$)}. Therefore any model of **S** is also a model of $\mathcal{Res}^n(\mathbf{S})$. Since $\mathcal{Res}^n(\mathbf{S})$ does not have any model, **S** does not have any model. Therefore **S** is unsatisfiable. ■

Lemma 4.6: (lifting lemma) If C'_1 and C'_2 are instances of C_1 and C_2 respectively and C′ is a resolvent of C'_1 and C'_2, then there is a resolvent C of C_1 and C_2 such that C′ is an instance of C.

Proof It can be assumed that there is no common variable between C_1 and C_2. If there is then the variables are renamed accordingly. Suppose $C' = (C'_1\theta_p - \{L'_1\theta_p\}) \cup (C'_2\theta_p - \{L'_2\theta_p\})$, where θ_p is an mgu of the set of atoms occurring in L'_1 and L'_2. Since C'_i is an instance of C_i, $C'_i = C_i\alpha$, $i = 1, 2$, for some substitution α. Let $L_i^1, ..., L_i^{n_i}$ be the literals of C_i corresponding to L'_i, for $i = 1, 2$, that is, $L_i^1\alpha = ... = L_i^{n_i}\alpha = L'_i$.

When $n_i > 1$, suppose β_i is an mgu for $\{L_i^1, ..., L_i^{n_i}\}$ and let $L_i = L_i^1\beta_i = ... = L_i^{n_i}\beta_i$, $i = 1, 2$. Then L_i is a literal in the factor $C_i\beta_i$ of C_i. When $n_i = 1$, let $\beta_i = \varepsilon$ and $L_i = L'_i$. Then L'_i is an instance of L_i. Since the atoms occurring in L'_1 and L'_2 are unifiable and L'_i is an instance of L_i, the atoms occurring in L_1 and L_2 are unifiable. Let θ be an mgu in this case. Let

$$\begin{aligned} C &= ((C_1\beta_1)\theta - \{L_1\theta\}) \cup ((C_2\beta_2)\theta - \{L_2\theta\}) \\ &= (C_1(\beta_1\beta_2\theta) - \{L_1^1, ..., L_1^{n1}\}(\beta_1\beta_2\theta))\text{-}(C_2(\beta_1\beta_2\theta) - \{L_2^1, ..., L_2^{n2}\}(\beta_1\beta_2\theta)) \end{aligned}$$

since β_i does not act on L_j^k, $i \neq j$, $i, j = 1, 2$, $1 \leq k \leq n_i$. Now

$$\begin{aligned} C' &= (C'_1\theta_p - \{L'_1\theta_p\}) \cup (C'_2\theta_p - \{L'_2\theta_p\}) \\ &= (C_1(\alpha\theta_p) - \{L_1^1, ..., L_1^{n1}\}(\alpha\theta_p))\text{-}(C_2(\alpha\theta_p) - \{L_2^1, ..., L_2^{n2}\}(\alpha\theta_p)) \end{aligned}$$

Since $\beta_1\beta_2\theta$ is more general than $\alpha\theta_p$, therefore C′ is an instance of C. Hence the lemma. ■

Definition 4.14: If **S** is any set of clauses and **P** is any set of terms, then the *saturation* of **S** over **P**, denoted as $\mathcal{Ground}_{\mathbf{P}}(\mathbf{S})$, is the set of all ground clauses obtained from members of **S** by replacing variables with members of **P**. Occurrences of the same variable in any one clause are replaced by occurrences of the same term. When **P** is $\mathcal{HU}(\mathbf{S})$, then $\mathcal{Ground}_{\mathbf{P}}(\mathbf{S})$ is simply $\mathcal{Ground}(\mathbf{S})$.

Lemma 4.7: Let **S** be any set of clauses and **P** be any subset of $\mathcal{HU}(\mathbf{S})$, then $\mathcal{Res}(\mathit{Ground}_{\mathbf{P}}(\mathbf{S})) \subseteq \mathit{Ground}_{\mathbf{P}}(\mathcal{Res}(\mathbf{S}))$.

Proof Suppose $C' \in \mathcal{Res}(\mathit{Ground}_{\mathbf{P}}(\mathbf{S}))$. Then there are two clauses C_1 and C_2 in **S** and their ground instances $C_1\alpha_1$ and $C_2\alpha_2$ such that C′ is a resolvent of $C_1\alpha_1$ and $C_2\alpha_2$. Then by the lifting lemma (4.6), C′ is an instance of C, where C is a resolvent of C_1 and C_2. Since C is a member of $\mathcal{Res}(\mathbf{S})$ and C′ is a ground instance of C, $C' \in \mathit{Ground}_{\mathbf{P}}(\mathcal{Res}(\mathbf{S}))$. Hence $\mathcal{Res}(\mathit{Ground}_{\mathbf{P}}(\mathbf{S})) \subseteq \mathit{Ground}_{\mathbf{P}}(\mathcal{Res}(\mathbf{S}))$. ■

EXAMPLE 4.10

$\mathbf{S} = \{P(a) \vee \neg Q(x), Q(b)\}$

$\mathbf{P} = \{a\}$

$\mathcal{HU}(\mathbf{S}) = \{a, b\}$

$\mathcal{Res}(\mathbf{S}) = \{P(a) \vee \neg Q(x), Q(b), P(a)\}$

$\mathit{Ground}_{\mathbf{P}}(\mathcal{Res}(\mathbf{S})) = \{P(a) \vee \neg Q(a), Q(b), P(a)\}$

$\mathit{Ground}_{\mathbf{P}}(\mathbf{S}) = \{P(a) \vee \neg Q(a), Q(b)\}$

$\mathcal{Res}(\mathit{Ground}_{\mathbf{P}}(\mathbf{S})) = \{P(a) \vee \neg Q(a), Q(b)\}$

$\mathcal{Res}(\mathit{Ground}_{\mathbf{P}}(\mathbf{S})) \subseteq \mathit{Ground}_{\mathbf{P}}(\mathcal{Res}(\mathbf{S}))$

$\mathcal{Res}(\mathit{Ground}_{\mathbf{P}}(\mathbf{S})) \neq \mathit{Ground}_{\mathbf{P}}(\mathcal{Res}(\mathbf{S}))$

Hence the converse of Lemma 4.7 is not necessarily true.

Corollary 4.1: If **S** is any set of clauses and **P** is any subset of $\mathcal{HU}(\mathbf{S})$, then $\mathcal{Res}^i(\mathit{Ground}_{\mathbf{P}}(\mathbf{S})) \subseteq \mathit{Ground}_{\mathbf{P}}(\mathcal{Res}^i(\mathbf{S}))$, for all $i \geq 0$.

Proof This corollary is established by induction on i:

- *Base step* $i = 0$. Then $\mathcal{Res}^0(\mathit{Ground}_{\mathbf{P}}(\mathbf{S})) = \mathit{Ground}_{\mathbf{P}}(\mathbf{S}) = \mathit{Ground}_{\mathbf{P}}(\mathcal{Res}^0(\mathbf{S}))$.
- *Induction step* Suppose the result is true for $i = n$. Then

$\mathcal{Res}^{n+1}(\mathit{Ground}_{\mathbf{P}}(\mathbf{S}))$	$= \mathcal{Res}(\mathcal{Res}^n(\mathit{Ground}_{\mathbf{P}}(\mathbf{S})))$	By definition
	$\subseteq \mathcal{Res}(\mathit{Ground}_{\mathbf{P}}(\mathcal{Res}^n(\mathbf{S})))$	For $i = n$
	$\subseteq \mathit{Ground}_{\mathbf{P}}(\mathcal{Res}(\mathcal{Res}^n(\mathbf{S})))$	By Lemma 4.7
	$= \mathit{Ground}_{\mathbf{P}}(\mathcal{Res}(\mathcal{Res}^{n+1}(\mathbf{S})))$	By definition

Hence the corollary. ■

The basic version of Herbrand's theorem stated in Chapter 3 can be restated as follows.

Theorem 4.3: If **S** is any finite set of clauses then **S** is unsatisfiable if and only if for some finite subset **P** of $\mathcal{HU}(\mathbf{S})$, $\mathcal{G}round_{\mathbf{P}}(\mathbf{S})$ is unsatisfiable.

Proof Left as an exercise. ■

Theorem 4.4: If **S** is any finite set of clauses then **S** is unsatisfiable if and only if for some finite subset **P** of $\mathcal{HU}(\mathbf{S})$ and some $n \geq 0$, $\mathcal{R}es^n(\mathcal{G}round_{\mathbf{P}}(\mathbf{S}))$ contains $\square$.

Proof Since **S** and **P** are finite, $\mathcal{G}round_{\mathbf{P}}(\mathbf{S})$ is also finite. Hence the theorem follows from Theorems 4.2 and 4.3. ■

Theorem 4.5: If **S** is any finite set of clauses then **S** is unsatisfiable if and only if for some finite subset **P** of $\mathcal{HU}(\mathbf{S})$ and some $n \geq 0$, $\mathcal{G}round_{\mathbf{P}}(\mathcal{R}es^n(\mathbf{S}))$ contains $\square$.

Proof Follows from Theorem 4.4 and Corollary 4.1. ■

Theorem 4.6: (resolution theorem) If **S** is any finite set of clauses then **S** is unsatisfiable if and only if $\mathcal{R}es^n(\mathbf{S})$ contains $\square$, for some $n \geq 0$.

Proof The set $\mathcal{G}round_{\mathbf{P}}(\mathcal{R}es^n(\mathbf{S}))$ will contain $\square$ if and only if $\mathcal{R}es^n(\mathbf{S})$ contains $\square$ (since the replacement of variables by terms cannot produce $\square$ from a non-empty clause in $\mathcal{R}es^n(\mathbf{S})$). Hence the theorem follows from Theorem 4.5. ■

4.3 Refutation procedure

This section provides a procedure based on the resolution theorem (4.6) to derive the empty clause from an unsatisfiable set of clauses. Later in this section some techniques are provided to improve the efficiency of the procedure.

Definition 4.15: Let **S** be a set of clauses (called *input clauses*). A *derivation* (or *deduction*) in **S** is a sequence of clauses $C_1, C_2, \ldots$ such that each C_i either is in **S** or is a resolvent of C_j and C_k, where $1 \leq i \leq n$, $1 \leq j < i$ and $1 \leq k < i$. In the latter case, C_i is a *derived clause*. A derivation is either *finite* or *infinite* according to the length of its sequence.

Definition 4.16: A *refutation* of **S** is a finite derivation $C_1, ..., C_n$ in **S** such that $C_n = \square$.

The following theorem is the completeness theorem of a system of logic whose sole inference rule is the resolution principle stated in Section 4.1.

Theorem 4.7: A finite set **S** of clauses is unsatisfiable if and only if there is a refutation of **S**.

Proof Immediate from Theorem 4.6. ■

One of the ways to find a refutation from a set of unsatisfiable clauses is to compute the sequence $\mathbf{S}$, $\mathcal{Res}(\mathbf{S})$, $\mathcal{Res}^2(\mathbf{S})$, ... until $\mathcal{Res}^n(\mathbf{S})$ contains $\square$. However, this procedure would be very inefficient. To illustrate, a series of examples are provided below. Examples 4.11–4.13 demonstrate some refutations and Example 4.14 demonstrates the satisfiability of a set of clauses through an exhaustive search.

EXAMPLE 4.11

S =	1.	$\neg P(a)$	
	2.	$P(x) \vee \neg Q(x)$	
	3.	$P(x) \vee \neg R(f(x))$	
	4.	$Q(a) \vee R(f(a))$	
$\mathcal{Res}(\mathbf{S}) = \mathbf{S} \cup$	5.	$\neg Q(a)$	1 and 2
	6.	$\neg R(f(a))$	1 and 3
	7.	$P(a) \vee R(f(a))$	2 and 4
	8.	$P(a) \vee Q(a)$	3 and 4
$\mathcal{Res}^2(\mathbf{S}) = \mathcal{Res}(\mathbf{S}) \cup$	9.	$R(f(a))$	1 and 7
	10.	$Q(a)$	1 and 8
	11.	$P(a)$	2 and 8
	12.	$P(a)$	3 and 6
	13.	$P(a)$	3 and 7
	14.	$R(f(a))$	4 and 5
	15.	$Q(a)$	4 and 6
$\mathcal{Res}^3(\mathbf{S}) = \mathcal{Res}^2(\mathbf{S}) \cup$	16.	$\square$	1 and 11
	...		

EXAMPLE 4.12

S =	1.	$P(x) \vee Q(x)$
	2.	$\neg P(x) \vee \neg Q(x)$
	3.	$\neg P(x) \vee Q(x)$
	4.	$\neg Q(a)$

$\mathcal{Res}(\mathbf{S}) = \mathbf{S} \cup$	5.	$Q(x) \vee \neg Q(x)$	1 and 2
	6.	$Q(x)$	1 and 3
	7.	$P(a)$	1 and 4
	8.	$\neg P(x)$	2 and 3
	9.	$\neg P(a)$	3 and 4

$\mathcal{Res}^2(\mathbf{S}) = \mathcal{Res}(\mathbf{S}) \cup$	10.	$P(x) \vee Q(x)$	1 and 5
	11.	$Q(x)$	1 and 8
	12.	$Q(a)$	1 and 9
	13.	$\neg P(x) \vee \neg Q(x)$	2 and 5
	14.	$\neg P(x)$	2 and 6
	15.	$\neg Q(a)$	2 and 7
	16.	$\neg P(x) \vee Q(x)$	3 and 5
	17.	$Q(a)$	3 and 7
	18.	$\neg Q(a)$	4 and 5
	19.	$\square$	4 and 6
	...		

EXAMPLE 4.13

S =	1.	$P(x)$
	2.	$P(a)$
	3.	$\neg P(x) \vee R(x)$
	4.	$\neg R(a)$

$\mathcal{Res}(\mathbf{S}) = \mathbf{S} \cup$	5.	$R(a)$	1 and 3
	6.	$R(a)$	2 and 3
	7.	$\neg P(a)$	3 and 4

$\mathcal{Res}^2(\mathbf{S}) = \mathcal{Res}(\mathbf{S}) \cup$	8.	$\square$	1 and 7
		...	

EXAMPLE 4.14

$\mathbf{S} =$ 1. $P(x) \vee R(f(a))$
2. $\neg P(x) \vee \neg R(g(x))$
3. $P(b)$
4. $R(g(a))$

$\mathcal{Res}(\mathbf{S}) = \mathbf{S} \cup$ 5. $R(f(a)) \vee \neg R(g(a))$ 1 and 2
6. $\neg R(g(b))$ 2 and 3
7. $\neg P(a)$ 2 and 4

$\mathcal{Res}^2(\mathbf{S}) = \mathcal{Res}(\mathbf{S}) \cup$ 8. $R(f(a))$ 1 and 7
9. $R(f(a))$ 4 and 5

$\mathcal{Res}^3(\mathbf{S}) = \mathcal{Res}^2(\mathbf{S})$

Many irrelevant redundant clauses have been generated in each of the above examples. In Example 4.11, only the clauses 1, 8 and 11 need to be generated to show that the set of clauses is unsatisfiable. The other clauses are redundant. In Example 4.12, clause 5 is a tautology. A tautology is true in any interpretation, therefore if a tautology is deleted from an unsatisfiable set of clauses, the remaining set of clauses must still be unsatisfiable. In Example 4.13, clause $R(a)$ is generated twice and this is due to the presence of both $P(x)$ and $P(a)$ in $\mathbf{S}$. $P(a)$ is irrelevant in this case. In Example 4.14, satisfiability of the set $\mathbf{S}$ will not depend on clause 1 as there is no clause in $\mathcal{Res}^n(\mathbf{S})$ with an occurrence of a literal $\neg A$ such that A unifies $R(f(a))$. Hence in this example, the given set $\mathbf{S}$ of clauses is satisfiable if and only if the set of clauses in $\mathbf{S}$ other than clause 1 is satisfiable.

To avoid the inefficiencies that would be caused for the above reasons, the refutation procedure incorporates a number of *search principles*. These are similar to the ones incorporated in the Davis–Putnam procedure described in Chapter 3.

(1) *Purity principle* Let $\mathbf{S}$ be any finite set of clauses. A literal L occurring in a clause $C \in \mathbf{S}$ is said to be *pure* if there is no clause in D for which a resolvent $(C\theta - \{L\theta\}) \cup (D\theta - \{M\theta\})$ exists. The *purity principle* is then stated as follows. From a finite set $\mathbf{S}$ of clauses any clause C containing a pure literal can be deleted from $\mathbf{S}$. Then $\mathbf{S}$ is satisfiable if and only if the resulting set $\mathbf{S} - \{C\}$ is satisfiable.

(2) *Subsumption principle* A clause C *subsumes* a clause D (or D is *subsumed by* C), where $C \neq D$, if there exists a substitution θ such that all the literals that occur in $C\theta$ also occur in D. The *subsumption principle* is then stated as

follows. From a finite set **S** of clauses, any clause D which is subsumed by a clause in $\mathbf{S}-\{D\}$ can be deleted. Then **S** is satisfiable if and only if the resulting set $\mathbf{S}-\{D\}$ is satisfiable.

(3) *Tautology principle* From a finite set **S** of clauses, any clause C which is a tautology can be deleted. Then **S** is satisfiable if and only if the remaining set of clauses $\mathbf{S}-\{C\}$ is satisfiable.

(4) *Replacement principle* The replacement principle can be stated as follows. Suppose C and D are two clauses and R is a resolvent of C and D which subsumes one of C and D. Then in adding R by the resolution principle, one of C and D which R subsumes can be simultaneously deleted.

EXAMPLE 4.15

Consider the set $\mathbf{S} = \{P(a), \neg P(x) \vee P(f(x)), \neg P(a) \vee Q(a)\}$. The literal $P(f(x))$ in **S** is pure and hence the clause $\neg P(x) \vee P(f(x))$ can be deleted from **S** giving the resulting set as $\{P(a), \neg P(a) \vee Q(a)\}$ which is satisfiable. Hence **S** is also satisfiable.

EXAMPLE 4.16

Suppose $\mathbf{S} = \{P(x), P(f(a)) \vee Q(a)\}$. Consider $\theta = \{x/f(a)\}$, $C = P(x)$ and $D = P(f(a)) \vee Q(a)$. Then D is subsumed by C as $C\theta \subseteq D$.

The above search principles can be used to delete some of the redundant and irrelevant clauses generated during the refutation procedure. In spite of this, there are still many irrelevant clauses (see Examples 4.11–4.14) which cannot be deleted that are generated during the refutation procedure. *Refinement* of resolution is necessary to achieve an efficient theorem proving procedure.

4.4 Refinements of the resolution principle

As mentioned earlier, many refinements of the resolution principles (Chang, 1970; Kowalski and Kuehner, 1971; Loveland, 1969; Robinson, 1965a; Robinson and Wos, 1969; Wos *et al.*, 1968) have been proposed. This section provides some in line with the mainstream development of the text.

4.4.1 Input resolution

Definition 4.17: *Input resolution* (Chang, 1970) requires that one of the parent clauses of each resolution operation must be an input clause, that is, not a derived clause. An *input derivation* is a derivation in which every resolution is an input resolution. An *input refutation* is an input derivation of $\Box$. Input resolution is incomplete as is evident from the following example.

EXAMPLE 4.17

Consider the set $\mathbf{S} = \{P(x) \vee Q(x),\ P(x) \vee \neg Q(x),\ \neg P(x) \vee Q(x),\ \neg P(x) \vee \neg Q(x)\}$. Input resolution is able to derive $P(x)$, $\neg P(x)$, $Q(x)$ and $\neg Q(x)$ but cannot resolve them with each other because none of these four clauses is a required input clause.

4.4.2 Unit resolution

Definition 4.18: *Unit resolution* (Chang, 1970) requires that at least one of the parent clauses or its factor in each resolution operation be a unit clause. A *unit derivation* is a derivation in which every resolution is a unit resolution. A *unit refutation* is a unit derivation of $\Box$.

Unit and input resolutions are equivalent to each other, in other words, there is a unit refutation from an unsatisfiable set of clauses $\mathbf{S}$ if and only if there is an input refutation from $\mathbf{S}$. Example 4.17, in considering the set $\{P(x) \vee Q(x),\ P(x) \vee \neg Q(x),\ \neg P(x) \vee Q(x),\ \neg P(x) \vee \neg Q(x)\}$, illustrated that input resolution is incomplete and hence so is unit resolution because of their equivalence. Unit resolution is obviously incomplete because an unsatisfiable set of clauses does not necessarily contain a clause which has a unit factor and it is true for this set. Both unit and input resolutions are complete for sets of Horn clauses.

4.4.3 Linear resolution

Linear resolution is an extension of input resolution in which at least one of the parent clauses to each resolution operation must be either an input clause or an ancestor clause of the parent.

Definition 4.19: Let **S** be a set of clauses and C be a member of **S**. Then a *linear derivation* of C_n from **S** with top clause C is a finite sequence $C_0 = C, C_1, ..., C_n$ of clauses such that for each $i = 0, 1, ..., n-1$:

(1) C_{i+1} is a resolvent of C_i (called a *centre clause* or *near parent*) and another clause B_i (called a *side clause*), and

(2) each B_i is

  (a) either in **S** and in that case B_i is the *input parent* of C_{i+1},

  (b) or an *ancestor* of each C_j $(0 \leq j < i)$ and in that case B_i is the *far parent* of C_{i+1}.

In the above definition of linear derivation, each clause C_{i+1} is said to have been obtained by *linear resolution*. A *linear refutation* is a linear derivation of $\emptyset$.

Linear derivation is constrained by the fact that a new clause is always derived from the preceding clause of the deduction by resolving against an earlier clause of the deduction. Linear resolution is complete. The following is an example of linear refutation.

EXAMPLE 4.18

Let $\mathbf{S} = \{\neg P(x), P(x) \vee \neg Q(x), P(x) \vee \neg R(x), Q(a) \vee R(a)\}$

(1) Consider the following derivation with $\neg P(x)$ as the top clause:

$C_0 = \neg P(x)$ $\quad B_0 = P(x) \vee \neg Q(x)$
$C_1 = \neg Q(x)$ $\quad B_1 = Q(a) \vee R(a)$
$C_2 = R(a)$ $\quad B_2 = P(x) \vee \neg R(x)$
$C_3 = P(a)$ $\quad B_3 = C_0$
$C_4 = \square$

(2) Consider the following derivation with $Q(a) \vee R(a)$ as the top clause:

$C_0 = Q(a) \vee R(a)$ $\quad B_0 = P(x) \vee \neg Q(x)$
$C_1 = R(a) \vee P(a)$ $\quad B_1 = P(x) \vee \neg R(x)$
$C_2 = P(a)$ $\quad B_2 = \neg P(x)$
$C_3 = \square$

For linear derivations from a set **S** of clauses with common top clause C, the whole search space is represented as a tree, called a *search tree*.

Definition 4.20: A *search tree* $\mathcal{T}$ is defined as follows:

(1) The root of $\mathcal{T}$ is labelled by C.

(2) Suppose N is a node in $\mathcal{T}$ and the nodes from the root to N are labelled by $C_1 = C, C_2, ..., C_n$. Then for each linear derivation $C_1, C_2, ..., C_n, C_{n+1}$, a node labelled by C_{n+1} is an *immediate descendant* of N.

EXAMPLE 4.19

A partial search tree for the set $\{P \vee Q, \neg P, \neg Q \vee R, \neg Q \vee \neg R \vee S, P \vee \neg S\}$ with $P \vee Q$ as the top clause is shown in Figure 4.1.

4.4.4 Set of support

Resolution is often used to prove a theorem C from a set of axioms $C_1, ..., C_n$ and to prove this, it is shown that $C_1 \wedge \cdots \wedge C_n \wedge \neg C$ is unsatisfiable. The axiom set $\{C_1, ..., C_n\}$ is usually taken as satisfiable. Hence this axiom set, together with that are created by resolution from the axiom set (called *axiom clauses*), are always satisfiable. Therefore a refutation cannot be found by using axiom clauses only. The set-of-support strategy (Wos *et al.*, 1968) takes advantage of this fact and avoids resolving clauses in the axiom clauses only.

Definition 4.21: A subset $\mathbf{S}_1$ of a set **S** of clauses is called a *set of support* of **S** if and only if $\mathbf{S}-\mathbf{S}_1$ is satisfiable. A *set-of-support resolution* is a resolution when two clauses are resolved upon only if both are not from $\mathbf{S}-\mathbf{S}_1$. A *set-of-support derivation* is a derivation in which every resolution is a set of support and a *set-of-support refutation* is a set-of-support derivation of $\square$.

Set-of-support resolution is complete from the following point of view. If $\mathbf{S}_1$ is a subset of an unsatisfiable set **S** of clauses such that $\mathbf{S}-\mathbf{S}_1$ is satisfiable then there exists a set-of-support deduction of $\square$ from **S** with $\mathbf{S}_1$ as a set of support.

EXAMPLE 4.20

Suppose the set **S** consists of the following clauses:

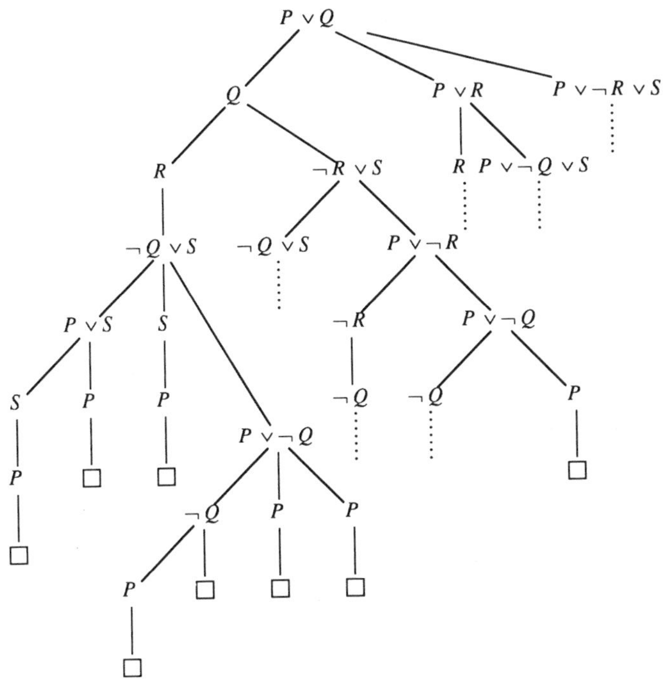

Figure 4.1 A search tree for linear derivation.

$\neg P(x, y) \vee \neg Q(x)$
$P(x, y) \vee \neg Q(x)$
$Q(a)$

Clearly **S** is unsatisfiable. Let $\mathbf{S}_1 = \{\neg P(x, y) \vee \neg Q(x)\}$ be a set-of-support and $\mathbf{S}-\mathbf{S}_1$ is satisfiable. A set-of-support derivation is given as follows.

1.	$\neg P(x, y) \vee \neg Q(x)$	Given
2.	$P(x, y) \vee \neg Q(x)$	Given
3.	$Q(a)$	Given
4.	$\neg P(a, y)$	1 and 3
5.	$\neg Q(a)$	2 and 4
6.	$\square$	3 and 5

In the above refutation, no resolution has been performed on 2 and 3.

4.4.5 Linear resolution with selection function

Linear resolution with selection function (or *SL-resolution*) (Kowalski and Kuehner, 1971) is a restricted form of linear resolution. The main restriction is effected by a selection function which chooses from each clause one single literal to be resolved upon in that clause. SL-resolution operates on *chains* rather than clauses and hence strictly is not a form of resolution. It does, however, employ ideas of unification and resolution.

Definition 4.22: A chain is a string of *A-literals* and *B-literals*. *Input chains* are chains formed from a set of input clauses, that is, the input chain corresponding to the clause $L_1 \vee L_2 \vee \cdots \vee L_n$ is just $L_1 L_2 \cdots L_n$.

All the literals in an input chain are B-literals. The literal that is resolved upon is saved in the result as an A-literal. A-literals are bracketed to distinguish them from B-literals. An A-literal (resp. B-literal) in a chain is said to have *status* A-literal (resp. B-literal).

Definition 4.23: Two B-literals in a chain are members of the same *cell* if they are not separated by an A-literal.

EXAMPLE 4.21

Consider the chain C = $P(x) \neg Q(x) [R(x)] [S(x)] T(x)$. The literals $P(x)$, $\neg Q(x)$ and $T(x)$ are the B-literals of C and $R(x)$, $S(x)$ are the A-literals of C. The chain C has two cells: one contains $P(x)$ and $\neg Q(x)$ and the other one contains $T(x)$. The former cell is the leftmost cell of the chain C and $P(x)$ is the leftmost literal in the chain C.

Definition 4.24: A *selection function* maps a chain C whose leftmost literal is a B-literal to one of the literals occurring in the leftmost cell of C.

Definition 4.25: A chain can be considered as a string whose elements come from the domain of A-literals and B-literals. In this context, a *subchain* of a chain $L_1 \cdots L_n$ is either an *empty chain* (a chain consisting of no A- or B-literals) or a chain of the form $L_i L_{i+1} \cdots L_j$, where $1 \le i \le n$, $1 \le j \le n$ and $i \le j$.

Definition 4.26: Let S be the set of input clauses. Then for each factor C′ of a clause in S and for each literal L in C′, exactly one sequence C is chosen which consists of all literals in C′ with L as the rightmost in C. Then C is called an *input* *chain* from **S**.

The following description of SL-resolution is a modified description of the original one (Kowalski and Kuehner, 1971) appropriate for this text.

Definition 4.27: Let **S** be a set of clauses and $\mathbf{S}_0$ be a set of support. An *SL-derivation* from **S** is a sequence of chains $C_1, ..., C_n$ satisfying the following conditions:

(1) C_1 is an input chain from $\mathbf{S}_0$.

(2) C_{i+1} is obtained from C_i by *truncation* if and only if the following conditions hold:

(a) The leftmost literal in C_i is an A-literal.

(b) C_{i+1} is the longest subchain of C_i whose leftmost literal is a B-literal. The status of a literal in C_{i+1} is same as its status in C_i.

(3) C_{i+1} is obtained from C_i by *reduction* if and only if the following conditions hold:

(a) The leftmost literal in C_i is a B-literal.

(b) C_i is not obtained from C_{i-1} by truncation.

(c) The leftmost cell of C_i contains a B-literal L and either

(i) C_i contains a B-literal M which is not in the leftmost cell of C_i and unifies with L with an mgu θ (*factoring*), or

(ii) C_i contains an A-literal N which is not the leftmost A-literal of C_i and the complement of N unifies with L with an mgu θ (*ancestor resolution*).

(d) $C_{i+1} = C'_i\theta$, where C'_i is obtained from C_i by deleting the occurrence of L in C_i. The status of a literal $K\theta$ in C_{i+1} is the same as the status as the literal K in C_i.

(4) C_{i+1} is obtained from C_i by *extension* with an input chain D if and only if the following conditions are satisfied:

(a) The leftmost literal in C_i is a B-literal.

(b) C_i and D have no common variables.

(c) The selected literal L in C_i and the complement of the rightmost literal M in D are unifiable with an mgu θ.

(d) Then C_{i+1} is the chain $(D' L C'_i)\theta$, where C'_i is obtained by removing the occurrence of L from C_i and D′ is obtained by removing the rightmost literal from B. The status of the literal $L\theta$ in C_{i+1} is A-literal. Each literal $M\theta$ in C_{i+1} has the same status as the literal M in C_i or M in D depending on wherever M occurs.

(5) C_{i+1} is *admissible*, that is, if C_{i+1} is not derived from C_i through step 3, then no two literals occurring at distinct positions in C_i have the same atom.

A *SL-refutation* is a SL-derivation of the empty chain (□). SL-resolution is also complete, that is, for every unsatisfiable set of clauses **S** and a set of support $\mathbf{S}_0$ and selection function ϕ, there exists an SL-refutation of **S**.

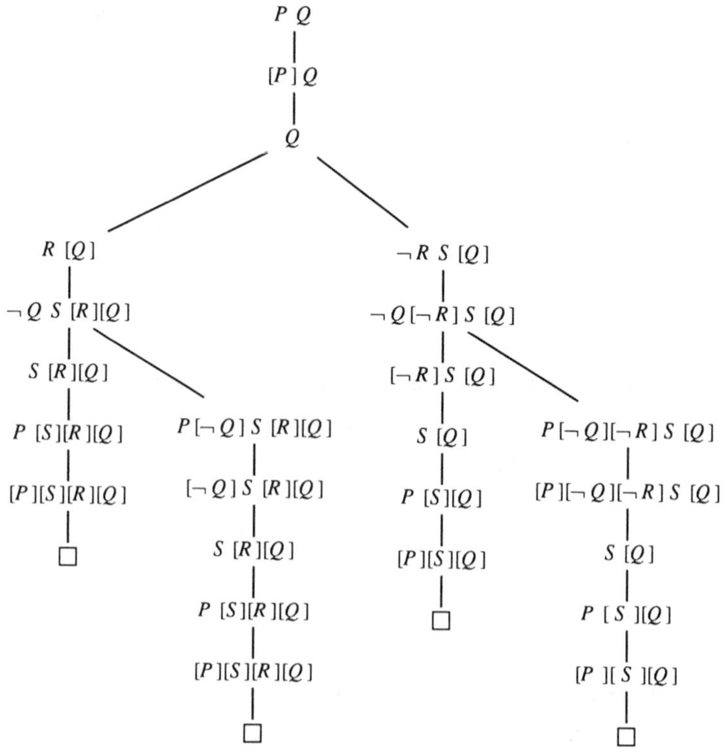

Figure 4.2 A search tree for SL-derivation.

EXAMPLE 4.22

Suppose $\mathbf{S} = \{P \vee Q, \neg P, \neg Q \vee R, \neg Q \vee \neg R \vee S, P \vee \neg S\}$ and the set of support $\mathbf{S}_0 = \{P \vee Q\}$. Then $\mathbf{S} - \mathbf{S}_0$ is satisfiable. An SL-derivation for the set $\mathbf{S}$ is given below.

Step 1:	$P\ Q$	Chosen from $\mathbf{S}_0$
Step 2:	$[P]\ Q$	Extension with $\neg P$
Step 3:	Q	Truncation
Step 4:	$R\ [Q]$	Extension with $R\ \neg Q$
Step 5:	$\neg Q\ S\ [R][Q]$	Extension with $\neg Q\ S\ \neg R$
Step 6:	$S\ [R][Q]$	Reduction
Step 7:	$P\ [S][R][Q]$	Extension with $P\ \neg S$
Step 8:	$[P][S][R][Q]$	Extension with $\neg P$
Step 9:	$\varnothing$	Truncation

A complete SL search tree for the set $\mathbf{S}$ with $P \vee Q$ as the top clause is shown in Figure 4.2. The reduction in the number of branches is observable by comparing with Figure 4.1.

Exercises

4.1 Construct an mgu (if one exist) in each of the following sets of expressions:

(a) $\{P(x, b), P(a, y)\}$

(b) $\{P(f(x), g(x)), P(y, g(y))\}$.

(c) $\{P(x, f(y), y), P(f(y_1), f(g(z)), g(a))\}$

(d) $\{P(x_1, f(y_1, b)), P(g(x_2), f(h(y_2), z)), P(g(a), f(h(c), b))\}$

4.2 Find the composite unifier $\alpha\beta$ in each of the following cases:

(a) $\alpha = \{x/z, y/f(z)\}, \beta = \{z/a\}$

(b) $\alpha = \{x/f(y), y/g(z)\}, \beta = \{y/g(a), z/a\}$

4.3 Show that each of the following sets of clauses is unsatisfiable by constructing a refutation by the resolution principle and also by its refinements, for example, liner resolution, SL-resolution, input and unit resolution. Also, draw search trees wherever applicable.

(a) $\{\neg P(x), P(x) \vee \neg Q(x), P(x) \vee \neg R(x), Q(x) \vee R(x)\}$

(b) $\{\neg P(x, y),\ P(x, y) \vee \neg Q(x, z) \vee \neg P(z, y),\ P(x, y) \vee \neg Q(x, y),$
$Q(a, b), Q(b, c)\}$

PART III

Logic Programming

5

Logic programming

This chapter introduces the concepts of logic programming. Program clauses are classified according to their syntactic structures. Several categories of logic programs are presented and the different kinds of semantics that can be attributed to a logic program are defined. Detailed studies on individual classes of logic programs are carried out in the following three chapters.

5.1 What is logic programming?

Kowalski (1979b) represented the analysis of an algorithm by the equation

Algorithm = Logic + Control

that is, given an *algorithm* for solving a particular problem, the *logic component* specifies the knowledge which can be used in solving the problem and the *control component* determines the way this knowledge can be used to arrive at a solution to the problem. To clarify the concepts of logic and control components, consider the following definition of factorial, which is specified by using standard mathematical symbols:

$$
\begin{aligned}
Fact(n) &= 1 && \text{when } n = 0 \\
&= n * Fact(n-1) && \text{when } n > 0
\end{aligned}
$$

Two different conventional algorithms for computing a factorial are developed below.

Algorithm 5.1

Input: n
Step 1: $Fact = 1$
Step 2: If $n = 0$ then return $Fact$
Step 3: $Fact = Fact * n$, $n = n-1$, go to step 2

Algorithm 5.1 computes a factorial in a *top-down* manner, that is, the algorithm starts from the goal to find the factorial of n and then reduces this to the goal to find the factorial of $n - 1$, and so on. Consider the following algorithm which computes the factorial of a number in a *bottom-up* manner, that is, the search for the solution of the factorial of n starts from the assertions present in the logic component ($Fact(0) = 1$) and then derives a number of new assertions (for example, $Fact(1) = 1$, $Fact(2) = 2$) until the desired solution is found.

Algorithm 5.2

Input: n
Step 1: $Fact = 1$, $n_1 = 0$
Step 2: If $n_1 = n$ then return $Fact$
Step 3: $n_1 = n_1 + 1$, $Fact = Fact * n_1$, go to step 2

Both algorithms generate the same answers but the efficiency and the consumption of storage space differ. The symbolized definition of factorial constitutes the logic component of both algorithms. The two algorithms constitute two different control components for the same logic component.

In a *logic programming* system a programmer specifies the logic component of an algorithm, called the *logic program*, using the notion of mathematical logic. For example, the definition of factorial as the logic component in a logic programming system is expressed by a well-formed formula in mathematical logic as

$$Fact(0, 1) \wedge \forall n \forall n_1 \forall v \forall v_1 (Fact(n, v) \leftarrow n > 0 \wedge n_1 = n - 1 \wedge Fact(n_1, v_1) \wedge v = n * v_1)$$

or, equivalently, as a set of Horn clauses as

$$Fact(0, 1)$$
$$\forall n \forall n_1 \forall v \forall v_1 (Fact(n, v) \leftarrow n > 0 \wedge n_1 = n - 1 \wedge Fact(n_1, v_1) \wedge v = n * v_1)$$

where the interpretation of $Fact(x, y)$ is that number y is the factorial of number x and the other symbols are given their usual meaning. The control component in a logic programming system either can be expressed by the programmer through a separate control-specifying language or can be determined entirely by the logic programming system itself. The efficiency of an algorithm can be increased by tuning its control component without changing its logic component.

Although a logic program lacks sufficient procedural information for the system to do anything other than make an exhaustive search to find the correct execution path, separating the logic component from the control component has several advantages, including those pertaining to the correctness of the algorithm, program improvement and modification.

In a logic programming system the logic component of an algorithm is specified in mathematical logic. More generally, in a *declarative programming* environment the programmer specifies the logic component of an algorithm in a standard symbolized manner. Thus *functional programming* (Hudak, 1989) is also declarative and the logic component of an algorithm in such an environment is specified through function declarations.

5.2 Program clauses and goals

A non-empty clause can be rewritten as

$$M_1 \vee \cdots \vee M_p \vee \neg N_1 \vee \cdots \vee \neg N_q, \qquad p + q \geq 1 \tag{5.1}$$

where M_is and N_js are positive literals and variables are implicitly universally quantified over the whole disjunction. Every closed wff may be rewritten in clausal form (see Chapter 3). The above clause can be written in the form of a *program clause* (Gallaire *et al.*, 1984) as

$$M'_1 \vee \cdots \vee M'_k \leftarrow N_1 \wedge \cdots \wedge N_q \wedge \neg M'_{k+1} \wedge \cdots \wedge \neg M'_p \qquad k \geq 1, q \geq 0, p \geq 0 \tag{5.2}$$

or, in the form of a *goal* as

$$\leftarrow N_1 \wedge \cdots \wedge N_q \wedge \neg M'_1 \wedge \cdots \wedge \neg M'_p, \qquad p + q \geq 1 \tag{5.3}$$

where each M'_i is an M_j, for some j. The general definitions of a program clause and a goal are given below.

Definition 5.1: A *program clause* (or *general clause* or simply *clause*) is a formula of the form

$$A_1 \vee \cdots \vee A_m \leftarrow L_1 \wedge \cdots \wedge L_n, \qquad m \geq 1, n \geq 0 \tag{5.4}$$

where $A_1 \vee \cdots \vee A_m$ is the *head* (or *conclusion* or *consequent*) of the program clause and $L_1 \wedge \cdots \wedge L_n$ the *body* (or *condition* or *antecedent*). Each A_i is an atom and each L_j is either an atom (a *positive condition*) or a negated atom (a *negative condition*). Any variables in A_1, ..., A_m, L_1, ..., L_n are assumed to be universally quantified over the whole formula. Each A_i (resp. L_i) is said to have *occurred* in the head (resp. body) of clause (5.4). If $m > 1$ then the general clause (5.4) is *indefinite*.

The various forms of a general clause for different values of m and n are the following:

(1) $m = 1, n = 0$, that is, clause (5.4) has the form

$$A \leftarrow \tag{5.5}$$

in which the body is empty and the head is a single atom. This clause is called a *unit clause* or *unit assertion*.

(2) $m \geq 1, n = 0$, that is, clause (5.4) has the form

$$A_1 \vee \cdots \vee A_m \leftarrow \tag{5.6}$$

in which the body is empty and the head is a disjunction of atoms. This clause is called a *positive clause* or an *assertion*.

(3) $m = 1, n \geq 0$ and each L_i is an atom, that is, clause (5.4) has the form

$$A \leftarrow B_1 \wedge \cdots \wedge B_n \tag{5.7}$$

in which A and B_is are atoms. This clause is called a *definite clause*.

(4) $m = 1, n \geq 0$, that is, clause (5.4) has the form

$$A \leftarrow L_1 \wedge \cdots \wedge L_n \tag{5.8}$$

in which A is an atom and L_is are literals. This clause is a *normal clause*.

(5) $m \geq 1, n \geq 0$, that is, clause (5.4) has the form

$$A_1 \vee \cdots \vee A_m \leftarrow B_1 \wedge \cdots \wedge B_n \tag{5.9}$$

in which A_is and B_js are atoms. This clause is a *disjunctive clause* or *non-Horn clause*.

Thus a unit clause is a special form of a definite clause; a definite clause is a special form of normal clause and also a special form of a disjunctive clause; and so on. A unit clause or an assertion is written by omitting the symbol '$\leftarrow$'. The following example contains various types of clauses involved with the problem of representing numbers.

EXAMPLE 5.1

Clause	**Type**
C1. $Even(0)$	Unit
C2. $Positive(x) \vee Negative(x)$	Assertion
C3. $Even(s(x)) \leftarrow Integer(x) \wedge Odd(x)$	Definite
C4. $Even(x) \leftarrow Integer(x) \wedge \neg Odd(x)$	Normal
C5. $Even(x) \vee Odd(x) \leftarrow Integer(x)$	Disjunctive
C6. $Integer(x) \vee Fraction(x) \leftarrow Real(x) \wedge \neg Irrational(x)$	General
C7. $Even(s(s(x))) \leftarrow Integer(x) \wedge Even(x)$	Definite

Clause C1 represents '0 is even', clause C2 represents 'everything is either positive or negative', and so on. Although clauses C4 and C5 are logically equivalent, the semantics of a logic program which includes clause C4 may be different if the program replaces C4 by C5. In such cases, the use of the negation symbol '$\neg$' becomes a default rule which may be different from the classical negation studied so far. But it is always clear from the context which particular approach has been taken.

Definition 5.2: A *normal goal* (or *denial* (Quine, 1980) or simply *goal*) is a formula of the form

$$\leftarrow L_1 \wedge \cdots \wedge L_n, \qquad n \geq 1 \tag{5.10}$$

where each L_i is either an atom or a negated atom. The conjunction $L_1 \wedge \cdots \wedge L_n$ is the *body* of the goal. Variables occurring in the goal are assumed to be universally quantified over the whole of the goal. When all the literals in the above goal are positive, that is, when goal (5.10) takes the form

$$\leftarrow B_1 \wedge \cdots \wedge B_n, \qquad n \geq 1 \tag{5.11}$$

where each B_i is an atom, then the goal is a *definite goal*. Thus a definite goal is a special form of a normal goal.

EXAMPLE 5.2

The goal

$$\leftarrow Integer(x) \wedge \neg Even(x)$$

is a normal goal whereas

$$\leftarrow Integer(x) \wedge Positive(x)$$

is a definite goal.

The classification of program clauses and goals is listed in Table 5.1.

Table 5.1 Different forms of program clauses and goals (A, A_is and B_js are atoms, L_ks are literals).

Form	*Name*
$\leftarrow B_1 \wedge \cdots \wedge B_n, n \geq 1$	Definite goal
$\leftarrow L_1 \wedge \cdots \wedge L_n, n \geq 1$	Normal goal
A	Unit clause
$A \leftarrow B_1 \wedge \cdots \wedge B_n, n \geq 1$	Definite clause
$A \leftarrow L_1 \wedge \cdots \wedge L_n, n \geq 1$	Normal clause
$A_1 \vee \cdots \vee A_m, m \geq 1$	Assertion
$A_1 \vee \cdots \vee A_m \leftarrow B_1 \wedge \cdots \wedge B_n, m \geq 1, n \geq 0$	Disjunctive clause
$A_1 \vee \cdots \vee A_m \leftarrow L_1 \wedge \cdots \wedge L_n, m \geq 1, n \geq 0$	General clause

Definition 5.3: A *subgoal of a goal* G is a literal occurring in G. A *subgoal of a rule* R is a literal occurring in the body of R.

5.3 Definite, normal and general programs

Definition 5.4: A *general program* (or simply *program*) is a finite set of general clauses. A *disjunctive program* is a finite set of disjunctive clauses. A *normal program* is a finite set of normal clauses. A *definite program* is a finite set of definite clauses. The classification of programs is listed in Table 5.2.

The number of clauses in a program does not necessarily have to be finite although it is so in most practical purposes. An objective of the formal theoretical developments of logic programming is to be able to treat the clauses in a program as proper axioms of some formal axiomatic theory. According to the definition of a formal axiomatic theory (see Chapter 3), there must be an effective procedure to determine all the axioms of the theory. This obviously does not restrict the number of proper or logical axioms of the theory to a finite number.

A definite program is a special form of a normal program and also a special form of a general program. Similarly, a normal program is a special form of a general program. The set of clauses in Example 5.1 constitutes a general program. In writing a set of clauses to represent a program, the same variables may be used in two different clauses. If there are any common variables between two different clauses then they are renamed before they are used.

EXAMPLE 5.3

Program:

C1. $Undergraduate(x) \vee Postgraduate(x) \leftarrow Student(x) \wedge \neg Research(x)$

C2. $Mother(x, y) \vee Father(x, y) \leftarrow Parent(x, y)$

Table 5.2 Different types of program (A, A_is and B_js are atoms, L_ks are literals).

Structure of clauses	*Program type*
$A \leftarrow B_1 \wedge \cdots \wedge B_n, n \geq 0$	Horn or definite
$A \leftarrow L_1 \wedge \cdots \wedge L_n, n \geq 0$	Normal
$A_1 \vee \cdots \vee A_m \leftarrow B_1 \wedge \cdots \wedge B_n, m \geq 1, n \geq 0$	Disjunctive or non-Horn
$A_1 \vee \cdots \vee A_m \leftarrow L_1 \wedge \cdots \wedge L_n, m \geq 1, n \geq 0$	General

C3. $Sponsor(x, y) \leftarrow Guardian(x, y) \wedge Employed(x) \wedge \neg Stipend(y)$
C4. $Guardian(x, y) \leftarrow Student(y) \wedge Parent(x, y)$
C5. $Likes(Janique, Logic) \vee Likes(Janique, Bookkeeping)$
C6. $Undergraduate(Subrata)$
C7. $Student(Janique)$
C8. $Research(Janique)$
C9. $Likes(x, Games)$
C10. $Likes(Subrata, Mathematics)$

The clauses C1, C2 and C5 make the above program general. In this program, the non-ground atom $Likes(x, Games)$ represents 'everyone likes games'.

In the context of the program of Example 5.3, one can have a definite goal

$$\leftarrow Sponsor(x, Subrata) \tag{5.12}$$

to find who is sponsoring Subrata. Similarly a normal goal of the form

$$\leftarrow Likes(x, Mathematics) \wedge \neg Research(x) \tag{5.13}$$

will find those non-research students who like mathematics. If $x_1, ..., x_p$ are all the free variables in a goal of the form (5.10), then the goal in the context of a program **P** is interpreted as a request for a constructive proof for the formula

$$\exists x_1, ..., \exists x_p (L_1 \wedge \cdots \wedge L_n) \tag{5.14}$$

This means that one should find a substitution θ for the free variables in the goal such that $(L_1 \wedge \cdots \wedge L_n)\theta$ is true according to the semantics of the program.

5.4 Hierarchical, recursive and stratified programs

Programs have so far been classified by looking at the structure of the individual clauses. Further subclassifications of programs can be achieved by looking at their constituent set of clauses as a whole. This classification can be facilitated by the use of dependency graphs. Consider the class of normal programs.

Definition 5.5: The *dependency graph* of a normal program **P** has a node for each predicate symbol occurring in **P** and a directed edge from the node for predicate Q to the node for predicate P whenever predicate Q is in the body of some clause and P is in the head of the same clause. An edge from node Q to node P is *positive* iff

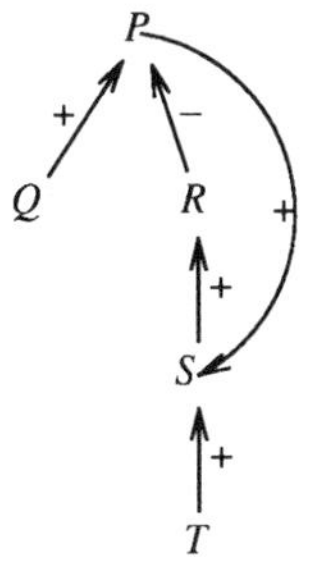

Figure 5.1 The dependency graph for the program of Example 5.4.

there is a clause C in **P** in which P is in the head of C, and Q is the predicate symbol of a positive literal in the body of C. The edge is *negative* if Q is the predicate symbol of a negative literal in the body of C. The *length* of a cycle in a dependency graph is the number of edges occurring in the cycle.

EXAMPLE 5.4

Program: $P(x) \leftarrow Q(x) \wedge \neg R(x)$
$R(x) \leftarrow S(x)$
$S(x) \leftarrow T(x, y) \wedge P(y)$
$Q(a)$
$T(a, b)$

The dependency graph for the above program is shown in Figure 5.1. The set of clauses in this example contains nodes P, Q, R, S and T. The edges from Q to P, from S to R, from T to S and from P to S are positive while the edge from R to P is negative.

Definition 5.6: If the dependency graph for a normal program does not contain any cycles then the program is *hierarchical.*

Having cycles in the dependency graph of a program **P** implies that some predicates of **P** are directly or indirectly defined by themselves. This, of course, complicates the structure of a program and goal evaluations in the context of that program. This class of programs are formally classified through the following definitions.

Definition 5.7: Let **P** be a normal program and Γ be the dependency graph for **P**. A predicate P occurring in **P** is *recursive* if it occurs in a cycle of Γ. Two predicates P and Q are *mutually recursive* if they both occur in a cycle of Γ.

EXAMPLE 5.5

The predicate P in the program of Example 5.4 is recursive and the predicates P and R are mutually recursive.

EXAMPLE 5.6

The program formed by excluding the indefinite clauses from the program of Example 5.3 is an example of an hierarchical normal program.

Definition 5.8: If the dependency graph for a normal program contains a cycle then the program is *recursive*. A recursive normal program is *directly recursive* if its dependency graph does not contain a cycle of length greater than one.

EXAMPLE 5.7

Program: $Append(Nil, x, x)$

$Append(List(x, y), z, List(x, z')) \leftarrow Append(y, z, z')$

The above program is directly recursive. The normal program in Example 5.4 is recursive but not directly recursive.

Normal programs allow negated atoms in their bodies. When this happens, one should be careful about the meaning of the program. Consider the following example.

EXAMPLE 5.8

Program: $Outside(a) \leftarrow \neg\, Member(a)$

$Member(a) \leftarrow \neg\, Outside(a)$

The dependency graph of the above program contains a cycle involving negative edges, that is, a recursion via negation.

In Example 5.8, it is not clear whether $Outside(a)$ is true or $Member(a)$ is true in the program. This kind of situation can be prevented by not allowing a recursion via negation.

Definition 5.9: A normal program is *stratified* (Chandra and Harel, 1985; Apt *et al.*, 1988) if each cycle of the dependency graph is formed by positive edges only although the remainder of the graph may contain negative edges.

Clearly every hierarchical program can be regarded as a specific stratified program and all definite programs are stratified.

EXAMPLE 5.9

Program: $ClearPath(x, y) \leftarrow Path(x, y) \wedge \neg Obstruction(x, y)$

$ClearPath(x, y) \leftarrow ClearPath(x, z) \wedge ClearPath(z, y)$

$Path(a, b)$

$Path(b, c)$

The above is stratified but neither definite nor hierarchical.

EXAMPLE 5.10

The normal program in Example 5.4 is not a stratified program. However, the modified version given below is now stratified.

Program: C1. $P(x) \leftarrow Q(x) \wedge \neg R(x)$

C2. $R(x) \leftarrow S(x)$

C3. $S(x) \leftarrow T(x, y) \wedge \neg U(y)$

C4. $S(x) \leftarrow U(x)$

C5. $Q(a)$

C6. $R(a)$

C7. $T(a, b)$

An alternative definition of stratified normal programs can be given by introducing the notions of stratification among the definitions of predicate symbols of programs.

Definition 5.10: Suppose **P** is a normal program. The definition of a predicate symbol P is the subset of **P** consisting of all clauses with P occurring in their heads.

EXAMPLE 5.11

Consider the program of Example 5.10. The definitions of predicate symbols P, Q, R, S, T and U are {C1}, {C5}, {C2, C6}, {C3, C4}, {C7} and {} respectively.

Definition 5.11: A normal program $\mathbf{P}$ is regarded as stratified if there is a partition

$$\mathbf{P} = \mathbf{P}_1 \cup \cdots \cup \mathbf{P}_n$$

such that the following two conditions hold for $i = 1, 2, ..., n$.

(1) If an atom A occurs positively in the body (that is, A occurs in the body) of a clause in $\mathbf{P}_i$ then the definition of its predicate symbol is contained within $\mathbf{P}_j$ with $j \leq i$.

(2) If an atom A occurs negatively in the body (that is, $\neg A$ occurs in the body) of a clause in $\mathbf{P}_i$ then the definition of its predicate symbol is contained within $\mathbf{P}_j$ with $j < i$.

The program $\mathbf{P}$ is said to be stratified by $\mathbf{P}_1 \cup \cdots \cup \mathbf{P}_n$ and each $\mathbf{P}_i$ is called a *stratum* of $\mathbf{P}$. The *level* of a predicate symbol is the index of the strata within which it is defined.

EXAMPLE 5.12

The program of Example 5.10 is stratified by $\mathbf{P}_1 \cup \mathbf{P}_2 \cup \mathbf{P}_3$, where $\mathbf{P}_3 = \{C1\}$, $\mathbf{P}_2 = \{C2, C3, C4, C6\}$ and $\mathbf{P}_1 = \{C5, C7\}$. An alternative way the program can be stratified is by $\mathbf{P}_1 \cup \mathbf{P}_2 \cup \mathbf{P}_3 \cup \mathbf{P}_4$, where $\mathbf{P}_4 = \{C1\}$, $\mathbf{P}_3 = \{C2, C6\}$, $\mathbf{P}_2 = \{C3, C4, C7\}$ and $\mathbf{P}_1 = \{C5\}$.

The following lemma provides the equivalence between Definitions 5.9 and 5.11.

Lemma 5.1: A normal program $\mathbf{P}$ is stratified (following Definition 5.10) if and only if in its dependency graph there are no cycles containing a negative edge.

Proof Suppose $\mathbf{P}$ is stratified. If there is a negative (resp. positive) edge from a predicate symbol P to another predicate symbol Q in the dependency graph of $\mathbf{P}$, then the level of P is less than (resp. less than or equal to) the level of Q. Thus there are no cycles in the dependency graph through a negative edge.

To prove the converse, define a relation ρ on the set of all predicate symbols $\mathbf{S}$ occurring as nodes in the dependency graph of $\mathbf{P}$ as follows: if $P, Q \in \mathbf{S}$, then

$P \rho Q$ if and only if either $P = Q$ or P and Q are connected in a cycle.

The relation ρ is an equivalence relation as for all $P, Q, R \in \mathbf{S}$:

(1) $P = P$ and hence $P \rho P$.

(2) If P and Q are connected in a cycle then Q and P are also connected in a cycle. Thus $P \rho Q$ implies $Q \rho P$.

(3) If P and Q are connected in a cycle and Q and R are connected in a cycle, then P and R are also connected in a cycle. Thus $P \rho Q$ and $Q \rho R$ imply $P \rho R$.

By the equivalence theorem (see Chapter 2), $\mathbf{S}$ can be partitioned into disjoint subsets $\mathbf{S}_1, \ldots, \mathbf{S}_n$ such that each pair of elements in each $\mathbf{S}_i$ $(1 \leq i \leq n)$ is connected in a cycle, but for every $P \in \mathbf{S}_i$ and $Q \in \mathbf{S}_j$, $1 \leq i \leq n$ and $1 \leq j \leq n$ and $i \neq j$, P and Q are not connected in a cycle. If a directed graph is formed where $\mathbf{S}_i$s are nodes and an $\mathbf{S}_i$ is connected to an $\mathbf{S}_j$ if an element of $\mathbf{S}_i$ is connected to an element of $\mathbf{S}_j$ in the dependency graph of $\mathbf{P}$, then this graph will not contain any cycles. Hence the numbers 1, ..., n can be assigned unambiguously (but not uniquely) to the $\mathbf{S}_i$s so that if there is an edge from a member of $\mathbf{S}_j$ to a member of $\mathbf{S}_i$, then the number assigned to $\mathbf{S}_j$ is strictly less than the number assigned to $\mathbf{S}_i$.

Let $\mathbf{P}_j$ be the subset of the program $\mathbf{P}$ containing the definitions of all the predicate symbols which lie within an $\mathbf{S}_j$ whose assigned number is i. Now $\mathbf{P}$ can be proved to be stratified by $\mathbf{P}_1 \cup \cdots \cup \mathbf{P}_n$. Indeed if P is defined within some $\mathbf{P}_i$ and refers to Q, then Q lies in the same component or lies in a component with a smaller number. In other words the definition of Q is contained in $\mathbf{P}_j$ with $j \leq i$. If this reference is negative, then Q lies in a component with the smallest number because, by assumption, there is no cycle through a negative edge. Thus the definition of Q is then contained in $\mathbf{P}_j$ with $j < i$. ■

Definition 5.12: A *level mapping* $\mathcal{L}$ of a normal program is a mapping from its set of predicates to the set of non-negative integers. If L is a literal, then the literal level $\mathcal{L}(L)$ is the level of the predicate symbol of L. The level of a clause C, denoted by $\mathcal{L}$(C), is the maximum level of any predicate symbol in C.

A third alternative equivalent definition of stratified normal programs in terms of level mapping will now be established.

Lemma 5.2: A program is stratified if it has a level mapping such that, for every normal clause C, the level of the predicate symbol of every positive condition in C is less than or equal to the level of the predicate symbol in the head of C, and the level of the predicate of every negated condition in C is less than the level of the predicate symbol in the head of C.

Proof Straightforward from Definition 5.11. ■

The definition of hierarchical, recursive and stratified programs will now be generalized for the case of general programs.

Definition 5.13: Let **P** be a general program. Suppose C is a clause in **P** and A is an atom occurring in the head of C. The *possible form* of C with respect to A, denoted *pos* (C, A), is the clause obtained from C by replacing its head by A.

According to this definition, the possible form of a normal clause C with respect to the only atom in its head is the clause C and the possible form of an atom or disjunctive atoms with respect to the atom A appearing in it, is the atom A.

Definition 5.14: A normal program that comprises at least one possible form of each of the clauses of **P** is called a *possible form* of the general program **P**.

EXAMPLE 5.13

The general program of Example 5.3 has 27 possible forms, one of which is the union of the set of all normal clauses of the program with the following three possible forms

$$Undergraduate(x) \leftarrow Student(x) \wedge \neg Research(x)$$
$$Mother(x, y) \leftarrow Parent(x, y)$$
$$Likes(Janique, Logic)$$

corresponding to the three indefinite clauses of the program.

Definition 5.15: A general program is hierarchical (resp. recursive and stratified) if each of its possible forms is hierarchical (resp. recursive and stratified).

Definition 5.16: A program **P** is *separate* if the intersection is empty between the set of all predicate symbols occurring in the assertions of **P** and the set of all predicate symbols occurring in the heads of clauses of **P** with non-empty bodies.

EXAMPLE 5.14

The program of Example 5.3 is separate whereas the program of Example 5.10 is not. This is because the predicate symbol R in the program of Example 5.10 is in the assertion $R(a)$ as well as in the head of the clause $R(x) \leftarrow S(x)$ whose body is non-empty.

5.5 Semantics of programs

The semantics of a program deals with its meaning. Three standard ways of defining semantics of programs are introduced in this section: declarative, fixpoint and procedural.

The *declarative semantics* of a program deals with the interpretation of the language of the program including meaning, logical implications and truth. The declarative semantics for a program can be defined by selecting one or more of its models. These models determine which substitution of a given goal is correct in the context of the program.

The *procedural semantics* (or *operational semantics*) of a program deals with well-formed formulae and their syntax, axioms, rules of inference and proofs within the language of the program. This semantics defines the input/output relations computed by a program in terms of the individual operations evoked by the program inside the machine. Procedural semantics refers to a computational method, called *proof procedure*, for obtaining the meaning of a program.

Fixpoint semantics (Fitting, 1985; Lassez *et al.*, 1982; Kolaitis and Papadimitriou, 1988; van Emden and Kowalski, 1976; van Gelder, 1989) defines the meaning of a program to be the input/output relation which is the minimal fixpoint of transformation T_P associated with the program P. This operator builds the intended model of the program in a step-by-step process.

Van Emden and Kowalski investigated first the semantics of Horn logic as a programming language (van Emden and Kowalski, 1976) and compared the declarative semantics of a program with the classical model-theoretic semantics, operational semantics with classical proof-theoretic semantics and fixpoint semantics by the fixpoint operator T_P corresponding to a program $\mathbf{P}$.

All logical consequences of a program can be considered as positive information. Declarative, procedural and fixpoint semantics are sometimes only concerned with the positive information about a program that can be derived from that program. The negative information is not explicitly stored in a program and it is assumed by default. This additional implicit negative information cannot be proved from the program by normal inference rules such as modus ponens. *Rules for inferring negative information* are rules that infer this additional implicit negative information. Hence a rule for inferring negative information defines the *semantics for negative informations* in the program and is given in either a declarative or a procedural manner. This rule will be studied alongside the other three kinds of semantics mentioned above.

EXAMPLE 5.15

Consider the following program **P**:

Program: $Undergraduate(x) \leftarrow Student(x)$
$Student(Daniel)$
$Likes(Robert, Logic)$

Several different semantics for the above program can be defined as follows:

(1) Declarative semantics – a fact which is in a minimal model of **P** is taken as true.
(2) Procedural semantics – a fact which can be derived from **P** is taken as true.
(3) Semantics for negative information – a fact which is in $\mathcal{HB}(\mathbf{P})$ and not in at least one minimal model of **P** is taken as false.

Then the declarative and procedural semantics coincide and are represented by the set

$$\{Student(Daniel), Undergraduate(Daniel), Likes(Robert, Logic)\}$$

According to these two semantics, the above set is the set of all true facts in the context of **P**. The semantics for negative information generates the set

$$\mathcal{HB}(\mathbf{P}) - \{Student(Daniel), Undergraduate(Daniel), Likes(Robert, Logic)\}$$

and thus, for example, $Student(Robert)$ is taken as false in the context of **P** according to the semantics for negative information.

Let $\mathcal{R}$ be a rule for inferring negative information for a particular class (such as definite or stratified or normal) of programs and **P** be a program from that class. Then $\mathcal{R}(\mathbf{P})$ will denote the set of negative facts that can be inferred from **P** by the application of $\mathcal{R}$. The following properties (Ross and Topor, 1988) are expected to be satisfied in a typical program **P** of this class:

- *Concise* Use of $\mathcal{R}$ should enable a useful reduction in the amount of negative information that would otherwise have to be stored in the form of clauses of $\mathbf{P}$. In other words, the set of facts $\mathcal{R}(\mathbf{P})$ is relatively large compared to $\mathbf{P}$. This reflects the property that in a typical program the number of facts which are true is much less than the whole Herbrand base associated with the database. In the context of the program $\mathbf{P}$ of Example 5.15, the number of true facts is 3 compared to 8 which is the size of $\mathcal{HB}(\mathbf{P})$.
- *Efficient* It should be relatively easy to determine whether an item of negative information can be inferred from $\mathbf{P}$ by $\mathcal{R}$. In other words, the decision procedure of $\mathcal{R}(\mathcal{P})$ should be relatively efficient.
- *Consistency* If the program $\mathbf{P}$ is consistent, then $\mathbf{P} \cup \mathcal{R}(\mathbf{P})$ should be consistent. Although this is the case for Example 5.15, it may not always be true. Consider the program $\mathbf{P} = \{Undergraduate(Didier) \vee Postgraduate(Didier)\}$ and the associated semantics for negative information is the one defined in Example 5.15. The program $\mathbf{P}$ has two minimal models $\{Undergraduate(Didier)\}$ and $\{Postgraduate(Didier)\}$. According to the semantics for negative information, both $Undergraduate(Didier)$ and $Postgraduate(Didier)$ are false in the context and thus $\mathcal{R}(\mathbf{P}) = \{\neg Undergraduate(Didier), \neg Postgraduate(Didier)\}$. Therefore $\mathbf{P} \cup \mathcal{R}(\mathbf{P})$ is inconsistent.
- *Decreasing* No more negative clauses should be inferred by $\mathcal{R}$ after adding clauses to $\mathbf{P}$ that can be inferred from $\mathbf{P}$ itself. In other words, if $\mathbf{P} \subseteq \mathbf{P}'$ then $\mathcal{R}(\mathbf{P}) \subseteq \mathcal{R}(\mathbf{P}')$.
- *Invariant* The clauses inferred by $\mathcal{R}$ should depend only on the models for $\mathbf{P}$. In other words, if $\mathbf{P} \equiv \mathbf{P}'$ then $\mathcal{R}(\mathbf{P}) = \mathcal{R}(\mathbf{P}')$

The decision as to whether the rule $\mathcal{R}$ should interpret disjunction inclusively or exclusively is rather controversial. In the case of the example assertion

$$Age(Janique, 27) \vee Age(Janique, 30)$$

of a program, the exclusive interpretation of disjunction is desirable. For example, if it is positively known that the age of Janique is 27 then there is no point in considering Janique's age as 30. On the other hand, the disjunction in

$$Likes(Janique, Logic) \vee Likes(Janique, Bookkeeping)$$

is inclusive rather than exclusive. That is, even if it is positively known that Janique likes logic it would be unwise to conclude that Janique does not like bookkeeping.

Situations may arise when it would not be possible to assign properly the meaning or truth value to a particular piece of information. For example, given the fact that

$$Likes(Janique, Logic) \vee Likes(Janique, Bookkeeping)$$

is a clause of a program, it is not clear whether or not Janique likes logic. These kinds of information would obviously be treated in a different way from positive or negative information. If there is a possibility of reaching such a situation they should be mentioned (if it is necessary) as part of the declarative semantics.

Detailed studies of semantics on individual classes of logic programs are carried out in the next three chapters.

Exercise

5.1 Classify the following program clauses as definite, normal, general, and so on:

$$Prime(x) \leftarrow Natural(x) \wedge \neg Factor(x)$$
$$Sort(x, y) \leftarrow Permutation(x, y) \wedge sorted(y)$$
$$SuccessfulDeletion(x, y, y') \leftarrow In(x, y) \wedge Delete(x, y, y')$$
$$Solve(Conj(x, y)) \leftarrow Solve(x) \wedge Solve(y)$$
$$Permutation(x, List(y, z)) \leftarrow Permutation(z', z) \wedge Append(t, t', z') \wedge Append(t, List(y, t'), x)$$
$$Traverse(t) \leftarrow Traverse(Root(t)) \wedge Traverse(Left(t)) \wedge Traverse(Right(t))$$
$$Subgroup(x, y, u, v) \leftarrow Subset(x, y) \wedge Group(x, u, v)$$
$$Dependent(x, y) \leftarrow Parent(y, x) \wedge Employed(y) \wedge \neg Employed(x)$$
$$Element(z, x) \vee Element(z, y) \leftarrow Set(x) \wedge Set(y) \wedge \neg Empty(Intersection(x, y)) \wedge Element(z, Union(x, y))$$
$$Cinema(x) \vee Pub(x) \leftarrow Day(x) \wedge \neg Dry(x)$$
$$Likes(x, y) \vee Likes(x, z) \leftarrow Compulsory(x, y) \wedge Additional(x, z)$$

6

Definite programs

This chapter deals with the semantics of definite programs. Declarative semantics is studied by employing classical model-theoretic semantics and procedural semantics by employing the SLD-resolution scheme. Unless otherwise stated, in this chapter the terms 'program' and 'goal' will always mean 'definite program' and 'definite goal' respectively. Recall that a definite program is defined as a finite set of definite clauses of the form

$$A \leftarrow A_1 \wedge \cdots \wedge A_m, \qquad m \geq 0 \tag{6.1}$$

and a definite goal is defined as

$$\leftarrow B_1 \wedge \cdots \wedge B_n, \qquad n \geq 1 \tag{6.2}$$

where A, A_is and B_js are atoms.

6.1 Declarative semantics

The only declarative semantics of a definite program studied here is that given in van Emden and Kowalski (1976) and is formally defined as follows. Let $\mathbf{P}$ be a definite program. Then the declarative semantics of $\mathbf{P}$, denoted as $\mathcal{M}(\mathbf{P})$, is defined as

$$\mathcal{M}(\mathbf{P}) = \{A \mid A \in \mathcal{HB}(\mathbf{P}) \text{ and } \mathbf{P} \models A\}$$

which means that $\mathcal{M}(\mathbf{P})$ is the set of all ground atoms of the Herbrand base of $\mathbf{P}$ which are logical consequences of $\mathbf{P}$. The following theorem can be considered as an alternative definition of the semantics in terms of Herbrand models of $\mathbf{P}$.

Theorem 6.1: Let $\mathbf{P}$ be a program and $\mathcal{HM}(\mathbf{P})$ be the set of all Herbrand models of $\mathbf{P}$. Then $\mathcal{M}(\mathbf{P}) = \{A \mid A \in \cap\mathcal{HM}(\mathbf{P})\}$.

Proof

$A \in \mathcal{M}(\mathbf{P})$
iff $\mathbf{P} \models A$
iff $\mathbf{P} \cup \{\neg A\}$ has no model
iff $\mathbf{P} \cup \{\neg A\}$ has no Herbrand model
iff $\neg A$ is false in all Herbrand models of $\mathbf{P}$
iff A is true in all Herbrand models of $\mathbf{P}$
iff $A \in \cap\mathcal{HM}(\mathbf{P})$ ■

Theorem 6.2 establishes the *model intersection property* of a set of Horn clauses.

Theorem 6.2: Suppose $\mathbf{P}$ is a consistent set of Horn clauses and $hm(\mathbf{P})$ is a non-empty set of Herbrand models of $\mathbf{P}$. Then $\cap\, hm(\mathbf{P})$ is also a model of $\mathbf{P}$.

Proof If possible, do not let $\cap\, hm(\mathbf{P})$ be a Herbrand model of $\mathbf{P}$. Then there is a clause C in $\mathbf{P}$ and a ground instance θ of C such that $C\theta$ is false in $\cap\, hm(\mathbf{P})$. If C has the form $A \leftarrow A_1 \wedge \cdots \wedge A_n$, then $A\theta \notin \cap\, hm(\mathbf{P})$ and $A_1\theta, \ldots, A_n\theta \in \cap\, hm(\mathbf{P})$. Therefore for some $\mathbf{M} \in hm(\mathbf{P})$, $A\theta \notin \mathbf{M}$ and $A_1\theta, \ldots, A_n\theta \in \mathbf{M}$. Hence C is false in $\mathbf{M}$ which contradicts the assumption that $\mathbf{M}$ is a model of $\mathbf{P}$. The other case when C has the form of a negative Horn clause is similar. ■

In view of Theorem 6.2 it can be said that $\cap\, \mathcal{HM}(\mathbf{P})$ is also a Herbrand model and hence the minimal model of $\mathbf{P}$. Thus the declarative semantics of a definite program is equal to its minimal model.

EXAMPLE 6.1

Consider the following program **P**:

Program: C1. $P(x, y) \leftarrow Q(x, y)$

C2. $P(x, y) \leftarrow Q(x, z) \wedge P(z, y)$

C3. $Q(a, b)$

C4. $Q(b, c)$

Then $\mathcal{M}(\mathbf{P}) = \{Q(a, b), Q(b, c), P(a, b), P(b, c), P(a, c)\}$. Any other model of **P**, for example $\{Q(a, b), Q(b, c), P(a, b), P(b, c), P(a, c), P(b, a), P(a, a)\}$, contains **P**.

6.2 Fixpoint semantics

Suppose **P** is a program. Then an interpretation of **P** can be characterized by a subset of $\mathcal{HB}(\mathbf{P})$. In a stricter sense there is a one-to-one correspondence between the set of all Herbrand interpretations of **P**, denoted as $\mathcal{HI}(\mathbf{P})$, and the power set $\mathcal{P}(\mathcal{HB}(\mathbf{P}))$. However, the power set of a set forms a lattice wrt the usual set-inclusion relationship. Hence the set $\mathcal{HI}(\mathbf{P})$ of all interpretations of **P** forms a lattice and is called the *lattice of Herbrand interpretations* of **P**.

Lemma 6.1: Let Δ be a directed subset of the lattice of Herbrand interpretation of a definite program. Then $\{A_1, ..., A_n\} \subseteq lub(\Delta)$ iff $\{A_1, ..., A_n\} \subseteq \mathbf{I}$, for some $\mathbf{I} \in \Delta$.

Proof Suppose $\{A_1, ..., A_n\} \subseteq lub(\Delta)$ and $lub(\Delta) = \mathbf{J}$. If possible, do not let A_k $(1 \leq k \leq n)$ belong to any member of Δ. In this case, the least upper bound of Δ would be $\mathbf{J} - \{A_k\}$, violating the fact that **J** is the least upper bound of Δ. Hence each A_i, $i = 1, 2, ..., n$, must belong to one of the members of Δ.

Suppose $\mathbf{J}_1, ..., \mathbf{J}_n$ are members of Δ such that $A_i \in \mathbf{J}_i$, $i = 1, ..., n$. Since Δ is directed, the upper bound of $\{\mathbf{J}_1, ..., \mathbf{J}_n\}$, say **I**, will be a member of Δ and $\{A_1, ..., A_n\} \subseteq \mathbf{I}$.

Conversely, if $\{A_1, ..., A_n\} \subseteq \mathbf{I}$, for some $\mathbf{I} \in \Delta$, then naturally $\{A_1, ..., A_n\} \subseteq lub(\Delta)$. ■

Now the fixpoint mapping $T_{\mathbf{P}}: \mathcal{HI}(\mathbf{P}) \rightarrow \mathcal{HI}(\mathbf{P})$ is defined as follows. For $\mathbf{I} \in \mathcal{HI}(\mathbf{P})$

$$\mathrm{T}_{\mathbf{P}}(\mathbf{I}) = \{A \in \mathcal{HB}(\mathbf{P}) \mid \text{there exists a clause } \mathrm{C} = A' \leftarrow A_1 \wedge \cdots \wedge A_n \text{ in } \mathbf{P} \text{ such that } A = A'\theta \text{ and } \{A_1\theta, ..., A_n\theta\} \subseteq \mathbf{I} \text{ for some ground substitution } \theta \text{ of } \mathrm{C}\}$$

EXAMPLE 6.2

Consider the program of Example 6.1. Now, if $\mathbf{I} = \emptyset$, then $\mathrm{T}_{\mathbf{P}}(\mathbf{I}) = \{Q(a,b), Q(b,c)\}$. If $\mathbf{I} = \{Q(a,b), Q(b,c), P(c,d)\}$, then $\mathrm{T}_{\mathbf{P}}(\mathbf{I}) = \{Q(a,b), Q(b,c), P(c,d), P(a,b), P(b,c), P(b,d)\}$.

Theorem 6.3 provides an important continuity property of the operator $\mathrm{T}_{\mathbf{P}}$.

Theorem 6.3: Let $\mathbf{P}$ be a definite program. Then the mapping $\mathrm{T}_{\mathbf{P}}$ is continuous and hence monotonic.

Proof Suppose Δ is a directed subset of $\mathcal{HI}(\mathbf{P})$.

Then	$A \in \mathrm{T}_{\mathbf{P}}(lub(\Delta))$
iff	there is a clause $A' \leftarrow A_1 \wedge \cdots \wedge A_n$ in $\mathbf{P}$ and its ground instance θ such that $A = A'\theta$ and $\{A_1\theta, ..., A_n\theta\} \subseteq lub(\Delta)$
iff	there is a clause $A' \leftarrow A_1 \wedge \cdots \wedge A_n$ in $\mathbf{P}$ and its ground instance θ such that $A = A'\theta$ and $\{A_1\theta, ..., A_n\theta\} \subseteq \mathbf{I}$, for some $\mathbf{I} \in \Delta$, (by Lemma 6.1)
iff	$A \in \mathrm{T}_{\mathbf{P}}(\mathbf{I})$ for some $\mathbf{I} \in \Delta$
iff	$A \in lub(\mathrm{T}_{\mathbf{P}}(\Delta))$

Hence for any directed subset Δ of $\mathcal{HI}(\mathbf{P})$, $\mathrm{T}_{\mathbf{P}}(lub(\Delta)) = lub(\mathrm{T}_{\mathbf{P}}(\Delta))$. Therefore, $\mathrm{T}_{\mathbf{P}}$ is continuous. ■

Let $\mathbf{P}$ be a program. An interpretation $\mathbf{I}$ is *closed* under the transformation $\mathrm{T}_{\mathbf{P}}$ iff $\mathrm{T}_{\mathbf{P}}(\mathbf{I}) \subseteq \mathbf{I}$. Let $\mathcal{C}(\mathbf{P})$ be the set of all closed interpretation of $\mathbf{P}$. Then the fixpoint semantics of $\mathbf{P}$ is

$$\mathcal{F}(\mathbf{P}) = \{A \mid A \in \cap\mathcal{C}(\mathbf{P})\}$$

6.3 Equivalence between declarative and fixpoint semantics

The following theorem establishes the equivalence between declarative and fixpoint semantics.

Theorem 6.4: Let $\mathbf{P}$ be a program. Then $\mathcal{M}(\mathbf{P}) = \mathcal{F}(\mathbf{P})$, that is, $\models_{\mathbf{I}} \mathbf{P}$ iff $\mathrm{T}_{\mathbf{P}}(\mathbf{I}) \subseteq \mathbf{I}$ for all Herbrand interpretations $\mathbf{I}$ of $\mathbf{P}$.

Proof Suppose $\models_{\mathbf{I}} \mathbf{P}$ and $\mathbf{I} \in \mathcal{HI}(\mathbf{P})$ is a model of $\mathbf{P}$. Let $A \in \mathrm{T}_{\mathbf{P}}(\mathbf{I})$. By the definition of $\mathrm{T}_{\mathbf{P}}$, there exists a clause $\mathrm{C} = A' \leftarrow A_1 \wedge \cdots \wedge A_n$ in $\mathbf{P}$ and ground instances θ of C such that $A = A'\theta$ and $\{A_1\theta, ..., A_n\theta\} \subseteq \mathbf{I}$. Since $\mathbf{I}$ is a model of $\mathbf{P}$, $\mathrm{C}\theta$ is true in $\mathbf{I}$, that is, $A'\theta \leftarrow A_1\theta \wedge \cdots \wedge A_n\theta$ is true in I. Since each $A_i\theta$, $i = 1, ..., n$, is true in $\mathbf{I}$, $A'\theta$ is also true in $\mathbf{I}$. Therefore $A \in \mathbf{I}$ and hence $\mathrm{T}_{\mathbf{P}}(\mathbf{I}) \subseteq \mathbf{I}$.

Conversely, suppose $\mathrm{T}_{\mathbf{P}}(\mathbf{I}) \subseteq \mathbf{I}$. If possible, do not let $\mathbf{I}$ be a model of $\mathbf{P}$. This means that $\mathbf{I}$ falsifies some ground instances $\mathrm{C}\theta$ of a clause $\mathrm{C} = A \leftarrow A_1 \wedge \cdots \wedge A_n$ and $\{A_1\theta, ..., A_n\theta\} \subseteq \mathbf{I}$ but $A\theta \notin \mathbf{I}$. This violates the definition of $\mathrm{T}_{\mathbf{P}}$. Hence $\mathbf{I}$ is a model of $\mathrm{T}_{\mathbf{P}}$. ■

Theorem 6.5: Let $\mathbf{P}$ be a definite program. Then $\mathcal{M}(\mathbf{P}) = \mathit{lfp}(\mathrm{T}_{\mathbf{P}}) = \mathrm{T}_{\mathbf{P}} \uparrow \omega$.

Proof
$$\begin{aligned} \mathcal{M}(\mathbf{P}) &= \mathit{glb}\ \{\mathbf{I} \mid \mathbf{I} \in \mathcal{HM}(\mathbf{P})\} & \\ &= \mathit{glb}\ \{\mathbf{I} \mid \mathbf{I} \subseteq \mathrm{T}_{\mathbf{P}}(\mathbf{I})\} & \text{By Theorem 6.4} \\ &= \mathit{lfp}(\mathrm{T}_{\mathbf{P}}) & \text{By Knaster–Tarski theorem} \\ &= \mathrm{T}_{\mathbf{P}} \uparrow \omega & \text{Since } \mathrm{T}_{\mathbf{P}} \text{ is continuous} \end{aligned}$$
■

6.4 Procedural semantics

The procedural semantics of a definite program is studied in this section using the *SLD-resolution* (*SL-resolution for Definite clauses*) schemes. A more specialized scheme, called SLD-AL resolution, will be introduced in the context of deductive database query evaluation. First, the resolution scheme and its properties are considered.

6.4.1 SLD-resolution

Definition 6.1: Let **P** be a definite program and G be a goal. An *unrestricted SLD-derivation* of $\mathbf{P}\cup\{G\}$ consists of a sequence $G_0 = G, G_1, \ldots$ of goals, a sequence $C_1, C_2, \ldots$ of variants of clauses in **P** (called the *input clauses* of the derivation) and a sequence $\theta_1, \theta_2, \ldots$ of *substitutions*. Each non-empty goal G_i contains one atom, which is the *selected atom* of G_i. The clause G_{i+1} is said to be derived from G_i and C_i with substitutions θ_i and is carried out as follows. Suppose G_i is

$$\leftarrow A_1 \wedge \cdots \wedge A_k \wedge \cdots \wedge A_m \qquad m \geq 1$$

and A_k is the selected atom. Let $C_i = A \leftarrow B_1 \wedge \cdots \wedge B_n$ be any clause in **P** such that A and A_k are unifiable with any unifier θ. Then G_{i+1} is

$$\leftarrow (A_1 \wedge \cdots \wedge A_{k-1} \wedge B_1 \wedge \cdots \wedge B_n \wedge A_{k+1} \wedge \cdots \wedge A_m)\theta$$

and θ_{i+1} is θ. An *unrestricted SLD-refutation* is a derivation ending at an empty clause.

Definition 6.2: The definitions of *SLD-derivation* and *SLD-refutation* are exactly as above except for considering only the most general unifier, rather than a unifier, of the selected atom and the conclusion of the input clause. Lemma 6.2 proves that if an unrestricted refutation of $\mathbf{P}\cup\{G\}$ exists then there also exists one for which every substitution is an mgu.

Lemma 6.2: Let **P** be a definite program and $G = \leftarrow A_1 \wedge \cdots \wedge A_k \wedge \cdots \wedge A_m$ ($m \geq 1$) be a goal and θ be a substitution. If there exists a refutation of $\mathbf{P}\cup\{G\theta\}$ with $A_k\theta$ as the first selected atom, then there exists a refutation of $\mathbf{P}\cup\{G\}$ with A_k as the first selected atom.

Proof One can assume that θ does not act on any of the variables in **P**. Suppose $A' \leftarrow B_1 \wedge \cdots \wedge B_n$ is the first selected clause in the refutation of $\mathbf{P}\cup\{\leftarrow A_1\theta \wedge \cdots \wedge A_k\theta \wedge \cdots \wedge A_m\theta\}$. Then $A_k\theta\theta_p = A'\theta_p$ for some substitution θ_p. By the assumption

$$\mathbf{P}\cup\{\leftarrow (A_1\theta \wedge \cdots \wedge A_{k-1}\theta \wedge B_1 \wedge \cdots \wedge B_n \wedge A_{k+1}\theta \wedge \cdots \wedge A_m\theta)\theta_p\}$$

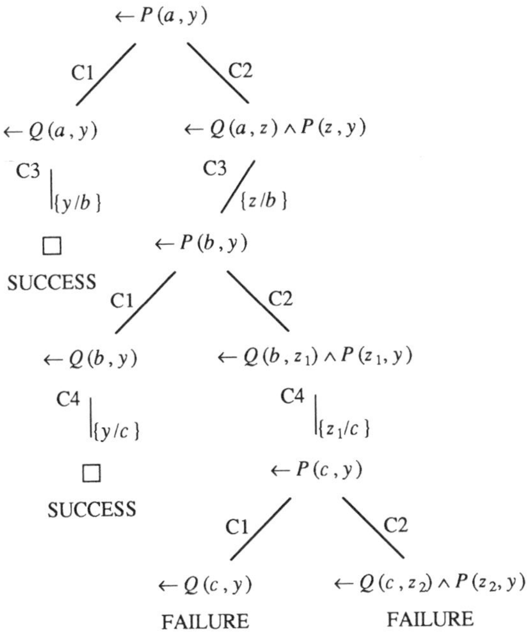

Figure 6.1 An SLD-tree with leftmost literal selection strategy.

has an SLD-refutation. Since θ does not act on any of the variables of **P**, $A' = A'\theta$ and $B_i = B_i\theta$, $i = 1, ..., n$. Hence $A_k\theta\theta_p = A'\theta\theta_p$ and by the above there exists a refutation of $\mathbf{P}\cup\{G\}$ with A_k as the first selected atom, $\theta\theta_p$ as the first substitution and $A' \leftarrow B_1 \wedge \cdots \wedge B_n$ as the first input clause. ■

In the definitions of SLD-derivation and SLD-refutation most general unifiers are considered to reduce the *search space* for the refutation procedure. A search space for the SLD-refutation procedure is an *SLD-tree* as defined below.

Definition 6.3: Let **P** be a definite program and G be a goal or an empty clause. An *SLD-tree* for $\mathbf{P}\cup\{G\}$ has G as root and each node is either a goal or an empty clause. Suppose

$$\leftarrow A_1 \wedge \cdots \wedge A_k \wedge \cdots \wedge A_n \qquad n \geq 1$$

is a non-empty node with selected atom A_k. Then this node has a descendant for every clause $A \leftarrow B_1 \wedge \cdots \wedge B_m$ such that A and A_k are unifiable with an mgu θ. The descendant is

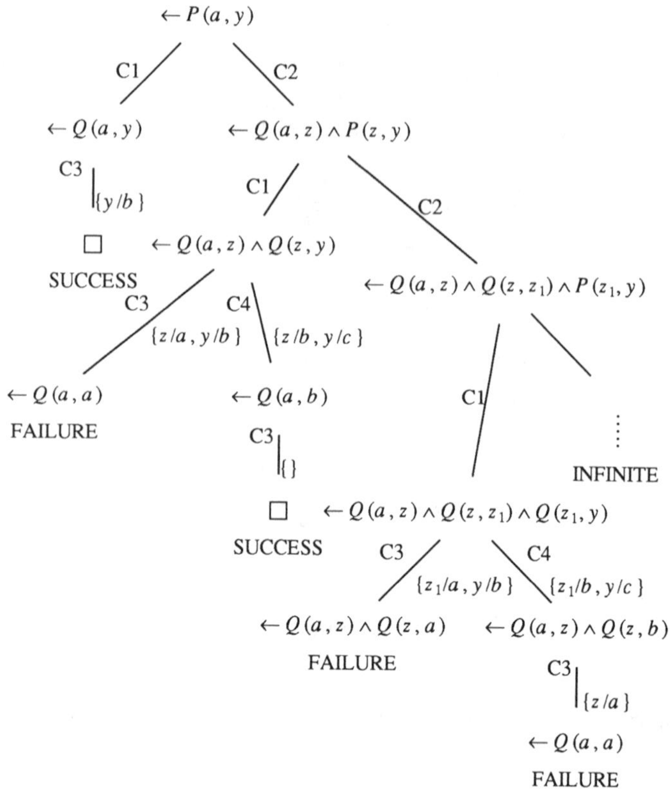

Figure 6.2 An SLD-tree with rightmost literal selection strategy.

$$\leftarrow (A_1 \wedge \cdots \wedge A_{k-1} \wedge B_1 \wedge \cdots \wedge B_m \wedge A_{k+1} \wedge \cdots \wedge A_n)\theta$$

Each path in an SLD-tree is an SLD-derivation and a path ending at an empty clause is an SLD-refutation. The search space is the totality of derivations constructed to find an SLD-refutation.

Definition 6.4: An SLD-derivation may be finite or infinite. An SLD-refutation is a successful SLD-derivation. A failed SLD-derivation is one that ends in a non-empty goal with the property that the selected atom in this goal does not unify with the head of any program clause. Branches corresponding to successful derivation in an SLD-tree are called *success branches*, branches corresponding to infinite derivations are called *infinite branches* and branches corresponding to failed derivations are called *failed branches*. All branches of a *finitely failed SLD-tree* are failed branches.

In general, a given $\mathbf{P} \cup \{G\}$ has different SLD-trees depending on which atoms are selected atoms. Consider the program of Example 6.1 and the goal $\leftarrow P(a, y)$. The tree in Figure 6.1 (resp. Figure 6.2) is based on a literal selection strategy which selects the leftmost (resp. rightmost) literal from a goal. The tree in Figure 6.2 has an infinite branch whereas all the branches of the tree in Figure 6.1 are finite.

It is worth clarifying at this stage why the SLD-resolution is a special case of SL-resolution. SLD-resolution deals with definite clauses only and does not perform any factoring or ancestor resolution operation. Owing to the latter reason, SLD-resolution gives the freedom to select an arbitrary literal from a goal rather than from only the leftmost cell. Also, the removal of an A-literal from a clause is automatic.

6.5 Equivalence between declarative and procedural semantics

The equivalence between declarative and procedural semantics for definite programs is basically the soundness and completeness of SLD-resolution wrt their minimal models. The soundness theorem of SLD-resolution is a corollary of Theorem 6.6 which is due to Apt and van Emden (1982).

Theorem 6.6: Let $\mathbf{P}$ be a definite program and G be a goal $\leftarrow A_1 \wedge \cdots \wedge A_m$ such that there exists an SLD-refutation of $\mathbf{P} \cup \{G\}$ with the substitution $\theta_1, \ldots, \theta_n$ and variants $C_1, \ldots, C_n$. Then, for every atom A in $G\theta_1 \cdots \theta_n$, $[A] \subseteq T_{\mathbf{P}} \uparrow n$, where $[A]$ is the set of all ground instances of the atom A over $\mathcal{HB}(\mathbf{P})$.

Proof The theorem is proved by induction on the length of refutation n.

Suppose first that $n = 1$. Then the goal G has the form $\leftarrow A_1$ and there is a unit clause A' in $\mathbf{P}$ such that $A_1\theta_1 = A'\theta_1$. Since A' is a unit clause, $[A'] \subseteq T_{\mathbf{P}} \uparrow 1$.

Suppose the result is true for refutation of length $n-1$ and consider a refutation of $\mathbf{P} \cup \{G\}$ of length n. If A_j $(1 \le j \le m)$ is an atom from G, consider the following two cases:

(1) A_j is a selected atom from G in the refutation of $\mathbf{P} \cup \{G\}$. If C_i is $A' \leftarrow B_1 \wedge \cdots \wedge B_p$, then $A_j\theta_1$ is an instance of A'. If $p = 0$, then $[A'] \subseteq T_{\mathbf{P}} \uparrow 1$ and $[A_j\theta_1 \cdots \theta_n] \subseteq [A_j\theta_1] \subseteq [A'] \subseteq T_{\mathbf{P}} \uparrow 1$. If $p > 0$, then G_1 has the form

$$\leftarrow (A_1 \wedge \cdots \wedge A_{j-1} \wedge B_1 \wedge \cdots \wedge B_p \wedge A_{j+1} \wedge \cdots \wedge A_m)\theta_1$$

By the induction hypothesis, $[B_i\theta_1 \cdots \theta_n] \subseteq T_P\uparrow(n-1)$, for $i = 1, ..., p$. Hence by the definition of T_P, $[A'\theta_1 \cdots \theta_n] = [A_j\theta_1 \cdots \theta_n] \subseteq T_P\uparrow n$.

(2) A_j is not a selected atom from G in the refutation of $\mathbf{P}\cup\{G\}$. Then $A_j\theta_1$ occurs in G_1. By induction hypothesis, $[A_j\theta_1 \cdots \theta_n] \subseteq T_P\uparrow(n-1)$. Since T_P is monotonic, $T_P\uparrow(n-1) \subseteq T_P\uparrow n$ and hence $[A_j\theta_1 \cdots \theta_n] \subseteq T_P\uparrow n$. ■

Corollary 6.1: (soundness of SLD-resolution) Let **P** be a definite program and G a definite goal such that $\mathbf{P}\cup\{G\}$ has an SLD-refutation with substitution θ. Then $\mathbf{P}\cup\{G\}$ is inconsistent.

Proof By Theorem 6.6, $A\theta \subseteq T_P\uparrow\omega$, for every atom A in G. Since T_P is continuous, $lfp(T_P) = T_P\uparrow\omega$ (see Chapter 2). Hence $A\theta \in lfp(T_P) = \cap\mathcal{HM}(\mathbf{P})$. This implies that G$\theta$ is not true in $\cap\mathcal{HM}(\mathbf{P})$ and hence not true in every model of **P**. Thus G is not true in every model of **P**. Therefore $\mathbf{P}\cup\{G\}$ is inconsistent. ■

Definition 6.5: The *success set* of a definite program **P**, denoted as $\mathcal{S}(\mathbf{P})$, is the set of all $A \in \mathcal{HB}(\mathbf{P})$ such that $\mathbf{P}\cup\{\leftarrow A\}$ has an SLD-refutation.

Corollary 6.2: The success set of a definite program **P** is contained in its least model, that is, $\mathcal{S}(\mathbf{P}) \subseteq \cap\mathcal{HM}(\mathbf{P})$.

Proof Let $A \in \mathcal{HB}(\mathbf{P})$ and $\mathbf{P}\cup\{\leftarrow A\}$ has a refutation. Hence according to Theorem 6.6, $A \in T_P\uparrow\omega = lfp(T_P) = \cap\mathcal{HM}(\mathbf{P})$. Hence $\mathcal{S}(\mathbf{P}) \subseteq \cap\mathcal{HM}(\mathbf{P})$. ■

Corollary 6.3: Let **P** be a program and $\leftarrow$Q be a goal such that $\mathbf{P}\cup\{\leftarrow Q\}$ has an SLD-refutation with substitution θ. Then Qθ is a logical consequence of **P**.

Proof By Theorem 6.6, every atom A occurring in Qθ is in $\cap\mathcal{HM}(\mathbf{P})$. Hence Q$\theta$ is true in $\cap\mathcal{HM}(\mathbf{P})$. ■

The converse of Corollary 6.2 is also true as is evident from Lemma 6.3.

Lemma 6.3: The least model of a definite program is contained in its success set, that is, $\cap\mathcal{HM}(\mathbf{P}) \subseteq \mathcal{S}(\mathbf{P})$.

Proof Suppose $A \in \cap\mathcal{HM}(\mathbf{P}) = \cap\mathcal{M}(\mathbf{P})$. By Theorem 6.5, $A \in lfp(\mathrm{T}_\mathbf{P})$. Hence $A \in \mathrm{T}_\mathbf{P}\uparrow k$, for some finite k. In the remainder of the proof, it will be shown by induction on k that $A \in \mathrm{T}_\mathbf{P}\uparrow k$ implies $\mathbf{P}\cup\{\leftarrow A\}$ has an SLD-refutation.

If $k = 1$, then $A \in \mathrm{T}_\mathbf{P}\uparrow 1$ implies that A is a variable-free instance of a unit clause in $\mathbf{P}$. Hence $\mathbf{P}\cup\{\leftarrow A\}$ has an SLD-refutation of length 1.

Suppose $A \in \mathrm{T}_\mathbf{P}\uparrow(k+1)$, that is, there exists a clause $A' \leftarrow B_1 \wedge \cdots \wedge B_m$ in $\mathbf{P}$ and its ground instance θ such that $A = A'\theta$ and $\{B_1\theta, ..., B_m\theta\} \subseteq \mathrm{T}_\mathbf{P}\uparrow k$. By the induction hypothesis there exists a refutation of $\mathbf{P}\cup\{\leftarrow B_i\theta\}$, for $i = 1, ..., n$. Since each $B_i\theta$ is ground, there exists a refutation of $\mathbf{P}\cup\{\leftarrow A\}$ with the first input clause being $A' \leftarrow B_1 \wedge \cdots B_m$ and the first substitution θ. ■

Some lemmas must be established before proving the completeness result of SLD-resolution.

Definition 6.6: Let $\mathbf{P}$ be a program and G be a goal. Then G is *k-refutable* ($k \geq 1$) if every SLD-tree for $\mathbf{P}\cup\{\mathrm{G}\}$ has a success branch of length at most n.

Lemma 6.4: Let $\mathbf{P}$ be a program and G be a goal. For any substitution θ, if $\mathrm{G}\theta$ is k-refutable then G is k-refutable.

Proof The lemma is proved by induction on k. The case when $k = 1$ is straightforward.

Suppose G is $\leftarrow A_1 \wedge \cdots \wedge A_k \wedge \cdots \wedge A_n$ and consider an arbitrary SLD-tree of $\mathbf{P}\cup\{\mathrm{G}\}$. Suppose A_k is the selected atom at the root and $A \leftarrow B_1 \wedge \cdots \wedge B_m$ is a clause in $\mathbf{P}$ such that A and A_k unify with an mgu θ_p. Since $\mathrm{G}\theta$ is k-refutable

$$\leftarrow (A_1\theta \wedge \cdots \wedge A_{k-1}\theta \wedge B_1 \wedge \cdots \wedge B_m \wedge A_{k+1}\theta \wedge \cdots \wedge A_n\theta)\theta_p$$

is $(k-1)$refutable. Assume θ does not act on the variables of $\mathbf{P}$ and then $A = A\theta$ and $B_i = B_i\theta$, $i = 1, ..., n$. Suppose α is an mgu of A and A_k and write $\theta\theta_p = \alpha\alpha_p$, for some α_p. Substituting $\theta\theta_p$ by $\alpha\alpha_p$ in the above goal, one can say that

$$\leftarrow (A_1 \wedge \cdots \wedge A_{k-1} \wedge B_1 \wedge \cdots \wedge B_m \wedge A_{k+1} \wedge \cdots \wedge A_n)\alpha\alpha_p$$

is $(k-1)$refutable. By the induction hypothesis,

$$\leftarrow (A_1 \wedge \cdots \wedge A_{k-1} \wedge B_1 \wedge \cdots \wedge B_m \wedge A_{k+1} \wedge \cdots \wedge A_n)\alpha$$

is k-refutable. Since α is an mgu of A_k, which occurs in G, and is the head of the clause $A \leftarrow B_1 \wedge \cdots \wedge B_m$, the above goal is the direct descendant of the considered SLD-tree for $\mathbf{P} \cup \{G\}$. This proves that G is k-refutable. Hence the lemma. ■

Lemma 6.5: (switching lemma) Let **P** be a program and G be a goal. Suppose $\mathbf{P} \cup \{G\}$ has an SLD-refutation $G_0 = G, G_1, ..., G_n = \square$ with input clauses $C_1, ..., C_n$, mgu $\theta_1, ..., \theta_n$. Suppose A_p is the selected atom in G_{m-1} and A_q is the selected atom in G_m $(0 < m \leq n)$. Then there exists another SLD-refutation of $\mathbf{P} \cup \{G\}$ in which A_q is selected in G_{m-1} instead of A_p and A_p is selected in G_m instead of A_q. The input clauses in the new refutation are $C_1, ..., C_{m+1}, C_m, ..., C_n$.

Proof Suppose C_i is

$$H^i \leftarrow B_1^i \wedge \cdots \wedge B_{n_i}^i$$

G_{m-1} is

$$\leftarrow A_1 \wedge \cdots \wedge A_p \wedge \cdots \wedge A_q \wedge \cdots \wedge A_r$$

Therefore, G_m is

$$\leftarrow (A_1 \wedge \cdots \wedge B_1^m \wedge \cdots \wedge B_{n_m}^m \wedge \cdots \wedge A_q \wedge \cdots \wedge A_r)\theta_m$$

G_{m+1} is

$$\leftarrow (A_1 \wedge \cdots \wedge B_1^m \wedge \cdots \wedge B_{n_m}^m \wedge \cdots \wedge$$
$$B_1^{m+1} \wedge \cdots \wedge B_{n_{m+1}}^{m+1} \wedge \cdots \wedge A_r)\theta_m \theta_{m+1}$$

Then $A_q \theta_m \theta_{m+1} = H^{m+1}\theta_{m+1} = H^{m+1}\theta_m \theta_{m+1}$. Then one can unify A_q and H^{m+1}. If β_m is an mgu of A_q and H^{m+1} then $\theta_m \theta_{m+1} = \beta_m \sigma$, for some substitution σ. Also, $H^m \sigma = H^m \beta_m \sigma$ (one can assume that β_m does not act on any of the variables of C_m) $= H^m \theta_m \theta_{m+1} = A_p \theta_m \theta_{m+1} = A_p \beta_m \sigma$. Hence unification of H^m and $A_p \beta_m$ is possible. Let β_{m+1} be an mgu in this case. Then $\sigma = \beta_m \sigma_1$, for some σ_1. Therefore $\theta_m \theta_{m+1} = \beta_m \beta_{m+1} \sigma_1$ Thus the two atoms can be selected in reverse order.

If it is possible to show that the $(m + 1)$th goal in the new refutation is a variant of G_{m+1} then the remainder of the new refutation can be completed in the same way as that given. In the new refutation, every goal would just be a variant of the given refutation.

Since $A_p \beta_m \beta_{m+1} = H^m \beta_m \beta_{m+1}$ and θ_m is an mgu of A_p and H^m, there exists a substitution α such that $\beta_m \beta_{m+1} = \theta_m \alpha$. Now, $A_q \theta_m \alpha = A_q \beta_m \beta_{m+1} = H^{m+1}\beta_m \beta_{m+1} = H^{m+1}\theta_m \alpha = H^{m+1}\alpha$. So α unifies $A_q \theta_m$ and H^{m+1}. Since θ_{m+1} is an mgu of $A_q \theta_m$ and H^{m+1}, $\alpha = \theta_{m+1}\sigma_2$, for some σ_2. Hence $\beta_m \beta_{m+1} = \theta_m \theta_{m+1}\sigma_2$. Hence the $(m+1)$th goal is a variant of G_{m+1}. Hence the lemma. ■

Lemma 6.6: Suppose $A_1, ..., A_n$ are atoms with no variables in common. If each A_i is k_i-refutable, $i = 1, ..., n$, then $\leftarrow A_1 \wedge \cdots \wedge A_n$ is $(k_1 + \cdots + k_n)$-refutable.

Proof Consider an SLD-tree for $\mathbf{P} \cup \{\leftarrow A_i\}$, $1 \le i \le n$. Since $\leftarrow A_i$ is k_i-refutable, this tree will contain a success branch of length m_i, where $m_i \le k_i$ Suppose C_1, ..., C_{m_i} are the input clauses along this success branch. By applying Lemma 6.5, a success branch can be found in any SLD-tree of $\mathbf{P} \cup \{\leftarrow A_i\}$ with input clauses C'_1, ..., C'_{m_i} such that the sequence C'_1, ..., C'_{m_i} is a permutation of C_1, ..., C_{m_i}. By following one such success branch for each i $(1 \le i \le n)$, a success branch B in an SLD-tree of $\mathbf{P} \cup \{\leftarrow A_1 \wedge \cdots \wedge A_n\}$ of length p, where $1 \le p \le k_1 + \cdots + k_n$, can be found for the following reason. Each SLD-refutation of $\mathbf{P} \cup \{\leftarrow A_i\}$, $1 \le i \le n$, is practically embedded into B. Also, two embedded refutations $\mathbf{P} \cup \{\leftarrow A_i\}$ and $\mathbf{P} \cup \{\leftarrow A_j\}$ in B, where $i \ne j$, $1 \le i \le n$ and $1 \le j \le n$, are independent in the sense that they will not share any variables in the course of construction of B. ■

Lemma 6.7: If A is in the least model of $\mathbf{P}$, then for some k, $\leftarrow A$ is k-refutable.

Proof Since A is in the least model of $\mathbf{P}$, $A \in \cap \mathcal{HM}(\mathbf{P})$. By Theorem 6.5, $\cap \mathcal{HM}(\mathbf{P}) = lfp(T_\mathbf{P})$, and thus $A \in lfp(T_\mathbf{P})$. Since $T_\mathbf{P}$ is continuous, $A \in T_\mathbf{P}\uparrow k$, for some finite k. In the remainder of the proof, it will shown by induction on k that $A \in T_\mathbf{P}\uparrow k$ implies $\leftarrow A$ is k-refutable.

If $k = 1$, then $A \in T_\mathbf{P}\uparrow 1$ implies that A is a ground instance of a unit clause in $\mathbf{P}$. Hence $\mathbf{P} \cup \{\leftarrow A\}$ has an SLD-refutation of length 1. Thus $\leftarrow A$ is 1-refutable.

Suppose $A \in T_\mathbf{P}\uparrow(k+1)$, that is, there exists a clause $A' \leftarrow B_1 \wedge \cdots \wedge B_m$ in $\mathbf{P}$ and its ground instance θ such that $A = A'\theta$ and $\{B_1\theta, ..., B_m\theta\} \subseteq T_\mathbf{P}\uparrow k$. By the induction hypothesis, each $\leftarrow B_i\theta$ is k_i-refutable, for some k_i, $i = 1, ..., n$. Since $B_1\theta, ..., B_n\theta$ are ground atomic and therefore have no variables in common, by Lemma 6.6, $\leftarrow B_1\theta \wedge \cdots \wedge B_n\theta$ is $(k_1 + \cdots + k_n)$-refutable.

Since $A = A'\theta$, A and A' unify. Let α be an mgu in this case. Then there exists a substitution β such that $\theta = \alpha\beta$. Thus $\leftarrow (B_1 \wedge \cdots \wedge B_n)\alpha\beta$ is $(k_1 + \cdots + k_n)$-refutable. By Lemma 6.4, $\leftarrow (B_1 \wedge \cdots B_n)\alpha$ is also

$(k_1 + \cdots + k_n)$-refutable, and hence $\leftarrow A$ is $(k_1 + \cdots + k_n + 1)$-refutable. ■

The following completeness result for SLD-resolution is due to Hill (1974).

Theorem 6.7: (completeness of SLD-resolution) Let $\mathbf{P}$ be a program and G be a goal such that $\mathbf{P} \cup \{G\}$ is inconsistent. Then every SLD-tree with G as root contains a success branch.

Proof Suppose G is $\leftarrow A_1 \wedge \cdots \wedge A_n$. If $\mathbf{P} \cup \{G\}$ is inconsistent then G is not true in $\cap \mathcal{HM}(\mathbf{P})$. This implies that there exists a ground instance $G\theta$ of G such that $G\theta$ is not true in $\cap \mathcal{HM}(\mathbf{P})$ and thus $\{A_1\theta, ..., A_n\theta\} \subseteq \cap \mathcal{HM}(\mathbf{P})$. By Lemma 6.7, $A_i\theta$ is k_i-refutable, for some $k_i \geq 1$, $i = 1, ..., n$. Since $A_1\theta$, ..., $A_n\theta$ are ground atoms with no variables in common, by Lemma 6.6, $\leftarrow A_1\theta \wedge \cdots \wedge A_n\theta$ is $(k_1 + \cdots + k_n)$-refutable. Hence by Lemma 6.4, $\leftarrow A_1 \wedge \cdots \wedge A_n$ is also $(k_1 + \cdots + k_n)$-refutable. By the definition of k-refutability every SLD-tree with G as root has a success branch. ■

Another version of the above completeness result can be found Apt and van Emden (1982) and an even stronger form of the above completeness result has been established (Clark, 1979). These versions of the completeness theorems are stated below as Theorems 6.8 and 6.9 respectively without their proofs.

Theorem 6.8: (completeness of SLD-resolution) Let $\mathbf{P}$ be a program and G be a goal such that $\mathbf{P} \cup \{G\}$ is inconsistent. Then for each atom A_k in the goal G there exists an SLD-refutation of $\mathbf{P} \cup \{G\}$ with A_k as the first selected atom.

Theorem 6.9: (completeness of SLD-resolution) Let $\mathbf{P}$ be a program and $\leftarrow$Q be a goal such that $\mathbf{P} \cup \{\leftarrow Q\}$ is inconsistent. For every substitution θ of $\leftarrow$Q, if $Q\theta$ is a logical consequence of $\mathbf{P}$, then there exists an SLD-refutation of $\mathbf{P} \cup \{\leftarrow Q\}$ with answer substitution θ_p such that θ is more general than θ_p.

The completeness theorem (6.7) establishes the fact that any SLD-tree for $\mathbf{P} \cup \{G\}$ is complete for any choice of computation rule. This means that if $\mathbf{P} \cup \{G\}$ is inconsistent then for any choice of computation rule a refutation using the given computation rule can be found if a proper algorithm (for example, breadth-first) is employed to search the tree.

Let $\mathbf{P}$ be a definite program. Then the procedural or operational semantics of $\mathbf{P}$ with respect to SLD-resolution, denoted as $O(\mathbf{P}, \text{SLD})$, is defined as

$$O(\mathbf{P}, \text{SLD}) = \{A \mid A \in \mathcal{HB}(\mathbf{P}) \text{ and } \mathbf{P} \vdash A\}$$

where $\mathbf{P} \vdash A$ means that there exists either an SLD-refutation of $\mathbf{P} \cup \{\leftarrow A\}$.

6.6 Equivalence among semantics

The inference system adopted to determine the operational semantics is SLD-resolution which is sound and complete. Hence $\mathcal{M}(\mathbf{P}) = O(\mathbf{P}, \text{SLD})$ by the completeness of first-order logic. Also, from the equivalence between declarative and fixpoint semantics, $\mathcal{M}(\mathbf{P}) = \mathcal{F}(\mathbf{P})$. Thus if $\mathbf{P}$ is a definite program and SLD-resolution is used to determine operational semantics then $\mathcal{M}(\mathbf{P}) = O(\mathbf{P}, \text{SLD}) = \mathcal{F}(\mathbf{P})$.

6.7 Semantics for negation

The above-mentioned declarative, procedural and fixpoint semantics for definite programs are only concerned with the positive information of a program that can be derived from the program. *Closed World Assumption* (CWA) and *Negation As Failure* (NAF) rules are provided below for studying semantics for negative information in definite programs. Each of these is consistent for the class of definite databases and can be used in conjunction with the other three semantics introduced above to obtain the complete meaning of a definite program.

6.7.1 Closed world assumption

Given a program $\mathbf{P}$ and $A \in \mathcal{HB}(\mathbf{P})$, one of the ways to say that $\neg A$ may be inferred from $\mathbf{P}$ is if A is not a logical consequence of $\mathbf{P}$. This declarative definition for inferring negative information is what is called the closed world assumption and hence is considered as a rule for inferring negative information from a program. Thus

$$\mathcal{CWA}(\mathbf{P}) = \{A \in \mathcal{HB}(\mathbf{P}) \mid A \text{ is not a logical consequence of } \mathbf{P}\}.$$

The CWA rule is consistent for definite programs but may be inconsistent for normal programs and hence for general programs too. The following example demonstrates this.

EXAMPLE 6.3

Suppose $\mathbf{P} = \{P(a) \leftarrow \neg Q(a)\}$. The single clause of $\mathbf{P}$ can be rewritten as $P(a) \vee Q(a)$. Neither $P(a)$ nor $Q(a)$ is a logical consequence of $\mathbf{P}$. Therefore CWA infers $\neg P(a)$ as well as $\neg Q(a)$ and these two negated facts together with the clause of $\mathbf{P}$ are inconsistent.

The generalized closed world assumption for disjunctive programs and is introduced in Chapter 8.

6.7.2 Negation as failure

Given a program $\mathbf{P}$ and $A \in \mathcal{HB}(\mathbf{P})$, if A is not a logical consequence of $\mathbf{P}$ then each branch of an SLD-tree for $\mathbf{P} \cup \{\leftarrow A\}$ is either finitely failed or infinite. This operational aspect of the CWA provides a new rule for inferring negative information from a program and is called the negation as failure rule. The rule can be formally stated as follows. Suppose $\mathbf{P}$ is a definite program and $A \in \mathcal{HB}(\mathbf{P})$. If $\mathbf{P} \cup \{\leftarrow A\}$ has a finitely failed SLD-tree then A is not a logical consequence of A and hence $\neg A$ can be inferred from $\mathbf{P}$. Thus

$$\mathcal{NAF}(\mathbf{P}) = \{A \in \mathcal{HB}(\mathbf{P}) | \mathbf{P} \cup \{\leftarrow A\} \text{ has a finitely failed SLD-tree}\}$$

Naturally CWA is more powerful from the point of view that A may not be a logical consequence of $\mathbf{P}$ but every SLD-tree for $\mathbf{P} \cup \{\leftarrow A\}$ has an infinite branch. Consider the following example.

EXAMPLE 6.4

Suppose $\mathbf{P} = \{P(a) \leftarrow P(a)\}$. Clearly $P(a)$ is not a logical consequence of $\mathbf{P}$ and hence CWA infers $\neg P(a)$ from $\mathbf{P}$. But the only branch of the tree for $\mathbf{P} \cup \{\leftarrow P(a)\}$ is infinite.

If a system implementing the SLD-resolution procedure is not capable of detecting infinite branches then a task for finding whether A is a logical consequence or not would be incomplete in that system.

As far as the properties of rules for negative information are concerned, both CWA and NAF for definite programs are concise, consistent and decreasing.

Exercise

6.1 For each of the following examples:

(a) Compute the minimal model of the program through the fixpoint operator.

(b) Draw a complete SLD-tree for the goal.

EXAMPLE A

Program:

$$Groupoid(x, y) \leftarrow Closure(x, y)$$
$$Semigroup(x, y) \leftarrow Groupoid(x, y) \wedge Associative(x, y)$$
$$Monoid(x, y, z) \leftarrow Semigroup(x, y) \wedge Identity(x, y, z)$$
$$Group(x, y, z) \leftarrow Monoid(x, y, z) \wedge Inverse(x, y, z)$$
$$Subgroup(x, y, z, t) \leftarrow Subset(x, y) \wedge Group(x, z, t)$$
$$Subgroup(x, y, z, t) \leftarrow Subgroup(x, y_1, z, t) \wedge Subgroup(y_1, y, z, t)$$

$Subset(EvenInteger, Integer)$
$Subset(OddInteger, Integer)$
$Closure(Integer, Multiplication)$
$Closure(EvenInteger, Multiplication)$
$Closure(OddInteger, Multiplication)$
$Closure(Integer, Addition)$
$Closure(EvenInteger, Addition)$
$Closure(OddInteger, Multiplication)$
$Associative(x, Addition)$
$Associative(x, Multiplication)$
$Identity(x, Multiplication, 1)$
$Identity(Integer, Addition, 0)$
$Identity(EvenInteger, Addition, 0)$
$Inverse(Integer, Addition, 0)$
$Inverse(EvenInteger, Addition, 0)$

Goal: $\leftarrow Group(x, y)$.

EXAMPLE B

Program: $P(x, y) \leftarrow Q(x, y) \wedge R(x, y)$

$R(x, y) \leftarrow S(x, z) \wedge R(z, y)$

$S(x, y) \leftarrow T(x) \wedge U(y)$

$T(a)$ $Q(a, d)$

$U(b)$ $Q(a, c)$

$S(b, c)$

$V(d, f)$

Goal: $\leftarrow P(x, y) \wedge V(y, z)$

7

Normal programs

The material presented in this chapter relates to normal programs. The fixpoint operator $\mathbf{T_P}$ which was introduced in Chapter 6 will now be generalized for application to normal programs. The declarative semantics of normal programs is studied through a number of well-known proposals including program completion, well-founded semantics and perfect model semantics. SLDNF-resolution is also introduced in this chapter and a relation is established with its declarative counterpart, that is, program completion through the soundness and completeness result. Extended programs and goals which are more expressive than normal programs and goals are also presented in this chapter. It is shown that the extended programs and goals can be converted to normal programs and goals when the underlying semantics of programs is based on program completion. Another meaningful semantics of normal programs is given by means of a three-valued logic.

Recall that a normal program has been defined as a finite set of normal clauses of the form

$$A \leftarrow L_1 \wedge \cdots \wedge L_m, \qquad m \geq 0 \tag{7.1}$$

and that a normal goal has been defined as a clause of the form

$$\leftarrow M_1 \wedge \cdots \wedge M_n, \qquad n \geq 1 \tag{7.2}$$

where A is an atom and L_is and M_js are literals. Unless otherwise mentioned, any reference to programs and goals will always mean normal programs and normal goals.

7.1 Generalized fixpoint operator

A generalized fixpoint operator $\mathrm{T_P}$ in the case of a normal program $\mathbf{P}$ can be defined as follows:

$$\mathrm{T_P}(\mathbf{I}) = \{A \in \mathcal{HB}(\mathbf{P}) | \text{ there exists a clause } \mathrm{C} = A' \leftarrow L_1 \wedge \cdots \wedge L_n \text{ in } \mathbf{P} \text{ such that } A = A'\theta \text{ and } \mathbf{I} \models (L_1 \wedge \cdots \wedge L_n)\theta \text{ for some ground substitution } \theta \text{ of } \mathrm{C}\}$$

where $\mathbf{I} \subseteq \mathcal{HB}(\mathbf{P})$. As in the case of definite programs, the following result concerning this generalized fixpoint operator remains true.

Lemma 7.1: Let $\mathbf{P}$ be a normal program. Then $\mathbf{I}$ is a model of $\mathbf{P}$ if and only if $\mathrm{T_P}(\mathbf{I}) \subseteq \mathbf{I}$.

Proof Left as an exercise. ■

In the case of a definite program $\mathbf{P}$ and its associated fixpoint operator $\mathrm{T_P}$, the following properties hold:

(1) $\mathrm{T_P}$ is monotonic.

(2) The intersection of the two models of $\mathbf{P}$ is also a model of $\mathbf{P}$, and

(3) $\mathbf{P}$ has a least model.

In contrast to above these three properties, the following are true in general in the case of normal programs and their associated fixpoint operators:

(1) The fixpoint operator $\mathrm{T_P}$ of a normal program $\mathbf{P}$ is not necessarily monotonic.

(2) Intersection of two models of a normal program $\mathbf{P}$ is not necessarily a model of $\mathbf{P}$, and

(3) A normal program $\mathbf{P}$ may not have any least model.

The following example justifies the above claims.

EXAMPLE 7.1

Consider the program $\mathbf{P} = \{P \leftarrow \neg Q\}$.

(1) The Herbrand base of $\mathbf{P}$ is $\{P, Q\}$. Suppose $\mathbf{I}_1 = \emptyset$ and $\mathbf{I}_2 = \{Q\}$. Then $T_{\mathbf{P}}(\mathbf{I}_1) = P$ and $T_{\mathbf{P}}(\mathbf{I}_2) = \emptyset$. Thus $\mathbf{I}_1 \subseteq \mathbf{I}_2$ but not $T_{\mathbf{P}}(\mathbf{I}_1) \subseteq T_{\mathbf{P}}(\mathbf{I}_2)$. Hence $T_{\mathbf{P}}$ is not monotonic.

(2) $\{P\}$ and $\{Q\}$ are two models of $\mathbf{P}$ and their intersection is $\emptyset$ which is not a model of $\mathbf{P}$.

(3) $\mathbf{P}$ has two different models $\{P\}$ and $\{Q\}$ and each of these is minimal. Hence $\mathbf{P}$ does not have any least model.

While it is said that the program $\mathbf{P}$ has two minimal models $\{P\}$ and $\{Q\}$, the three different representations of the clause $P \leftarrow \neg Q$ in $\mathbf{P}$, namely $P \leftarrow \neg Q$ itself, $P \vee Q$ and $Q \leftarrow \neg P$, are not distinguished from each other. However, the intent of writing $P \leftarrow \neg Q$ is to say that P is true when Q is not; neither the reverse $Q \leftarrow \neg P$ of $P \leftarrow \neg Q$ is intended nor the disjunction $P \vee Q$. By distinguishing these representations from each other, the standard model for a stratified program is given in the following section.

7.2 Declarative and fixpoint semantics for stratified programs

Declarative semantics for a stratified program is given in terms of its supported model.

Definition 7.1: Suppose $\mathbf{P}$ is a stratified program. A model $\mathbf{M}$ of $\mathbf{P}$ is *supported* (Apt *et al.*, 1988) if for every member A of $\mathbf{M}$ there exists a clause $H \leftarrow \mathrm{B}$ in $\mathbf{P}$ and a ground instance θ of $H \leftarrow \mathrm{B}$ such that $A = H\theta$ and $\mathrm{B}\theta$ is true in $\mathbf{M}$.

EXAMPLE 7.2

Consider the program $\{P \leftarrow \neg Q\}$. The minimal model $\{P\}$ of this program is supported, but the minimal model $\{Q\}$ is not. The reason for taking Q false in the supported minimal model because there is no way to prove Q.

Now, suppose $\mathbf{P}$ is a normal program stratified by $\mathbf{P} = \mathbf{P}_1 \cup \cdots \cup \mathbf{P}_n$. Then define $\mathbf{M}_1, \ldots, \mathbf{M}_n$ as follows:

$$\mathbf{M}_1 = \cap\{\mathbf{M} | \mathbf{M} \text{ is a supported model of } \mathbf{P}_1\}$$
$$\mathbf{M}_i = \cap\{\mathbf{M} | \mathbf{M} \text{ is a supported model of } \mathbf{P}_1 \cup \cdots \cup \mathbf{P}_i \text{ and coincides with } \mathbf{M}_{i-1} \text{ on predicates of level less than } i\}, \text{ for } i = 2, \ldots, n.$$

Then the set $\mathbf{M}_n$ is the minimal supported model for the stratified program $\mathbf{P}$ and is taken as a declarative semantics for $\mathbf{P}$.

EXAMPLE 7.3

Consider the stratified program of Example 5.10 with stratification $\mathbf{P}_4 = \{C_1\}$, $\mathbf{P}_3 = \{C_2, C_6\}$, $\mathbf{P}_2 = \{C_3, C_4, C_7\}$, $\mathbf{P}_1 = \{C_5\}$. Then $\mathbf{M}_i$s are constructed as follows:

$$\mathbf{M}_1 = \{Q(a)\}$$
$$\mathbf{M}_2 = \{Q(a), T(a,b), S(a)\}$$
$$\mathbf{M}_3 = \{Q(a), T(a,b), S(a), R(a)\}$$
$$\mathbf{M}_4 = \{Q(a), T(a,b), S(a), R(a)\}$$

Fixpoint semantics is also defined by using the fixpoint operator introduced in Section 7.1. Let $\mathbf{P}$ be a normal program stratified by $\mathbf{P} = \mathbf{P}_1 \cup \cdots \cup \mathbf{P}_n$. Define the following sequence

$$\mathbf{M}_1 = T_{\mathbf{P}_1}\uparrow\omega(\varnothing)$$
$$\mathbf{M}_2 = T_{\mathbf{P}_2}\uparrow\omega(\mathbf{M}_1)$$
$$\vdots$$
$$\mathbf{M}_n = T_{\mathbf{P}_n}\uparrow\omega(\mathbf{M}_{n-1})$$

Then $\mathbf{M}_n$ is a minimal model of $\mathbf{P}$ and is considered to be the fixpoint semantics for $\mathbf{P}$.

Definition 7.2: For every stratified program $\mathbf{P}$, the above-defined declarative and fixpoint semantics coincide and are considered as the *standard model* $\mathbf{M}_{\mathbf{P}}$ for $\mathbf{P}$. Moreover, the model $\mathbf{P}$ is independent of the stratification of $\mathbf{P}$ (Apt *et al.*, 1988; Thayse, 1989).

There are normal programs that are not stratified and yet have an intuitive best minimal model. For example, neither the program $\{P(a) \leftarrow Q(a) \wedge \neg P(b), Q(a)\}$, nor the program $\{R(a) \leftarrow \neg R(b) \wedge \neg R(c), R(b) \leftarrow \neg R(a), R(c)\}$ (Grant and Minker, 1989) is stratified. Yet the models $\{P(a), Q(a)\}$ and $\{R(b),$

$R(c)\}$ appear to be the best minimal models of these two programs respectively. The stable model semantics and the well-founded approach are applicable for every normal program.

7.3 Stable model semantics

Stable model semantics (Gelfond and Lifschitz, 1988) is more general than the declarative or iterated fixpoint semantics for stratified programs described in Section 7.2 and is applicable to some normal programs that are not stratified.

Definition 7.3: Let $\mathbf{P}$ be a program and $\mathbf{M} \subseteq \mathcal{HB}(\mathbf{P})$. Let the set $\mathit{Stable}_{\mathbf{M}}(\mathbf{P})$ be obtained from $\mathit{Ground}(\mathbf{P})$ by the following two steps:

(1) Delete each rule from $\mathit{Ground}(\mathbf{P})$ that has a negative literal of the form $\neg A$ in its body and $A \in \mathbf{M}$, and

(2) Delete all negative literals in the bodies of the remaining rules.

$\mathit{Stable}_{\mathbf{M}}(\mathbf{P})$ is a set of ground definite clauses and therefore has a unique minimal model. If this model coincides with $\mathbf{M}$ then $\mathbf{M}$ is called a *stable model* of $\mathbf{P}$. If the program $\mathbf{P}$ has exactly one stable model then the model is called the *unique stable model* and is considered to be the *stable model semantics* for $\mathbf{P}$. The unique stable model of a stratified program $\mathbf{P}$ is identical to the standard model of $\mathbf{P}$ defined in Section 7.2.

The idea behind the above two-stage transformation is to simplify and reduce the number of clauses from $\mathit{Stable}_{\mathbf{M}}(\mathbf{P})$ and can be described as follows. If $\mathbf{M}$ is a set of ground atoms that is to be considered as a model then any rule that has a subgoal $\neg A$ with $A \notin \mathbf{M}$ is considered 'useless' and any subgoal $\neg A$ with $A \in \mathbf{M}$ is considered trivial.

EXAMPLE 7.4

Suppose $\mathbf{P} = \{P(a) \leftarrow \neg P(b)\}$ and $\mathbf{M} = \{P(a)\}$. Therefore $\mathit{Stable}_{\mathbf{M}}(\mathbf{P}) = \{P(a)\}$. The program $\mathbf{P}$ is not stratified. But $\mathbf{P}$ has a stable model $\{P(a)\}$.

EXAMPLE 7.5

Suppose $\mathbf{P} = \{P(x) \leftarrow Q(x, y) \wedge \neg P(y),\ Q(a, b)\}$ and $\mathbf{M} = \{P(b)\}$. Then $\mathit{Stable}_{\mathbf{M}}(\mathbf{P}) = \{P(a) \leftarrow Q(a, a), P(b) \leftarrow Q(b, a), Q(a, b)\}$. The minimal model of this program is $\{Q(a, b)\}$ and does not coincide with $\mathbf{M}$. Hence $\mathbf{M}$ is not a stable model. On the other hand, considering $\mathbf{M} = \{Q(a,b), P(a)\}$, $\mathit{Stable}_{\mathbf{M}}(\mathbf{P}) = \{P(a) \leftarrow Q(a,b),\ \ P(b) \leftarrow Q(b,b),\ \ Q(a,b)\}$. The minimal model of $\mathit{Stable}_{\mathbf{M}}(\mathbf{P})$ coincides with $\mathbf{M}$ and $\mathbf{M}$ is perfect.

EXAMPLE 7.6

Suppose $\mathbf{P} = \{\mathit{Male}(a) \leftarrow \neg \mathit{Female}(a),\ \mathit{Female}(a) \leftarrow \neg \mathit{Male}(a)\}$. If $\mathbf{M} = \{\mathit{Male}(a)\}$ then $\mathit{Stable}_{\mathbf{M}}(\mathbf{P}) = \{\mathit{Male}(a)\}$. If $\mathbf{M} = \{\mathit{Female}(a)\}$ then $\mathit{Stable}_{\mathbf{M}}(\mathbf{P}) = \{\mathit{Female}(a)\}$. Thus each of $\{\mathit{Male}(a)\}$ and $\{\mathit{Female}(a)\}$ is a stable model of $\mathbf{P}$. Therefore $\mathbf{P}$ has no unique stable model.

EXAMPLE 7.7

Suppose $\mathbf{P} = \{\mathit{Even}(0),\ \mathit{Even}(x) \leftarrow \neg \mathit{Even}(s(x))\}$. Therefore $\mathit{Ground}(\mathbf{P}) = \{\mathit{Even}(0),\ \mathit{Even}(0) \leftarrow \neg \mathit{Even}(s(0)),\ \mathit{Even}(s(0)) \leftarrow \neg \mathit{Even}(s(s(0))), \ldots\}$. If $\mathbf{M} = \{\mathit{Even}(0),\ \mathit{Even}(s(s(0))),\ \mathit{Even}(s(s(s(s(0))))), \ldots\}$, then $\mathit{Stable}_{\mathbf{M}}(\mathbf{P}) = \{\mathit{Even}(0),\ \mathit{Even}(s(s(0))),\ \mathit{Even}(s(s(s(s(0))))), \ldots\}$. Hence $\mathbf{M}$ is a stable model.

7.4 Well-founded model

A well-founded semantics (van Gelder *et al.*, 1988) of any normal logic program is defined by *well-founded partial models*. The literals in such a model $\mathbf{M}$ for a normal program $\mathbf{P}$ are true, their complements are false and the truth value of other literals are not determined by the program $\mathbf{P}$. If $\mathbf{M}$ is in fact a model of $\mathbf{P}$, then $\mathbf{P}$ is *well-behaved* and $\mathbf{M}$ is a *well-founded model.* The key idea behind developing such a model is to construct *unfounded sets.*

As a first step in constructing an unfounded set, the program $\mathbf{P}$ is extended by what is called a 'nonsensical' rule

$$\&(\&(\&)) \leftarrow \&(\&(\&))$$

where '$\&$' is a symbol that does not occur elsewhere in $\mathbf{P}$. According to the structure of this nonsensical rule, the symbol '$\&$' simultaneously represents a unary predicate symbol, a unary function symbol and a constant. The new Herbrand universe is the Herbrand universe of the extended program and the new Herbrand base (called $\mathcal{HB}(\mathbf{P})$ as usual) of a program $\mathbf{P}$ is constructed using an extended Herbrand universe of $\mathbf{P}$ not containing any atom under the predicate $\&$. Hence the ground instance of a clause will be obtained by instantiating its variables to elements of the extended Herbrand universe. The reason for extending a program by a nonsensical rule is to avoid the kind of problem demonstrated by the following example.

EXAMPLE 7.8

Consider the program **P** = $\{P(a) \leftarrow \neg Q(a,x),\ Q(x,x)\}$. The formula $\forall x Q(a,x)$ is expected to be false and that would make $P(a)$ true. Since the only element of $\mathcal{HU}(\mathbf{P})$ is a, the formula $\forall x Q(a,x)$ succeeds through the fact $Q(x,x)$ of **P** and therefore $P(a)$ becomes false. Suppose $\mathcal{HU}(\mathbf{P})$ is extended by another constant b through the addition of the fact $R(b)$ to **P**. Now $Q(a,b)$ is false in this extended program. Although the fact $R(b)$ is unrelated to the problem in finding the proof of $P(a)$, the fact $P(a)$ becomes true due to the addition of $R(b)$ to **P**. Extension of the Herbrand universe by the symbol '&' will always make $P(a)$ true.

Definition 7.4: A *partial interpretation* **PI** of a program **P** is a consistent set of literals whose atoms are in $\mathcal{HB}(\mathbf{P})$.

Definition 7.5: A set $\mathbf{S} \subseteq \mathcal{HB}(\mathbf{P})$ is called an unfounded set wrt a partial interpretation **PI** if for each atom $A \in \mathbf{S}$ and for each fully instantiated clause C of **P** whose head is A, at least one of the following conditions holds:

(1) A positive literal A' occurring in the body of C and $\neg A'$ is a member of **PI**.

(2) A negative literal $\neg A'$ occurring in the body of C and A' is a member of **PI**.

(3) At least one positive literal occurring in the body of C is a member of **S**.

The *greatest unfounded set* wrt **PI**, denoted as $\mathcal{GUS}_{\mathbf{P}}(\mathbf{PI})$ is the union of all sets that are unfounded.

Define the three operators $\mathrm{T}_{\mathbf{P}}$, $\mathrm{U}_{\mathbf{P}}$, and $\mathrm{V}_{\mathbf{P}}$, from the set of all partial interpretations to itself, as follows:

$$\mathrm{T}_{\mathbf{P}}(\mathbf{PI}) = \{A \in \mathcal{HB}(\mathbf{P}) \mid \text{there exists a clause } C = A' \leftarrow L_1 \wedge \cdots \wedge L_n \text{ in } \mathbf{P} \text{ such that } A = A'\theta \text{ and } \{L_1\theta, \ldots, L_n\theta\} \subseteq \mathbf{PI},\ i = 1, \ldots, n, \text{ for some ground substitution } \theta \text{ of C}\}$$

$$\mathrm{U}_{\mathbf{P}}(\mathbf{PI}) = \{\neg A \mid A \in \mathcal{GUS}_{\mathbf{P}}(\mathbf{PI})\}$$

$$\mathrm{V}_{\mathbf{P}}(\mathbf{PI}) = \mathrm{T}_{\mathbf{P}}(\mathbf{PI}) \cup \mathrm{U}_{\mathbf{P}}(\mathbf{PI})$$

Using the mapping V_P the set PI_{α}, for all countable ordinals α, is recursively defined as follows:

$$PI_0 = \emptyset$$
$$PI_{\alpha} = \bigcup_{\beta<\alpha} PI_{\beta}, \text{ if } \alpha \text{ is a limit ordinal}$$
$$PI_{k+1} = V_P(PI_k), \text{ if } k+1 \text{ is a successor ordinal}$$

It can be proved (van Gelder *et al.*, 1988) that the definition of **PI** is monotonic. Since $\mathcal{HB}(\mathbf{P})$ is countable, this definition of **PI** will reach a limit $\mathbf{PI}^*$. Now the well-founded semantics of the program **P** is given as follows. Suppose

$$PI^{*(+)} = \{A \in \mathcal{HB}(\mathbf{P}) \mid A \in PI^*\}$$
$$PI^{*(-)} = \{A \in \mathcal{HB}(\mathbf{P}) \mid \neg A \in PI^*\}$$
$$PI^{*(U)} = \mathcal{HB}(\mathbf{P}) - PI^{*(+)} \cup PI^{*(-)}$$

then all members of $\mathbf{PI}^{*(+)}$ are considered to be true and all members of $\mathbf{PI}^{*(-)}$ are considered to be false. The truth value of each member of $\mathbf{PI}^{*(U)}$ is undefined.

Definition 7.6: The set $\mathbf{PI}^*$ is the *well-founded partial model* for **P**. If $\mathbf{PI}^{*(U)} = \emptyset$, then $\mathbf{PI}^{*(+)}$ is the *well-founded model* for **P**.

The following example illustrates the step-by-step construction of a well-founded model.

EXAMPLE 7.9

Consider the following program **P**:

$$\mathbf{P}:\ P(a) \leftarrow Q(a) \wedge \neg P(b)$$
$$Q(a)$$
$$\&(\&(\&)) \leftarrow \&(\&(\&))$$

$$\mathcal{HB}(\mathbf{P}) = \{P(a), Q(a), P(b), Q(b)\}$$

Step 1: $PI_0 = \emptyset$

$\mathcal{GUS}_P(PI_0) = \{P(b), Q(b)\}$

$T_P(PI_0) = \{Q(a)\}$

$U_P(PI_0) = \{\neg P(b), \neg Q(b)\}$

$V_P(PI_0) = T_P(PI_0) \cup U_P(PI_0) = \{Q(a), \neg P(b), \neg Q(b)\}$

Step 2: $PI_1 = V_P(PI_0) = \{Q(a), \neg P(b), \neg Q(b)\}$

$\mathcal{GUS}_{\mathbf{P}}(\mathbf{PI}_1) = \{P(b), Q(b)\}$
$\mathrm{U}_{\mathbf{P}}(\mathbf{PI}_1) = \{\neg P(b), \neg Q(b)\}$
$\mathrm{T}_{\mathbf{P}}(\mathbf{PI}_1) = \{P(a), Q(a)\}$
$\mathrm{V}_{\mathbf{P}}(\mathbf{PI}_1) = \mathrm{T}_{\mathbf{P}}(\mathbf{PI}_1) \cup \mathrm{U}_{\mathbf{P}}(\mathbf{PI}_1) = \{P(a), Q(a), \neg P(b), \neg Q(b)\}$

Step 3: $\mathbf{PI}_2 = \mathrm{V}_{\mathbf{P}}(\mathbf{PI}_1) = \{P(a), Q(a), \neg P(b), \neg Q(b)\}$
$\mathcal{GUS}_{\mathbf{P}}(\mathbf{PI}_2) = \{P(b), Q(b)\}$
$\mathrm{U}_{\mathbf{P}}(\mathbf{PI}_2) = \{\neg P(b), \neg Q(b)\}$
$\mathrm{T}_{\mathbf{P}}(\mathbf{PI}_2) = \{P(a), Q(a)\}$
$\mathrm{V}_{\mathbf{P}}(\mathbf{PI}_2) = \mathrm{T}_{\mathbf{P}}(\mathbf{PI}_2) \cup \mathrm{U}_{\mathbf{P}}(\mathbf{PI}_2) = \{P(a), Q(a), \neg P(b), \neg Q(b)\}$

Step 4: $\mathbf{PI}_3 = \mathrm{V}_{\mathbf{P}}(\mathbf{PI}_2) = \{P(a), Q(a), \neg P(b), \neg Q(b)\}$

Thus $\mathbf{PI}^* = \mathbf{PI}_k = \mathbf{PI}_3$, $k \geq 3$. The model $\mathbf{PI}^*$ is a well-founded model for **P** and not a partial one.

If a program has a well-founded model then that model is its unique stable model. It was shown in Section 7.3 that the program $\{Male(a) \leftarrow \neg Female(a), Female(a) \leftarrow \neg Male(a)\}$ has two stable models. A well-founded partial model does not exist for this program. Hence stable model semantics is strictly more general than well-founded semantics.

7.5 Normal program completion

Another approach to studying declarative semantics for normal programs is program completion. According to this semantics, the clauses of a program **P** provide the if-parts of the definition of the predicates. The only-if parts in a program are implicitly defined and are obtained by completing each predicate symbol. Consider a normal program containing only the following two clauses defining the predicate *ClearPath*:

$$ClearPath(x, y) \leftarrow Path(x, y) \wedge \neg Obstruction(x, y)$$
$$ClearPath(a, b)$$

These two clauses jointly states that the path is clear from x to y if x is a and y is b or if there is a path from x to y and there is no obstruction from x to y. In other words

$$ClearPath(x, y) \leftarrow ClearPath(a, b) \vee Path(x, y) \wedge \neg Obstruction(x, y) \tag{7.3}$$

However, the definition leaves open the possibility that the path may be cleared from x to y for some other reason. What has been implicitly meant by the program is that the path is clear from x to y only if x is a and y is b or there is a path from x to y and there is no obstruction from x to y. In other words

$$ClearPath(x, y) \rightarrow ClearPath(a, b) \vee Path(x, y) \wedge \neg Obstruction(x, y) \tag{7.4}$$

Clauses (7.3) and (7.4) jointly give the completed definition of the predicate *ClearPath*. The formal definition of predicate and program completions are provided below.

Definition 7.7: Suppose that **P** is a program and

$$P(t_1, ..., t_n) \leftarrow L_1 \wedge \cdots \wedge L_m$$

is a clause in **P**. If the predicate symbol '=' is interpreted as the equality (or identity) relation, and $x_1, ..., x_n$ are variables not appearing elsewhere in the clause, then the above clause is equivalent to the clause

$$P(x_1, ..., x_n) \leftarrow x_1{=}t_1 \wedge \cdots \wedge x_n{=}t_n \wedge L_1 \wedge \cdots \wedge L_m$$

If $y_1, ..., y_p$ are the variables of the original clause then this can be transformed to

$$P(x_1, ..., x_n) \leftarrow \exists y_1 \cdots \exists y_p (x_1 = t_1 \wedge \cdots \wedge x_n = t_n \wedge L_1 \wedge \cdots \wedge L_m)$$

The above form is called the *general form of the clause.* Suppose there are exactly k clauses, $k \geq 0$, in **P** defining P (a clause C defines P if C has P in its head). Let

$$P(x_1, ..., x_n) \leftarrow E_1$$

.

.

.

$$P(x_1, ..., x_n) \leftarrow E_k$$

be the k clauses in general form. Then the *completed definition* of P is the formula

$$P(x_1, ..., x_n) \leftrightarrow E_1 \vee \cdots \vee E_k$$

Some predicate symbols in the program may not appear in the head of any program clause. For each such predicate Q, the *completed definition* of Q is the formula

$$\forall x_1 \cdots \forall x_n \neg Q(x_1, ..., x_n)$$

EXAMPLE 7.10

Let the predicate symbol P be defined by the following clauses:

$$P(a, z) \leftarrow Q(z, z') \wedge \neg R(z')$$
$$P(b, c)$$

Then the completed definition of P is

$$\forall x \forall y (P(x, y) \leftrightarrow$$
$$(\exists z \exists z' ((x = a) \wedge (y = z) \wedge Q(z, z') \wedge \neg R(z')) \vee ((x = b) \wedge (y = c))))$$

and the completed definitions of Q and R are $\forall x \forall y \neg Q(x, y)$ and $\forall x \neg R(x)$ respectively.

Definition 7.8: The *equality theory* $\mathcal{EQ}$ (or *identity theory*) for a completed program contains the following axioms:

(1) $c \neq d$, for all pairs c, d of distinct constants (the symbol $\neq$ stands for not equal, that is, $c \neq d$ stands for $\neg(c = d)$).

(2) $\forall x_1 \cdots \forall x_n \forall y_1 \cdots \forall y_m (f(x_1, ..., x_n) \neq g(y_1, ..., y_m))$, for all pairs f, g of distinct function symbols.

(3) $\forall x_1 \cdots \forall x_n (f(x_1, ..., x_n) \neq c)$, for each constant c and function symbol f.

(4) $\forall x (t[x] \neq x)$, for each term $t[x]$ containing x and different from x.

(5) $\forall x_1 \cdots \forall x_n \forall y_1 \cdots \forall y_n ((x_1 \neq y_1) \wedge \cdots \wedge (x_n \neq y_n) \rightarrow f(x_1, ..., x_n) \neq f(y_1, ..., y_n))$, for each function symbol f.

(6) $\forall x_1 \cdots \forall x_n \forall y_1 \cdots \forall y_n ((x_1 = y_1) \wedge \cdots \wedge (x_n = y_n) \rightarrow f(x_1, ..., x_n) = f(y_1, ..., y_n))$, for each function symbol f.

(7) $\forall x (x = x)$

(8) $\forall x_1 \cdots \forall x_n \forall y_1 \cdots \forall y_n ((x_1 = y_1) \wedge \cdots \wedge (x_n = y_n) \rightarrow (P(x_1, ..., x_n) \rightarrow P(y_1, ..., y_n)))$, for each predicate symbol P (including '=').

Note that Axioms 7 and 8 together imply that '=' is an equivalence relation.

Definition 7.9: The *completion* of **P** (Clark, 1978; Kunen, 1988; Lloyd, 1987), denoted by $Comp(\mathbf{P})$, is the collection of completed definitions of predicate symbols in **P** together with the equality theory.

The following example proves that the completion of a program may not be consistent.

EXAMPLE 7.11

Suppose $\mathbf{P} = \{P \leftarrow \neg P\}$. Apart from the equality axioms, $Comp(\mathbf{P})$ is $\{P \leftrightarrow \neg P\}$ which is inconsistent. But, $Comp(\mathbf{P})$ is consistent when **P** is stratified.

Theorem 7.1: Let **P** be a normal program. If **P** is stratified then $Comp(\mathbf{P})$ is consistent.

Proof Left as an exercise. ■

Theorem 7.2: Let **P** be a normal program. Then **I** is a model of $Comp(\mathbf{P})$ if and only if $T_{\mathbf{P}}(\mathbf{I}) = \mathbf{I}$.

Proof Left as an exercise. ■

When a program **P** is stratified, its declarative semantics given in terms of $Comp(\mathbf{P})$ does not necessarily coincide with its standard model $\mathbf{M}_{\mathbf{P}}$. Consider the following example.

EXAMPLE 7.12

Suppose $\mathbf{P} = \{P \leftarrow P, Q \leftarrow \neg P\}$. Apart from the equality axioms, $Comp(\mathbf{P})$ is $\{P \leftrightarrow P, Q \leftrightarrow \neg P\}$. Thus $Comp(\mathbf{P})$ reduces to $\{Q \leftrightarrow \neg P\}$ and hence neither P nor $\neg P$ is a logical consequence of $Comp(\mathbf{P})$. On the other hand, consider $\mathbf{P}_1 = \{P \leftarrow P\}$ and $\mathbf{P}_2 = \{Q \leftarrow \neg P\}$ and the program **P** can be stratified by $\mathbf{P}_1 \cup \mathbf{P}_2$. Thus

$$\mathbf{M}_1 = T_{\mathbf{P}_1}\uparrow\omega(\varnothing) = \varnothing$$
$$\mathbf{M}_2 = T_{\mathbf{P}_2}\uparrow\omega(\mathbf{M}_1) = \{Q\}$$

Hence $\mathbf{M}_{\mathbf{P}} = \{Q\}$ and P is not in $\mathbf{M}_{\mathbf{P}}$. Thus the standard model semantics infers $\neg P$.

7.6 SLDNF-resolution

SLDNF-resolution is thought of as a procedural counterpart of the declarative semantics given in terms of completed programs. This resolution scheme is, to a large extent, the basis of present-day logic programming. The resolution scheme is essentially SLD-resolution augmented by the 'negation as failure' (NAF) inference rule.

Most of the definitions and results in this section are due to Clark (1978), Lloyd (1987) and Shepherdson (1984). The definition of SLDNF-resolution is a formal inductive version (Lloyd, 1987) as opposed to the recursive version proposed by Clark (1978). This eases establishing its soundness results with respect to the completed programs. Some of the definitions given in Chapter 6 are generalized below.

Definition 7.10: Let G be a goal $\leftarrow L_1 \wedge \cdots \wedge L_m \wedge \cdots \wedge L_k$, and C be $A \leftarrow M_1 \wedge \cdots \wedge M_q$. Suppose L_m is a literal, called the *selected atom*, and θ is the mgu of A_m and A. Then the goal

$$\leftarrow (L_1 \wedge \cdots \wedge L_{m-1} \wedge M_1 \wedge \cdots \wedge M_q \wedge L_{m+1} \wedge \cdots \wedge L_k)\theta$$

is said to have been *derived* from G and C using mgu θ or a derived goal of G and C. The derived goal is also a resolvent of G and C. If $k = 1$ and $q = 0$ then the resolvent is the empty clause.

Definition 7.11: Let **P** be a program and G be a goal. An *SLDNF-refutation of rank 0* of $\mathbf{P} \cup \{G\}$ consists of a sequence $G_0 = G, G_1, ..., G_n = \square$ of goals, a sequence $C_1, ..., C_n$ of variants of clauses of **P** and a sequence $\theta_1, ..., \theta_n$ of mgus such that G_{i+1} is derived from G_i and C_{i+1} using θ_{i+1}.

Definition 7.12: Let **P** be a program and G be a goal. A *finitely failed SLDNF-tree of rank 0* for $\mathbf{P} \cup \{G\}$ is a finite tree satisfying the following:

(1) The root node is G.

(2) Each node of the tree is a goal and not an empty clause.

(3) Only atoms are selected at nodes in the tree.

(4) Suppose $\leftarrow L_1 \wedge \cdots \wedge L_m \wedge \cdots \wedge L_k$ $(k \geq 1)$ is a non-leaf node in the tree and the selected positive literal is L_m. Then this node has a descendant for each clause $A \leftarrow M_1 \wedge \cdots \wedge M_q$ in **P** such that L_m and A are unifiable:

$$\leftarrow (L_1 \wedge \cdots \wedge L_{m-1} \wedge M_1 \wedge \cdots \wedge M_q \wedge L_{m+1} \wedge \cdots \wedge L_k)\theta$$

where θ is an mgu of L_m and A.

(5) Suppose $\leftarrow L_1 \wedge \cdots \wedge L_m \wedge \cdots \wedge L_k$ $(k \geq 1)$ is a leaf node in the tree and the selected positive literal from this goal is L_m. Then there is no clause in **P** whose head unifies with L_m.

Definition 7.13: Let **P** be a program and G be a goal. An *SLDNF-refutation of rank r+1* of $\mathbf{P} \cup \{G\}$ consists of a sequence $G_0 = G, G_1, ..., G_n = \Box$ of goals, a sequence $C_1, ..., C_n$ of variants of clauses of **P** and a sequence $\theta_1, ..., \theta_n$ of mgus such that one of the following conditions holds:

(1) Each G_{i+1} is derived from G_i and C_{i+1} using θ_{i+1}.

(2) Suppose G_i is $\leftarrow L_1 \wedge \cdots \wedge L_m \wedge \cdots \wedge L_k$ $(k \geq 1)$ and the selected literal L_m is a ground negative literal $\neg A$ and there is a finitely failed SLDNF-tree of rank r for $\mathbf{P} \cup \{\leftarrow A\}$. Then G_{i+1} is

$$\leftarrow L_1 \wedge \cdots \wedge L_{m-1} \wedge \cdots \wedge L_{m+1} \wedge \cdots \wedge L_k$$

θ_{i+1} is an identity substitution and C_{i+1} is L_m.

Definition 7.14: Let **P** be a program and G be a goal. A *finitely failed SLDNF-tree of rank r + 1* for $\mathbf{P} \cup \{G\}$ is a finite tree satisfying the following:

(1) The root node is G.

(2) Each node of the tree is a goal and not an empty clause.

(3) Let $\leftarrow L_1 \wedge \cdots \wedge L_k$ $(k \geq 1)$ be a non-leaf node in the tree and suppose that a positive literal L_m is selected. Then this node has a descendant for each clause $A \leftarrow M_1 \wedge \cdots \wedge M_q$ in **P** such that L_m and A are unifiable and it is

$$\leftarrow (L_1 \wedge \cdots \wedge L_{m-1} \wedge M_1 \wedge \cdots \wedge M_q \wedge L_{m+1} \wedge \cdots \wedge L_k)\theta$$

where θ is an mgu of L_m and A.

(4) Let $\leftarrow L_1, ..., L_k$ $(k \geq 1)$ be a non-leaf node in the tree and suppose that the selected literal L_m is a ground negative literal of the form $\neg A$ and there is a finitely failed SLDNF-tree of rank r for $\mathbf{P} \cup \{\leftarrow A\}$. Then the single descendant of the node is

$$\leftarrow (L_1, ..., L_{m-1}, L_{m+1}, ..., L_k)$$

(5) Let $\leftarrow L_1, ..., L_k$ $(k \geq 1)$ be a leaf node in the tree and suppose that the literal L_m is selected. Then either

(a) L_m is positive and there is no clause in **P** whose head unifies with L_m, or

(b) L_m is a ground negative literal $\neg A$ and there is an SLDNF-refutation of $\mathbf{P} \cup \{\leftarrow A\}$ of rank r.

(c) A node which is the empty clause has no descendants.

Definition 7.15: An *SLDNF-refutation* of $\mathbf{P} \cup \{G\}$ is an SLDNF-refutation of rank r of $\mathbf{P} \cup \{G\}$, for some r. A *finitely failed SLDNF-tree* for $\mathbf{P} \cup \{G\}$ is a finitely failed SLDNF-tree of rank r for $\mathbf{P} \cup \{G\}$, for some r.

Definition 7.16: Let **P** be a program and G be a goal. An *SLDNF-derivation* of $\mathbf{P} \cup \{G\}$ consists of a sequence $G_0 = G, G_1, ...$ of goals, a sequence $C_1, C_2, ...$ of variants of clauses of **P** or negative literals, and a sequence $\theta_1, \theta_2, ...$ of substitutions satisfying the following:

(1) If the selected literal from G_i is an atom then G_{i+1} is derived from G_i and C_{i+1} using θ_{i+1}.

(2) If G_i is $\leftarrow L_1 \wedge \cdots \wedge L_k$ and the selected literal L_m in G_i is a ground negative literal $\neg A$ and there is a finitely failed SLDNF-tree for $\mathbf{P} \cup \{\leftarrow A\}$, then θ_{i+1} is the identity substitution, C_{i+1} is $\neg A$ and G_{i+1} is

$$\leftarrow L_1 \wedge \cdots \wedge L_{m-1} \wedge L_{m+1} \wedge \cdots \wedge L_k$$

(3) If the sequence $G_0, G_1, ...$ is finite, then either

(a) the last goal is empty, or

(b) the last goal is $\leftarrow L_1 \wedge \cdots \wedge L_k$ and the selected literal L_m is positive and there is no program clause whose head unifies with L_m, or

(c) the last goal is $\leftarrow L_1 \wedge \cdots \wedge L_k$ and the selected literal L_m is a ground negative literal $\neg A$ and there is an SLDNF-refutation of $\mathbf{P} \cup \{\leftarrow A\}$.

An SLDNF-derivation is finite if it consists of a finite sequence of goals; otherwise it is infinite. An SLDNF-derivation is successful if it is finite and the last goal is the empty goal. A successful SLDNF-derivation is indeed an SLDNF-refutation.

An SLDNF-derivation is failed if it is finite and the last goal is not the empty goal.

Definition 7.17: Let **P** be a program and G be a goal. An *SLDNF-tree* for $\mathbf{P} \cup \{G\}$ is a tree satisfying the following:

(1) Each node of the tree is a goal or an empty clause.

(2) The root node is G.

(3) Let $\leftarrow L_1 \wedge \cdots \wedge L_k$ $(k \geq 1)$ be a non-leaf node in the tree and suppose that a positive literal L_m is selected. Then this node has a descendant for each clause $A \leftarrow M_1 \wedge \cdots \wedge M_q$ in **P** such that L_m and A are unifiable. The descendant is

$$\leftarrow (L_1 \wedge \cdots \wedge L_{m-1} \wedge M_1 \wedge \cdots \wedge M_q \wedge L_{m+1} \wedge \cdots \wedge L_k)\theta$$

where θ is an mgu of L_m and A.

(4) Let $\leftarrow L_1, ..., L_k$ $(k \geq 1)$ be a non-leaf node in the tree and suppose that the selected literal L_m is a ground negative literal of the form $\neg A$ and there is a finitely failed SLDNF-tree for $\mathbf{P} \cup \{\leftarrow A\}$. Then the single descendant of the node is

$$\leftarrow (L_1, ..., L_{m-1}, L_{m+1}, ..., L_k)$$

(5) Let $\leftarrow L_1, ..., L_k$ $(k \geq 1)$ be a leaf node in the tree and suppose that the literal L_m is selected. Then either

  (a) L_m is positive and there is no clause in **P** whose head unifies with L_m, or

  (b) L_m is a ground negative literal $\neg A$ and there is an SLDNF-refutation of $\mathbf{P} \cup \{\leftarrow A\}$.

  (c) A node which is the empty clause has no descendants.

In an SLDNF-tree, a branch which terminates at an empty goal is a *success branch*, a branch which does not terminate is an *infinite branch* and a branch which terminates at a non-empty goal is a *failure branch.* An SLDNF-tree for which every branch is a failure branch is indeed a finitely failed SLDNF-tree. Each branch of an SLDNF-tree corresponds to an SLDNF-derivation.

When a positive literal in an SLDNF-resolution is selected, SLD-resolution is used to derive a new goal. When a ground negative literal is selected, a recursive process is established to apply the NAF rule.

Definition 7.18: Given a theorem proving procedure $\mathcal{P}$ and a set of clauses $\mathbf{S}$, a *computation* of $\mathbf{S}$ means an attempt to construct a derivation by $\mathcal{P}$ in $\mathbf{S}$.

Definition 7.19: Let $\mathbf{P}$ be a program and G be a goal. A computation of $\mathbf{P} \cup \{G\}$ represents an attempt to construct an SLDNF-derivation of $\mathbf{P} \cup \{G\}$.

According to the definition of SLDNF-resolution, a computation cannot proceed further from a goal with only non-ground negative literals left. The following definition caters for such a situation.

Definition 7.20: Let $\mathbf{P}$ be a program and G be a goal. A computation of $\mathbf{P} \cup \{G\}$ *flounders* if at some point in the computation a goal is reached which contains only non-ground negative literals.

EXAMPLE 7.13

If a program $\mathbf{P} = \{P(x) \leftarrow \neg Q(x), Q(a)\}$ then the computation of $\mathbf{P} \cup \{\leftarrow P(x)\}$ flounders but the computation of $\mathbf{P} \cup \{\leftarrow P(a)\}$ does not.

The notion of *constructive negation* (Chan, 1988) is introduced to deal with floundering goals. The following 'allowedness' restriction on programs and goals are also introduced in order to prevent floundering of any computation.

Definition 7.21: Let $\mathbf{P}$ be a program and G be a goal. A clause $A_1 \vee \cdots \vee A_m \leftarrow L_1 \wedge \cdots \wedge L_n$ in $\mathbf{P}$ is *allowed* (Clark, 1978; Lloyd, 1987) (or *range-restricted* (Gallaire *et al.*, 1984)) if every variable that occurs in the clause occurs in a positive literal of the body $L_1 \wedge \cdots \wedge L_n$. The whole program $\mathbf{P}$ is allowed if each of its clauses is allowed. A goal G is allowed if G is $\leftarrow L_1 \wedge \cdots \wedge L_n$ and every variable that occurs in G occurs in a positive literal of the body $\leftarrow L_1 \wedge \cdots \wedge L_n$.

If a program is range-restricted then, by definition, each of its assertions (that is, a clause with empty body) is ground.

Definition 7.22: Let $\mathbf{P}$ be a program and G be a goal $\leftarrow W$. An *answer substitution* for $\mathbf{P} \cup \{G\}$ is a substitution for the variables of G. A *computed answer* θ for $\mathbf{P} \cup \{G\}$ is the substitution obtained by restricting the composition $\theta_1 \cdots \theta_n$ to the variables of G, where $\theta_1, \ldots, \theta_n$ is the sequence of substitutions used in an SLDNF-refutation of $\mathbf{P} \cup \{G\}$. A computed answer for $\mathbf{P} \cup \{G\}$ will also be referred to as an answer substitution for the SLDNF-refutation of $\mathbf{P} \cup \{G\}$.

When a program **P** and a goal G are allowed, no computation of **P**∪{G} flounders and every computed answer for **P**∪{G} is a ground substitution for variables in G.

Definition 7.23: A *computation rule* is a function from a set of goals to a set of literals such that the value of the function for a goal is a literal, called the *selected literal*, in that goal. A computation rule is *safe* if negative literals may only be selected if they are ground.

7.7 Soundness and completeness of SLDNF-resolution

This section presents the soundness and completeness results of SLDNF-resolution with respect to program completion. A number of lemmas and theorems must be established to support the soundness result.

Lemma 7.2: Prove the following:

$$\mathcal{EQ} \vdash \forall x_1 \cdots \forall x_n (f(x_1, ..., x_n) = f(y_1, ..., y_n) \rightarrow \\ (x_1 = y_1) \wedge \cdots \wedge (x_n = y_n))$$

Proof Follows from the equality axiom

$$\forall x_1 \cdots \forall x_n ((x_1 \neq y_1) \vee \cdots \vee (x_n \neq y_n) \rightarrow f(x_1, ..., x_n) \neq f(y_1, ..., y_n)) \blacksquare$$

Lemma 7.3: Suppose $A = P(s_1, ..., s_n)$ and $B = P(t_1, ..., t_n)$ are two atoms and $\mathcal{EQ}$ is the equality theory. Then

(1) if A and B are unifiable with an mgu $\theta = \{x_1/e_1, ..., x_p/e_p\}$ then

$$\mathcal{EQ} \vdash \forall x_1 \cdots \forall x_n ((s_1 = t_1) \wedge \cdots \wedge (s_n = t_n) \leftrightarrow \\ (x_1 = e_1) \wedge \cdots \wedge (x_p = e_p))$$

(2) if A and B are not unifiable then

$$\mathcal{EQ} \vdash \forall x_1 \cdots \forall x_n ((s_1 = t_1) \wedge \cdots \wedge (s_n = t_n) \leftrightarrow \mathbf{F})$$

$$\mathcal{EQ} \vdash \neg \exists x_1 \cdots \exists x_n ((s_1 = t_1) \wedge \cdots \wedge (s_n = t_n))$$

Proof By induction on the number of steps k of an attempt to unify two atoms.

Base step $k = 1$, that is, the unification algorithm finds the substitution $\theta = \{x_1/e_1\}$ which is an mgu of A and B. Lemma 7.2 can be used to establish

$$\mathcal{EQ} \vdash \forall x_1((s_1 = t_1) \wedge \cdots \wedge (s_n = t_n) \rightarrow (x_1 = e_1))$$

Induction step Suppose the result holds for $k = p - 1$ and let the unification algorithm take p steps to decide whether A and B are unifiable or not. Let $\theta_1 = \{x_1/e_1\}$ be the first substitution. Consider the following two possibilities:

- *Subcase (a)* Suppose $P(s_1\theta_1, ..., s_n\theta_1)$ and $P(t_1\theta_1, ..., t_n\theta_1)$ are unifiable. Now, the unification algorithm will take $p - 1$ steps to find an mgu $\beta = \{x_2/e_2, ..., x_p/e_p\}$ of $P(s_1\theta_1, ..., s_n\theta_1)$ and $P(t_1\theta_1, ..., t_n\theta_1)$. Hence, by induction hypothesis

$$\mathcal{EQ} \vdash \forall((s_1\theta_1 = t_1\theta_1) \wedge \cdots \wedge (s_n\theta_1 = t_n\theta_1) \rightarrow (x_2 = e_2) \wedge \cdots \wedge (x_n = e_n))$$

  Since $e_1 = e'_1\{x_2/e_2, ..., x_k/e_k\}$, for some e'_1, the required result follows from the equality axioms 5, 6, 7 and 8.
- *Subcase (b)* Alternatively, suppose $P(s_1\theta_1, ..., s_n\theta_1)$ and $P(t_1\theta_1, ..., t_n\theta_1)$ are not unifiable. Then from the induction hypothesis

$$\mathcal{EQ} \vdash \neg\exists((s_1 = t_1)\theta_1 \wedge \cdots \wedge (s_n = t_n)\theta_1)$$

  Since θ_1 is the first substitution made by the unification algorithm

$$\mathcal{EQ} \vdash \neg\exists((s_1 = t_1) \wedge \cdots \wedge (s_n = t_n)) \blacksquare$$

Lemma 7.4: Let **P** be a normal program, G = $\leftarrow L_1 \wedge \cdots \wedge L_p \wedge \cdots \wedge L_q$ be a goal and $L_p = P(s_1, ..., s_n)$ be a selected positive literal from G.

(1) If $G_1, ..., G_m$ are all the derived goals resolving on L_p, then

$$Comp(\mathbf{P}) \vdash G \leftrightarrow G_1 \wedge \cdots \wedge G_m$$

(2) If $m = 0$, that is, there are no derived goals on L_p then $Comp(\mathbf{P}) \vdash$ G.

Proof Consider first the following two possibilities:

Case (a) If the completed definition of P is $\forall x_1 \cdots \forall x_n(\neg P(x_1, ..., x_n))$, then obviously $Comp(\mathbf{P}) \vdash$ G.

Case (b) Otherwise, suppose the completed definition of P has the form

$$\forall x_1 \cdots \forall x_n (P(x_1, ..., x_n) \leftrightarrow \mathrm{E}_1 \vee \cdots \vee \mathrm{E}_m)$$

where the definition of P is the set of clauses

$$Q_i(t_1^i, ..., t_{n_i}^i) \leftarrow M_1^i \wedge \cdots \wedge M_{r_i}^i,\ i = 1, ..., m$$

and each E_i is

$$\exists y_1^i \cdots \exists y_{k_i}^i ((x_1 = t_1^i) \wedge \cdots \wedge (x_n = t_{n_i}^i) \wedge M_1^i \wedge \cdots \wedge M_{r_i}^i)$$

Therefore, it follows that

$$Comp(\mathbf{P}) \vdash \leftarrow \neg \mathrm{G} \leftrightarrow \bigvee_{i=1}^{m} \exists y_1^i \cdots \exists y_{k_i}^i ((s_1 = t_1^i) \wedge \cdots \wedge (s_n = t_{n_i}^i) \wedge$$
$$L_1 \wedge \cdots \wedge L_{p-1} \wedge M_1^i \wedge \cdots \wedge M_{r_i}^i \wedge L_{p+1} \wedge \cdots \wedge L_q)$$

where $y_1^i, ..., y_{k_i}^i$ are the variables of the input clause

$$Q_i(t_1^i, ..., t_{n_i}^i) \leftarrow M_1^1 \wedge \cdots \wedge M_{r_i}^i,\ i = 1, ..., m$$

Therefore

$$Comp(\mathbf{P}) \vdash \mathrm{G} \leftrightarrow \bigwedge_{i=1}^{m} \neg \exists y_1^i \cdots \exists y_{k_i}^i ((s_1 = t_1^i) \wedge \cdots \wedge (s_n = t_{n_i}^i) \wedge$$
$$L_1 \wedge \cdots \wedge L_{p-1} \wedge M_1^i \wedge \cdots \wedge M_{r_i}^i \wedge L_{p+1} \wedge \cdots \wedge L_q)$$

If θ_i is an mgu of A_i and $P(s_1, ..., s_n)$, by Lemma 7.3

$$Comp(\mathbf{P}) \vdash \forall((s_1 = t_1^i) \wedge \cdots \wedge (s_n = t_{n_i}^i) \leftrightarrow \theta_i)$$

Hence by applying equality axioms,

$$Comp(\mathbf{P}) \vdash \exists y_1^i \cdots \exists y_{k_i}^i ((s_1 = t_1^i) \wedge \cdots \wedge (s_n = t_{n_i}^i) \wedge$$
$$L_1 \wedge \cdots \wedge L_{p-1} \wedge M_1^i \wedge \cdots \wedge M_{r_i}^i \wedge L_{p+1} \wedge \cdots \wedge L_q) \leftrightarrow$$
$$\exists y_1^i \cdots \exists y_{k_i}^i (L_1 \wedge \cdots \wedge L_{p-1} \wedge$$
$$M_1^i \wedge \cdots \wedge M_{r_i}^i \wedge L_{p+1} \wedge \cdots \wedge L_q)\theta_i, i = 1, ..., m$$

that is

$$Comp(\mathbf{P}) \vdash \mathrm{G} \leftrightarrow \bigwedge_{i=1}^{m} \neg \exists y_1^i \cdots \exists y_{k_i}^i (L_1 \wedge \cdots \wedge L_{p-1} \wedge$$
$$M_1^i \wedge \cdots \wedge M_{r_i}^i \wedge L_{p+1} \wedge \cdots \wedge L_q)\theta_i$$

that is

$$Comp(\mathbf{P}) \vdash G \leftrightarrow G_1 \wedge \cdots \wedge G_m \quad \blacksquare$$

Theorem 7.3: Let **P** be a program and $G = \leftarrow L_1 \wedge \cdots \wedge L_n$ be a goal. If $\mathbf{P} \cup \{G\}$ has a finitely failed SLDNF-tree then G is a logical consequence of $Comp(\mathbf{P})$.

Proof By induction on rank k of the SLDNF-tree.

Base step (rank) $k = 0$: according to the definition of SLDNF-tree of rank 0, only positive literals are selected at nodes in the tree. The result for this base case is established by applying further the induction principle on depth of the tree.

Base step (depth) $d = 0$, that is, the finitely failed SLDNF-tree has depth 0. Then L_1 is positive and the result follows from Lemma 7.4(2).

Induction step (depth) Suppose the finitely failed SLDNF-tree for $\mathbf{P} \cup \{G\}$ has a depth d. The result follows from Lemma 7.4(1) and the induction hypothesis for depth less than d.

Induction step (rank) Suppose the result holds for finitely failed SLDNF-trees of rank less than k. Consider a finitely failed SLDNF-tree of rank k. The result for this is also established by further applying the induction principle on the depth d.

Base Step (depth) d=0: consider the following two possibilities:

- *Subcase (a)* If the selected literal from G is positive then the result follows from Lemma 7.4(2).
- *Subcase (b)* if the selected literal L_1 is a ground negative literal $\neg A$, then $\mathbf{P} \cup \{\leftarrow A\}$ has an SLDNF-refutation of rank $k - 1$. Now, if the selected literal of a goal is positive, then the resolvent is a logical consequence of the goal and the input clause of the resolution. Also, each clause of **P** is a logical consequence of $Comp(\mathbf{P})$. Hence by applying the induction hypothesis for each SLDNF-tree of rank $k - 1$ in the refutation of $\mathbf{P} \cup \{\leftarrow A\}$, it can be shown that A is a logical consequence of $Comp(\mathbf{P})$. Since A is ground, $\forall(\leftarrow \neg A)$, that is, G is a logical consequence of $Comp(\mathbf{P})$.

Induction step (depth) Suppose that the finitely failed SLDNF-tree has depth d. Consider again the following two possibilities:

- *Subcase (a)* If the selected literal from G is positive then the result follows from Lemma 7.4(1) and the induction hypothesis for depth less than d.

- *Subcase (b)* If the selected literal L_p is a ground negative literal $\neg A$, then by induction hypothesis for depth less than d, the goal $\leftarrow L_1 \wedge \cdots \wedge L_{p-1} \wedge L_{p+1} \wedge \cdots \wedge L_n$ is a logical consequence of $Comp(\mathbf{P})$. Hence $\leftarrow L_1 \wedge \cdots \wedge L_n$ is also a logical consequence of $Comp(\mathbf{P})$. ■

Theorem 7.4: (soundness of SLDNF-resolution) Let **P** be a program and G = $\leftarrow L_1 \wedge \cdots \wedge L_n$ be a goal. If $\mathbf{P} \cup \{G\}$ has an SLDNF-refutation with substitutions $\theta_1, ..., \theta_m$, then

$$\forall((L_1 \wedge \cdots \wedge L_n)\theta_1 \cdots \theta_m)$$

is a logical consequence of $Comp(\mathbf{P})$.

Proof By induction on the length n of the refutation.

Base step $n = 1$, that is, $G = \leftarrow L_1$. Consider the following two possibilities:

- *Subcase (a)* If L_1 is positive then there is an atomic formula A in **P** such that $L_1\theta_1 = A\theta_1$. Since $L_1\theta_1$ is an instance of a unit clause in **P**, $\forall(L_1\theta_1)$ is a logical consequence of **P**. Since **P** is a logical consequence of $Comp(\mathbf{P})$, $\forall(L_1\theta_1)$ is a logical consequence of $Comp(\mathbf{P})$.
- *Subcase (b)* If L_1 is negative then L_1 is ground. Therefore, by Lemma 7.4, L_1 is a logical consequence of $Comp(\mathbf{P})$.

Induction step Suppose the result holds for any refutation of length $m - 1$. Consider an SLDNF-refutation of $\mathbf{P} \cup \{G\}$ whose length is m. Suppose $\theta_1, ..., \theta_m$ are substitutions for this refutation and $C_1 = A \leftarrow M_1 \wedge \cdots \wedge M_p$ is the first input clause. Let L_q be the selected literal from G. Consider the following two possibilities:

- *Subcase (a)* If L_q is positive then, by induction hypothesis,

$$\forall((L_1 \wedge \cdots \wedge L_{q-1} \wedge M_1 \wedge \cdots \wedge M_p \wedge \\ L_{q+1} \wedge \cdots \wedge L_n)\theta_1 \cdots \theta_m)$$

is a logical consequence of $Comp(\mathbf{P})$. If C_1 has a non-empty body, then

$$\forall((M_1 \wedge \cdots \wedge M_p)\theta_1 \cdots \theta_m)$$

is a logical consequence of $Comp(\mathbf{P})$, that is, $\forall(A\,\theta_1 \cdots \theta_m)$ is a logical consequence of $Comp(\mathbf{P})$, that is, $\forall(L_q\theta_1 \cdots \theta_m)$ is a logical consequence of $Comp(\mathbf{P})$. Also,

$$\forall((L_1 \wedge \cdots \wedge L_{q-1} \wedge L_{q+1} \wedge \cdots \wedge L_n)\,\theta_1 \cdots \theta_m)$$

is a logical consequence of $Comp(\mathbf{P})$. Therefore

$$\forall((L_1 \wedge \cdots \wedge L_n)\,\theta_1 \cdots \theta_m)$$

is a logical consequence of $Comp(\mathbf{P})$.

- *Subcase (b)* If L_q is a ground negative literal, by Theorem 7.3, L_q is a logical consequence of $Comp(\mathbf{P})$. Since L_q is ground, $\forall(L_q\theta_1 \cdots \theta_m)$ is also a logical consequence of $Comp(\mathbf{P})$. By induction hypothesis

$$\forall((L_1 \wedge \cdots \wedge L_{q-1} \wedge L_{q+1} \wedge \cdots \wedge L_n)\theta_1 \cdots \theta_m)$$

is a logical consequence of $Comp(\mathbf{P})$. Combining these two, $\forall((L_1 \wedge \cdots \wedge L_n)\theta_1 \cdots \theta_m)$ is a logical consequence of $Comp(\mathbf{P})$. ■

Although SLDNF-resolution is sound with respect to the completion, the resolution is not necessarily complete (Barbuti and Martelli, 1986; Cavedon and Lloyd, 1989; Jaffar *et al.*, 1983; Lloyd, 1987) even when the completion is consistent. The following example demonstrates this fact.

EXAMPLE 7.14

Suppose $\mathbf{P} = \{P \leftarrow Q,\ P \leftarrow \neg Q,\ Q \leftarrow Q\}$. The program $\mathbf{P}$ is stratified and hence $Comp(\mathbf{P})$ is consistent. The atom P is a logical consequence of $Comp(\mathbf{P})$ but $\mathbf{P} \cup \{\leftarrow P\}$ does not have an SLDNF-refutation.

This example also proves that the SLDNF-resolution is not even complete for stratified programs. Hence one should look for a class of programs which is less general than the stratified class of programs. In his paper Clark (1978) proved that the SLDNF-resolution is complete for an allowed hierarchical class of programs and goals. A further completeness result was also established for *structured programs* introduced by Barbuti and Martelli (1986). The completeness result has been pushed up to the class of allowed strict stratified programs (Cavedon and Lloyd, 1989; Baratelli and File, 1988) whose definition is given below.

Definition 7.24: Suppose **P** is a program and G is a goal. Define the two sets $\mathcal{Pos}$ and $\mathcal{Neg}$ as follows:

$$\mathcal{Pos}^0 = \{P \mid P(t_1, ..., t_p) \text{ is a literal occurring in G}\}$$
$$\mathcal{Neg}^0 = \{P \mid \neg P(t_1, ..., t_p) \text{ is a literal occurring in G}\}$$

$$\begin{aligned}\mathcal{Pos}^{i+1} = \{P \mid\ & Q(s_1, ..., s_q) \leftarrow L_1 \wedge \cdots \wedge P(t_1, ..., t_p) \wedge \cdots \wedge L_n \\ & \text{is in } \mathbf{P} \text{ and } Q \in \mathcal{Pos}^i \text{, or} \\ & Q(s_1, ..., s_q) \leftarrow L_1 \wedge \cdots \wedge \neg P(t_1, ..., t_p) \wedge \cdots \wedge L_n \\ & \text{is in } \mathbf{P} \text{ and } Q \in \mathcal{Neg}^i\}\end{aligned}$$

$$\begin{aligned}\mathcal{Neg}^{i+1} = \{P \mid\ & Q(s_1, ..., s_q) \leftarrow L_1 \wedge \cdots \wedge P(t_1, ..., t_p) \wedge \cdots \wedge L_n \\ & \text{is in } \mathbf{P} \text{ and } Q \in \mathcal{Neg}^i \text{, or} \\ & Q(s_1, ..., s_q) \leftarrow L_1 \wedge \cdots \wedge \neg P(t_1, ..., t_p) \wedge \cdots \wedge L_n \\ & \text{is in } \mathbf{P} \text{ and } Q \in \mathcal{Pos}^i\}\end{aligned}$$

$$\mathcal{Pos} = \bigcup_i \mathcal{Pos}^i$$
$$\mathcal{Neg} = \bigcup_i \mathcal{Neg}^i$$

Now, $\mathbf{P} \cup \{G\}$ is *strict* if $\mathcal{Pos} \cap \mathcal{Neg} = \emptyset$.

The above definition obviously excludes the case when $\mathbf{P} = \{P \leftarrow Q, P \leftarrow \neg Q, Q \leftarrow Q\}$ and $G = \leftarrow P$. The two sets $\mathcal{Pos}$ and $\mathcal{Neg}$ are respectively $\{P, Q\}$ and $\{Q\}$, and hence $\mathbf{P} \cup \{G\}$ does not satisfy the strictness condition.

An even stronger version has been provided has been provided by Decker (1991) through *generalized cover axioms*. This generalization includes cases like $\mathbf{P} = \{P(x, y) \leftarrow Q(x, y), Q(a, x) \leftarrow \neg R(y)\}$ and $G = \leftarrow P(b, x)$.

Correctness of an SLDNF-resolution can be maintained by weakening the safeness condition in the following way. Suppose a non-ground negative literal $\neg A$ is selected from a goal G. If the computation of $\mathbf{P} \cup \{\leftarrow A\}$ has a finitely failed SLDNF-tree, that is, if the negative subgoal $\neg A$ succeeds, then the rest of the computation of $\mathbf{P} \cup \{G\}$ can be continued in the usual manner. On the other hand, if $\mathbf{P} \cup \{\leftarrow A\}$ has an SLDNF-refutation, that is, if the subgoal $\neg A$ fails then a check is performed to make sure no bindings were made to any variables in the rest of the subgoals of G. If no such bindings were made then the subgoal $\neg A$ is allowed to fail and the rest of the computation can proceed in the usual manner. If such a binding was made then a different subgoal from G should be selected and the selection of the subgoal $\neg A$ is delayed.

EXAMPLE 7.15

Consider the program $\mathbf{P} = \{Q(b), P(a)\}$ and the goal $G = \leftarrow \neg Q(y) \wedge P(x)$. In the computation of $\mathbf{P} \cup \{G\}$, the non-ground negative literal $\neg Q(y)$ can be selected from G and the subgoal $\neg Q(y)$ can be taken as failed. The correctness of the computation can be maintained. This is possible because the variable y does not occur in the rest of the goal G. On the other hand, if one considers the goal $\leftarrow \neg Q(x) \wedge P(x)$ then selecting the non-ground negative literal $\neg Q(x)$ will affect completeness although $\mathbf{P}$ is hierarchical. Considering the program $\mathbf{P} = \{P(a)\}$ and the goal $\leftarrow \neg Q(x) \wedge P(x)$, the subgoal $\neg Q(x)$ can be selected first and can be taken as true.

7.8 Extended normal programs

The expressibility of normal programs is further increased by considering the class of extended normal programs which are more general than normal programs.

Definition 7.25: An *extended normal program clause* is a formula of the form

$$A \leftarrow W$$

where A is an atom and W is any formula. Any variables in A and any free variables in W are assumed to be universally quantified at the front of the program clause.

Definition 7.26: An *extended normal program* is a finite set of extended normal program clauses.

Definition 7.27: An *extended goal* is a formula of the form $\leftarrow$ W, where W is a formula and any free variables in W are assumed to be universally quantified at the front end of the goal.

The completion of an extended normal program is defined in the same fashion as in the case of normal programs. Here, each E_i in the completed definition of an n-ary predicate symbol P will have the form

$$\exists y_1 \cdots \exists y_k ((x_1 = t_1) \wedge \cdots \wedge (x_n = t_n) \wedge W_i)$$

where $y_1, ..., y_k$ are the variables occurring in A_i and the free variables in W_i.

Suppose $\mathbf{P}$ is an extended program and $G = \leftarrow W$ is an extended goal whose free variables are $x_1, ..., x_n$. Consider an n-ary predicate symbol *Answer* appearing neither in $\mathbf{P}$ nor in G. Then the goal G is transformed to the normal goal $\leftarrow Answer(x_1, ..., x_n)$ by adding the clause $Answer(x_1, ..., x_n) \leftarrow W$ to the extended program $\mathbf{P}'$. It is straightforward to verify that the goal G is a logical consequence of $Comp(\mathbf{P})$ if and only if $\leftarrow Answer(x_1, ..., x_n)$ is a logical consequence of $Comp(\mathbf{P}')$, where $\mathbf{P}'$ is $\mathbf{P} \cup \{Answer(x_1, ..., x_n) \leftarrow W\}$. Furthermore, for any substitution θ, $\forall x_1 \cdots \forall x_n (W\theta)$ is a logical consequence of $Comp(\mathbf{P})$ if and only if $\forall x_1 \cdots \forall x_n (Answer(x_1, ..., x_n)\theta)$ is a logical consequence of $Comp(\mathbf{P}')$. These two results justify the transformation from an extended goal to a normal goal.

An extended normal program $\mathbf{P}'$ is transformed into a normal program $\mathbf{P}$ by means of the following transformation (Lloyd and Topor, 1984):

(a) Replace $A \leftarrow W_1 \wedge \cdots \wedge W_{i-1} \wedge \neg(U \wedge V) \wedge W_{i+1} \wedge \cdots \wedge W_n$
by $A \leftarrow W_1 \wedge \cdots \wedge W_{i-1} \wedge \neg U \wedge W_{i+1} \wedge \cdots \wedge W_n$
and $A \leftarrow W_1 \wedge \cdots \wedge W_{i-1} \wedge \neg V \wedge W_{i+1} \wedge \cdots \wedge W_n$

(b) Replace $A \leftarrow W_1 \wedge \cdots \wedge W_{i-1} \wedge \forall x_1 \cdots \forall x_m U \wedge W_{i+1} \wedge \cdots \wedge W_n$
by $A \leftarrow W_1 \wedge \cdots \wedge W_{i-1} \wedge \neg \exists x_1 \cdots \exists x_m \neg U \wedge W_{i+1} \wedge \cdots \wedge W_n$

(c) Replace $A \leftarrow W_1 \wedge \cdots \wedge W_{i-1} \wedge \neg \forall x_1 \cdots \forall x_m U \wedge W_{i+1} \wedge \cdots \wedge W_n$
by $A \leftarrow W_1 \wedge \cdots \wedge W_{i-1} \wedge \exists x_1 \cdots \exists x_m \neg U \wedge W_{i+1} \wedge \cdots \wedge W_n$

(d) Replace $A \leftarrow W_1 \wedge \cdots \wedge W_{i-1} \wedge (U \leftarrow V) \wedge W_{i+1} \wedge \cdots \wedge W_n$
by $A \leftarrow W_1 \wedge \cdots \wedge W_{i-1} \wedge U \wedge W_{i+1} \wedge \cdots \wedge W_n$
and $A \leftarrow W_1 \wedge \cdots \wedge W_{i-1} \wedge \neg V \wedge W_{i+1} \wedge \cdots \wedge W_n$

(e) Replace $A \leftarrow W_1 \wedge \cdots \wedge W_{i-1} \wedge \neg(U \leftarrow V) \wedge W_{i+1} \wedge \cdots \wedge W_n$
by $A \leftarrow W_1 \wedge \cdots \wedge W_{i-1} \wedge V \wedge \neg U \wedge W_{i+1} \wedge \cdots \wedge W_n$

(f) Replace $A \leftarrow W_1 \wedge \cdots \wedge W_{i-1} \wedge (U \vee V) \wedge W_{i+1} \wedge \cdots \wedge W_n$
by $A \leftarrow W_1 \wedge \cdots \wedge W_{i-1} \wedge U \wedge W_{i+1} \wedge \cdots \wedge W_n$
and $A \leftarrow W_1 \wedge \cdots \wedge W_{i-1} \wedge V \wedge W_{i+1} \wedge \cdots \wedge W_n$

(g) Replace $A \leftarrow W_1 \wedge \cdots \wedge W_{i-1} \wedge \neg(U \vee V) \wedge W_{i+1} \wedge \cdots \wedge W_n$
by $A \leftarrow W_1 \wedge \cdots \wedge W_{i-1} \wedge \neg U \wedge \neg V \wedge W_{i+1} \wedge \cdots \wedge W_n$

(h) Replace $A \leftarrow W_1 \wedge \cdots \wedge W_{i-1} \wedge \neg\neg U \wedge W_{i+1} \wedge \cdots \wedge W_n$
by $A \leftarrow W_1 \wedge \cdots \wedge W_{i-1} \wedge U \wedge W_{i+1} \wedge \cdots \wedge W_n$

(i) Replace $A \leftarrow W_1 \wedge \cdots \wedge W_{i-1} \wedge \exists x_1 \cdots \exists x_m U \wedge W_{i+1} \wedge \cdots \wedge W_n$
by $A \leftarrow W_1 \wedge \cdots \wedge W_{i-1} \wedge U \wedge W_{i+1} \wedge \cdots \wedge W_n$

(j) Replace $A \leftarrow W_1 \wedge \cdots \wedge W_{i-1} \wedge \neg \exists x_1 \cdots \exists x_m U \wedge W_{i+1} \wedge \cdots \wedge W_n$
by $A \leftarrow W_1 \wedge \cdots \wedge W_{i-1} \wedge \neg P(y_1, ..., y_k) \wedge W_{i+1} \wedge \cdots \wedge W_n$
and $P(y_1, ..., y_k) \leftarrow \exists x_1 \cdots x_m U$
where $y_1, ..., y_k$ are the free variables in $\exists x_1 \cdots x_m U$ and P is a new predicate symbol not already in the program.

The above set of transformations is applied to every clause of **P′** until no more such transformations are possible. This process terminates after a finite number of steps.

The motivation behind introducing extended normal programs and extended goals is to allow the programs to be written in a larger subset of logic. At the same time, query evaluation in this extended system can be handled in the environment of usual normal programs and normal goals with the aid of the above transformation method. When the underlying semantics of a program has been given by its completion, the following result (Lloyd and Topor, 1984) justifies the transformation from an extended program to a normal program.

Lemma 7.5: Suppose **P′** is an extended program and **P** is a normal program obtained from **P′** by applying the above set of transformations. Then for any closed formula F in the language of **P′**, F is a logical consequence of *Comp*(**P′**) if and only F is a logical consequence of *Comp*(**P**).

Proof Left as an exercise. ■

EXAMPLE 7.16

This illustrates the above transformation process.

Step 1:	$ValidDept(x) \leftarrow \forall y (\exists z Manager(z, y, x) \leftarrow Worker(y, x))$	
Step 2.	$VD(x) \leftarrow \forall y (\exists z M(z, y, x) \leftarrow W(y, x))$	Abbr.
Step 3:	$VD(x) \leftarrow \neg \exists y \neg (\exists z M(z, y, x) \leftarrow W(y, x))$	Rule (b)
Step 4:	$VD(x) \leftarrow \neg \exists y (W(y, x) \wedge \neg \exists z M(z, y, x))$	Rule (d)
Step 5:	$VD(x) \leftarrow \neg P(x)$	Rule (j)
	$P(x) \leftarrow \exists y (W(y, x) \wedge \neg \exists z M(z, y, x))$	

Step 6: $VD(x) \leftarrow \neg P(x)$

$P(x) \leftarrow W(y, x) \wedge \neg \exists z M(z, y, x)$ Rule (i)

Step 7: $VD(x) \leftarrow \neg P(x)$

$P(x) \leftarrow W(y, x) \wedge \neg Q(y, x)$ Rule (j)

$Q(y, x) \leftarrow \exists z M(z, y, x)$

Step 8: $VD(x) \leftarrow \neg P(x)$

$P(x) \leftarrow W(y, x) \wedge \neg Q(y, x)$

$Q(y, x) \leftarrow M(z, y, x)$ Rule (i)

7.9 Negation as inconsistency

A resolution scheme is introduced in this section which is based on the notion of *Negation As Inconsistency* (NAI) (Gabby and Sergot, 1986). Unlike negation as failure (NAF), NAI is fully compatible with classical negation and NAF becomes a special-case NAI whenever NAF behaves logically correctly. The resolution scheme (*SLDNI-resolution*) introduced deals with a special class (say C) of programs and goals. A program clause in this class is a formula of the form $A \leftarrow$ F and a goal is a formula of the form $\leftarrow$ G, where F and G are *Normal Form negative formulae* (or *NF negative formulae*) (Ling, 1987) defined as follows:

(1) An atom is an NF negative formula.

(2) If A and B are NF negative formulae, so are $\neg$ A and A $\wedge$ B.

Free variables in a program clause or in a goal are assumed to be universally quantified over the whole formula. The general form of an NF negative formula is

$$A_1 \wedge \cdots \wedge A_m \wedge \neg \mathrm{F}_1 \wedge \cdots \wedge \neg \mathrm{F}_n$$

where each A_i is an atom and each F_j is an NF negative formula. The class C of programs and goals generalizes the class of normal programs and goals but is less general than the class of extended programs and goals. Any reference to programs, program clauses and goals in this section will always mean that they are from the class C.

SLDNI-resolution requires a program to be a quadruple $<\mathbf{P}, \mathbf{Q}, \mathbf{N}, \mathbf{M}>$, where **P** is a program, **Q** is a set of atoms and **M** and **N** are sets of goals. The goals of $\mathbf{N} \cup \mathbf{M}$ are not to succeed. Intuitively, $\mathbf{P} \cup \mathbf{Q}$ represents the positive information and $\mathbf{N} \cup \mathbf{M}$ represents the set of negative information. At the start of a computation both **Q** and **M** are empty and **P** and **N** do not have any variables in common. During the computation clauses and goals are added to **Q** and **M**. A program in such a form is considered inconsistent if some goal $G \in \mathbf{N} \cup \mathbf{M}$ succeeds from $\mathbf{P} \cup \mathbf{Q}$. Therefore a piece of information can only be negated if adding it to $\mathbf{P} \cup \mathbf{Q}$ causes the program to become inconsistent.

Definition 7.28: Let $G = \leftarrow G_1 \wedge \cdots \wedge G_n$ be a goal, where each G_i $(1 \leq i \leq n)$ is an NF negative formula and is associated with a program $<\mathbf{P}_i, \mathbf{Q}_i, \mathbf{N}_i, \mathbf{M}_i>$. By selecting G_p $(1 \leq p \leq n)$ from G, another goal G′ can be *derived* using SLDNI-resolution as follows:

(1) Suppose G_p is a positive literal and there exists a substitution θ such that $G_p\theta = A\theta$, for some clause $A \leftarrow H_1 \wedge \cdots \wedge H_q$ in $\mathbf{P}_p \cup \mathbf{Q}_p$. Then G′ is

$$\leftarrow (G_1 \wedge \cdots \wedge G_{p-1} \wedge H_1 \wedge \cdots \wedge H_q \wedge G_{p+1} \wedge \cdots \wedge G_n)\theta$$

where each $G_i\theta$ in this goal has $<\mathbf{P}_i, \mathbf{Q}_i\theta, \mathbf{N}_i, \mathbf{M}_i\theta>$ as its associated program and each $H_j\theta$ in this goal has the same $<\mathbf{P}_p, \mathbf{Q}_p\theta, \mathbf{N}_p, \mathbf{M}_p\theta>$ as its associated program.

(2) Suppose G_p is an NF negative formula of the form

$$\neg(A_1 \wedge \cdots \wedge A_r \wedge \neg F_1 \wedge \cdots \wedge \neg F_s)$$

Then G′ is

$$\leftarrow G_1 \wedge \cdots \wedge G_{p-1} \wedge H_1 \wedge \cdots \wedge H_q \wedge G_{p+1} \wedge \cdots \wedge G_n$$

for some goal $\leftarrow H_1 \wedge \cdots \wedge H_q$ in $\mathbf{N}_i \cup \mathbf{M}_p \cup \{\leftarrow F_1, \ldots, \leftarrow F_s\}$, where $i \neq p$ and each G_i in this goal has $<\mathbf{P}_i, \mathbf{Q}_i, \mathbf{N}_i, \mathbf{M}_i>$ as its associated program and each H_j in this goal has $<\mathbf{P}_p$, $\mathbf{Q}_p \cup \{A_1, \ldots, A_r\}$, $\mathbf{N}_p$, $\mathbf{M}_p \cup \{\leftarrow F_1, \ldots, \leftarrow F_s\}>$ as its associated program.

Suppose $<\mathbf{P}, \mathbf{Q}, \mathbf{N}, \mathbf{M}>$ is a program and $G = \leftarrow H_1 \wedge \cdots \wedge H_n$ is a goal. An *SLDNI-derivation* of $<\mathbf{P}, \mathbf{Q}, \mathbf{N}, \mathbf{M}> \cup \{G\}$ is a sequence $G_0 = G$, G_1, ..., where G_{i+1} is derived from G_i by SLDNI-resolution and the associated program for each H_i in G is same as $<\mathbf{P}, \mathbf{Q}, \mathbf{N}, \mathbf{M}>$. An *SLDNI-refutation* is an SLDNI-derivation of the empty clause.

EXAMPLE 7.17

This example constructs an SLDNI-refutation for the following program and goal:

$\mathbf{P}$: $\{P(x) \leftarrow Q(x), P(x) \leftarrow R(x)\}$

$\mathbf{N}$: $\{\leftarrow \neg Q(a) \wedge \neg R(a)\}$

G: $\leftarrow \neg\neg P(x)$

Derivation	*Programs associated with literals in goals*
$G = G_0 = \leftarrow \neg\neg P(x)$	$<\mathbf{P}, \{\}, \mathbf{N}, \{\}>$
$G_1 = \leftarrow \neg Q(a) \wedge \neg R(a)$	$<\mathbf{P}, \{\}, \mathbf{N}, \{\leftarrow P(x)\}>$
	$<\mathbf{P}, \{\}, \mathbf{N}, \{\leftarrow P(x)\}>$
$G_2 = \leftarrow P(x) \wedge \neg R(a)$	$<\mathbf{P}, \{Q(a)\}, \mathbf{N}, \{\leftarrow P(x)\}>$
	$<\mathbf{P}, \{\}, \mathbf{N}, \{\leftarrow P(x)\}>$
$G_3 = \leftarrow Q(x) \wedge \neg R(a)$	$<\mathbf{P}, \{Q(a)\}, \mathbf{N}, \{\leftarrow P(x)\}>$
	$<\mathbf{P}, \{\}, \mathbf{N}, \{\leftarrow P(x)\}>$
$G_4 = \leftarrow \neg R(a)$	$<\mathbf{P}, \{\}, \mathbf{N}, \{\leftarrow P(a)\}>$
$G_5 = \leftarrow P(a)$	$<\mathbf{P}, \{R(a)\}, \mathbf{N}, \{\leftarrow P(a)\}>$
$G_6 = \leftarrow R(a)$	$<\mathbf{P}, \{R(a)\}, \mathbf{N}, \{\leftarrow P(a)\}>$
$G_7 = \square$	

Both negative and indefinite data can be stored in a programming environment using NAI formalism. To store information of the form $\neg A$, where A is an atom, just $\leftarrow A$ is added to the negative part $\mathbf{N}$. To store an indefinite clause of the form $A_1 \vee \cdots \vee A_m \leftarrow L_1 \wedge \cdots \wedge L_n$, the goal $\leftarrow L_1 \wedge \cdots \wedge L_n \wedge \neg A_1 \wedge \cdots \wedge \neg A_m$ is added to $\mathbf{N}$. Although every clause can be stored in such a fashion, the NAI rule is still weaker than classical negation as is evident from the following example.

EXAMPLE 7.18

Consider the program $\mathbf{P} = \{P \leftarrow Q, P \leftarrow R, Q \vee R\}$. Now the atom P is a logical consequence of $\mathbf{P}$. But NAI formalism represents $\mathbf{P}$ as $<\{P \leftarrow Q, P \leftarrow R\}, \{\leftarrow \neg Q \wedge \neg R\}>$. No successful derivation can be carried out with $\leftarrow P$ as goal. However, the goal $\leftarrow \neg\neg P$ succeeds under NAI-derivation (see Example 7.17).

The NAI rule contains the NAF rule as a special case whenever NAF behaves logically correctly. But this is not so when NAF behaves logically incorrectly and an example of such a case is provided below.

EXAMPLE 7.19

For the program $\mathbf{P} = \{P \leftarrow \neg Q\}$ and $\mathbf{N} = \{\}$, NAF succeeds for the goal $\mathbf{P} \cup \{\leftarrow P\}$ but there is no successful NAI-derivation for $\{\leftarrow P\}$. This is because P is not a logical consequence of $\mathbf{P}$. But the same goal has an NAI-refutation when $\mathbf{N}$ is taken as $\{\leftarrow Q\}$ instead of the empty set.

There are some cases where SLDNF-resolution fails to generate answers but NAI formalism succeeds. One such case is demonstrated through the following example.

EXAMPLE 7.20

Suppose $\mathbf{P} = \{P(x) \leftarrow \neg R(x)\}$ and $\mathbf{N} = \{\leftarrow R(a)\}$. The goal $\leftarrow P(x)$ succeeds by NAI and generates $\{x/a\}$ as an answer substitution. But the computation of $\mathbf{P} \cup \{\leftarrow P(x)\}$ by SLDNF-resolution flounders.

7.10 Semantics by three-valued logic

In the case of a definite program $\mathbf{P}$, the operator $T_{\mathbf{P}}$ has both smallest and the biggest fixpoints and they give success set and ground failure set respectively for the program $\mathbf{P}$. Fitting (Fitting, 1986; Fitting and Ben-Jacob, 1988) defines an analogous operator $\phi_{\mathbf{P}}$ for normal programs, based on Kleene's (Kleene, 1967) strong three-valued logic, which is discussed in this section.

Definition 7.29: Suppose $\mathbf{P}$ is a separate program (see Chapter 11 for the definitions of separate programs, EDB and IDB predicates). A *(two-valued) interpretation* $\mathbf{I}$ of $\mathbf{P}$ ($\mathbf{I} \subseteq \mathcal{HB}(\mathbf{P})$ is considered as a mapping v with a domain $\mathcal{HB}(\mathbf{P})$ and a range as the set $\{\mathbf{T}, \mathbf{F}\}$ and is defined as follows:

$$\begin{aligned} v(A) &= \mathbf{T}, \text{ if } A \in \mathbf{I} \\ &= \mathbf{F}, \text{ if } A \notin \mathbf{I} \end{aligned}$$

To illustrate this concept of considering an interpretation as a mapping, consider the following example.

EXAMPLE 7.21

Let $\mathbf{P} = \{P(x) \leftarrow Q(x), Q(a)\}$. The set of all interpretations of this program and definitions of the associated mappings is given below:

$\mathbf{I}_0 = \varnothing$	$v_0(P(a)) = \mathbf{F}, v_0(Q(a)) = \mathbf{F}$
$\mathbf{I}_1 = \{P(a)\}$	$v_1(P(a)) = \mathbf{T}, v_1(Q(a)) = \mathbf{F}$
$\mathbf{I}_2 = \{Q(a)\}$	$v_2(P(a)) = \mathbf{F}, v_2(Q(a)) = \mathbf{T}$
$\mathbf{I}_3 = \{P(a), Q(a)\}$	$v_3(P(a)) = \mathbf{T}, v_3(Q(a)) = \mathbf{T}$

Definition 7.30: A *three-valued interpretation* of a program $\mathbf{P}$ can be considered as a mapping $v : \mathcal{HB}(\mathbf{P}) \rightarrow \{\mathbf{T}, \mathbf{F}, \perp\}$. The symbol '$\perp$' is read as 'undefined'.

Analogous to the fixpoint operator $T_\mathbf{P}$ in the case of two-valued interpretations, a mapping $\phi_\mathbf{P}$ is also considered from the set of all three-valued interpretations of $\mathbf{P}$ to the set of all three-valued interpretations of $\mathbf{P}$. The mapping is defined in the following manner:

$\phi_\mathbf{P}(v) = w$, where w is recursively defined as follows:

$w(A)$	$= \mathbf{T}$	if A is under an EDB predicate and $A \in \mathit{Ground}(\mathbf{P})$, or if there is a clause $A \leftarrow \mathrm{B}$ in $\mathit{Ground}(\mathbf{P})$ such that $v(M) = \mathbf{T}$ for every positive literal M occurring in B and $v(N) = \mathbf{F}$ for every negative literal $\neg N$ occurring in B.
	$= \mathbf{F}$	if A is under an EDB predicate and $A \notin \mathit{Ground}(\mathbf{P})$, and if there is a clause $A \leftarrow \mathrm{B}$ in $\mathit{Ground}(\mathbf{P})$ then $v(N) = \mathbf{T}$ for some negative literal $\neg N$ occurring in B, or $v(M) = \mathbf{F}$ for some positive literal M occurring in B.
	$= \perp$	otherwise.

The following example clarifies the definition of an extended fixpoint operator.

EXAMPLE 7.22

Consider a program $\mathbf{P} = \{P(a) \leftarrow Q(x) \wedge \neg P(b), Q(a)\}$

$\mathit{Ground}(\mathbf{P}) = \{P(a) \leftarrow Q(a) \wedge \neg P(b), P(a) \leftarrow Q(b) \wedge \neg P(b), Q(a)\}$

$\mathcal{HB}(\mathbf{P}) \quad = \{P(a), P(b), Q(a), Q(b)\}$

Since $\mathcal{HB}(\mathbf{P})$ has four elements, 3^4 different interpretations of $\mathbf{P}$ are possible. In particular, consider the following two interpretations v and w:

$v(Q(a)) = \mathbf{T}$	$w(Q(a)) = \mathbf{T}$
$v(Q(b)) = \mathbf{F}$	$w(Q(b)) = \mathbf{F}$
$v(P(a)) = \perp$	$w(P(a)) = \mathbf{T}$
$v(P(b)) = \mathbf{F}$	$w(P(b)) = \mathbf{F}$

It can easily be verified that $\phi_{\mathbf{P}}(v) = w$.

The operator $\phi_{\mathbf{P}}$ is an order-preserving operator on the space of three-valued interpretations and has a least fixed point. This fixed point gives meaningful semantics for a logic program. Semantics given by using $\phi_{\mathbf{P}}$ does not require any stratification assumption.

Exercises

7.1 For each of the following stratified programs derive the standard model by computing (a) the minimal supported model, (b) the fixpoint, (c) the unique stable model, and (d) the well-founded model. Also, compute the completion for each of the programs.

Program:

$Open(x, y) \leftarrow Open(x, z) \wedge Open(z, y)$
$Open(x, y) \leftarrow Road(x, y) \wedge \neg Closed(x, y)$
$Closed(x, y) \leftarrow RoadWork(x, y)$
$Closed(x, y) \leftarrow Accident(x, y)$
$Closed(x, y) \leftarrow SpecialEvent(x, y)$
$Road(Junction\,1, Junction\,2)$
$Road(Junction\,1, Junction\,3)$
$Road(Junction\,2, Junction\,4)$
$Road(Junction\,3, Junction\,4)$
$RoadWork(Junction\,2, Junction\,3)$

Program:

$Student(x, y) \leftarrow Registered(x, y) \wedge \neg Suspended(x)$
$FullTime(x, y) \leftarrow Student(x, y) \wedge FeesPaid(x)$
$PartTime(x, y) \leftarrow Student(x, y) \wedge ResearchAssociate(x, z)$
$Registered(a, Math)$
$Registered(b, Computer)$
$ResearchAssociate(b, Math)$

7.2 Convert the following extended normal program to its equivalent normal program and then try to construct a successful SLDNF-derivation for the goal $\leftarrow Group(x, y)$.

$$Group(x_{set}, y_{op}) \leftarrow$$
$$Closure(x_{set}, y_{op}) \wedge Associative(x_{set}, y_{op}) \wedge$$
$$Identity(x_{set}, y_{op}, z_{id}) \wedge Inverse(x_{set}, y_{op}, z_{id})$$

$$Closure(x_{set}, y_{op}) \leftarrow$$
$$\forall x_e \forall y_e \forall z_e (Element(x_{set}, z_e) \leftarrow Element(x_{set}, x_e) \wedge$$
$$Element(x_{set}, y_e) \wedge Operation(x_{set}, y_{op}, x_e, y_e, z_e))$$

$$Associative(x_{set}, y_{op}) \leftarrow$$
$$\forall x_e \forall y_e \forall z_e \forall x_e^1 \forall x_e^2 \forall y_e^1 \forall y_e^2 (Equal(x_e^2, y_e^2) \leftarrow$$
$$Element(x_{set}, x_e) \wedge Element(x_{set}, y_e) \wedge Element(x_{set}, z_e) \wedge$$
$$Operation(x_{set}, y_{op}, x_e, y_e, x_e^1) \wedge Operation(x_{set}, y_{op}, x_e^1, z_e, x_e^2) \wedge$$
$$Operation(x_{set}, y_{op}, y_e, z_e, y_e^1) \wedge Operation(x_{set}, y_{op}, x_e\ y_e^1, y_e^2))$$

$$Identity(x_{set}, y_{op}, z_{id}) \leftarrow$$
$$Element(x_{set}, z_{id}) \wedge \forall x_e \forall x_e^1 \forall y_e^1 (Equal(x_e, x_e^1) \wedge Equal(x_e^1, y_e^1) \leftarrow$$
$$Element(x_{set}, x_e) \wedge Operation(x_{set}, y_{op}, x_e, z_{id}, x_e^1) \wedge$$
$$Operation(x_{set}, y_{op}, z_{id}, x_e, y_e^1))$$

$$Inverse(x_{set}, y_{op}, z_{id}) \leftarrow$$
$$Element(x_{set}, z_{id}) \wedge \forall x_e \exists x_{inv} \forall x_e^1 \forall y_e^1 (Equal(x_e^1, z_{id}) \wedge$$
$$Equal(y_e^1, z_{id}) \leftarrow Element(x_{set}, x_e) \wedge Element(x_{set}, x_{inv}) \wedge$$
$$Operation(x_{set}, y_{op}, x_e, x_{inv}, x_e^1) \wedge Operation(x_{set}, y_{op}, x_{inv}, x_e, y_e^1))$$

Element (*Integer* 3, 1)
Element (*Integer* 3, 2)
Element (*Integer* 3, 3)
Element (*Complex* 4, 1)
Element (*Complex* 4, −1)
Element (*Complex* 4, *i*)
Element (*Complex* 4, −*i*)
Operation (*Integer* 3, *PlusMod* 3, *x*, *y*, *mod* (*x*+*y*, 3))
Operation (*Integer* 3, *MultMod* 3, *x*, *y*, *mod* (*x***y*, 3))
Operation (*Complex*, *Multcplx*, 1, *x*, *x*)
Operation (*Complex*, *Multcplx*, −1, −1, 1)
Operation (*Complex*, *Multcplx*, −1, *i*, −*i*)
Operation (*Complex*, *Multcplx*, −1, −*i*, *i*)
Operation (*Complex*, *Multcplx*, *i*, *i*, −1)
Operation (*Complex*, *Multcplx*, *i*, −*i*, 1)
Operation (*Complex*, *Multcplx*, −*i*, −*i*, −1)
Operation (*Complex*, *Multcplx*, *x*, *y*, *z*) ←
    Operation (*Complex*, *Multcplx*, *y*, *x*, *z*)

8

Disjunctive programs and general programs

This chapter discusses disjunctive as well as general programs. Circumscription is also introduced in this chapter to allow dealing with arbitrary first-order formulae rather than just program clauses. It should be noted that results related to general programs are also applicable to disjunctive programs as the latter are a subclass of the former. Recall that a general program is defined as a finite set of clauses of the form

$$A_1 \vee \cdots \vee A_m \leftarrow L_1 \wedge \cdots \wedge L_n, \qquad m \geq 1, n \geq 0 \tag{8.1}$$

and a *goal* is defined as a clause of the form

$$\leftarrow M_1 \wedge \cdots \wedge M_r, \qquad r \geq 1 \tag{8.2}$$

where A_is are atoms and L_js and M_js are literals. An alternative form of clause (8.1) is

$$A_1 \vee \cdots \vee A_m \leftarrow M_1 \wedge \cdots \wedge M_p \wedge \neg N_1 \wedge \cdots \wedge \neg N_q \tag{8.3}$$

where A_is, M_js and N_ks are atoms. Each clause in a *disjunctive program* has the same form as (8.1) except that each L_i is an atom instead of a literal. A *definite goal* has the form of (8.2), where each M_i is an atom.

8.1 Disjunctive programs

This section focuses on declarative and procedural semantics for disjunctive programs. Semantics for negation for this class of programs are studied using the generalized closed world assumption, the disjunctive database rule. The fixpoint operator is generalized to give fixpoint semantics for this class of programs.

8.1.1 Minimal model semantics for disjunctive programs

Unlike definite programs, a disjunctive program does not necessarily possess a unique smallest *minimal model*. For example, the disjunctive program $\{P \vee Q\}$ has three models $\{P\}$, $\{Q\}$ and $\{P, Q\}$ and none of them is the smallest. But each of $\{P\}$ and $\{Q\}$ is smaller than $\{P, Q\}$ and is called a minimal model. Therefore, a model $\mathbf{M}$ for a disjunctive program $\mathbf{P}$ is minimal if no other model of $\mathbf{P}$ is strictly smaller than $\mathbf{M}$. A ground atom A is taken as true if and only if it is true in all minimal models for $\mathbf{P}$. Also, the ground assertions logically implied by $\mathbf{P}$ are exactly the ones that are true in all minimal models. In other words, if D is a ground assertion, then $\mathbf{P} \models \mathrm{D}$ if and only if D is true in every minimal model for $\mathbf{P}$.

EXAMPLE 8.1

Consider the program $\mathbf{P} = \{P(a), P(a) \vee Q(a), Q(b), R(x) \vee S(x) \leftarrow Q(x)\}$. The two minimal models of $\mathbf{P}$ are $\{P(a), Q(b), R(b)\}$ and $\{P(a), Q(b), S(b)\}$.

8.1.2 Fixpoint semantics for disjunctive programs

The fixpoint operator defined for definite programs is now generalized to give fixpoint semantics for disjunctive programs (Minker and Rajasekar, 1989). First, though, the concept of the Herbrand base must be extended.

Definition 8.1: The *extended Herbrand base* (also known as *disjunctive Herbrand base*), denoted as $\mathcal{EHB}(\mathbf{P})$, is the set of all assertions formed by using distinct atoms from $\mathcal{HB}(\mathbf{P})$.

EXAMPLE 8.2

If $\mathbf{P} = \{P(a), Q(a) \vee Q(b)\}$, then $\mathcal{HB}(\mathbf{P}) = \{P(a), Q(a), Q(b)\}$ and therefore $\mathcal{EHB}(\mathbf{P}) = \{P(a), Q(a), Q(b), P(a) \vee Q(a), P(a) \vee Q(b), Q(a) \vee Q(b), P(a) \vee Q(a) \vee Q(b)\}$.

An extended fixpoint operator $T_P: \mathcal{P}(\mathcal{EHB}(\mathbf{P})) \rightarrow \mathcal{P}(\mathcal{EHB}(\mathbf{P}))$ in the case of disjunctive programs has been defined as follows (Minker and Rajasekar, 1989):

$T_P(\mathbf{S}) = \{A' \in \mathcal{EHB}(\mathbf{P}) |$ $D \leftarrow B_1 \wedge \cdots \wedge B_n$ is a clause in $\mathcal{G}round(\mathbf{P})$ and $B_1 \vee D_1, ..., B_n \vee D_n$ are in $\mathbf{S}$, where each D_i is a disjunction (may be empty) of atoms and A' is the smallest factor of $D \vee D_1 \vee \cdots \vee D_n\}$

The operator is a direct generalization of the fixpoint operator defined for definite programs in Chapter 6. The least fixpoint of the operator T_P characterizes the minimal models of $\mathbf{P}$. Consider the following example which constructs the least fixpoint of a program.

EXAMPLE 8.3

Consider the program $\mathbf{P} = \{P(a), P(a) \vee Q(a), Q(b), R(x) \vee S(x) \leftarrow Q(x)\}$.

$$T_P \uparrow 1 = \{P(a), P(a) \vee Q(a), Q(b)\}$$
$$T_P \uparrow 2 = \{P(a), P(a) \vee Q(a), Q(b), R(a) \vee S(a) \vee P(a), R(b) \vee S(b)\}$$
$$T_P \uparrow \omega = T_P \uparrow 2$$

8.1.3 SLI-resolution

SLI-resolution (Minker and Rajasekar, 1988) (SL-resolution for Indefinite clauses) is the counterpart of SLD-resolution for handling disjunctive programs and it closely follows SL-resolution. The resolution scheme operates on admissible and minimal t-clauses. The definition of a t-clause is given below.

Definition 8.2: A t*-clause* τ is a labelled tree together with a marking relation. The root of the tree is a distinguished symbol ε and other nodes are labelled with literals. Every non-terminal node of the tree is marked by '*'. A marked literal is an A-literal and an unmarked literal is a B-literal. A tree is equivalently represented by a well-parenthesised expression. Every literal which is immediately followed by an open parenthesis is a marked literal.

EXAMPLE 8.4

The t-clause $(\varepsilon^* \ A \ (B^* \ C \ (D^* \ \neg E \ F)) \ G)$ represents the tree in Figure 8.1.

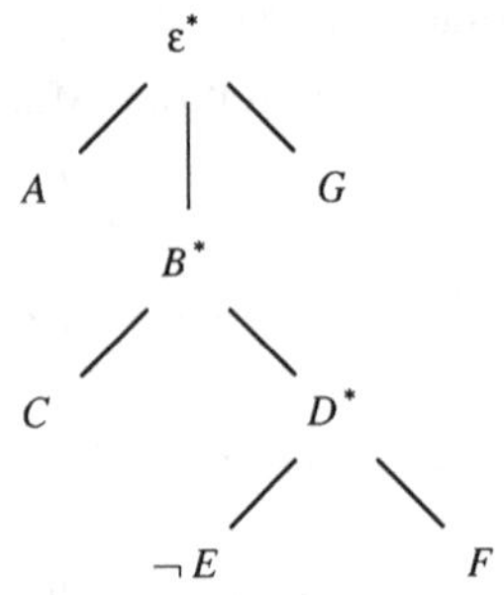

Figure 8.1 A t-clause.

Every disjunctive clause $A_1 \vee \cdots \vee A_m \leftarrow M_1 \wedge \cdots \wedge M_n$ is represented as a t-clause by

$$(\varepsilon^* \; A_1 \; \cdots \; A_m \; \neg M_1 \; \cdots \; \neg M_n).$$

In an SLI-resolution scheme, a literal is marked if it has been selected in an SLI-derivation and resolved with a program clause. The resolvent is attached as a subtree to the literal resolved upon. The resolvent clause is then made admissible and minimal by performing factoring, ancestory resolution and truncation as in the case of SL-resolution. The following two sets of literals are used during the resolution process:

$\Gamma_L = \{M | M$ is a B-literal and M is one node off the path from the parent of $L\}$
$\Delta_L = \{N | N$ is an A-literal and N is on the path between root and $L\}$

EXAMPLE 8.5
In Figure 8.1, $\Gamma_F = \{C\}$ and $\Delta_F = \{B^*, D^*\}$.

The above two sets Γ_L and Δ_L are used in the definitions of *t-factoring*, *t-ancestory* and *t-truncation*.

Definition 8.3: A t-clause D is obtained from another t-clause C by t-factoring if and only if

(1) C is $(e_1 \, L \, e_2 \, M \, e_3)$, and
(2) L and M have the same sign and unify with an mgu θ, and

(3) L is in Γ_M (resp. M is in Γ_L), and

(4) D is $(e_1\theta\, L\theta^*\ e_2\theta\, e_3\theta)$ (resp. $(e_1\theta\, e_2\theta\, M\theta^*\ e_3\theta)$)

Definition 8.4: A t-clause D is obtained from another t-clause C by t-ancestory if and only if

(1) C is $(e_1\,(L\ e_2\,(e_3\,M\ e_4)\,e_5\,)\,e_6)$, and

(2) L and M are complementary to each other and their atoms unify with an mgu θ, and

(3) L is in Δ_M, and

(4) D is $(e_1\theta\,(L\theta^*\ e_2\theta\,(e_3\theta\, e_4\theta)\,e_5\theta\,)\,e_6\theta)$

Definition 8.5: A t-clause D is obtained from another t-clause C by t-truncation if and only if

(1) C is $(e_1\,(L^*)\,e_2)$ (resp. (ε^*)), and

(2) D is $(e_1\,e_2)$ (resp. □).

Clearly, the above notions of factoring, ancestory and truncation are similar to those used in the SL-resolution.

Definition 8.6: A t-clause C is said to be a *tranfac-derivation* (truncation, ancestory and factoring) of another t-clause C_0 if there exists a sequence of t-clauses C_0, C_1, ..., C_n such that each C_{i+1} is obtained from C_i by either t-truncation, t-ancestory or t-factoring.

Definition 8.7: A t-clause is admissible, or equivalently a t-clause is said to satisfy the admissibility condition, if it cannot be factored or ancestory resolved. A t-clause is minimal or equivalently a t-clause is said to satisfy the minimality condition, if it cannot be truncated.

In other words, a t-clause C is said to satisfy the admissibility condition if for every occurrence of every B-literal L in a t-clause C

(1) no literal from Γ_L and the literal L have atoms unifying each other, and

(2) no literal from Δ_L and the literal L have the atoms unifying each other.

Similarly, if there is no A-literal in a t-clause C which is a terminal node, then C is said to satisfy the minimality condition.

Definition 8.8: An *SLI-derivation* of a t-clause C_n from a disjunctive program **P** with top t-clause $(\varepsilon^* \neg C)$ is a sequence of t-clauses $C_1, ..., C_n$ satisfying the following conditions:

(1) C_1 is a tranfac-derivation of C.

(2) Each C_{i+1} $(0 \leq i < n)$ is obtained from C_i and a program clause B_{i+1} in the following way:

  (a) C_i has the form $(\varepsilon^* \; e_1 \, L \, e_2)$ and B_{i+1} has the form $(\varepsilon^* \; e_3 \, M \, e_4)$ and L is a *selected literal.*

  (b) L and M are complementary and their atoms unify with an mgu θ.

  (c) C'_{i+1} is $(\varepsilon^* \; e_1\theta \, (L\theta^* \; e_3\theta \, e_4\theta) \, e_2\theta)$.

  (d) C_{i+1} is a tranfac-derivation of C'_{i+1}.

  (e) C_{i+1} satisfies the admissibility and minimality conditions.

An *SLI-refutation* from a program **P** with top t-clause $(\varepsilon^* \neg C)$ is an SLI-derivation of an empty clause $\square$. The following example demonstrates an SLI-refutation.

EXAMPLE 8.6

Consider the following program **P** and goal G:

$\mathbf{P} = \{P \leftarrow Q, P \leftarrow R \wedge S, Q \vee R, S\}$
$G = \leftarrow P$

t-clause representation of **P** is

$$\{(\varepsilon^* \; P \; \neg Q), (\varepsilon^* \; P \; \neg R \; \neg S), (\varepsilon^* \; Q \; R), (\varepsilon^* \; S)\}$$

t-clause representation of G is $(\varepsilon^* \; \neg P)$

Step 1:	$(\varepsilon^* \; P \; \neg Q)$	Given clause
Step 2:	$(\varepsilon^* \; P \; \neg R \; \neg S)$	Given clause
Step 3:	$(\varepsilon^* \; Q \; R)$	Given clause
Step 4:	$(\varepsilon^* \; S)$	Given clause
Step 5:	$(\varepsilon^* \; \neg P)$	Given goal
Step 6:	$(\varepsilon^* \; (\neg P^* \; \neg Q))$	Derivation (steps 1 and 5)

Step 7:	$(\varepsilon^* (\neg P^* (\neg Q^* R)))$	Derivation (steps 3 and 6)
Step 8:	$(\varepsilon^* (\neg P^* (\neg Q^* (R^* P \neg S))))$	Derivation (steps 2 and 7)
Step 9:	$(\varepsilon^* (\neg P^* (\neg Q^* (R^* \neg S))))$	Ancestory (step 8)
Step 10:	$(\varepsilon^* (\neg P^* (\neg Q^* (R^* \neg S^*))))$	Derivation (steps 4 and 9)
Step 11:	$\square$	Truncation (step 10)

SLINF-resolution (Minker and Rajasekar, 1988) is a further extension of SLI-resolution for deriving assertions from top clauses.

8.1.4 Equivalence among semantics

The success set in the case of a disjunctive program **P** is defined as follows:

$$\mathcal{S}(\mathbf{P}) = \{A_1 \vee \cdots \vee A_n \in \mathcal{EHB}(\mathbf{P}) \mid \text{there is an SLI-refutation from } \mathbf{P} \text{ with top clause } (\varepsilon^* \neg A_1 \cdots \neg A_n)\}$$

The following theorem (Minker and Rajasekar, 1989) establishes the equivalence between declarative, procedural and fixpoint semantics in disjunctive programs.

Theorem 8.1: Suppose **P** is a disjunctive program and D is an assertion. Then the following statements are equivalent:

(1) D is a logical consequence of **P**.

(2) D is true in every minimal model of **P**.

(3) D is a logical consequence of $T_{\mathbf{P}} \uparrow \omega$.

(4) D is a member of $\mathcal{S}(\mathbf{P})$.

Proof Left as an exercise. ■

8.1.5 The generalized closed world assumption

By considering the disjunctive program $\{P(a) \vee Q(a)\}$, it can be concluded (see Chapter 6) that the CWA rule may be inconsistent for disjunctive programs and hence for general programs too. The *Generalized Closed World Assumption* (GCWA) (Minker, 1988a) generalizes the concept of CWA. GCWA is a rule for inferring negative information from disjunctive programs and is defined in terms of minimal models as follows. The rule GCWA states that $\neg A$ may be inferred from a disjunctive program **P** if A is not in any minimal model for **P**. Thus

$$\mathcal{GCWA}(\mathbf{P}) = \{\neg A \mid A \text{ is not in any minimal model for } \mathbf{P}\}$$

The syntactic definition of GCWA can be given as follows. Consider a set $\mathbf{S}$ consisting of all disjunctions of the form $A_1 \vee \cdots \vee A_n$, where each A_i is a ground atom and $A_1 \vee \cdots \vee A_n$ is derivable from $\mathbf{P}$, and any proper subdisjunction of $A_1 \vee \cdots \vee A_n$ is not derivable from $\mathbf{P}$. The unit clauses of $\mathbf{S}$ are *definitely true* in $\mathbf{P}$. Atoms occurring in a disjunction containing at least two literals are *possibly true* in $\mathbf{P}$. An atom of $\mathcal{HB}(\mathbf{P})$ which does not occur in any disjunction of $\mathbf{S}$ can be taken as *definitely false* or negative.

EXAMPLE 8.7

$\mathbf{P} = \{P(a), P(a) \vee Q(a), Q(b), R(x) \vee S(x) \leftarrow Q(x)\}$

$\mathcal{HB}(\mathbf{P}) = \{P(a), P(b), Q(a), Q(b), R(a), R(b), S(a), S(b)\}$

$\mathbf{S} = \{P(a), Q(b), R(b) \vee S(b)\}$

$\mathcal{A}tom(\mathbf{S}) = \{P(a), Q(b), R(b), S(b)\}$

$\mathcal{GCWA}(\mathbf{P}) = \{\neg P(b), \neg Q(a), \neg R(a), \neg S(a)\}$

Thus $P(a)$ and $Q(b)$ are definitely true in $\mathbf{P}$, $R(b)$ and $S(b)$ are possibly true in $\mathbf{P}$ and the negation of each member of GCWA($\mathbf{P}$) is definitely false. In Example 8.7, that the ground atom $Q(a)$ has been taken as false demonstrates that GCWA is not inclusive. In the domain of normal programs, the NAF rule is more powerful than the GCWA. The following example demonstrates one such case.

EXAMPLE 8.8

Consider the program $\{P(a) \leftarrow \neg Q(a)\}$. Now, $P(a)$ can be inferred as definitely true and $Q(a)$ can be inferred as definitely false from the program by applying the NAF rule. On the other hand, GCWA treats the program as the disjunctive program $\{P(a) \vee Q(a)\}$ and infers each of $P(a)$ and $Q(a)$ as possibly true only.

The GCWA is concise, consistent and invariant, but neither decreasing nor inclusive. The GCWA reduces to the CWA for definite programs and thus the GCWA is a consistent extension of the CWA.

The set of all definitely true facts in a disjunctive program $\mathbf{P}$ is its success set $\mathcal{S}(\mathbf{P})$. Thus minimal model semantics can be used in conjunction with the GCWA to obtain the complete meaning of disjunctive programs.

8.1.6 The extended generalized closed world assumption

The GCWA rule can only infer ground negative literals from a disjunctive program. The *Extended Generalized Closed World Assumption* (EGCWA) (Yahya and Henschen, 1985) extends the GCWA to infer ground negative clauses from disjunctive programs. The semantic definition of the EGCWA is given as follows. A negative ground clause $\neg A_1 \vee \cdots \vee \neg A_n$ can be inferred from a program $\mathbf{P}$ if and only if it is true in every minimal model for $\mathbf{P}$. Thus

$$\mathcal{EGCWA}(\mathbf{P}) = \{\neg A_1 \vee \cdots \vee \neg A_n \mid \text{none of the minimal models of } \mathbf{P} \text{ should contain all of } A_1, ..., A_n\}$$

EXAMPLE 8.9

Suppose $\mathbf{P} = \{P(a), P(b) \vee Q(b)\}$. The minimal models of $\mathbf{P}$ are $\{P(a), P(b)\}$ and $\{P(a), Q(b)\}$. Then GCWA($\mathbf{P}$) = $\{\neg Q(a)\}$ and EGCWA($\mathbf{P}$) infers $\neg Q(a)$, $\neg P(a) \vee \neg Q(a)$, $\neg P(b) \vee \neg Q(a)$, $\neg P(b) \vee \neg Q(b)$ and so on.

The syntactic definition of the EGCWA is given as follows. A non-unit ground negative clause $\neg A_1 \vee \cdots \vee \neg A_n$ may not be assumed if and only if there exists a positive or empty disjunction K such that, for all i $(1 \le i \le n)$, $A_i \vee \mathrm{K}$ is a logical consequence of $\mathbf{P}$ whereas K is not. The EGCWA reduces to the GCWA if every element of EGCWA($\mathbf{P}$) is a unit clause. Thus the EGCWA is a consistent extension of the GCWA and hence the CWA too.

8.1.7 The weakly generalized closed world assumption

The *Weakly Generalized Closed World Assumption* (WGCWA) is a rule for inferring negative information from disjunctive programs and is defined in terms of the fixpoint operator $\mathrm{T}_{\mathbf{P}}$ as follows:

$$\mathcal{WGCWA}(\mathbf{P}) = \{\neg A \mid A \in \mathcal{HB}(\mathbf{P}) - \mathcal{A}tom(\mathrm{T}_{\mathbf{P}} \uparrow \omega)\}$$

where $\mathcal{A}tom(\mathbf{S})$ is the set of all atoms occurring in the clauses of $\mathbf{S}$. The following example demonstrates why the WGCWA is weaker than the GCWA.

EXAMPLE 8.10

Consider the following program $\mathbf{P}$:

$$\begin{aligned}
\mathbf{P} = \quad & \{P(x) \vee Q(x) \leftarrow R(x), R(a), P(a)\} \\
\mathcal{HB}(\mathbf{P}) = \quad & \{P(a), Q(a), R(a)\} \\
\mathrm{T}_{\mathbf{P}} \uparrow \omega = \quad & \{P(a), R(a), P(a) \vee Q(a)\} \\
\mathcal{A}tom(\mathrm{T}_{\mathbf{P}} \uparrow \omega) = \quad & \{P(a), Q(a), R(a)\} \\
\mathcal{GCWA}(\mathbf{P}) = \quad & \{\neg Q(a)\} \\
\mathcal{WGCWA}(\mathbf{P}) = \quad & \{\}
\end{aligned}$$

Another semantics for negation for disjunctive programs, which is equivalent to the above WGCWA and which interprets disjunction inclusively, is introduced below.

8.1.8 The disjunctive database rule

The *Disjunctive Database Rule* (DDR) (Ross and Topor, 1988) is expressed in terms of closed sets which are defined as follows.

Definition 8.9: Let $\mathbf{P}$ be a program and $\mathbf{S}$ be a subset of $\mathcal{HB}(\mathbf{P})$. Then $\mathbf{S}$ is a *closed set* of $\mathbf{P}$ if for every element A of $\mathbf{S}$, and for every clause C in $\mathcal{G}round(\mathbf{P})$ such that A is in the head of C, there exists an atom B in the body of C such that B is in $\mathbf{S}$. The union of the set of closed sets of a program $\mathbf{P}$ is also a closed set and is defined as the *greatest closed set* of $\mathbf{P}$, denoted by $\mathcal{GCS}(\mathbf{P})$.

By the DDR, a ground atom A can be taken as false in $\mathbf{P}$ or $\neg A$ can be inferred from $\mathbf{P}$ by the DDR if A is in $\mathcal{GCS}(\mathbf{P})$, that is

$$\mathcal{DDR}_d(\mathbf{P}) = \{\neg A \mid A \in \mathcal{GCS}(\mathbf{P})\}$$

If $\mathbf{P}$ is a disjunctive program and $\mathbf{I}$ is a Herbrand interpretation of $\mathbf{P}$ then consider an alternative definition of fixpoint mapping for disjunctive program:

$$\mathrm{T}_{\mathbf{P}}(\mathbf{I}) = \{A \in \mathcal{HB}(\mathbf{P}) \mid \text{C is in } \mathcal{G}round(\mathbf{P}), A \text{ is in the head of C and for all } B \text{ in the body of C}, B \in \mathbf{I}\}$$

This definition also generalizes the definition given in Chapter 6 for definite programs. The mapping is continuous and monotonic and hence $\mathrm{T}_{\mathbf{P}} \uparrow \omega$ is the fixpoint of $\mathrm{T}_{\mathbf{P}}$. The fixpoint definition of the DDR is

$$\mathcal{DDR}_f(\mathbf{P}) = \{\neg A \mid A \in \mathcal{HB}(\mathbf{P}) - \mathrm{T}_{\mathbf{P}} \uparrow \omega\}$$

The declarative definition and the fixpoint definition coincide, that is

$$\mathcal{DDR}_d(\mathbf{P}) = \mathcal{DDR}_f(\mathbf{P}) = \mathcal{DDR}(\mathbf{P})$$

The definition of DDR can be extended to layered programs and is described below.

Definition 8.10: Let $(\mathbf{P}, \mathcal{L})$ be a layered disjunctive program where $\mathbf{P}$ is a disjunctive program and $\mathcal{L}$ is a level mapping. Then $\mathbf{S}$ is a closed set of $(\mathbf{P}, \mathcal{L})$ if for every element A of $\mathbf{S}$, and for clause C in $\mathcal{Ground}(\mathbf{P})$, if A is in the head of C then either

(1) there is an atom B occurring in C such that $\mathcal{L}(B) > \mathcal{L}(A)$, or
(2) there is an atom B in the body of C such that B is in $\mathbf{S}$.

As in the case of disjunctive programs, the union of all closed sets of a layered program is also a closed set and called the greatest closed set.

The definition of the DDR for a layered program $(\mathbf{P}, \mathcal{L})$ is that $\neg A$ can be inferred from $(\mathbf{P}, \mathcal{L})$ if A is in $\mathcal{GCS}(\mathbf{P}, \mathcal{L})$, that is

$$\mathcal{DDR}_d(\mathbf{P}, \mathcal{L}) = \{\neg A \mid A \in \mathcal{GCS}(\mathbf{P}, \mathcal{L})\}$$

The mapping $\mathrm{T}_{(\mathbf{P},\, \mathcal{L})}$ for defining the fixpoint semantics can be given as follows. Let $(\mathbf{P}, \mathcal{L})$ be a layered program and $\mathbf{I}$ be a Herbrand interpretation of $\mathbf{P}$.

$$\mathrm{T}_{(\mathbf{P},\, \mathcal{L})} = \{A \in \mathcal{HB}(\mathbf{P}) \mid \text{C is a clause in } \mathcal{Ground}(\mathbf{P}),\ A \text{ is in the head of C, } \mathcal{L}(A) = \mathcal{L}(C), \text{ and for each } B \text{ in the body of C, } B \in \mathbf{I}\}$$

The fixpoint definition of the DDR for a layered program $(\mathbf{P}, \mathcal{L})$ is defined as follows:

$$\mathcal{DDR}_f(\mathbf{P}, \mathcal{L}) = \{\neg A \mid A \in \mathcal{HB}(\mathbf{D}) - \mathrm{T}_{(\mathbf{P},\, \mathcal{L})}\uparrow\omega\}$$

The declarative definition and the fixpoint definition for layered program coincide, that is

$$\mathcal{DDR}_d(\mathbf{P}, \mathcal{L}) = \mathcal{DDR}_d(\mathbf{P}, \mathcal{L}) = \mathcal{DDR}(\mathbf{P}, \mathcal{L})$$

Now, a procedural definition of the DDR for layered program, called PL-resolution, is developed and a NAF-like rule called the *Negation as Positive Failure* (NPF) rule is defined in the context of this resolution.

Definition 8.11: Let G be a definite goal $\leftarrow M_1 \wedge \cdots \wedge M_p$ and C be the clause

$$A_1 \vee \cdots \vee A_m \leftarrow B_1 \wedge \cdots \wedge B_n$$

and $\mathcal{L}$ be a level mapping and the selected atom for the goal is M_q, $1 \leq q \leq p$. Then the goal

$$\leftarrow (M_1 \wedge \cdots \wedge M_{q-1} \wedge B_1 \wedge \cdots \wedge B_n \wedge M_{q+1} \wedge \cdots \wedge M_p)\theta$$

is *positively derived* from G and C, where $\mathcal{L}(A_r) = \mathcal{L}(\mathrm{C})$, for some r, and θ is an mgu of M_q and A_r.

Definition 8.12: A *Positive Linear derivation* (PL-derivation) of a layered program $(\mathbf{P}, \mathcal{L})$ and a goal G consists of a sequence $G_0 = G$, G_1, ... of goals, a sequence C_1, C_2, ... of variants of clauses from **P** and a sequence θ_1, θ_2, ... of mgus such that G_{i+1} is positively derived from G_i and C_{i+1} using θ_{i+1}.

The definitions of successful PL-derivation, failed PL-derivation and finitely failed PL-tree are similar to the definitions in the case of SLD-resolution.

Lemma 8.1: Let $(\mathbf{P}, \mathcal{L})$ be a layered program and A be a ground atom. If $A \in T_{(\mathbf{P}, \mathcal{L})}\uparrow n$, for some n, then $(\mathbf{P}, \mathcal{L}) \cup \{\leftarrow A\}$ has a successful PL-derivation.

Proof Similar to the case of definite programs. ■

The NPF rule states that $\neg A$ cannot be inferred if $(\mathbf{P}, \mathcal{L}) \cup \{\leftarrow A\}$ has a finitely failed PL-tree. Thus

$$\mathcal{NPF}(\mathbf{P}) = \{\neg A \mid (\mathbf{P}, \mathcal{L}) \cup \{\leftarrow A\} \text{ has a finitely failed PL-tree}\}$$

Theorem 8.2: (soundness of NPF rule) Let $(\mathbf{P}, \mathcal{L})$ be a layered program and A be a ground atom. If $(\mathbf{P}, \mathcal{L}) \cup \{\leftarrow A\}$ has a finitely failed PL-tree then $\neg A$ is inferred from $(\mathbf{P}, \mathcal{L})$ by the DDR.

Proof If possible let $\neg A$ be inferred from $(\mathbf{P}, \mathcal{L})$ by the DDR. Then $A \in T_{(\mathbf{P}, \mathcal{L})}\uparrow n$, for some n. By Lemma 8.1, $(\mathbf{P}, \mathcal{L}) \cup \{\leftarrow A\}$ has a successful PL-derivation which contradicts the fact that $(\mathbf{P}, \mathcal{L}) \cup \{\leftarrow A\}$ has a finitely failed PL-tree. ■

However, the NPF rule is sound but it is not complete as it is evident from the following examples (Ross and Topor, 1988).

EXAMPLE 8.11

Suppose a program $\mathbf{P}$ contains only the clause $P(x) \leftarrow P(x)$ and the level mapping $\mathcal{L}$ assigns the predicate P to 0. The greatest closed set of $\mathbf{P}$ is $\{P(a)\}$. Again, $\neg P(a)$ can be inferred by the DDR but the PL-tree for $(\mathbf{P}, \mathcal{L}) \cup \{\leftarrow P(a)\}$ is not finitely failed.

EXAMPLE 8.12

Suppose a program $\mathbf{P}$ contains only the clause $P(x) \leftarrow P(f(x))$ and the level mapping $\mathcal{L}$ assigns the predicate P to 0. $\mathcal{HB}(\mathbf{P}) = \{P(a), P(f(a)), ...\}$. The greatest closed set of $\mathbf{P}$ is $\{P(a), P(f(a)), P(f(f(a))), ...\}$. Since $P(a)$ is in $\mathcal{GCS}(\mathbf{P}, \mathcal{L})$, $\neg P(a)$ can be inferred by the DDR. But the PL-tree for $(\mathbf{P}, \mathcal{L}) \cup \{\leftarrow P(a)\}$ is not finitely failed.

An improved version of the NPF resolution, called *Acyclic Negation as Positive Failure resolution* (ANPF resolution) is developed in the following. ANPF resolution is different from NPF resolution to take account of infinite derivation.

Definition 8.13: Suppose $(\mathbf{P}, \mathcal{L})$ is a layered program. An *APL-derivation* of $(\mathbf{P}, \mathcal{L}) \cup \{G\}$ consists of a sequence $G_0 = G, G_1, ...$ of goals, a sequence $C_1, C_2, ...$ of variants of clauses from $\mathbf{P}$ and a sequence $\theta_1, \theta_2, ...$ of mgus such that G_{i+1} is positively derived from G_i and C_{i+1} using θ_{i+1} and for every pair of distinct ancestors A and B of the selected atoms A_m in G_i, $A\theta_1 \cdots \theta_i \neq B\theta_1 \cdots \theta_i$.

The definitions of successful APL-derivation, failed APL-derivation and finitely failed APL-tree are given accordingly.

The ANPF rule states that $\neg A$ may be inferred if $(\mathbf{P}, \mathcal{L}) \cup \{\leftarrow A\}$ has a finitely failed APL-tree. Thus

$\mathcal{ANPF}(\mathbf{P}) = \{\neg A \mid (\mathbf{P}, \mathcal{L}) \cup \{\leftarrow A\}$ has a finitely failed APL-tree$\}$

EXAMPLE 8.13

The ANPF rule can infer $\neg P(a)$ from the program $\{P(x) \leftarrow P(x)\}$ but cannot infer the same from the program $\{P(x) \leftarrow P(f(x))\}$.

The soundness of the ANPF rule follows from the fact that if $(\mathbf{P}, \mathcal{L}) \cup \{G\}$ has a successful PL-derivation then $(\mathbf{P}, \mathcal{L}) \cup \{G\}$ also has a successful APL-derivation.

The ANPF rule is complete wrt DDR for a *ground APL-tree* and in function-free programs. The definition of a ground APL-tree is as follows.

Definition 8.14: Suppose $(\mathbf{P}, \mathcal{L})$ is a layered program and G is a goal. Suppose a non-failed PL-derivation for $(\mathbf{P}, \mathcal{L}) \cup \{G\}$, say BR, is given by the sequence $G_0 = G, G_1, \ldots$ and the sequence $\theta_1, \theta_2, \ldots$ of mgus. Then BR is *grounded* if for every $i \geq 0$ and for every variable x in G_i, there exists $j > i$ such that $\theta_{i+1}, \ldots, \theta_j$ is a ground substitution for x. An APL-tree is ground if every non-failed branch of the tree is ground.

The following lemma is needed to establish the completeness result for the ANPF rule.

Lemma 8.2: Let $(\mathbf{P}, \mathcal{L})$ be a layered program and A be a ground atom. If $(\mathbf{P}, \mathcal{L}) \cup \{\leftarrow A\}$ has a successful APL-derivation then $A \in T_{(\mathbf{P}, \mathcal{L})} \uparrow n$ for some $n \geq 0$.

Proof The lemma can be proved as in the case of definite programs by using the following two facts:

(1) In the definition of the fixpoint operator $T_{(\mathbf{P}, \mathcal{L})}$, the atom selected from the head of a ground clause to be included in $T_{(\mathbf{P}, \mathcal{L})}(\mathbf{I})$ has the maximum level of all the atoms occurring in the clause.

(2) At any particular stage of the APL-derivation, the level of the selected atom is equal to the level of the variants for that stage. ■

Theorem 8.3: (completeness of ANPF rule) Let $(\mathbf{P}, \mathcal{L})$ be a function-free layered disjunctive program and A be a function-free ground atom. If $\neg A$ is inferred from $(\mathbf{P}, \mathcal{L})$ by the DDR, then every ground APL-tree for $(\mathbf{P}, \mathcal{L}) \cup \{\leftarrow A\}$ is finitely failed.

Proof If possible, suppose not every branch of the ground APL-tree for $(\mathbf{P}, \mathcal{L}) \cup \{\leftarrow A\}$ is finitely failed. Then $(\mathbf{P}, \mathcal{L}) \cup \{\leftarrow A\}$ has either a successful derivation or an infinite derivation. If $(\mathbf{P}, \mathcal{L}) \cup \{\leftarrow A\}$ has a successful APL-derivation, by Lemma 8.2, $A \in T_{(\mathbf{P}, \mathcal{L})} \uparrow n$ for some $n \geq 0$. From the equivalence of declarative and fixpoint semantics, $\neg A$ can be inferred from $(\mathbf{P}, \mathcal{L})$ by the DDR which contradicts the initial assumption.

Alternatively, if $(\mathbf{P}, \mathcal{L}) \cup \{\leftarrow A\}$ has an infinite grounded APL-derivation, say BR, with sequence $G_0 = G, G_1, \ldots$ of goals and $\theta_1, \theta_2, \ldots$ of mgus, then there exists an infinite sequence $A_1, A_2 \ldots$ of atoms from the sequence $G_0, G_1, \ldots$ such that A_i is the parent of A_{i+1}. As BR is an APL-derivation, there are no integers j, k, such that $j \neq k$ and $A_j\theta_1 \cdots \theta_p = A_k\theta_1 \cdots \theta_p$, for some $p \geq j, k$. The number of elements in $\mathcal{HB}(\mathbf{P})$ (say N) is finite as the program is function-free. Since the considered APL-derivation is grounded, for every integer $i \geq 1$, there exists an integer n_i such that $A\theta_1 \cdots \theta_{n_i}$ is ground. Hence at some stage of the derivation BR, an instantiated version of the sequence $A_1, A_2, \ldots$ will have N' different ground atoms where N' is greater than N. This contradicts the fact that $\mathcal{HB}(\mathbf{P})$ contains only N elements.

Hence the initial assumption is incorrect and every ground APL-tree for $(\mathbf{P}, \mathcal{L}) \cup \{\leftarrow A\}$ is finitely failed. ■.

8.2 General programs

This section deals with the class of general programs. Differential declarative semantics for general programs are studied by several proposals including generalized completion, semantics by possible forms and perfect model semantics. Resolution schemes like possible resolution give a flavour of the operational semantics for general programs.

8.2.1 General program completion

Similar to the case of normal programs, a type of completion for a general program $\mathbf{P}$, called *weak completion* (Lobo *et al.*, 1988; Minker and Rajasekar, 1988), is obtained by completing each predicate in the program and by adding the necessary equality axioms. The equality predicate symbol '=' is considered as usual. Predicates occurring in $\mathbf{P}$ are completed as follows. Suppose

$$P_1(t_1^1, \ldots, t_{p_1}^1) \vee \cdots \vee P_m(t_1^m, \ldots, t_{p_m}^m) \leftarrow L_1 \wedge \cdots \wedge L_n \tag{8.4}$$

is a general clause. Then execute the following steps with clause (8.4) as input.

- Step 1: Transform clause (8.4) to

$$\begin{array}{c} P_1(x_1^1, \ldots, x_{p_1}^1) \vee \cdots \vee P_m(x_1^m, \ldots, x_{p_m}^m) \leftarrow \\ (x_1^1 = t_1^1) \wedge \cdots \wedge (x_{p_m}^m = t_{p_m}^m) \wedge L_1 \wedge \cdots \wedge L_n \end{array} \tag{8.5}$$

where the variables x_i^js do not appear in clause (8.4).

- Step 2: Transform clause (8.5) to

$$\begin{array}{c} P_1(x_1^1, \ldots, x_{p_1}^1) \vee \cdots \vee P_m(x_1^m, \ldots, x_{p_m}^m) \leftarrow \\ \exists y_1 \cdots \exists y_q \, ((x_1^1 = t_1^1) \wedge \cdots \wedge (x_{p_m}^m = t_{p_m}^m) \wedge L_1 \wedge \cdots \wedge L_n) \end{array} \tag{8.6}$$

where $y_1, \ldots, y_q$ are the variables occurring in clause (8.4).

- Step 3: Split clause (8.6) into as many clauses as the number of atoms in its head as

$$\begin{array}{c} P_1(x_1^1, \ldots, x_{p_1}^1) \leftarrow \\ \exists y_1 \cdots \exists y_q \, ((x_1^1 = t_1^1) \wedge \cdots \wedge (x_{p_m}^m = t_{p_m}^m) \wedge L_1 \wedge \cdots \wedge L_n) \\ \vdots \\ P_m(x_1^m, \ldots, x_{p_m}^m) \leftarrow \\ \exists y_1 \cdots \exists y_q \, ((x_1^1 = t_1^1) \wedge \cdots \wedge (x_{p_m}^m = t_{p_m}^m) \wedge L_1 \wedge \cdots \wedge L_n) \end{array} \tag{8.7}$$

The above three-step transformations are applied to each clause in **P**. Let P be the predicate that appears in the head of some clause in **P** and let there be k transformed clauses with P in the head. Then the transformed set of clauses has the form

$$\begin{array}{l} P(x_1, \ldots, x_n) \leftarrow \mathrm{E}_1 \\ \quad\vdots \\ P(x_1, \ldots, x_n) \leftarrow \mathrm{E}_k \end{array} \tag{8.8}$$

where each E_i has the same form as the body of (8.6). The completed definition of the predicate P is the formula

$$\forall x_1 \cdots \forall x_n (P(x_1, \ldots, x_n) \rightarrow \mathrm{E}_1 \vee \cdots \vee \mathrm{E}_k) \tag{8.9}$$

When a predicate Q does not appear in the head of any program clause in **P** but appears in the body of some program clause in **P**, then completed definition of Q is the formula

$$\forall x_1 \cdots \forall x_n \neg Q(x_1, \ldots, x_n) \tag{8.10}$$

The weak completion of **P**, also denoted as $Comp(\mathbf{P})$, is the collection of completed definitions for each predicate of **P** together with the equality axioms. The completed program semantics for negative information in a general program **P** is as follows:

$$\mathcal{WCP}(\mathbf{P}) = \{\neg A \mid Comp(\mathbf{P}) \models \neg A\}$$

EXAMPLE 8.14

$$\begin{aligned} \mathbf{P} = \{&P(y) \vee Q(y) \leftarrow R(y), \\ &P(a) \leftarrow S(y) \wedge \neg T(a), \\ &R(a)\} \end{aligned}$$

$$\begin{aligned} Comp(\mathbf{P}) = \mathbf{P} \cup \{&\forall x (P(x) \rightarrow (\exists y (x = y \wedge R(y)) \vee \exists y (x = a \wedge S(y) \wedge \neg T(a)))), \\ &\forall x (Q(x) \rightarrow (\exists y (x = y \wedge R(y)))), \\ &\forall x (R(x) \rightarrow x = a), \\ &\forall x (\neg S(x)), \\ &\forall x (\neg T(x))\} \end{aligned}$$

As opposed to the case of normal programs, only one-sided implication is used in (8.9). If the implication is replaced by an if-and-only-if condition, the positive information that can be inferred from **P** may get modified. In the above example, if the clause $\forall x (Q(x) \rightarrow (\exists y (x = y \wedge R(y))))$ is replaced by $\forall x (Q(x) \leftrightarrow (\exists y (x = y \wedge R(y))))$ then $Q(a)$ would be a logical consequence of $Comp(\mathbf{P})$ which was obviously not intended in **P**.

Note that the completion of every general program is not necessarily consistent and this can be shown by considering the general program $\{P \leftarrow \neg P\}$. However, the completion of an arbitrary disjunctive program can be shown to be consistent.

Completed normal programs are used to study the NAF rule. Completed disjunctive programs are used to study the rule *Negation As Finite Failure for Non-Horn* (that is, disjunctive) (NAFFNH) programs. This rule is incorporated in the SLINF-resolution (Minker and Rajasekar, 1988). The soundness and completeness of this scheme with respect to the completion of disjunctive programs can be stated as follows. Let **P** be a definite program and A be a ground atom. Then $\mathbf{P} \cup \{\leftarrow A\}$ has a finitely failed SLINF-tree if and only if $\neg A$ is a logical consequence of $\mathit{Comp}(\mathbf{P})$. In a disjunctive program $\mathbf{P}$, $\mathcal{WCP}(\mathbf{P}) = \mathcal{WGCWA}(\mathbf{P})$.

8.2.2 Semantics by possible forms

The semantics of general programs introduced here is an improved version of the one described by Das (1990). By this semantics, the declarative concept of determining the truth functionality of a ground literal with respect to a general program is based on Clark's idea of completed normal programs. To define the declarative semantics, a general program is transformed to the set of its possible forms and the semantics is given in terms of the completion of each of these possible forms. A ground atom which can be derived from the completion of each of the possible forms associated with the general program is taken as true in the program: if its negation can be derived from the completion of each of them, it is taken to be false; otherwise, it is unknown. The procedural semantics is based on two mutually recursive resolution schemes. These two resolution schemes coincide and reduce to the mechanism of simple SLDNF-resolution when the program is normal.

Declarative semantics

Let $\mathbf{P}$ be a program. Let $\{\mathbf{P}_1, ..., \mathbf{P}_n\}$ be the set of all possible forms of $\mathbf{P}$ such that the completion of each $\mathbf{P}_i$ is consistent. Then the Herbrand base $\mathcal{HB}(\mathbf{P})$ can be partitioned into three subsets:

$$\mathit{DefTrue}(\mathbf{P}) = \bigcap_{i=1}^{n} \{A \mid A \in \mathcal{HB}(\mathbf{P}) \text{ and } \mathit{Comp}(\mathbf{P}_i) \vdash A\}$$

$$\mathit{DefFalse}(\mathbf{P}) = \bigcap_{i=1}^{n} \{A \mid A \in \mathcal{HB}(\mathbf{P}) \text{ and } \mathit{Comp}(\mathbf{P}_i) \vdash \neg A\}$$

$$\mathit{Unknown}(\mathbf{P}) = \mathcal{HB}(\mathbf{P}) - \mathit{DefTrue}(\mathbf{P}) \cup \mathit{DefFalse}(\mathbf{P})$$

The set of all facts in $\mathit{DefTrue}(\mathbf{P})$ can be taken as definitely true in $\mathbf{P}$ whereas the set of all facts in $\mathit{DefFalse}(\mathbf{P})$ are definitely false in $\mathbf{P}$. The facts in $\mathit{Unknown}(\mathbf{P})$ are possibly true in $\mathbf{P}$. Note that a fact becomes possibly true due to the presence of recursion among program clauses and also due to the presence of indefinite clauses in the program. Consider the following example.

EXAMPLE 8.15

If $\mathbf{P} = \{P(a) \leftarrow P(a)\}$, then the fact $P(a)$ becomes possibly true, that is, $P(a) \in \mathit{Unknown}(\mathbf{P})$. Also, $P(a)$ is possibly true in the program $\{P(a) \vee Q(a)\}$.

Clearly, when the program is normal the above definition of semantics reduces to the normal program completion. The definite resolution mechanism determines the elements of the set $\mathit{DefTrue}(\mathbf{P})$. The possible resolution mechanism is able to determine the set constituting of elements which are either in the set $\mathit{Unknown}(\mathbf{P})$ or in the set $\mathit{DefTrue}(\mathbf{P})$. An element of the Herbrand base which cannot be determined even by the possible resolution mechanism can be taken to be false and hence is a member of $\mathit{DefFalse}(\mathbf{P})$.

Procedural semantics

Procedural semantics is based on two mutually recursive resolution schemes, one for possible resolution and one for definite resolution.

Possible resolution

Each derivation of a possible resolution constructs a sequence of positive programs and a sequence of negative programs. A positive program corresponds to a possible form and negative programs help to keep track of the ground negative atoms resolved during a derivation. The marking process of clauses helps to construct different possible forms and also to avoid redundant computations. All the clauses in the program are unmarked before the start of a derivation.

Definition 8.15: Let $\mathbf{P}$ be a program, G be a goal and $\mathcal{R}$ be a computation rule. Initially, none of the clauses in $\mathbf{P}$ is marked as possibly used with respect to atoms occurring in their heads. A *possible derivation* for $\mathbf{P} \cup \{G\}$ via $\mathcal{R}$ consists of a sequence $\mathbf{P}_0^+ = \mathbf{P}, \mathbf{P}_1^+, \mathbf{P}_2^+, \ldots$ of positive programs, a sequence $\mathbf{P}_0^- = \{\}, \mathbf{P}_1^-, \mathbf{P}_2^-, \ldots$ of negative programs, a sequence $G_0 = G, G_1, G_2, \ldots$ of goals, a sequence $C_1, C_2, \ldots$ of variants of ground negative literals or program clauses from the possible forms of $\mathbf{P}$, and a sequence $\theta_1, \theta_2, \ldots$ of substitutions satisfying the following:

(1) For each i, G_i is $\leftarrow L_1 \wedge \cdots \wedge L_m \wedge \cdots \wedge L_p$, the selected literal L_m in G_i is

(a) A positive literal and L_m unifies with the head of a normal clause C = $A \leftarrow M_1 \wedge \cdots \wedge M_n$ in $\mathbf{P}_i^+$ with an mgu θ_{i+1}. Then C_{i+1} is C, $\mathbf{P}_{i+1}^+$ and $\mathbf{P}_{i+1}^-$ are respectively $\mathbf{P}_i^+$ and $\mathbf{P}_i^-$, and G_{i+1} is $\leftarrow (L_1 \wedge \cdots \wedge L_{m-1} \wedge M_1 \wedge \cdots \wedge M_n \wedge L_{m+1} \wedge \cdots \wedge L_p)\theta_{i+1}$.

(b) A positive literal and L_m unifies with an atom A occurring in the head of an indefinite clause C = H $\leftarrow M_1 \wedge \cdots \wedge M_n$ of $\mathbf{P}_i^+$ with an mgu θ_{i+1} and C has not been possibly used with respect to A. If for every member A' of $\mathbf{P}_i^-$, $\mathbf{P}_i^+ \cup \{pos(C, A)\} \cup \{\leftarrow A'\}$ has a finitely failed definite tree (introduced in the next subsection) then C_{i+1} is $pos(C, A)$, $\mathbf{P}_{i+1}^+$ and $\mathbf{P}_{i+1}^-$ are respectively $\mathbf{P}_i^+ \cup \{pos(C, A)\}$ and $\mathbf{P}_i^-$, and G_{i+1} is $\leftarrow (L_1 \wedge \cdots \wedge L_{m-1} \wedge M_1 \wedge \cdots \wedge M_n \wedge L_{m+1} \wedge \cdots \wedge L_p)\theta_{i+1}$. Finally, C is marked as possibly used with respect to A.

(c) A ground negative literal $\neg A$ and $\mathbf{P}_i^+ \cup \{\leftarrow A\}$ has a finitely failed definite tree. In this case, θ_{i+1} is an identity substitution, C_i is $\neg A$, $\mathbf{P}_{i+1}^+$ and $\mathbf{P}_{i+1}^-$ are respectively $\mathbf{P}_i^+$ and $\mathbf{P}_i^- \cup \{A\}$, and G_{i+1} is $\leftarrow L_1 \wedge \cdots \wedge L_{m-1} \wedge L_{m+1} \wedge \cdots \wedge L_p$.

(2) If the sequence $G_0, G_1, \ldots$ of goals is finite, then the last goal G_n of the sequence either is empty or has the form $\leftarrow L_1 \wedge \cdots \wedge L_m \wedge \cdots \wedge L_p$, where L_m is selected and

(a) L_m is an atom and there is no program clause in $\mathbf{P}_n^+$ for which any of the literals occurring in its head unifies with L_m, or

(b) L_m is an atom and there are program clauses $\{D_1, \ldots, D_l\}$ in $\mathbf{P}_n^+$ such that for each j, one of the atoms A occurring in the head H_j of D_j unifies with L_m. But, for each j, there exists a literal A' in $\mathbf{P}_n^-$ such that $\mathbf{P}_n^+ \cup \{pos(D_j, A)\} \cup \{\leftarrow A'\}$ has a definite refutation (introduced in the next subsection), or

(c) L_m is a ground negative literal of the form $\neg A$ and $\mathbf{P}_n^+ \cup \{\leftarrow A\}$ has a definite refutation.

When a goal is refuted by a possible resolution with an answer substitution θ, it can be said that the goal bound with the answer substitution θ is true in the last program of the sequence of positive programs. The sequence of negative programs keeps track of the ground negative atoms occurring in goals which have been inferred false by step 1(c). Thus a member of $\mathbf{P}_i^-$ is false in $\mathbf{P}_i^+$, for every i. To clarify the definition, consider Example 8.16.

EXAMPLE 8.16

Consider the following program **P**:

Program: $P(x) \leftarrow Q(x) \wedge \neg R(x) \wedge S(x)$

$R(a) \leftarrow S(a)$

$Q(a)$

$Q(b)$

$S(a) \vee S(b)$

Goal: $\leftarrow P(x)$

As each of the possible forms of **P** is hierarchical in nature, their completions are consistent. At the first step of execution of the goal $\leftarrow P(x)$ in the context of the above program, the selected literal $P(x)$ is resolved with the first clause of **P** producing $\leftarrow Q(x) \wedge \neg R(x) \wedge S(x)$ as the next goal. The next selected literal from this goal, $Q(x)$, unifies with $Q(a)$ yielding $\leftarrow \neg R(a) \wedge S(a)$. To execute step 1(c) on the selected negative literal $\neg R(a)$, a definite refutation of the goal $\leftarrow R(a)$ is attempted in the constructed positive program (which is **P** itself). As this is not possible, $\neg R(a)$ is taken as true and the only literal remaining in the goal is $S(a)$. At this stage the positive and negative programs are respectively **P** and $\{R(a)\}$.

To process the goal $\leftarrow S(a)$, it is possible to resolve it against the first atom $S(a)$ of the indefinite fact $S(a) \vee S(b)$. In this case, the positive program is updated by adding $S(a)$ to it, resulting in a definite refutation of the goal $\leftarrow R(a)$ in the updated positive program, where $R(a)$ has been taken from the latest negative program. The second clause of **P** is the main source of this refutation as it implicitly infers $R(a)$ from $S(a)$ which is inconsistent with $\neg R(a)$ which has already been inferred from the program. The resolution of the goal $\leftarrow Q(x) \wedge \neg R(x) \wedge S(x)$ with the fact $Q(b)$ will lead to the answer substitution $\{x/b\}$ since the inclusion of $S(b)$ in the positive program does not implicitly infer $R(b)$ at any stage.

The process of marking clauses in step 1(b) is necessary to construct different possible forms and also to avoid redundant answers. In the above example, when $S(a)$ is added to the positive program, it supersedes the indefinite fact $S(a) \vee S(b)$. In any subsequent use of $S(a)$, the definite fact $S(a)$ will be used rather than $S(a) \vee S(b)$.

Referring to the above, consider the case when the literal $S(a)$ is selected from the goal $\leftarrow \neg R(a) \wedge S(a)$, instead of $\neg R(a)$. In that case, the indefinite fact $S(a) \vee S(b)$ is the obvious candidate for resolving with the goal, causing the addition of the fact $S(a)$ to the positive program. It is quite clear that inferring the only negative literal selected from the resolved goal $\leftarrow \neg R(a)$ is not possible in the updated program due to the presence of the rule $R(a) \leftarrow S(a)$ and the fact $S(a)$.

The definitions of finite, infinite, successful, failed possible derivations, possible refutation, possible tree, finitely failed possible tree, and so on are defined in the usual way.

If each possible form of a program **P** is hierarchical, then the possible resolution in **P** is guaranteed to terminate, provided that the definite resolution of step 1(c) for resolving negative literals terminates.

Definite resolution

The definition of a definite derivation is given using a linear resolution theorem proving approach with a special rule for resolving any ground negative literal occurring in the body of a clause. First, the definitions of a clause and a goal are generalized to allow a different kind of literal in their bodies.

Definition 8.16: An *extended clause* has the form (8.1), where each L_i is a literal or a *deferred literal* of the form $Def\ A$, where A is an atom. An *extended goal* has the form (8.2), where each L_i is either a literal or a deferred literal.

Definition 8.17: Let R be a clause of the form (8.1). Then a *definite form* of R with respect to A_p, $1 \le p \le m$, denoted by *def* (R, A_p), is the extended clause

$$A_p \leftarrow L_1 \wedge \cdots \wedge L_n \wedge Def\ A_1 \wedge \cdots \wedge Def\ A_{p-1} \wedge$$
$$Def\ A_{p+1} \wedge \cdots \wedge Def\ A_m$$

According to the above definition, the definite form of a definite clause is the clause itself.

Definition 8.18: Let R be a clause of the form (8.3). Then a *semi-contrapositive form* of R with respect to M_r, $1 \le r \le p$, denoted by $con(R, M_r)$, is the extended clause

$$M_r \leftarrow M_1 \wedge \cdots \wedge M_{r-1} \wedge M_{r+1} \wedge \cdots \wedge M_p \wedge \neg N_1 \wedge \cdots \wedge \neg N_q \wedge$$
$$Def\ A_1 \wedge \cdots \wedge Def\ A_m$$

According to the above definition, semi-contrapositive forms of facts as well as rules containing only negative literals in their bodies are not defined.

Definition 8.19: Let G be a goal of the form (8.2). Then a semi-contrapositive form of G with respect to a positive (resp. deferred) literal L_r, $1 \le r \le n$, denoted by $con(G, L_r)$, is the extended clause

$$A \leftarrow L_1 \wedge \cdots \wedge L_{r-1} \wedge L_{r+1} \wedge \cdots \wedge L_n$$

where L_r is A (resp. $Def\ A$).

Definition 8.20: An *extended computation rule* is a function which maps an extended goal to either a literal or a deferred literal, called the *selected literal*, in that goal.

Definition 8.21: Let **P** be a program, G be an extended goal and $\mathcal{R}$ be an extended computation rule. A *definite derivation* for $\mathbf{P} \cup \{G\}$ via $\mathcal{R}$ consists of a sequence $G_0 = G$, G_1, G_2, ... of extended goals, a sequence C_1, C_2, ... of variants of extended clauses, and a sequence θ_1, θ_2, ... of substitutions satisfying the following. For each i, G_i is $\leftarrow L_1 \wedge \cdots \wedge L_m \wedge \cdots \wedge L_p$, the selected literal L_m in G_i is a

(1) Positive literal and L_m unifies with

(a) the head of a normal clause $C = A \leftarrow M_1 \wedge \cdots \wedge M_n$ in **P** with an mgu θ_{i+1}. Then C_i is C and G_{i+1} is

$$\leftarrow (L_1 \wedge \cdots \wedge L_{m-1} \wedge M_1 \wedge \cdots \wedge M_n \wedge L_{m+1} \wedge \cdots \wedge L_p)\theta_{i+1}$$

(b) an atom A_p occurring in the head of an indefinite clause C = $A_1 \vee \cdots \vee A_p \vee \cdots \vee A_l \leftarrow M_1 \wedge \cdots \wedge M_n$ of **P** with an mgu θ_{i+1}. Then C_{i+1} is $def(C, A_p)$ and G_{i+1} is

$$\leftarrow (L_1 \wedge \cdots \wedge L_{m-1} \wedge M_1 \wedge \cdots \wedge M_n \wedge L_{m+1} \wedge \cdots \wedge L_p \wedge$$
$$Def\ A_1 \wedge \cdots \wedge Def\ A_{p-1} \wedge Def\ A_{p+1} \wedge \cdots \wedge Def\ A_l)\theta_{i+1}$$

(c) an atom A with an mgu θ, where $Def\ A$ (say, L'_l) occurs in $G_k\theta_1 \cdots \theta_i$ $(0 \le k \le i-1)$ and $G_k\theta_1 \cdots \theta_i$ has the form $\leftarrow L'_1 \wedge \cdots \wedge L'_q$. Then C_{i+1} is $con(G_k, Def\ A)$ and G_{i+1} is

$$\leftarrow (L_1 \wedge \cdots \wedge L_{m-1} \wedge L'_1 \wedge \cdots \wedge L'_{l-1} \wedge$$
$$L'_{l+1} \wedge \cdots \wedge L'_q \wedge L_{m+1} \wedge \cdots \wedge L_p)\theta$$

(2) a ground negative literal $\neg A$ and $\mathbf{P} \cup \{\leftarrow A\}$ has a finitely failed possible tree. In this case, θ_{i+1} is the identity substitution, C_i is $\neg A$, and G_{i+1} is $\leftarrow L_1 \wedge \cdots \wedge L_{m-1} \wedge L_{m+1} \wedge \cdots \wedge L_p$.

(3) a deferred literal *Def* A and

(a) there is a clause $C = A_1 \vee \cdots \vee A_l \leftarrow B_1 \wedge \cdots \wedge B_p \wedge \cdots \wedge B_s$ such that A unifies with the atom B_p with an mgu θ_{i+1}. Then C_{i+1} is $con(C, B_p)$ and G_{i+1} is

$$\leftarrow (L_1 \wedge \cdots \wedge L_{m-1} \wedge B_1 \wedge \cdots \wedge B_{p-1} \wedge B_{p+1} \wedge \cdots \wedge B_s \wedge Def\ A_1 \wedge \cdots \wedge Def\ A_l \wedge L_{m+1} \wedge \cdots \wedge L_p)\theta_{i+1}$$

(b) A unifies with a positive literal L'_l occurring in $G_k\theta_1 \cdots \theta_i$ $(0 \le k \le i-1)$ with an mgu θ and $G_k\theta_1 \cdots \theta_i$ has the form $\leftarrow L'_1 \wedge \cdots \wedge L'_q$. Then C_{i+1} is $con(G_k, L'_l)$ and G_{i+1} is

$$\leftarrow (L_1 \wedge \cdots \wedge L_{m-1} \wedge L'_1 \wedge \cdots \wedge L'_{l-1} \wedge L'_{l+1} \wedge \cdots \wedge L'_q \wedge L_{m+1} \wedge \cdots \wedge L_p)\theta$$

The above resolution scheme can obviously be improved by using other refinements such as factoring and tautology elimination. Again, the terms finite, infinite and successful definite derivations, definite refutation, definite tree, success, failure and infinite branches of a definite tree, and finitely failed definite tree are defined in the usual way.

To illustrate the two resolution schemes together, consider the following example of a definite resolution.

EXAMPLE 8.17

Consider the following program $\mathbf{P}$:

Program:
R1. $P(x) \leftarrow Q(x)$
R2. $P(x) \leftarrow R(x)$
R3. $Q(x) \vee R(x) \leftarrow S(x) \wedge \neg T(x)$
R4. $T(x) \leftarrow U(x) \wedge \neg V(x)$
R5. $V(b) \leftarrow U(b) \wedge W(b)$
F1. $S(a)$
F2. $S(b)$
F3. $S(c)$

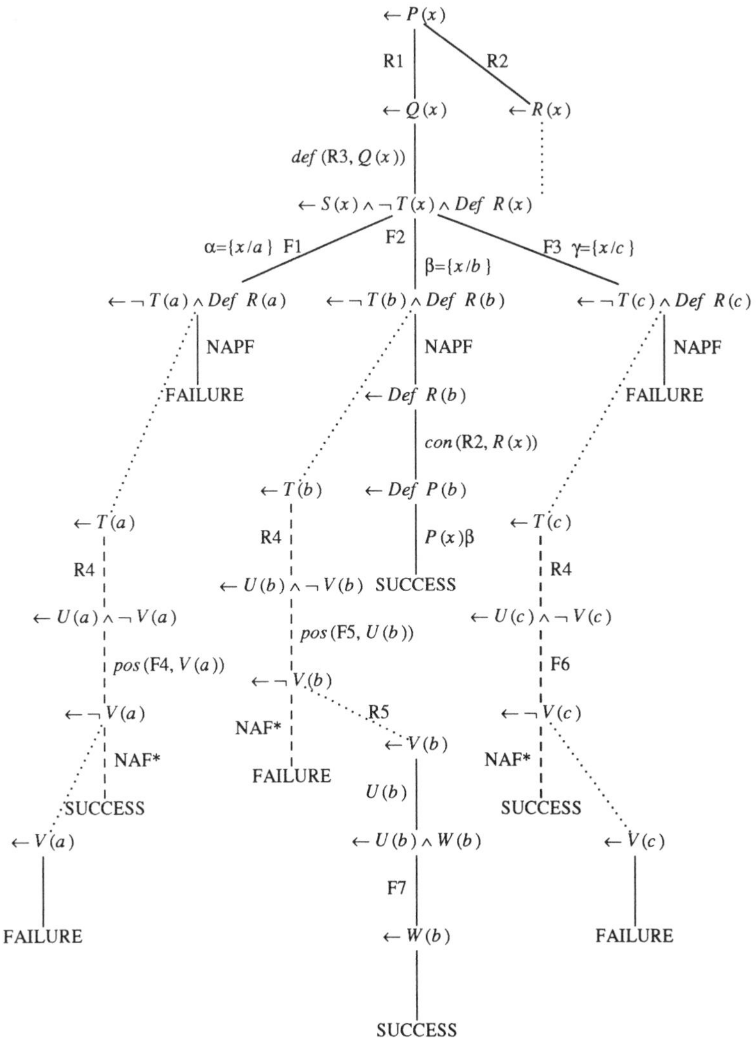

Figure 8.2 A partial search space in the case of Example 8.17.

F4. $U(a) \vee V(d)$

F5. $U(b) \vee V(d)$

F6. $U(c)$

F7. $W(b)$

Goal: $\leftarrow P(x)$

As each of the possible forms of the program above is hierarchical in nature, their completions are consistent. Figure 8.2 shows one possible partial search space for finding definite derivations of the goal $\leftarrow P(x)$. In the search tree, branches indicated by solid lines represent branches of a definite tree whereas branches indicated by dashed lines represent a possible tree. A dotted line indicates a subgoal generation due to the selection of a negative or a deferred literal from a goal. Selected clauses and sometimes variable bindings are also shown beside the respective branch. NAPF represents an application of the NAPF rule and NAF* represents negation as failure like a rule in the transformed program. For example, in the definite tree generated from the goal $\leftarrow V(b)$ the fact $U(b)$ has been taken as definite in the transformed program although its occurrence is indefinite in the program of Example 8.17. The reason is its use as a possible form of the indefinite fact $U(b) \vee V(d)$.

The definite resolution is an adaptation of linear resolution (including ancestor resolution) to incorporate the NAPF rule. Hence by inheriting the completeness property of linear resolution, the definite resolution becomes complete provided the incorporated NAPF rule is complete. Also, its compatibility with the NAPF rule (that is, negative facts inferred by the NAPF rule are consistent with the program) follows naturally because the inferred negative facts are consistent with every possible form of the program.

The definite derivation corresponding to the middle branch of the tree in Figure 8.2 is given in Table 8.1 and the possible derivation for goal $\leftarrow T(b)$ is given in Table 8.2.

Table 8.1 A definite derivation.

Goals	*Variants*	*Subst.*
$G_0 = G\ (= M) = \leftarrow P(x)$		
$G_1 = \leftarrow Q(x)$	$C_1 = R1 = P(x) \leftarrow Q(x)$	$\theta_1 = \{\}$
$G_2 = \leftarrow S(x) \wedge \neg T(x) \wedge Def\ R(x)$	$C_2 = def\,(R3, Q(x))$	$\theta_2 = \{\}$
	$= Q(x) \leftarrow S(x) \wedge \neg T(x)$	
$G_3 = \leftarrow \neg T(b) \wedge Def\ R(b)$	$C_3 = F2 = S(b)$	$\theta_3 = \{x/b\}$
$G_4 = \leftarrow Def\ R(b)$	$C_4 = \neg T(b)$	$\theta_4 = \{\}$
$G_5 = \leftarrow Def\ P(b)$	$C_5 = con\,(R2, R(x))$	$\theta_5 = \{\}$
	$= R(x) \leftarrow Def\ P(x)$	
G_6 = SUCCESS	$C_6 = M\beta$	$\theta_6 = \{\}$

Table 8.2 A possible derivation.

+ *Progs*	– *Progs*	*Goals*	*Variants*	*Subst.*
$\mathbf{P}_0^+ = \mathbf{P}$	$\mathbf{P}_0^- = \{\}$	$G_0 = \leftarrow T(b)$		
$\mathbf{P}_1^+ = \mathbf{P}_0^+$	$\mathbf{P}_1^- = \mathbf{P}_0^-$	$G_1 = \leftarrow U(b) \wedge \neg V(b)$	$C_1 = R4 = T(x) \leftarrow U(x) \wedge \neg V(x)$	$\theta_1 = \{\}$
$\mathbf{P}_2^+ = \mathbf{P}_1^+ \cup \{U(b)\}$	$\mathbf{P}_2^- = \mathbf{P}_1^-$	$G_2 = \leftarrow \neg V(b)$	$C_2 = pos(F5, U(b)) = U(b)$	$\theta_2 = \{\}$

Negation by all possible failure

Based on the two resolution strategies introduced in the previous two sections, the rule (procedural semantics) for inferring negative information denoted by *Negation by All Possible Failure* (NAPF), is defined as follows. The negation of a fact A is taken as true in a program $\mathbf{P}$ if $\mathbf{P} \cup \{\leftarrow A\}$ has a finitely failed possible tree. Thus

$$\mathcal{NAPF}(\mathbf{P}) = \{\neg A \mid \mathbf{P} \cup \{\leftarrow A\} \text{ has a finitely failed possible tree}\}$$

The NAPF rule is consistent because a ground atom is taken as false in the context of a program $\mathbf{P}$ if it is not true in any of the possible forms of $\mathbf{P}$. The conciseness property of the NAPF rule is inherited from the NAF rule. The rule is also inclusive because to obtain all possible forms of a program it is necessary to consider all possible combinations of possible forms for each of its indefinite clauses. Consider the following example.

EXAMPLE 8.18

The possible forms of the program $\{P, P \vee Q\}$ are $\{P\}$ and $\{P, Q\}$. Hence there is a world of the program where both P and Q are true.

The equivalence between the declarative and procedural concepts of negative information in an arbitrary program (at least when each possible form is hierarchical in nature) follows in the same way as for normal programs in Chapter 7. The result in the case of normal programs establishes that SLDNF-resolution can infer those items of information which are declaratively given in terms of the completion of the program. In the context of general programs, the possible and definite resolution schemes can infer items of information which are given in the previous two subsections in terms of the completion of the possible forms of the program. The following theorem states the soundness results for the NAPF rule and the two resolution schemes.

Theorem 8.4: (soundness of NAPF rule and definite and possible resolution) Suppose $\mathbf{P}$ is a general program and $A \in \mathcal{HB}(\mathbf{P})$. Then

(1) If $\mathbf{P} \cup \{\leftarrow A\}$ has a finitely failed possible tree then A is definitely false in $\mathbf{P}$. In other words, $\mathcal{NAPF}(\mathbf{P}) \subseteq \mathcal{DefFalse}(\mathbf{P})$.

(2) If $\mathbf{P} \cup \{\leftarrow A\}$ has a definite refutation then A is definitely true in $\mathbf{P}$.

(3) If $\mathbf{P} \cup \{\leftarrow A\}$ has a possible refutation then A is either definitely or possibly true in $\mathbf{P}$.

Proof Left as an exercise. ■

8.2.3 Perfect model semantics

In a general program $\mathbf{P}$, the class of all perfect models (Przymusinski, 1988a, 1988b) for $\mathbf{P}$ is a subclass of the class of all minimal models. Perfect models capture the meaning of general programs. These models are singled out from the class of minimal models with the help of preference relations between models. The *priority relations* $<$ and $\leq$ need to be defined among the elements of $\mathcal{HB}(\mathbf{P})$ and also a definition of preferability among models of $\mathbf{P}$ is required.

Definition 8.22: Suppose A and B are two elements of $\mathcal{HB}(\mathbf{P})$. Then

(1) $A \leq B$, that is, the priority of A is less than or equal to the priority of B if and only if

   (a) there is a ground instance C of clause for $\mathbf{P}$ such that A occurs in the head of C and B occurs in the body of C, or

   (b) there is a ground instance C of a clause from $\mathbf{P}$ such that both A and B occur in the head of C, or

   (c) there exists C in $\mathcal{HB}(\mathbf{P})$ such that $A \leq C$ and $C \leq B$.

(2) $A < B$, that is, the priority of B is higher than the priority of A if and only if

(a) there is a ground instance C of a clause from **P** such that $\neg B$ occurs in the body of C and A occurs in the head of C, or

(b) there exists C in $\mathcal{HB}(\mathbf{D})$ such that $A \leq C$ and $C < B$ or $A < C$ and $C \leq B$.

(3) If $A < B$ then $A \leq B$.

(4) Nothing else satisfies $<$ or $\leq$.

EXAMPLE 8.19

$\mathbf{P} = \{S(a) \leftarrow \neg S(b), P(x) \vee Q(x) \leftarrow R(x) \wedge \neg S(x), R(a)\}$

$\mathcal{HB}(\mathbf{P}) = \{P(a), P(b), Q(a), Q(b), R(a), R(b), S(a), S(b)\}$

$\mathcal{G}round(\mathbf{P}) = \{S(a) \leftarrow \neg S(b), P(a) \vee Q(a) \leftarrow R(a) \wedge \neg S(a),$
$P(b) \vee Q(b) \leftarrow R(b) \wedge \neg S(b), R(a)\}$

By 1(a), $P(a) \leq R(a), Q(a) \leq R(a), P(b) \leq R(b), Q(b) \leq R(b)$.

By 1(b), $P(a) \leq Q(a), Q(a) \leq P(a), P(b) \leq Q(b), Q(b) \leq P(b)$.

By 2(a), $S(a) < S(b), P(a) < S(a), Q(a) < S(a), P(b) < S(b), Q(b) < S(b)$.

Hence $X < S(a) < S(b)$, where $X \in \{P(a), P(b), Q(a), Q(b), R(a), R(b)\}$.

The idea behind constructing perfect models from a set of given models is to minimize the set of higher priority atoms in the given models as much as possible.

Definition 8.23: Suppose **M** and **N** are two models and **N** is obtained from **M** by possibly adding and/or removing some elements from **M**. Then **N** is *preferable* to **M** ($\mathbf{N} \ll \mathbf{M}$) if for every element A in $\mathbf{N} - \mathbf{M}$ there is an element B in $\mathbf{M} - \mathbf{N}$ such that $A < B$. A model **M** of **P** is *perfect* if there is no model preferable to **M**. The relation $\ll$ is called the *preference relation.*

EXAMPLE 8.20

The minimal models of the program $\mathbf{P} = \{S(a) \leftarrow \neg S(b), P(x) \vee Q(x) \leftarrow R(x) \wedge \neg S(x), R(a)\}$ are as follows:

$\mathbf{M}_1 = \{R(a), S(a)\}$
$\mathbf{M}_2 = \{R(a), S(b), P(a)\}$
$\mathbf{M}_3 = \{R(a), S(b), Q(a)\}$

Since $S(a) < S(b)$ and $S(a) \in \mathbf{M}_1 - \mathbf{M}_2$,
$S(b) \in \mathbf{M}_2 - \mathbf{M}_1$, therefore $\mathbf{M}_1 \ll \mathbf{M}_2$.
For the same reason, $\mathbf{M}_1 \ll \mathbf{M}_3$.

Proposition 8.1: Every perfect model is minimal.

Proof if $\mathbf{M}$ is a perfect model and not minimal then there is a minimal model $\mathbf{N}$ such that $\mathbf{N} \subseteq \mathbf{M}$. Since $\mathbf{N} - \mathbf{M}$ is empty, by the definition of preferable relation, $\mathbf{N} \ll \mathbf{M}$. Hence $\mathbf{N}$ is preferable to $\mathbf{M}$. By the definition of the prefect model, $\mathbf{N}$ and $\mathbf{M}$ coincide. ■

Not every minimal model is perfect as it is evident from the following example.

EXAMPLE 8.21

The program $\mathbf{P} = \{P \leftarrow \neg Q\}$ has two minimal models $\{P\}$ and $\{Q\}$. The model $\{P\}$ is preferable to $\{Q\}$ and therefore it is perfect.

EXAMPLE 8.22

The program $\mathbf{P} = \{P \leftarrow \neg Q, Q \leftarrow \neg P\}$ has two minimal models $\{P\}$ and $\{Q\}$. Neither of these two is perfect as $\{P\} << \{Q\}$ and $\{Q\} << \{P\}$.

Proposition 8.2: In a disjunctive program $\mathbf{P}$, a model is perfect if and only if it is minimal.

Proof Suppose a model $\mathbf{M}$ of $\mathbf{P}$ is perfect. Then by Proposition 8.1 it is minimal.

Conversely, suppose $\mathbf{M}$ is a minimal model of $\mathbf{P}$. If $\mathbf{M}$ is not perfect, then there is a model $\mathbf{N}$ preferable to $\mathbf{M}$. Since $\mathbf{N}$ is preferable to $\mathbf{M}$, for every $A \in \mathbf{N} - \mathbf{M}$ there is an element $B \in \mathbf{M} - \mathbf{N}$ such that $A < B$. Now in disjunctive programs, the priority relation $<$ is empty. Hence $\mathbf{N} - \mathbf{M}$ is empty, that is, $\mathbf{N} \subseteq \mathbf{M}$. Since $\mathbf{M}$ is minimal, $\mathbf{N} = \mathbf{M}$. Hence there is no other model preferable to $\mathbf{M}$, therefore $\mathbf{M}$ is perfect. ■

The class of stratified normal programs do not include many important normal programs. The class of stratified programs is extended to a class called *locally stratified programs* and is defined in the following. Its connection with perfect models will be established later.

Definition 8.24: A program $\mathbf{P}$ is *locally stratified* if it is possible to decompose $\mathcal{HB}(\mathbf{P})$ into disjoint sets, called *strata*, $\mathbf{H}_0$, $\mathbf{H}_1$, ... so that for every ground substitution θ of a clause

$$A_1 \vee \cdots \vee A_m \leftarrow M_1 \wedge \cdots \wedge M_p \wedge \neg N_1 \wedge \cdots \wedge \neg N_q$$

the following conditions are satisfied:

(1) Each $A_i\theta$ belongs to the stratum $\mathbf{H}_i$.

(2) Each $M_i\theta$ belongs to $\cup\{\mathbf{H}_j | j \leq i\}$.

(3) Each $N_i\theta$ belongs to $\cup\{\mathbf{H}_j | j < i\}$.

The sequence $\mathbf{H}_0$, $\mathbf{H}_1$, ... is a local stratification of $\mathbf{P}$. In the definition of a stratified program $\mathbf{P}$, the set of all predicate symbols occurring in a program $\mathbf{P}$ is finitely decomposed. On the other hand, the above definition of locally stratified program decomposes the Herbrand base $\mathcal{HB}(\mathbf{P})$. This decomposition may be infinite.

Proposition 8.3: Every stratified normal program is locally stratified.

Proof Suppose $\mathbf{P}$ is a stratified program and let $\mathbf{P} = \mathbf{P}_0 \cup \mathbf{P}_1 \cup \cdots \cup \mathbf{P}_n$ be a decomposition of $\mathbf{P}$. With a decomposition of $\mathcal{HB}(\mathbf{P}) = \mathbf{H}_0 \cup \mathbf{H}_1 \cup \cdots \cup \mathbf{H}_n$, where $\mathbf{H}_i = \{A \in \mathcal{HB}(\mathbf{P}) |$ the definition of the predicate symbol of A belongs to $\mathbf{P}_i\}$, the program can be proved to be locally stratified. ■

The converse of the above proposition may not hold as is evident from Example 8.23.

EXAMPLE 8.23

Consider the following program which defines the set of all even integers:

$\mathbf{P}$: $Even(0)$

$Even(s(x)) \leftarrow \neg\, Even(x)$

where s is the successor function. The program is not stratified but is a locally stratified program with the decomposition of Herbrand base $\{Even(0), Even(s(0)), Even(s(s(0))), \ldots\}$ as $\{Even(0)\} \cup \{Even(s(0))\} \cup \{Even(s(s(0)))\} \cup \ldots$.

The connection between a locally stratified program and perfect models is that every locally stratified program has at least one perfect model. The set of all locally stratified programs $\mathbf{P}$ is independent of the choice of stratification of $\mathcal{HB}(\mathbf{P})$. Also, if the program $\mathbf{P}$ is stratified normally, then the perfect model is unique and coincides with the standard model for a stratified program as constructed in Chapter 7.

Proposition 8.2 shows that the class of perfect models for general programs is a natural extension of the class of minimal models for disjunctive programs. On this basis, perfect model semantics is stated as follows. A sentence is considered true in a general program **P** if and only if it is true in all perfect models of **P**. The *Perfect Model Rule* (PMR) for inferring negative information from a general program **P** is given as follows:

$$\mathcal{PMR}(\mathbf{P}) = \{\neg A \in \mathcal{HB}(\mathbf{P}) | A \text{ is not in any perfect model of } \mathbf{P}\}$$

Well-founded semantics coincides with perfect model semantics on locally stratified programs. If **P** is a locally stratified program then it has a unique stable model which is identical to its perfect model. The model $\{P\}$ of the program $\{P \leftarrow \neg P\}$ is perfect but not stable.

8.3 Circumscription

First-order logic is *monotonic* because the theorems of a first-order theory are always a subset of a theorem of any extension to the theory. This means that if **A** and **B** are two sets of axioms such that $\mathbf{A} \subseteq \mathbf{B}$, then $\mathcal{Theorem}(\mathbf{A}) \subseteq \mathcal{Theorem}(\mathbf{B})$, where $\mathcal{Theorem}(\mathbf{S}) = \{F | \mathbf{S} \vdash F\}$. The rules of inference (modus ponens and generalization) associated with first-order logic are called *monotonic rules of inference*. On the other hand, a *non-monotonic logic* (Davis, 1980; Ginsberg, 1987; McCarthy, 1980; McDermott and Doyle, 1980) can invalidate old theorems in introducing new axioms. Rules of inference in such a logic are called *non-monotonic rules of inference*.

All rules of inferring negative information are non-monotonic rules of inference and are used along with the rules of inference of first-order logic. For example, answering definite queries in the context of a definite program **P** can be thought of as deriving information from a non-monotonic logical system. This logical system consists of first-order logical axioms, monotonic rules of inference (MP and Gen), axioms of **P** as proper axioms and the CWA (or NAF defined by SLD-resolution) as the non-monotonic rule of inference. If a ground atom A is not derivable from a first-order system with the set of proper axioms **P** then the CWA rule will infer $\neg A$ from the system. Once the ground atom A is added to **P** as a proper axiom, the CWA rule no longer derives $\neg A$. Hence $\mathbf{P} \subseteq \mathbf{P} \cup \{A\}$, but it is not true that $\mathcal{Theorem}(\mathbf{P}) \subseteq \mathcal{Theorem}(\mathbf{P} \cup \{A\})$.

McCarthy's *circumscription* (1980, 1984) is also a formalized non-monotonic rule of inference that can be used along with the rules of inference of first-order logic. This rule can be formally stated as follows. Let an n-ary predicate symbol P occur in a first-order sentence A. Suppose $A[P/\phi]$ denotes the result of replacing all occurrences of P in A by the predicate expression ϕ (either a predicate symbol or a suitable λ-abstraction (see Chapter 17)). The circumscription of P in A is the sentence schema

$$A[P/\phi] \wedge \forall x_1 \cdots \forall x_n (\phi(x_1, ..., x_n) \rightarrow P(x_1, ..., x_n)) \\ \rightarrow \forall x_1 \cdots \forall x_n (P(x_1, ..., x_n) \rightarrow \phi(x_1, ..., x_n)) \tag{8.11}$$

The above formula is better expressed in second-order logic (see Chapter 17) by putting a quantifier $\forall \phi$ in front of (8.11). Formula (8.11) can be regarded as asserting that the only tuples $<x_1, ..., x_n>$ that satisfy P are those that have to, assuming the sentence A. The first conjunction $A[P/\phi]$ in the condition of (8.11) expresses the assumption that ϕ satisfies the conditions satisfied by P. The second conjunct in the condition of (8.11) expresses the assumption that the entities satisfying ϕ are a subset of those that satisfy P. If both the conjuncts in the condition of (8.11) are satisfied, then the conclusion asserts the converse of the second conjunct and hence ϕ and P must coincide.

Circumscribing several predicates $P_1, ..., P_m$ in $A[P_1, ..., P_m]$, a generalized version of (8.11) is obtained as

$$A[P_1/\phi_1, ..., P_m/\phi_m] \wedge \forall x_1^1 \cdots \forall x_{n_1}^1 (\phi_1(x_1^1, ..., x_{n_1}^1) \rightarrow P_1(x_1^1, ..., x_{n_1}^1)) \wedge \\ \cdots \wedge \forall x_1^m \cdots \forall x_{n_m}^m (\phi_m(x_1^m, ..., x_{n_m}^1) \rightarrow P_m(x_1^m, ..., x_{n_m}^m)) \rightarrow \\ \forall x_1^1 \cdots \forall x_{n_1}^1 (P_1(x_1^1, ..., x_{n_1}^1) \rightarrow \phi_1(x_1^1, ..., x_{n_1}^1)) \wedge \cdots \wedge \\ \forall x_1^m \cdots \forall x_{n_m}^m (P_m(x_1^m, ..., x_{n_m}^1) \rightarrow \phi_m(x_1^m, ..., x_{n_m}^m)) \tag{8.12}$$

EXAMPLE 8.24

Consider the following program **P**:

Program: *Student* (*Daniel*) ∨ *Employee* (*Daniel*)
Student (*Didier*)
Brother (*Daniel*, *Didier*)
$\forall x$ (*Student* (x) → *Grant* (x))

The last clause in **P** is equivalent to the program clause *Grant* (x) ← *Student* (x). Sentence A is considered as the conjunction of the above three clauses, that is

$$(Student(Daniel) \vee Employee(Daniel)) \wedge Student(Didier) \wedge \\ \forall x (Student(x) \rightarrow Grant(x)) \tag{8.13}$$

Circumscribing the predicate *Student* gives the sentence schema as

$$(\phi(Daniel) \vee Employee(Daniel)) \wedge \phi(Didier) \wedge \forall x(\phi(x) \rightarrow Student(x)) \rightarrow \forall x(Student(x) \rightarrow \phi(x)) \tag{8.14}$$

The other clauses in **P** (for example *Brother*(*Daniel*, *Didier*) and $\forall x(Student(x) \rightarrow Grant(x)))$ can also appear as a conjunct on the left-hand side of ormula (8.14). These additional conjuncts are cancelled by themselves. Substituting 'x=*Didier*' in place of $\phi(x)$, formula (8.14) can be transformed to

$$(Daniel = Didier \vee Employee(Daniel)) \wedge Didier = Didier \wedge \forall x(x = Didier \rightarrow Student(x)) \rightarrow \forall x(Student(x) \rightarrow x = Didier)$$

that is

$$Employee(Daniel) \wedge Student(Didier) \rightarrow \forall x(Student(x) \rightarrow x = Didier)$$

Using *Student*(*Didier*) of **P**, this formula can be transformed to

$$Employee(Daniel) \rightarrow \forall x(Student(x) \rightarrow x = Didier) \tag{8.15}$$

Formula (8.15) states that '$\vee$' occurring in the first clause of **P** is exclusive, that is, if Daniel is an employee then the only student is Didier. Therefore, Daniel is not a student in this case. Circumscription is non-monotonic because if one adds another fact *Student*(*Robert*), then (8.15) no longer holds.

Circumscribing the predicate *Grant* gives the sentence schema (8.13) as

$$\forall x(Student(x) \rightarrow \phi(x)) \wedge \forall x(\phi(x) \rightarrow Grant(x)) \rightarrow \forall x(Grant(x) \rightarrow \phi(x)) \tag{8.16}$$

Substituting 'x = *Didier*' in place of $\phi(x)$ occurring in (8.16),

$$\forall x(Student(x) \rightarrow x = Didier) \wedge \forall x(x = Didier \rightarrow Grant(x)) \rightarrow \forall x(Grant(x) \rightarrow x = Didier)$$

Using *Grant*(*Didier*) of **P**, this formula can be transformed to

$$\forall x(Student(x) \rightarrow x = Didier) \rightarrow \forall x(Grant(x) \rightarrow x = Didier)$$

which asserts that if *Didier* is the only student then the only student who receives the grant is Didier.

The model-theoretic counterpart of circumscription is *minimal entailment* which is introduced below.

Definition 8.25: A sentence B is minimally entailed by a sentence A if and only if B is true in all minimal models of A. Since the definition of circumscription is with respect to some predicates $P_1, ..., P_m$, this usage of 'minimal model' above is also with respect to $P_1, ..., P_m$ and is clarified below.

Definition 8.26: Let $\mathbf{M}$ and $\mathbf{N}$ be models of A. Then $\mathbf{M}$ is a *submodel of* $\mathbf{N}$ in $P_1, ..., P_m$, denoted by $\mathbf{M} \leq_{P_1, ..., P_m} \mathbf{N}$, if $\mathbf{M}$ and $\mathbf{N}$ have the same domain. All other predicate symbols in A besides $P_1, ..., P_m$ have the same extensions in $\mathbf{M}$ and $\mathbf{N}$, but the extensions of $P_1, ..., P_m$ in $\mathbf{M}$ are included in its extension in $\mathbf{N}$.

Now the definition of minimal model which is based on this definition is given in usual manner.

Definition 8.27: A model $\mathbf{M}$ of A is minimal in $P_1, ..., P_m$ if and only if there is no other model $\mathbf{M}'$ of A in $P_1, ..., P_m$ such that $\mathbf{M}'$ is a proper submodel of $\mathbf{M}$.

If a sentence B is minimally entailed by A (or A minimally entails B) then it is denoted as $A \models_{P_1, ..., P_m} B$. Also, the notation $A \vdash_{P_1, ..., P_m} B$ means that the sentence B can be obtained from the result of circumscribing $P_1, ..., P_m$ in A.

Theorem 8.5 If $A \vdash_{P_1, ..., P_m} B$ then $A \models_{P_1, ..., P_m} B$.

Proof Suppose $\mathbf{M}$ is a model of A minimal in $P_1, ..., P_m$. Let $P'_1, ..., P'_m$ be predicates satisfying the left-hand side when substituting for $\phi_1, ..., \phi_n$ respectively. Since

$$\forall x_1^i \cdots \forall x_{n_i}^i (P'_i(x_1^i, ..., x_{n_i}^i) \rightarrow P_i(x_1^i, ..., x_{n_i}^i))$$

holds, for all i $(1 \leq i \leq m)$, P_i is an extension of P'_i. If the right-hand side of (8.12) were not satisfied, P_i would be a proper extension of P'_i for each i. In that case a proper submodel $\mathbf{M}'$ of $\mathbf{M}$ is obtained by letting $\mathbf{M}'$ agree with $P'_1, ..., P'_m$ on $P_1, ..., P_m$ respectively. This contradicts the fact that $\mathbf{M}$ is minimal. ■

Exercises

8.1 Derive negative information from the following disjunctive programs by applying every relevant rule introduced in the first half of this chapter:

Program:
$$P(x) \leftarrow Q(x)$$
$$P(x) \leftarrow R(x)$$
$$Q(x) \leftarrow S(x)$$
$$Q(x) \leftarrow T(x)$$
$$S(a) \vee T(a)$$

Program:
$$P(x) \leftarrow Q(x) \wedge R(x)$$
$$Q(a) \vee R(a)$$

Program:
$$P(x) \leftarrow Q(x) \wedge R(x)$$
$$Q(a) \vee Q(b)$$
$$R(a) \vee R(b)$$

Program:
$$P(x, x, f(x)) \vee P(y, x, z) \leftarrow P(x, y, z)$$
$$Q(x, z) \leftarrow P(x, y, z)$$
$$Q(x, y) \vee Q(x, z) \leftarrow R(x) \wedge P(y, z, u) \wedge Q(x, u)$$
$$R(a)$$
$$P(a, f(c), f(b))$$

8.2 Generate a definite tree for the following programs and goals:

Program:
$$P(x, y) \leftarrow Q(x, y) \wedge R(x)$$
$$Q(x, y) \leftarrow S(x, y) \wedge \neg P'(x)$$
$$R(x) \leftarrow U(x)$$
$$R(x) \leftarrow V(x)$$
$$U(x) \vee V(x) \leftarrow T(x) \wedge \neg W(x)$$
$$T(a) \qquad T(b)$$
$$S(a, c)$$
$$S(b, c)$$
$$W(c) \vee W(a)$$

Goal:
$$\leftarrow P(x, y)$$

Program: $Manager(x, y) \leftarrow Superior(x, y) \wedge Officer(x)$

$Worker(x) \leftarrow Clerk(x)$

$Worker(x) \leftarrow Typist(x)$

$Clerk(x) \vee Typist(x) \leftarrow Employee(x) \wedge \neg Officer(x)$

$Employee(x) \leftarrow Officer(x)$

$Superior(b, a)$

$Superior(c, a)$

$Employee(a)$

$Employee(b)$

$Officer(c)$

$Officer(b) \vee Clerk(b)$

Goal: $\leftarrow Worker(x)$

8.3 Compute the completed program for each of the two general programs of Exercise 8.2 and also compute all the perfect models.

9

Prolog

This chapter presents the logic programming language Prolog using a standard C-Prolog (Clocksin and Mellish, 1984) type of syntax to represent Prolog programs and goals. The main topics discussed in this chapter include the syntax of Prolog programs, the style of their execution, semantics and usefulness of extralogical features and meta-programming.

9.1 Programs and goals

Prolog (Bratko, 1986; Colmerauer *et al.*, 1973; Clocksin and Mellish, 1984; Maier and Warren, 1988; O'Keefe, 1985; Roussel, 1975; Sterling and Shapiro, 1986) is a logic programming language and a *normal Prolog program* is a normal logic program. Hence according to the definition of a normal logic program, a normal Prolog program is a finite set of normal clauses. Similarly, a *normal Prolog goal* is a normal goal. Some additional extralogical features from outside the framework of first-order logic have been incorporated within normal Prolog programs and goals. These extra features allow (among other things) the achievement of the following:

(1) Performance enhancement by reducing the search space, that is, by pruning the redundant branches of search trees (for example, using the *cut* symbol).

(2) Increasing readability (for example, using *if-then/or* constructs).

(3) Input/output operations (for example, using *read/write* predicates).

(4) Clause management (for example, using *assert/retract* predicates).

(5) Set-type evaluation in addition to the resolution-based tuple-at-a-time approach (for example, using *setof/bagof* predicates).

(6) Meta-programming (for example, using *clause*, *call* predicates).

To incorporate these features the syntax of normal Prolog programs (and normal Prolog goals) is extended using some special symbols, special predicates and special constructs. Prolog programs and Prolog goals are simply these extended normal Prolog programs and extended normal goals respectively. A definite or pure Prolog program is a finite set of definite clauses without any use of extralogical features. In a similar manner, a definite or pure Prolog goal is a definite goal without any use of extralogical features. Each literal occurring in a goal or in the body of a clause is called a Prolog subgoal.

9.2 Syntax

A standard C-Prolog type of syntax is now introduced for dealing with the normal Prolog programs and goals in the rest of the book. Extralogical symbols, predicates and constructs are introduced in the relevant sections.

(1) In general, constants, functions and predicate symbols of a Prolog program begin with a lower-case letter (or the 'dollar' symbol) or may comprise any string of characters enclosed in single quotes.

(2) Variables begin with at least one upper-case letter (or the 'underline' symbol). The symbol '_' on its own is a special type of variable called the 'don't know' variable. Discrete occurrences of this particular variable in a program clause or in a goal are considered different from each other.

(3) The symbols for '$\wedge$' (and sign), '$\vee$' (or sign), '$\leftarrow$' (implication) and '$\neg$' (negation) are '`,`', '`;`', '`:-`' and '`not`' respectively.

(4) Arithmetic function symbols (for example, +, −, *, /) and some comparison predicates (such as <, >) may be written in their infix forms. For example, the addition of two numbers `a` and `b` is usually expressed as `a+b` rather than `+(a,b)` (although this is also perfectly correct syntax).

(5) Arithmetic assignment is achieved by the predicate `is` and the arithmetic equality symbol is represented by the symbol `=:=`.

(6) The unification of two terms is performed using the symbol `=` whereas to check whether or not two terms are syntactically equal (that is, the equality symbol) the symbol `==` is used.

In describing a goal or a subgoal or a piece of code, the occurrence of an expression of the form `<type>` or `<type_n>` can be replaced by an arbitrary expression which is of type `type`. So, for example, a subgoal `square<(<integer_1>, <integer_2>)` means the arguments of the predicate `square` are arbitrary integers.

With the above conventions under the C-Prolog syntax a normal Prolog clause has the form

```
<atom>:- <literal_1>, <literal_2>, ..., <literal_m>.
```

where `m` ≥ 0. Every clause in a Prolog program or a goal is terminated with the symbol '`.`'. As an example, the normal clause

$$Even(x) \leftarrow Integer(x) \wedge \neg Odd(x)$$

in the syntax of first-order logic is expressed in Prolog syntax as

```
even(X):- integer(X), not odd(X).
```

A goal to a Prolog program is expressed by the symbol `?-` followed by a conjunction of literals and then terminated with '`.`'. Hence a normal Prolog goal has the form

```
?- <literal_1>, <literal_2>, ..., <literal_n>.
```

As an example of a goal, the goal to find all non-square even numbers is

```
?- even(X), not square(X).
```

Commands to a Prolog interpreter are in the form of goals.

9.3 Theoretical background

The inference mechanism adopted in a standard Prolog system (considered as a Prolog interpreter throughout the text) is the same as SLDNF-resolution with the following restrictions:

(1) The computation rule in standard Prolog systems always selects the leftmost literal in a goal (it follows a leftmost literal selection strategy).

(2) Standard Prolog uses the order of clauses in a program as the fixed order in which clauses are to be tried, that is, the search tree is searched depth-first.

(3) Prolog omits the occur check condition for unifying two expressions.

Therefore, the search trees in the context of the execution of normal Prolog programs and goals are similar in structure to SLDNF-trees. Given a Prolog program and a goal, the search tree is unique because of the fixed computation rule and the fixed clause order in which they are fetched for the purpose of resolution. For the convenience of the reader, the definition of search tree is provided below in the terminology of Prolog.

Definition 9.1: Suppose **P** is a normal Prolog program and G is a Prolog goal. Then the *search tree* $\mathcal{T}$ for $\mathbf{P} \cup \{G\}$ (or the search tree for G wrt **P**) is defined as follows:

(1) The root of $\mathcal{T}$ is G.

(2) A leaf node of $\mathcal{T}$ is either a goal (a failure node) or an empty clause (a success node).

(3) Suppose the node N is

```
?- <literal_1>, <literal_2>, ..., <literal_n>
```

and the leftmost literal '`<literal_1>`' is positive. Suppose

```
<atom_1>:-<literal_conjunction_1>
  .
  .
  .
<atom_p>:-<literal_conjunction_p>
```

are the only clauses of **P** such that <literal_1> and each of <atom_i> unifies with an mgu <substitution_i>. The order shown for these clauses is the order in which they will be tried for resolution with the goal of node N. Then N has p descendants and they are (from left to right)

```
?- (<literal_conjunction_1>, <literal_2>, ...,
        <literal_n>)<substitution_1>
 .
 .
 .
?- (<literal_conjunction_p>, <literal_2>, ...,
        <literal_n>)<substitution_p>.
```

If for some i, <literal_conjunction_i> is true, that is, the clause <atom_i>:-<literal_conjunction_i> is a fact then the corresponding descendant is

```
?- (<literal_2>, ..., <literal_n>)<substitution_i>.
```

This becomes the empty clause □ when $n = 0$.

(4) Suppose the node N is

```
?- <literal_1>, <literal_2>, ..., <literal_n>
```

and the leftmost literal <literal_1> is a negative literal of the form not <atom> (The search tree construction does not stop even if the leftmost literal is non-ground and the answer in this case may be incorrect.) Then a recursive process is established to apply the negation as failure (NAF) rule, that is, to find the search tree for the goal ?- <atom> wrt **P**. If all the branches of this tree result in failure then the only descendant of N is

```
?- <literal_2>, ..., <literal_n>
```

without any substitution of its variables; otherwise if the system is able to find a success node of the search tree without going into an infinite loop then N is considered as a failure node.

In the above definition a success branch corresponds to a successful Prolog derivation which causes some instantiations to the variables of G and is an answer to the goal G. The following example constructs a Prolog search tree.

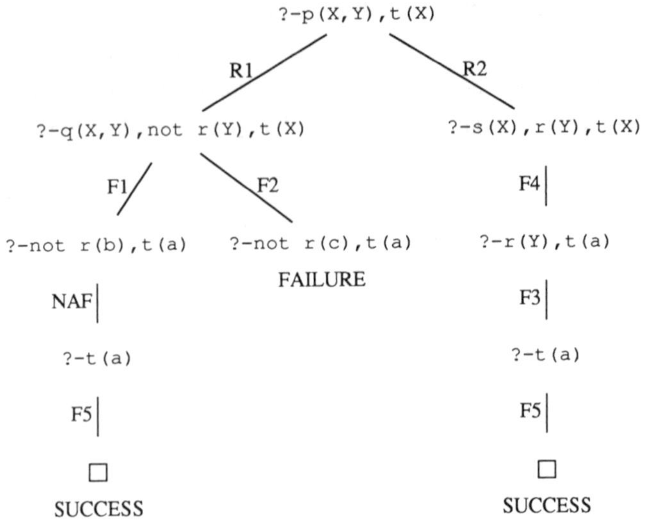

Figure 9.1 A Prolog search tree.

EXAMPLE 9.1

Consider the following Prolog program **P** and goal G:

Program:
R1. `p(X,Y):-q(X,Y),not r(Y).`
R2. `p(X,Y):-s(X),r(Y).`
F1. `q(a,b).`
F2. `q(a,c).`
F3. `r(c).`
F4. `s(a).`
F5. `t(a).`

Goal: `?-p(X,Y),t(X)`

The Prolog search tree for **P**∪{G} is given in Figure 9.1. The leftmost branch is a successful derivation and is given below.

Goals	*Input clauses*	*Substitutions*
`?-p(X,Y),t(X)`	R1	{X/X,Y/Y}
`?-q(X,Y),not r(Y),t(X)`	F1	{X/a,Y/b}
`?-not r(b),t(a)`	`not r(b)`	{}
`?-t(a)`	`t(a)`	{}
□		

9.4 Backtracking

When a complete search tree for a goal wrt a program is generated without going into a loop, all success branches of the tree generate all answers to the goal G. In Example 9.1, there are two answers to the goal `?-p(X,Y), t(X)` and these correspond to the two success branches of Figure 9.1. These two answers are {`X/a,Y/b`} and {`X/a,Y/a`}. Since the search tree is generated depth-first, the leftmost branch is generated first and therefore the answer {`X/a,Y/b`} results.

To try to find the next alternative answer, the user can initiate *backtracking* which is a request for an alternative solution. Backtracking after detecting a failure branch is automatic. Hence after the user initiates backtracking, all subsequent backtrackings are automatic until the interpreter finds an alternative answer to the goal. In the case of the above example, when backtracking is initiated after the first answer has been generated, the system must try to find an alternative solution for the last subgoal `t(a)` to find an alternative answer for the original goal. Since there is no more `t(a)` in the program, the last but one subgoal is tried. This is the negative subgoal `not R(b)` which cannot generate any new answers.

Backtracking further, the subgoal `q(X,Y)` is resolved against the second fact `q(a,c)` under the predicate `q` and another descendant `?-not r(c),t(a)` is created from the node `?-q(X,Y),not r(Y),t(X)`. The selected subgoal `not r(c)` from this node does not succeed and hence this node is considered a failure node. The interpreter backtracks automatically to the root node and generates the rightmost success branch eventually.

9.5 The cut

Prolog provides an extralogical system predicate called the *cut* (`!`) to reduce the search space. This reduction is achieved by dynamically pruning redundant branches of the search tree. A normal clause with one cut looks like

```
<atom>:- <literal_1>, ..., <literal_i>, !,
              <literal_i+1>, ..., <literal_n>.
```

On finding a solution, the cut prunes all alternative solutions to the conjunction `<literal_1>, ..., <literal_i>`, but does not affect the conjunction `<literal_i+1>, ..., <literal_n>`. To illustrate this, consider the following examples.

EXAMPLE 9.2

Refer to Example 9.1 given earlier. The search tree for $\mathbf{P} \cup \{G\}$, where G is the goal `?-p(X,Y),!,t(X),` is same as the one in Figure 9.1 excluding its rightmost branch. Due to the presence of the cut symbol in the goal the alternative solution `p(X,Y)` (with the help of R2) is pruned.

EXAMPLE 9.3

Again refer to Example 9.1. If the rule R1 is replaced `p(X,Y):-q(X,Y),!,not r(b),` then the new search tree contains only the leftmost branch of Figure 9.1.

Cuts are divided into two different categories. *Green cuts* prune only those branches of the search tree that do not lead to any new solutions. Hence removal of those cuts from a program does not change the declarative meaning of the program. Consider the following program which computes the absolute value of an integer `X` and illustrates the use of a green cut in a program:

```
absolute(X, X):-X >= 0, !.
absolute(X, Y):-X < 0, Y is -X.
```

Without using the cut in the first clause a redundant check would be performed when calculating the absolute value of a non-negative integer using a goal such as `?-absolute(3, Z).` By using a cut this redundant check is eliminated.

All other cuts are *red cuts* and they do affect the declarative meaning of a program. Red cuts should be used in a program with special care. Consider the following example illustrating the use of a red cut:

```
absolute(X, X):-X >= 0, !.
absolute(X, Y):-Y is -X.
distance(X, Y, Z):-Z1 is X-Y, absolute(Z1, Z).
```

The cut in the above program is absolutely essential. In its absence a goal of the form `?-distance(2, -3, Z)` would instantiate `Z` to 5 first and then to –5 upon backtracking which is obviously incorrect.

9.6 Special constructs and connectives

To increase the readability of a Prolog program and also, to some extent, the efficiency, a few extra connectives and constructs have been introduced. When the or-connective '`;`' is used in program clauses (and also in goals) as

```
<atom>:-<lit_conj_1>,
    (lit_conj_2;lit_conj_3),lit_conj_4.
```

this single clause is interpreted as a combination of two clauses

```
<atom>:-<lit_conj_1>, lit_conj_2, lit_conj_4
<atom>:-<lit_conj_1>, lit_conj_3, lit_conj_4
```

where `lit_conj` is an abbreviation of `literal_conjunction`. In the body of a Prolog program clause an occurrence of an expression of the form

```
<lit_conj_1> -> <lit_conj_2>; <lit_conj_3>
```

using the special conditional if–then construct (`->`) can be thought of as an alternative form of an atom (not a first-order atom)

```
<predicate_symbol>(<lit_conj_1>,
    <lit_conj_2>,<lit_conj_3>)
```

where the definition of `<predicate_symbol>` is

```
<predicate_symbol>(<lit_conj_1>, <lit_conj_2>, _):-
    <lit_conj_1>, !, <lit_conj_2>.
<predicate_symbol>(_, _, <lit_conj_3>):-
    <lit_conj_3>.
```

The above use of the cut is red. An example of the use of the construct `->` is to define the absolute value of a number `X` as in the program

```
absolute(X, Y):- X >= 0 -> Y = X; Y is -X.
```

where `Y` gives the absolute value of `X`.

9.7 Negation

Following SLDNF-resolution, Prolog provides a form of negation based on the negation as failure principle. The negation of `<atom>` is written in Prolog as `not <atom>` and can be implemented using the cut as follows:

```
not X :- X, !, fail.
not X.
```

The first of the above clauses prunes the other branches of the SLDNF-tree for the goal `?- X` when a success branch is found and marks the original goal as failed. This way of inferring negation may fail to generate all answers as is evident from the following example.

EXAMPLE 9.4

Program:
```
p(a).
q(b).
```
Goals:
```
?- p(X), not q(X).
?- not q(X), p(X).
```

The above pair of goals is the same except for the order of the literals. With leftmost literal selection strategy, the first goal succeeds and returns `X = a` as an answer. However, the second goal has a finitely failed search tree wrt to the program and therefore does not generate any answers.

As was pointed out in the description of SLDNF-resolution, negative literals should be selected only when they are ground. If at some stage of a computation the goal contains only non-ground negative literals then the computation flounders. When programs and goals are considered to be range-restricted, a literal selection strategy can always be found such that computations never flounder. Under Prolog's leftmost literal selection strategy, even if considered programs and goals are range-restricted, a computation may flounder. This can be demonstrated by considering the program of Example 9.4 and its second goal. However, by rearrangement of the literals in the goals as well as in the bodies of the program clauses it is always possible to make the negative literals ground before their selection. One of the ways to achieve this is by placing all negative literals in a goal or in the body of a clause after all the positive literals. By applying this strategy to the program and the second goal of Example 9.4, it is reduced to the first one.

It is again worth mentioning here that if a non-ground negative literal `not A` is chosen from a goal and if the goal `?-A` has a finitely failed search tree wrt the program then the computation can be continued without fear of losing any answers.

9.8 Equality

The symbol '=' in Prolog is treated as an unifying relation, that is, a subgoal of the form

```
<expression_1> = <expression_2>
```

succeeds when `<expression_1>` and `<expression_2>` unify. Such a success will cause instantiation to the variables of `<expression_1>` and `<expression_2>` giving an mgu of `<expression_1>` and `<expression_2>`. For example, the goal

```
?- f(X,b) = f(a,Y).
```

will succeed with variables `X` and `Y` instantiated to `a` and `b` respectively, that is, the goal returns {`X/a`, `Y/b`} as an mgu.

When the two arguments of the predicate = are equal, the mgu in this case can be taken as an identity substitution. The predicate \= is just the negation of the predicate = and is defined using the cut and fail combination as follows:

```
<expression_1> \= <expression_2>:-
    <expression_1> = <expression_2>, !, fail.
_ \= _.
```

Since Prolog omits the occur check condition when unifying two expressions, goals of the form

```
?- X = f(X).
```

do not fail although the normal unification procedure would, of course, fail to unify the two expressions `X` and `f(X)`. Prolog, however, would instantiate `X` to the infinite string `f(f(f(f(f(....`

The predicate == is used to check whether or not two terms are syntactically equal. The subgoal

```
?- f(X,b) == f(a,Y).
```

fails as its constituent terms `f(X,b)` and `f(a,Y)` are not syntactically equal.

The predicate `\==` is the negation of `==` and can be defined using the cut and fail combination in the same way as `\=` was defined by `=`.

9.9 List

A list structure is a sequence of any finite number of term structures. In Prolog it is represented as

```
[<expression_1>, ..., <expression_n>]
```

where each of <expression_1>, ..., <expression_n> is a member of the list. The expression <expression_1> is called the *head* of the list and the list [<expression_2>, ..., <expression_n>] is called the *tail* of the list. The *empty list*, denoted as `[]`, does not have any members. A list in Prolog is abbreviated as [<expression>|<list>] in which <expression> is the head and <list> is the tail. Thus the goal

```
?- [H|T] = [a, b, c, d].
```

would succeed and instantiates `H` to `a` and `T` to `[b, c, d]`.

A list structure can be thought of as a functional value $list(H, T)$ which is when the one-to-one function symbol *list* is applied on its two arguments H and T. The functional value $list(H, T)$ is also a list in which H is the head and T is the tail. As an application of list structure, consider the following Prolog program which checks whether a given structure is a member of a list or not:

```
member(X, [Y|_]):-X == Y.
member(X, [_|T]):-member(X, T).
```

The subgoal `member(X,L)` succeeds when `X` is a member of `L`.

Another useful operation on lists is to join two lists together to form another. The following Prolog program serves this purpose:

```
append([], L, L).
append([X|L1], L2, [X|L3]):-append(L1, L2, L3).
```

The subgoal `append(L1,L2,L3)` succeeds when the list `L3` is obtained by appending `L2` to `L1`.

9.10 Arithmetic

The arithmetic function symbols (*, /, +, −, mod, div) are interpreted function symbols in Prolog. The assignment of the value of an arithmetic expression to a variable is achieved by the binary predicate symbol `is`. A subgoal of the form

```
<variable> is <arithmetic_expression>
```

causes an evaluation of `<arithmetic_expression>` giving a value and then `<variable>` is instantiated to this value. For example, the subgoal

```
?- X is 2+3*5.
```

succeeds and instantiates `X` to 17. Equality testing between the values of two arithmetic expressions is carried out in Prolog by means of the predicate `=:=`. Hence a subgoal of the form

```
<arithmetic_expression_1> =:=
    <arithmetic_expression_2>
```

succeeds when the value of `<arithmetic_expression_1>` is equal to that of `<arithmetic_expression_2>`. Thus the goal

```
?- 2+3*5 =:= 57/3-2.
```

succeeds. Other arithmetic binary predicates are < (strictly less than), > (strictly greater than), <= (less than or equal to), >= (greater than or equal to). The arguments of these predicates and also the predicate `=:=` should be ground.

9.11 Input/output

A Prolog program can read data from several input files (called *input streams*) and can output data to several output files (called *output streams*). However only one input stream and one output stream can be active at any time during the execution of the program. Reading input from a user's terminal and outputing data to a user's terminal are considered as input and output to a special file named `user`. At the beginning of the execution of a program these two streams are open. The subgoal

```
see( <file_name> )
```

succeeds if the file <file_name> exists. The subgoal will cause the current input stream to switch to <file_name>. The existence of a file can be tested by the predicate exists. The subgoal

```
exists( <file_name> )
```

succeeds if the file <file_name> exists in the current directory. In dealing with output streams, the subgoal

```
tell( <file_name> )
```

always succeeds and causes the current output stream to switch to file_name.

Reading a term from the current input stream is accomplished by the unary predicate read and writing a term to the current output stream is done by the predicate write. Hence the subgoal

```
read( <variable> )
```

succeeds with an instantiation of the variable <variable> to a term from a current input file. When the end of the current input file is reached, <variable> is instantiated to end_of_file. Each term of the input file must be followed by '.' and a carriage return. In a similar way, the subgoal

```
write( <term> )
```

succeeds and causes the term <term> to be written on the current output stream. The subgoal

```
tab( <integer> )
```

succeeds and writes <integer> number of spaces on the current output stream. Also the nullary predicate nl causes the start of a new line on the current output stream. Current input and output streams can be closed by the nullary predicates seen and told respectively. Consider the following program to display the contents of a file on the terminal (assuming the current output stream is user) using the predicates read and write:

```
display_file( FileName ):-
    exists( FileName ),
    see( FileName ),
    repeat,
        read( Term ),
        ( Term = end_of_file ->
            !, seen ;
            write( Term ), write('.'), nl, fail ).
```

A goal of the form

```
?- display_file( <file_name> ).
```

displays the contents of the file `<file_name>` on the terminal but the variable names occurring in any terms therein are replaced by suitable internal variable names.

As opposed to reading and writing terms, single characters from the input or output streams can also be read or written with the help of the unary predicates `get0` and `put`. For example, a single character can be read from an input stream by using a subgoal of the form

```
get0( <variable> )
```

and `<variable>` will be instantiated to the ASCII character code for the character read. A subgoal of the form

```
put( <variable> )
```

displays the character whose ASCII character code is `<variable>`. The above program to display the contents of a file can be rewritten using the two predicates `get0` and `put` as follows:

```
display_file( FileName ):-
    exists( FileName ),
    see( FileName ),
    repeat,
        get0( Char ),
        ( Char = 26 ->   % ASCII code for control-Z
            !, seen ;
            put( Char ), fail ).
```

In this case the variable names will be displayed as they were in the input file.

9.12 Clause management

To read clauses from a file the `consult` predicate is used. Hence a command

```
?- consult( <file_name> ).
```

reads the clauses from the file <file_name> into the Prolog interpreter. An alternative syntax for this is

```
?- [ <file_name> ].
```

A number of different files can be consulted as

```
?- [ <file_name_1>, ..., <file_name_n> ].
```

This is useful where different parts of a program are held in a number of different files, for example. A command of the form

```
?- reconsult( <file_name> ).
```

results in the clauses in the file being added to the existing clause set. At the same time any clauses with the same predicate symbol and arity in their heads as those in <file_name> are deleted from the existing clause set. An alternative syntax for reconsulting the file is

```
?- [ -<file_name> ].
```

A sequence of files can be consulted and reconsulted. As an example consider the command

```
?- [ <file_name_1>, -<file_name_2>, <file_name_3> ].
```

which causes <file_name_1> to be consulted, then <file_name_2> to be reconsulted on the resultant set of clauses and then <file_name_3> to be consulted on the resultant set of clauses. Consulting or reconsulting the special file `user` causes the system to read in clauses from the terminal until `end_of_file` is entered.

An individual clause can be added to an existing set of clauses by the command

```
?- assert( <clause> ).
```

There are two different versions of the `assert` predicate, namely `asserta` and `assertz`. The former causes the clause to be placed towards the beginning of the existing set of clauses before any other clauses with same head predicate and the latter will place it at the end after any clauses with the same head predicate. Deleting a clause from an existing set of clauses is achieved by

```
?- retract( <clause> ).
```

Considering `clause` as a term, Prolog attempts to unify it with an existing clause. The first clause for which this unification succeed is deleted from the existing clause set. The command

```
?- retractall( <clause> ).
```

deletes all the clauses whose heads unify with `clause`. The command

```
?- abolish( <predicate_symbol>, <integer> ).
```

causes the deletion of all clauses whose head predicate symbol is `<predicate_symbol>` with arity `<integer>`.

9.13 Set evaluation

The evaluation strategy for producing answers in pure Prolog is basically tuple-at-a-time, that is, branches of the search tree are explored one after another using a depth-first strategy with backtracking. Every success branch produces an answer. When Prolog tries to find another success branch through backtracking, all information about the previous branch of the computation is lost. Hence in a way there is no connection between the computation of answers coming from two different branches of the search tree.

The `setof` predicate enables one to accumulate different answers to a query and thus provides a set-at-a-time evaluation strategy. The syntax of this predicate is outside the framework of first-order logic and can be given as

```
setof( <term>, <conjunction>, <list> )
```

The above subgoal is true when `<list>` is the sorted set of instances of `<term>` for which the goal `<conjunction>` succeeds. A slightly different version of the `setof` predicate is `bagof` whose syntax is similar to the above, that is

```
bagof( <term>, <conjunction>, <list> )
```

The semantics of the above subgoal is given as true when `<list>` is the multiset (that is, a well-defined collection of elements, not necessarily distinct) of all instances of `<term>` for which `?- <conjunction>` succeeds. Consider a program containing the following clauses:

```
father(a, q).
father(a, p).
father(a, q).
father(b, s).
father(b, r).
father(b, s).
father(c, t).
```

A goal to find all the children of `a` can be given as

```
?- setof(X, father(a, X), L).
```

which causes an instantiation of `L` as

```
L = [p,q]
```

On the other hand, the goal

```
?- bagof(X, father(a, X), L).
```

causes an instantiation of `L` to

```
L = [q,p,q]
```

The predicate `setof` can have multiple solutions. The goal

```
?- setof(X, father(Y, X), L).
```

causes an instantiation of `Y` and `L` as

```
L = [p,q]
Y = a
```

respectively. Upon backtracking, the next instantiation of `Y` and `L` would be

```
L = [r,s]
Y = b
```

and so on. The same goal can be interpreted as to find all `X`s such that `father(Y, X)` is true for some `Y` and is expressed as

```
?- setof(X, Y^father(Y, X), L).
```

The instantiation to `L` would be

```
L = [p,q,r,s,t]
```

The predicate `bagof` has similar interpretations in the above two cases but does not discard any duplicate elements from a list.

The system predicate `setof` can be implemented by using some of the predicates already introduced. Consider one such alternative implementation to find all solutions without backtracking:

```
set_of(Term, Goal, Instance):-
    assert(term_goal(Term, Goal)),
    set_of([], UInstance),
    sort(UInstance, Instance),
    retract(term_goal(_,_)).
set_of(L, UInstance):-
    term_goal(Term, Goal),
    Goal,
    not member(Term, L), !,
    set_of([Term|L], UInstance).
set_of(UInstance, UInstance).

member(H, [H|_]):-!.
member(H, [_|T]):-member(H, T).
```

A major drawback in the above implementation is that each time a new solution is generated the search tree corresponding to the goal `Goal` is traversed from the beginning and not from the point where the last solution is found. A further alternative implementation can be achieved by using the `assert` and `retract` predicates. This implementation would be particularly difficult in the presence of rules.

9.14 Meta-programming

A meta-program analyses, transforms and simulates other programs by treating them as data. Meta-programming is inherent in the nature of logic programming and Prolog is no exception to this. Some examples of meta-programming (Abramson and Rogers, 1989; Hill and Lloyd, 1989) are as follows. A translator (or a compiler) for a particular language is a meta-program which takes programs written in that language as input. The output for the translator (or compiler) is another program in another language. An editor can also be viewed as a meta-program which treats other program as data.

An interpreter for a language, called a *meta-interpreter* (Abramson and Rogers, 1989; Sterling and Lakhotia, 1988; Sterling and Shapiro, 1986), is also a meta-program. If the language of a meta-interpreter $\mathcal{M}$, that is, the language in which $\mathcal{M}$ is written, coincides with the language for which $\mathcal{M}$ is written, then the meta-interpreter $\mathcal{M}$ is called a *meta-circular interpreter*. Since program and data are uniformly expressed as clauses in logic programming environments, writing a meta-circular interpreter is an inherent feature.

Consider an example of a meta-circular interpreter written in Prolog which simulates Prolog-like execution by selecting the rightmost atom from a goal:

```
solve(true).
solve((B, A)):- solve(B), solve(A).
solve(not A):- not solve(A).
solve(A):- clause(A, B), solve(B).
```

Another example is the meta-program which transforms a set of definite rules (with no occurrence of constant symbols) to another program by *saturating* each non-recursive predicate occurring in the body of a rule. For example, the following Prolog version of some definite program

```
a(X, Y):- p(X, Y).
a(X, Y):- p(X, Z), a(Z, Y).
p(X, Y):- f(X, Y).
p(X, Y):- m(X, Y).
m(X, Y):- f(Z, Y), h(Z, X).
```

can be transformed to the following Prolog program:

```
a(X, Y):- f(X, Y).
a(X, Y):- f(Z, Y), h(Z, X).
a(X, Y):- f(X, Z), a(Z, Y).
a(X, Y):- f(Z1, Z), h(Z1, X), a(Z, Y).
p(X, Y):- f(X, Y).
p(X, Y):- f(Z, Y), h(Z, X).
m(X, Y):- f(Z, Y), h(Z, X).
```

To write this meta-program, suppose the program clauses are stored under a unary predicate rule in the form of rule(<rule>). Then, in the following meta-program, the subgoal saturate(<rule_1>, <rule_2>) succeeds only when <rule_2> is obtained from <rule_1> by the saturation process described above:

```
base( P ):- not rule((P:-_)).

recursive(P):- rule((P:-B)), recursive(P, B), !.

recursive(H, H).
recursive(H, (B,Bs)):-
    recursive(H, B); recursive(H, Bs).
recursive(H, H1):-
    rule((H1:-B)), recursive( H, B ).

expand((B,Bs), (ExpB,ExpBs)):-!,
    expand(B, ExpB), expand(Bs, ExpBs).
expand(H, H):- (recursive( H ); base(H)), !.
expand(H, ExpB):- rule((H:-B)),  expand(B, ExpB).
```

Exercises

9.1 Write a program to generate all possible permutations of a given sequence of numbers.

9.2 A number is *perfect* if the sum of all of its proper factors (excluding the number itself) is equal to the number. For example, 6, 28, 496 are perfect numbers. Write a program to generate as many of these numbers as possible.

9.3 Suppose **S** is a non-empty set and ⊕ and ⊗ are binary operations defined on **S**. Then consider the following algebraic properties (Blyth and Robertson, 1986; Herstein, 1964) defined on **S** wrt these operations:

(a) (**S**, ⊕) is called a *semigroup* if the following conditions are satisfied:

(i) $a, b \in \mathbf{S}$ implies that $a \oplus b \in \mathbf{S}$ (*closure*).

(ii) $a, b, c \in \mathbf{S}$ implies that $a \oplus (b \oplus c) = (a \oplus b) \oplus c$ (*associative*).

(b) (**S**, ⊕) is called a *group* if the following conditions are satisfied:

(i) (**S**, ⊕) is a semigroup.

(ii) There exists an element $e \in \mathbf{S}$ such that $a \oplus e = e \oplus a = a$ for all $a \in \mathbf{S}$ (*existence of identity*).

(iii) For every $a \in \mathbf{S}$ there exists an element $a^{-1} \in \mathbf{S}$ such that $a \oplus a^{-1} = a^{-1} \oplus a = e$ (*existence of inverse*).

(c) (**S**, ⊕) is called an *abelian group* if the following conditions are satisfied:

(i) (**S**, ⊕) is a group.

(ii) For all $a, b \in \mathbf{S}$, $a \oplus b = b \oplus a$ (*commutative*).

(d) (**S**, ⊕, ⊗) is called a *ring* if the following conditions are satisfied:

(i) (**S**, ⊕) is an abelian group.

(ii) (**S**, ⊗) is a semigroup.

(iii) For all $a, b, c \in \mathbf{S}$, $a \otimes (b \oplus c) = (a \otimes b) \oplus (a \otimes c)$ and $(b \oplus c) \otimes a = (b \otimes a) \oplus (c \otimes a)$ ($\otimes$ is *distributive* over $\oplus$).

(e) $(\mathbf{S}, \oplus, \otimes)$ is called a *field* if

(i) **S** has at least two elements.

(ii) $(\mathbf{S}, \oplus)$ is an abelian group with the identity element e.

(iii) $(\mathbf{S} - \{e\}, \otimes)$ is a group.

(iv) $\otimes$ is *distributive* over $\oplus$.

For example, $(\{0, 1, 2\}, \oplus, \otimes)$ is a field where the two binary operations are defined by the following composition table:

$\oplus$	0	1	2
0	0	1	2
1	1	2	0
2	2	0	1

$\otimes$	0	1	2
0	0	0	0
1	0	1	2
2	0	2	1

By representing sets and composition tables by a suitable data structure, write a Prolog program to verify all the above algebraic properties in a given set with operations.

9.4 Write a Prolog program to solve the famous eight queens problem which is to place eight queens on the empty chess board in such a way that no two queens cross each other. The following is one such arrangement and the position of the queens are shown by the symbol * (the symbol # is relevant in Exercise 9.5 only).

					*		
		*					
				*			
						*	
*				#			
			*	#			
	*			#			
				#			*

9.5 A farmer has a plot of land like the chess board of Exercise 9.4 containing four trees at positions shown by the symbol #. The farmer wants to distribute the land equally (the same shape and area) among four children in such a way that every child receives his/her share with a tree in it. Each such area is composed of 16 squares and every pair of squares of the area of each child is edge connected (two squares S1 and S2 are edge connected if either they have a common edge or there exists another square S3 such that S1 is edge connected to S3 and S3 is edge connected to S1). Write a Prolog program which will achieve the required partition.

9.6 Write a Prolog program to sort a list of numbers using the quick sort algorithm.

9.7 Write a Prolog program to build a binary tree from a given list of numbers such that for every node N of the tree, the left child of N is less than N and the right child of N is greater than or equal to N. Traverse the tree in the order of left, root and right to print the sorted version of the initial input list.

9.8 Write a Prolog meta-program for checking the syntax of normal Prolog programs.

9.9 Write a meta-interpreter which simulates the Prolog-like execution of pure Prolog programs and goals by always selecting an instantiated literal under a non-recursive predicate symbol, if one exists. If there is no such literal the leftmost literal selection strategy should be followed.

9.10 Write a program to convert an extended program to its equivalent normal program (see Chapter 7 for the set of transformations).

PART IV

Deductive Databases

10

Deductive databases

This chapter introduces the deductive database model, different categories of deductive databases and their model-theoretic and proof-theoretic views. A number of differences are observed between deductive database systems and logic programming systems and a connection is established to allow deductive databases to be viewed as logic programs. The concept of transactions in the context of deductive databases is also discussed.

10.1 Deductive database model

A *data model* consists of the following:

(1) A mathematical notation for the formal description of data and its relationships, and

(2) A technique for the manipulation of data such as answering queries and checking integrity.

The first-order language is used as a mathematical notation for describing data in a *deductive database model* and data is manipulated in such models by the evaluation of logical formulae. The approach of taking first-order logic as the theoretical foundation of *deductive database systems* (Gallaire, 1983; Gallaire *et al.*, 1984; Gray and Lucas, 1988; Leung and Lee, 1988; Lloyd, 1983; Topor *et al.*, 1984) has several advantages:

(1) Logic itself has a well-understood semantics.

(2) Logic can be used as a uniform language for expressing facts, rules, queries and integrity constraints.

(3) The well-developed theory of logic can be used to solve a number of database problems, including those of null values and indefinite data.

(4) The use of a single rule may replace many explicit facts. This provides an expressive and economic environment for data modelling.

(5) The concept of the deductive database generalizes the concept of *relational databases* (Brodie and Manola, 1989; Date, 1986; Gardarin and Valduriez, 1989; Ullman, 1984).

Definition 10.1: A *database clause* is a program clause, that is, a formula of the form

$$A_1 \vee \cdots \vee A_m \leftarrow L_1 \wedge \cdots \wedge L_n \qquad m \geq 1, n \geq 0$$

where each A_i is an atom and each L_j is a literal. A *rule* is a database clause with a non-empty body (that is, $n > 0$). A *fact* is a ground atom. Thus when a database is range-restricted each of its unit clauses becomes a fact. The terms definite, normal, disjunctive and general (or indefinite) rules and definite and indefinite facts are defined accordingly.

Definition 10.2: A *database query* (or simply *query*) is a goal, that is, a formula of the form

$$\leftarrow L_1 \wedge \cdots \wedge L_n \qquad n \geq 1$$

where each L_i is a literal.

Definition 10.3: A *general deductive database* (or *general database* or *deductive database*) is defined as a pair $(\mathbf{D}, \mathcal{L})$, where $\mathbf{D}$ is a finite set of database clauses and $\mathcal{L}$ is a first-order language. It is assumed that $\mathcal{L}$ has at least two symbols, one representing a constant symbol and another one representing a predicate symbol. A *definite* (resp. *normal*) database is a deductive database $(\mathbf{D}, \mathcal{L})$ where $\mathbf{D}$ contains only definite (resp. *normal*) clauses. A *relational database* is a deductive database $(\mathbf{D}, \mathcal{L})$ where $\mathbf{D}$ contains only definite facts. Hence, a relational database is a special form of a definite or normal or general database, a definite database is a special form of a normal or general database, and so on.

10.2 Deductive database systems versus logic programming systems

Although the structure of database clauses and program clauses are the same, a number of differences have been observed between deductive database systems and logic programming systems:

(1) In a typical deductive database system the number of facts is large compared to the number of rules. This is not the case in a typical logic programming system.

(2) A deductive database system partitions the set of predicate symbols into two disjoint sets, namely, a set of *base predicates* and a set of *virtual predicates*. Under this partition, each fact in the database is a fact under some base predicate symbol and the head of each rule is an atom under some virtual predicate. This kind of partition helps to store the clauses in a uniform fashion. On the other hand, a logic programming system does not make such a partition.

(3) The underlying language of a deductive database system is function free (apart from some common arithmetic functions). On the other hand, usage of functions is very common in a logic programming environment.

(4) Clauses in deductive database systems are considered range restricted, whereas a logic programming system, in general, does not impose such a restriction on clauses.

(5) In most theoretical developments of logic programming (such as the theory of program completion) the set of constant, function and predicate symbols for the underlying language has always been constructed using only symbols occurring in the program. On the other hand, the underlying language of a deductive database system is constructed using a predefined schema.

(6) Deductive database systems have a proper interface for data description and manipulation and this is done possibly through a high-level language. In logic programming systems the facility for manipulating clauses is very primitive.

(7) Deductive database systems have facilities for expressing and verifying integrity constraints which are properties that the data of a database is required to satisfy. There is no such concept in a logic programming system

(not to be confused with constraint logic programming).

(8) Deductive database systems place emphasis on efficiency while logic programming systems place it on functionalities. For example, occur check condition, function symbols, and so on, which have limited practical use, may be excluded from a deductive database system to achieve efficiency. On the other hand, the functionalities of a typical logic programming system are increased by incorporating function symbols, partial evaluation, occur check condition, and so on, and also by handling more general clauses rather than only definite ones.

(9) A typical implementation of a deductive database system stresses the efficient management of data (for example, the efficient retrieval of facts) while a logic programming system stresses the efficiency of the inference mechanism.

(10) Most deductive database queries seek all solutions and hence the procedural semantics of deductive databases are sometimes given in a set-at-a-time evaluation manner (such as fixpoint computation type) as opposed to tuple-at-a-time which is typical of a resolution-based refutation procedure in logic programming systems.

(11) The terminology used in logic programming systems differs from that used in deductive database systems. Logic programming terminology is inherited from mathematical logic and resolution theorem proving whereas deductive database terminology is inherited from that used in conventional database systems. Table 10.1 lists a set of equivalent terms used in deductive database systems and logic programming systems.

Despite the differences listed above between what is called a logic programming system and a deductive database system, theoretical studies (such as semantics) on logic programs and deductive databases can be made from the same point of view. In fact, the theoretical study of deductive databases can be performed by considering them as a subclass of logic programs provided the set of constant, function and predicate symbols for their underlying languages are the same. This means that the symbols for the underlying language of a deductive database system should be constructed using only symbols occurring in the set of clauses constituting the deductive database.

Consider the points of difference between deductive database systems and logic programming systems. Points (6), (7) and (9)–(11) are merely differences in the kind of facilities, notations and conveniences between logic programming systems and deductive database systems. Hence they do not otherwise change the semantics of a deductive database from a logic program. Points (1)–(4) and (8)

Table 10.1 Deductive database and logic programming terminology compared.

Deductive database	*Logic program*
Schema	Language
Relation symbol	Predicate symbol
Argument	Attribute
Database clause	Program clause
Fact	Ground unit clause
Indefinite fact	Ground non-unit assertion
Rule	Program clause (non-empty body)
Query	Goal
Integrity constraint	Closed formula

make deductive databases more specific than logic programs and hence they can still be studied as a subclass of logic programs. The difference between their underlying languages (point (5)) can also be removed by considering the language $\mathcal{L}$ of the database $(\mathbf{D}, \mathcal{L})$ as one constructed using only the symbols appearing in $\mathbf{D}$. Keeping this restriction in mind, all the results introduced in Chapters 5–8 relevant to programs and goals can be taken as valid in the context of databases and queries respectively. In particular, the procedural semantics introduced in Chapters 6–8 can be taken as *query evaluation procedures* in the appropriate class of databases. However, from the point of view of conventional databases, it can be shown that query evaluation in normal databases can be achieved by the SLDNF-resolution scheme.

10.3 Model theory versus proof theory

A database can be considered from the viewpoint of logic as:

(1) an interpretation of a first-order theory, or
(2) a first-order theory.

From the interpretation viewpoint, queries and integrity constraints are formulae that are to be evaluated using the semantic definition of truth. From the theory viewpoint, queries are considered to be theorems that are to be proved and integrity constraints are either considered to be theorems that are to be proved or formulae that are to be consistent with the theory. These two approaches are referred to as the *model-theoretic view* (or *relational structure view*) and the *proof-theoretic view* (or *logic database view*) (Gallaire *et al.*, 1984; Grant and Minker, 1989; Nicolas and Gallaire, 1978) respectively. The interpretation view and the theory view formalize the concepts of conventional and deductive databases respectively.

The idea behind the proof-theoretic view of a database $(\mathbf{D}, \mathcal{L})$ is to construct a theory $\mathcal{T}$, called a *proof theory* of $(\mathbf{D}, \mathcal{L})$, using the clauses of **D** and with $\mathcal{L}$ as language. Then an *answer to a query* $\leftarrow$ Q would be to find a substitution θ such that $\mathcal{T} \vdash Q\theta$. It is clear that when the language $\mathcal{L}$ of a database $(\mathbf{D}, \mathcal{L})$ is taken as the one constructed by using only the symbols occurring in **D**, any procedural semantics in the context of logic programs can serve as a vehicle for deduction from an underlying proof theory $\mathcal{T}$ (provided the semantics of **D** has been agreed as the semantics of $\mathcal{T}$) to find answers to the queries. For example, $Comp(\mathbf{D})$ can be taken as a proof theory of a database $(\mathbf{D}, \mathcal{L})$ and SLDNF-resolution can be used to find answers to the queries. This fact will be established in the following sections starting from the concepts of conventional databases.

10.4 Model theory for relational databases

Consider the range-restricted class of relational databases (that is, facts are ground) such that their languages do not contain any function symbols. The following hypotheses are made on such a class of relational databases for evaluating queries:

(1) The closed world assumption (CWA) states that all information that is not true in the database is assumed to be false ($\neg R(a_1, ..., a_n)$ is assumed to be true if and only if the fact $R(a_1, ..., a_n)$ is not explicitly present in the database). A more generalized form of CWA was introduced in Chapter 5.

(2) The *unique name assumption* (UNA) states that constants with different names are different.

(3) The *domain closure assumption* (DCA) states that there are no constants other than those in the language of the database.

EXAMPLE 10.1

Consider the following relational database:

Database: *Undergraduate (Subrata)*
Student (Janique)
Research (Janique)
Likes (Subrata, Mathematics)

(1) From the CWA it can be said that the tuple $\neg$ *Likes* (*Janique* , *Mathematics*) is assumed to be true, that is, Janique does not like mathematics.

(2) From the UNA it can be said that the two constants *Janique* and *Subrata* uniquely identify two different students.

(3) From the DCA it can be said that *Philosophy* is not a valid constant.

Let ($\mathbf{D}$, $\mathcal{L}$) be a relational database such that $\mathbf{D}$ is range restricted and $\mathcal{L}$ does not contain any function symbols. Then the database can be taken as an interpretation of the first-order theory consisting of the language $\mathcal{L}$ and the variables of $\mathcal{L}$ as ranging over the domain in this interpretation. The evaluation of logical formulae of $\mathcal{L}$ in this interpretation is based on:

$$R(a_1, ..., a_n) \text{ is true if and only if } R(a_1, ..., a_n) \in \mathbf{D}$$

This method of evaluation preserves the properties of the CWA, DCA and UNA. The least Herbrand model of the constructed theory contains exactly the information it is intended to store.

Although a relational database is generally considered as an interpretation of a first-order theory (from a model-theoretic point of view), it can also be considered from a proof-theoretic point of view in the following manner.

Let ($\mathbf{D}$, $\mathcal{L}$) be a relational database such that $\mathbf{D}$ is range restricted and $\mathcal{L}$ does not contain any function symbols. The proof-theoretic view of this relational database is obtained by constructing a theory $\mathcal{T}$ underlying the language $\mathcal{L}$. The proper axioms of the theory $\mathcal{T}$ are as follows:

(1) *Assertions* For each fact $R(a_1, ..., a_n) \in \mathbf{D}$, the assertions $R(a_1, ..., a_n)$.

(2) *The completion axioms* For each relation symbol R, if $R(a_1^1, ..., a_n^1)$, ..., $R(a_1^m, ..., a_n^m)$ denote all the facts under R, the completion axiom for R

$$\forall x_1, ..., \forall x_n (R(x_1, ..., x_n) \rightarrow$$
$$(x_1 = a_1^1 \wedge \cdots \wedge x_n = a_n^1) \vee \cdots \vee (x_1 = a_1^m \wedge \cdots \wedge x_n = a_n^m)$$

(3) *The unique name axioms* If $a_1, ..., a_p$ are all constant symbols of $\mathcal{L}$, then

$$(a_1 \neq a_2), ..., (a_1 \neq a_p), (a_2 \neq a_3), ..., (a_{p-1} \neq a_p)$$

(4) *The domain closure axioms* If $a_1, ..., a_p$ are all constant symbols of $\mathcal{L}$, then

$$\forall x ((x = a_1) \vee \cdots \vee (x = a_p))$$

(5) *Equality axioms* The following axioms

$$\forall x (x = x)$$
$$\forall x \ \forall y ((x = y) \rightarrow (y = x))$$
$$\forall x \ \forall y \ \forall z ((x = y) \wedge (y = z) \rightarrow (x = z))$$
$$\forall x_1 \cdots \forall x_n (P(x_1, ..., x_n) \wedge (x_1 = y_1) \wedge \cdots \wedge (x_n = y_n) \rightarrow P(y_1, ..., y_n))$$

The following theorem establishes the equivalence between the two approaches, namely the model-theoretic and the proof-theoretic views.

Theorem 10.1: For any formula U in $\mathcal{L}$, $\mathcal{T} \vdash$ U if and only if U is true in **D**.

Proof Left as an exercise. ■

10.5 Proof theory for deductive databases

Deductive databases are generally considered as a first-order theory and this section is devoted to constructing a proof theory for the class of normal databases. A proof theory for definite databases is a special case of that for a normal database. The construction of a proof theory for general databases is left as an exercise.

Let (**D**, $\mathcal{L}$) be a normal database. As in the case of relational databases, a proof-theoretic view of **D** is obtained by constructing a theory $\mathcal{T}$ underlying the language $\mathcal{L}$. The proper axioms of the theory $\mathcal{T}$ are as follows:

(1) *Completion axioms* Obtained by completing each predicate symbol of $\mathcal{L}$ (as defined in Chapter 7) according to the clauses of **D**.

(2) *Equality and unique name axioms* Axioms of the equality theory (defined in Chapter 7) according to the constant, function and predicate symbols of $\mathcal{L}$.

(3) *Domain closure axiom* If $a_1, ..., a_p$ are all the elements of $\mathcal{L}$ and $f_1, ..., f_q$ are all the function symbols of $\mathcal{L}$, then the domain closure axiom (Lloyd, 1987; Mancarella *et al.*, 1988) is as follows:

$$\forall x ((x{=}a_1) \vee \cdots \vee (x{=}a_p) \vee (\exists x_1 \cdots \exists x_m (x{=}f_1(x_1, ..., x_m))) \vee \cdots \vee (\exists y_1 \cdots \exists y_n (x{=}f_q(y_1, ..., y_n))))$$

Since **D** is a normal database, the above proof-theoretic view reduces to *Comp*(**D**) plus the above domain closure axiom.

10.6 Deductive databases as logic programs

If $\mathcal{T}$ is the proof theory of a normal database (**D**, $\mathcal{L}$) as constructed in the previous section, then $\mathcal{T}$ reduces to *Comp*(**D**) plus the domain closure axiom of $\mathcal{T}$. The domain closure axiom from $\mathcal{T}$ may be avoided by dealing with range-restricted queries and clauses and thus the proof theory of a normal database is reduced to *Comp*(**D**). It was shown in Chapter 7 that there is an equivalence (sound but not always complete) between the *Comp*(**D**) and SLDNF-resolution. Hence, from the operational point of view (that is, for the purpose of query evaluation) a normal database, under some restrictions, consists of the following:

(1) A set of normal clauses each of whose elements is range restricted.

(2) SLDNF-resolution.

A proof theory $\mathcal{T}$ for a definite database (**D**, $\mathcal{L}$) can be constructed in exactly the same way as for normal databases. However, from the operational point of view a definite database will consist of the following:

(1) A set of definite clauses each of whose elements is range restricted.

(2) SLD-resolution.

10.7 Transactions on deductive databases

Definition 10.4: A *transaction* on a deductive database is a finite sequence of the *operations* (or *actions*) of *insertion*, *deletion* or *updating* of clauses.

As a deductive database is viewed as a set of clauses (the proof-theoretic view) rather than their models (the model-theoretic view), no deletion or update operations are allowed on any fact (either definite or indefinite) which is implicit in the database (it is not present in the database, but can be derived from the database). Discussions related to the problem of updating implicit tuples can be found in Bancilhon and Spyratos (1981), Dayal and Bernstein (1978), Fagin *et al.* (1986), Guessoum and Lloyd (1990, 1991) and Naqvi and Krishnamurthy (1988). An update of a clause which is explicitly present in a deductive database will be taken (except in Chapter 16) as a deletion followed by an addition.

Throughout the rest of the text, an insert (resp. delete) operation in a transaction is written as 'insertfact C' or 'insertrule C' (resp. 'deletefact C' or 'deleterule C'), depending on the type of the clause C.

Definition 10.5: A transaction is said to have been *committed* successfully if the entire sequence of operations forming the transaction completes successfully.

The main reasons for failing to complete a transaction include the violation of an integrity constraint by operations in the transaction, a system failure, an infinite computation or some user interrupt.

Exercise

10.1 Develop a proof-theory for general databases using the definition of general program completion given in Chapter 8.

11

Query evaluation

This chapter establishes a number of basic characteristics of the process of query evaluation. It then describes in some detail a representative selection of query evaluation strategies for definite databases and definite goals. Note that query processing in parallel environments will be discussed in Chapter 15. Recall that a definite program (or definite database) has been defined as a finite set of definite clauses of the form

$$A \leftarrow B_1 \wedge \cdots \wedge B_m, \qquad m \geq 0 \tag{11.1}$$

and a definite goal (or definite query) has been defined as a formula of the form

$$\leftarrow B_1 \wedge \cdots \wedge B_n, \qquad n \geq 1 \tag{11.2}$$

where A and B_is are atoms and free variables occurring in each of the clauses and (11.1) and (11.2) are assumed to be universally quantified over the clause. Databases and queries are assumed to be definite for this chapter.

11.1 What is query evaluation?

An answer to a query $\leftarrow$ Q in the context of a database **D** is a substitution θ such that Qθ is true according to the chosen declarative semantics of **D**. For example, if the 'completed database' semantics is chosen as the declarative semantics of **D** then a substitution θ is an answer to the query $\leftarrow$ Q if Qθ is a logical consequence of *Comp*(**D**), that is, *Comp*(**D**) $\vdash$ Qθ. Similarly, if the 'minimal model' semantics is chosen as declarative semantics of **D** then a substitution θ is an answer to the query $\leftarrow$ Q if Qθ is true in every minimal model of **D**.

As has been pointed out previously, different semantics given on a particular class of programs may not necessarily agree. The above two agree for the class of definite databases. For the class of normal programs they may be different as is evident from the following example. According to the minimal model semantics, an answer to the query $\leftarrow P(x)$ in the context of the normal database $\{P(a) \leftarrow \neg P(a)\}$ is $\{x/a\}$; but the completed database semantics in this case is inconsistent. In this chapter, the minimal model (that is, the completed database) semantics has been chosen as the standard one for the purpose of query evaluation.

The subject of query evaluation deals with finding answers to queries from different databases. A *query evaluation procedure* (or *method* or *strategy*) finds answers to queries in the context of a class of databases while obeying a specified semantics for that class of databases. When a database is considered as a logic program (see Chapter 10), each of the theorem proving procedures introduced so far may serve as a query evaluation procedure. In the main, theorem proving procedures generalize query evaluation procedures. However, query evaluation procedures may additionally incorporate a number of special techniques to achieve efficient clause management to answer generations.

Another way of looking at the subject of query evaluation is to deal with the computation of a subset of the model of the considered database. The query to be evaluated on this database corresponds to this particular subset of the model. The computation of the fixpoint of a definite program (definite database) in Chapter 6 yields the whole model of the database and the computation can be restricted to a subset of this model by looking at the query patterns. This type of computation is referred to as *bottom-up* and is particularly efficient for typical all-solution type database queries. A few methods will be introduced in this chapter which follow bottom-up computation.

11.2 Characteristics of query evaluation methods

This section describes the characteristics (Das, 1991b) which a typical query evaluation method might possess. These characteristics may be used to categorize and compare different query evaluation methods. Also, the overall suitability of a particular method can be judged from its basic characteristics.

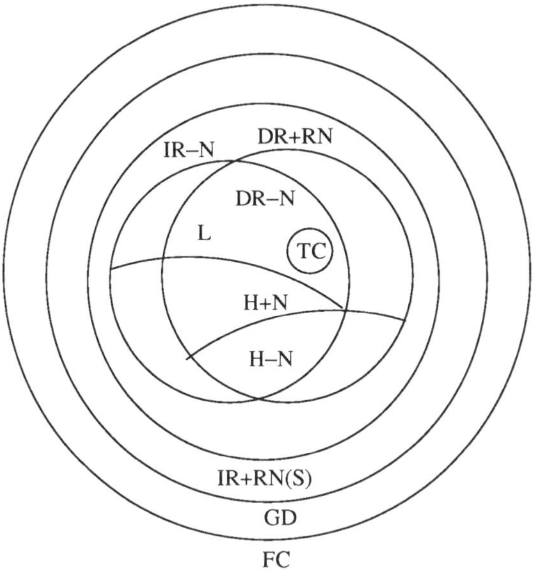

Figure 11.1 Different classes of rules: H–N – Hierarchical without Negation; H+N – Hierarchical with Negation; DR–N – Directly Recursive without Negation; TC – Transitive Closure; DR+RN – Directly Recursive with Restricted Negation; IR–N – Indirectly Recursive without Negation; L – Linear; IR+N – Indirectly Recursive with Restricted Negation; S – Stratified; GD – General Definite; FC – Full Clausal.

11.2.1 Application domain

The application domain for a query processing strategy is the class of databases that it can handle. To a large extent, this was discussed in Chapter 5. However, the classification provided there does not fully serve the type of applications in the context of deductive databases. This section handles the same problem in a more refined way and uses database terminology. Different application domains are introduced using the concept of dependency graphs in order of the complexity of their implementations. They are also shown diagrammatically in Figure 11.1.

If the dependency graph for a database **D** contains neither cycles nor negative edges, then **D** is said to be *hierarchical without negation* (H–N). An example of a hierarchical database of family relations is as follows (only the set of rules is given):

$\mathbf{S}_1$: R1. $Mother(x, y) \leftarrow Father(z, y) \wedge Husband(z, x)$

R2. $Parent(x, y) \leftarrow Father(x, y)$

R3. $Parent(x, y) \leftarrow Mother(x, y)$

R4. $Wife(x, y) \leftarrow Husband(y, x)$

R5. $Married(x, y) \leftarrow Husband(x, y)$

R6. $Married(x, y) \leftarrow Wife(x, y)$

R7. $Dependent(x, y) \leftarrow Parent(y, x) \wedge Employed(y) \wedge Student(x)$

R8. $Guardian(x, y) \leftarrow Dependent(y, x)$

The set of rules $\mathbf{S}_1$ can be extended by permitting the inclusion of negation. For example, if the dependent relation in $\mathbf{S}_1$ is defined as follows:

$\mathbf{S}_2$: $Dependent(x, y) \leftarrow Married(y, x) \wedge Employed(y) \wedge \neg Employed(x)$

then a database containing the resultant set $\mathbf{S}_1 \cup \mathbf{S}_2$ of rules will be hierarchical with negation. In other words if the dependency graph of a database **D** does not contain any cycles but does contain a negative edges, then **D** is called *hierarchical with negation* (H+N).

If one adds to $\mathbf{S}_1$ the following two rules defining the family relations *Ancestor* and *Samegen*, then a database containing the resultant set $\mathbf{S}_1 \cup \mathbf{S}_3$ of rules becomes directly recursive:

$\mathbf{S}_3$: $Ancestor(x, y) \leftarrow Parent(x, y)$

$Ancestor(x, y) \leftarrow Parent(x, z) \wedge Ancestor(z, y)$

$Samegen(x, y) \leftarrow Equal(x, y)$

$Samegen(x, y) \leftarrow Parent(u, x) \wedge Samegen(u, v) \wedge Parent(v, y)$

In other words if each cycle of the dependency graph of a database is of length 1 and is formed by a positive edge, and the graph does not contain any negative edge, then the set of rules is *directly recursive without negation* (DR–N). A *transitive closure* (TC) rule, that is, a rule of the form

$\mathbf{S}_4$: $Samegen(x, y) \leftarrow Samegen(x, z) \wedge Samegen(z, y)$

$Ancestor(x, y) \leftarrow Ancestor(x, z) \wedge Ancestor(z, y)$

falls into this category. Several methods (Agrawal and Jagadish, 1987, 1988; Han *et al.*, 1988; Ioannidis and Ramakrishnan, 1988; Valduriez and Khoshafian, 1988) have been proposed for processing queries in the presence of transitive closure type rules.

If each cycle of the dependency graph of a database is of length 1 and is formed by a positive edge although the remainder of the graph may contain negative edges, then the set of rules is *directly recursive with restricted negation* (DR+RN). A database whose set of rules is $\mathbf{S}_1 \cup \mathbf{S}_2 \cup \mathbf{S}_3$ is an example of a database with direct recursion with restricted negation.

If each cycle of the dependency graph of a database **D** is formed by positive edges only and the graph does not contain a negative edge, then **D** is *indirectly recursive without negation* (IR–N) (that is, definite). A graph of this kind may contain cycles of length more than 1. *Datalog* (Bancilhon and Ramakrishnan, 1989; Bancilhon *et al.*, 1986; Ceri *et al.*, 1990; Ullman, 1985) is another name for this class of database:

$\mathbf{S}_5$: $\quad Husband(x, y) \leftarrow Wife(y, x)$

A database whose set of rules is $\mathbf{S}_1 \cup \mathbf{S}_3 \cup \mathbf{S}_4 \cup \mathbf{S}_5$ is an example of a datalog but not directly recursive without negation.

Consider a set of rules from the datalog class. A rule R is linear (L) if at most one predicate occurring in the body of R is mutually recursive with respect to the predicate of the head of R. A database is linear if each of its rules is linear. This is a particular case of indirect recursion without negation. Each of the rules in $\mathbf{S}_3$ is linear but none of the rules in $\mathbf{S}_4$ is.

If each cycle of the dependency graph of a database is formed by positive edges only although the remainder of the graph may contain negative edges, then the set of rules is *indirectly recursive with restricted negation* (IR+RN). A graph of this kind may contain negative edges and cycles of length greater than 1. This class of databases is equivalent to the *stratified* (S) class. A database whose set of rules is $\mathbf{S}_1 \cup \cdots \cup \mathbf{S}_5$ is an example of a stratified database.

In the *general definite* (GD) (that is, normal) class of databases negation is unrestricted and recursion may be indirect:

$\mathbf{S}_6$: $\quad Father(x, y) \leftarrow Parent(x, y) \wedge \neg Mother(x, y)$

$\quad\quad Husband(x, y) \leftarrow Married(x, y) \neg Divorced(x, y)$

Suppose **D** is a database with the set of rules $\mathbf{S}_1 \cup \cdots \cup \mathbf{S}_6$. Then **D** is a database in which negation is unrestricted and recursion is complex. The dependency graph for **D** contains a cycle of length 2 involving the nodes *Father* and *Mother*. One of the edges of this cycle is positive and the other one is negative. This shows that this set of rules is indirectly recursive with negation unrestricted.

Full clausal (FC) form is the most general form of a database, in which a rule may have more than one positive literal in the conclusion. This kind of clause is used to represent indefinite data:

$$\mathbf{S}_7\text{:} \quad \mathit{Father}(x, y) \vee \mathit{Mother}(x, y) \leftarrow \mathit{Parent}(x, y)$$
$$\mathit{Husband}(x, y) \vee \mathit{Wife}(x, y) \leftarrow \mathit{Married}(x, y) \neg \mathit{Divorced}(x, y)$$

A database involving the set of rules in $\mathbf{S}_7$ is an example of a database in full clausal form.

11.2.2 Formalism

In an approach based on logic (that being the trend of this text), a query is evaluated on a database by using logical rewriting and the logical evaluation method in sequence. This entails the notions of unification, resolution, and so on. By contrast, in an approach based on *relational algebra* (Ullman, 1984) a query is solved by using an algebraic rewriting method and an algebraic evaluation method in sequence. In this case operations are expressed using the relational join, filter, and so on. In the functional approach, the problem of evaluation of a query is converted to the problem of evaluation of a set of functions on different domains of constants and tuples.

11.2.3 Technique

Computation of tuples by a bottom-up search technique (such as fixpoint computation) starts by considering the tuples explicitly present in the database and derives all tuples which can be inferred by substituting these into the body of a rule. This process is then repeated by applying rules to the set consisting of tuples explicitly present in the database together with those tuples which were inferred in the previous step. This process continues until no new tuples are derived.

A top-down query evaluation technique (such as SLD-resolution) starts from the query and derives answers by applying the rules using backward chaining. The concept of *forward chaining* and *backward chaining* are properties specifying the type of chaining adopted in the method. The forward chaining concept corresponds to the bottom-up technique and similarly, the backward chaining concept to the top-down technique.

Bottom-up evaluation may be inefficient for several reasons. During the iteration, the same tuple may be evaluated more than once. Optimization techniques could be applied to eliminate redundancy in the evaluation of tuples. Also, the bottom-up evaluation process may generate tuples not relevant to the user queries. In such cases, constant propagation is necessary to reduce this inefficiency.

Special methods for employing constant propagation are not necessary in the top-down approach as the computation starts from the goal itself. However, top-down evaluation may suffer from the problem of non-termination in the presence of a set of recursive rules. As a result, top-down approaches should employ a special kind of loop detection mechanism. A selection of methods are described in the following section following both the bottom-up and top-down techniques. These take into account the problems listed above.

11.2.4 Approaches

In a compiled approach (Henschen and Naqvi, 1984), the rules of the database and the user query (or its pattern) are transformed into another program focusing on relevant tuples. The transformed program is then run on the tuples of the database to get answers to the query. Hence, in the compiled approach, there is a clear separation between the compiled phase which compiles the query using rules, and the run phase which runs the compiled program on the tuples. By contrast, in an *interpreted* approach, the query is run directly using the rules and tuples of the database. Optimizations techniques are applied at run time.

In a compiled approach, the compilation phase is dependent on the query (or query pattern) and the rules of the database. Hence, recompilation is necessary on the arrival of each new query (or of a query of a different pattern) or on changing the set of rules of the database.

11.2.5 Answering techniques

A query evaluation method may compute either a single answer at a time or the set of all answers. The former technique is called tuple-at-a-time and the latter is set-at-a-time. A method can return an answer to a query by following either the tuple-at-a-time strategy or the set-at-a-time strategy or by using a combination of both approaches. A resolution-based query evaluation method falls into the category of tuple-at-a-time answering techniques.

The set-at-a-time approach to evaluation is ideal for some database queries though for others the computation of a large set of answers is very inefficient.

11.2.6 Modes of evaluation

In a *lazy* query evaluation mode, the query evaluation system will only determine answers to a query when driven by a request, and even then will produce only a subset of the set of all answers to a query rather than the full set. By contrast, in an *eager* query evaluation mode, the query evaluation method will go on producing answers to a query irrespective of the needs of the user.

Lazy/eager evaluation is not quite the same as the concept of answer computation strategy, that is, tuple-at-a-time or set-at-a-time. A lazy query evaluation mode can easily be incorporated into a method which follows a tuple-at-a-time evaluation technique, except if the method follows a bottom-up approach. Finding a successful derivation in an SLD-resolution involves computing one answer and then using backtracking if this is required. Hence, this is a tuple-at-a-time strategy. A lazy evaluation mode can be incorporated easily into this kind of tuple-at-a-time strategy as little work is done at every derivation compared to the generation of the complete search space.

To incorporate lazy evaluation successfully into an algorithm, the algorithm should be divided into several small steps of computation where each step is capable of generating some answers. Obviously SLD-resolution has the finest steps of this kind. On the other hand, in the naive and seminaive evaluation methods (see Section 11.3), which compute a set of answers at every step, a substantial amount of work is done at each step.

The eager evaluation mode is ideal when the set of all answers is required for most of the incoming queries. On the other hand, in a seat reservation system for example, it is usually sufficient to present a customer with a limited subset of options. If in this case eager evaluation mode were to be used, effort would be wasted in determining the set of all seats available.

11.2.7 Correctness

An algorithm for query evaluation is expected to satisfy the three properties: soundness, completeness and termination. An algorithm is sound if it does not produce as a result tuples which are not answers to the query; it is complete if it produces all results of the query; it has the termination property if every query is guaranteed to terminate in a finite amount of time.

A query evaluation procedure must possess the soundness property. Sometimes the termination property is not guaranteed because of the presence of recursive rules in the database (Minker and Nicolas, 1983). In this case the procedure also does not satisfy the property of completeness.

11.2.8 Objective

A *pure evaluation* algorithm accepts a program and a query as input and produces as output the answer to the query. Often some optimization can be done at evaluation time. An optimization strategy, on the other hand, assumes a pure query evaluation algorithm and optimizes either the program or the program and the goal (transforming to another set of clauses) to make the evaluation more efficient. For example, a Prolog interpreter accepts as input a database and a query and produces as output the answer to the query by SLDNF-resolution and a literal selection strategy which selects the leftmost literal from a goal. This evaluation mechanism can be thought of as a pure evaluation.

An optimization strategy for evaluating a query in a Prolog system may be based on an improved literal selection strategy which selects either the most instantiated literal or an instantiated base literal from a goal. With the limitation of a leftmost literal selection strategy, another way of achieving this optimization may be to transform each rule to another rule by rearranging the body literal. This optimization strategy is not compiled as it does not use the query. On the other hand, a compiled approach always has an inherent optimization strategy as it transforms the rules of the database and the user query to give another program focusing on relevant tuples.

Optimization strategies can be classified into two main categories: *syntactic* and *semantic*. Syntactic optimization deals with a program's syntactic features, whereas semantic optimization is concerned with the use of additional semantic knowledge of the database, for example, queries and integrity constraints. The optimization strategy mentioned above regarding the selection of the most instantiated literal from a Prolog goal is an example of syntactic optimization.

11.2.9 Representation of clauses

The representation of clauses in a database is either *mixed* or *separate*. For performance reasons, some methods need to have the set of database relations divided into two disjoint sets: one is the set of *base* or *extensional* database relations (or *EDB relations* or *EDB predicates*) and the other is the set of *derived* or *intensional* database relations (or *IDB relations* or *IDB predicates*), that is, predicates used for rule heads are disjoint from predicates used for facts. A database not satisfying this condition can always be transformed (Bancilhon and Ramakrishnan, 1989) into an equivalent database which satisfies the desired property. For example, the database $\{P(x) \leftarrow Q(x),\ P(a),\ Q(b)\}$ which is in mixed representation can be transformed into an equivalent separately represented database $\{P(x) \leftarrow Q(x), P(x) \leftarrow R(x), R(a), Q(b)\}$ through the introduction of a new base relation R.

The separate representation of clauses has an advantage over mixed representation as it stores the clauses in a uniform fashion.

11.3 Methods of query evaluation

Having established a set of basic characteristics in Section 11.2, a number of methods will now be introduced, each possessing some subset of these characteristics. The four methods introduced deal with function-free definite databases (that is, function-free datalog) and are capable of answering definite queries. The first is a resolution-based top-down evaluation strategy called SLD-AL-resolution (Vieille, 1986). The others are based on bottom-up evaluation strategy and are called *naive*, *seminaive* (Bancilhon *et al.*, 1986) and *magic sets* (Bancilhon *et al.*, 1986; Beeri and Ramakrishnan, 1987). Seminaive is an optimized version of naive and magic sets can be thought of as a further optimization over seminaive. Additional references for the other methods of query evaluation which have been proposed are provided in Chapter 17.

11.3.1 SLD-AL-resolution

SLD-AL-resolution (Vieille, 1989) extends SLD-resolution by adding the *admissibility test* and the *lemma technique* (AL technique) and by pruning redundant parts of the SLD-tree. The AL technique requires each subgoal to be answered only once while guaranteeing answer completeness. In some cases SLD-AL-trees are finite where the equivalent SLD-trees are infinite. The selection function used in the SLD-AL-resolution is called a *local selection function*. This always selects one of the most recently introduced literals. The definition of this selection function is detailed below.

Definition 11.1: Let N_1 be a node in an SLD-tree labelled by the goal $G_1 = \leftarrow A_1 \wedge \cdots \wedge A_p \wedge \cdots A_n$ and A_p be the selected literal from this goal. Suppose N_2 is an immediate descendant of N_1 obtained by resolving G_1 against the clause $A \leftarrow B_1 \wedge \cdots \wedge B_m$. The node N_2 is then labelled by the goal $G_2 = \leftarrow (A_1 \wedge \cdots \wedge A_{p-1} \wedge B_1 \wedge \cdots \wedge B_m \wedge A_{p+1} \wedge \cdots \wedge A_n)\theta$, where θ is an mgu of A_p and A. Then each $B_i\theta$ ($1 \le i \le m$) in the goal of N_2 is said to be *introduced* at the node N_1. Each A_i, $i = 1, ..., p-1, p+1, ..., n$ is said to be introduced at a node N_0 higher than N_1 (that is, an ancestor on the SLD-tree) if A_i in G_1 was introduced at N_0. Each A occurring in G_2 is said to be the *most recently introduced*, if A was introduced at a node N_0 and if no other literal in N_2 was introduced at a node strictly between N_0 and N_2. The node N_2 (resp. its subgoal) is called a *direct descendant* of N_1 (resp. of its subgoal) if the subgoal selected at N_2 was introduced at N_1. The *descendance* relationship is the transitive closure of the direct descendance relationship.

Definition 11.2: A local selection function is a selection function that always selects one of the most recently introduced literals.

Definition 11.3: Suppose N_1 and N_2 are two nodes in an SLD-tree with a local selection function. Then N_1–N_2 is called a *proof segment* for the selected atom A in N_1 if and only if N_2 is a descendant of N_1 on the tree and N_2 is the first node on this branch that does not contain any descendants of A. If θ is the substitution at N_1, N_1–N_2 is said to prove the lemma $A\theta$ and N_2 is a *proof node* for $A\theta$.

Example 11.1 clarifies the above definition of the local selection function and proof segment.

EXAMPLE 11.1

Database: R1. $P(x) \leftarrow Q(x) \wedge R(x)$
R2. $P(x) \leftarrow S(x) \wedge T(x)$
R3. $T(b) \leftarrow U(b)$
F1. $Q(a)$
F2. $R(a)$
F3. $S(b)$

Goal: $\leftarrow P(x)$

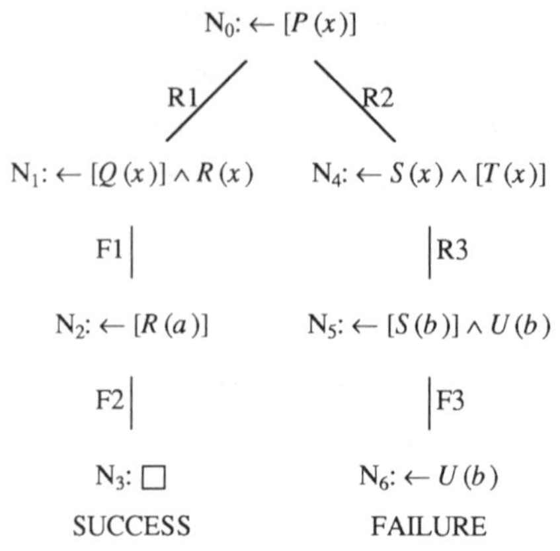

Figure 11.2 An SLD-tree in the case of Example 11.1 (bracketed literals are selected literals).

An SLD-tree for the database wrt the goal $\leftarrow P(x)$ is shown in Figure 11.2 where the selected literals have been placed within brackets. The ground atom $R(a)$ (= $R(x)\{x/a\}$) is introduced at node N_0 and not at node N_1, and $Q(x)$ is also introduced at N_0. The literals $Q(x)$ and $R(a)$ are most recently introduced literals in N_1 and N_2 respectively, whereas $S(b)$ in N_5 is not the most recently introduced as $U(b)$ has already been introduced between N_0 and N_5. The node N_1 is a direct descendant of N_0 but N_2 is not a direct descendant of N_1 as $R(a)$ was introduced in N_0 and not in N_1. The selection strategy along the left branch of the tree follows the property of a local selection function, whereas the selection strategy along the right branch fails to satisfy this property. This is because the selected literal at N_5 is not the most recently introduced. N_0–N_3 is a proof segment of $P(x)$ and similarly N_1–N_2 is a proof segment of $Q(x)$ but not N_1–N_3.

Each node of an SLD-AL-tree is labelled by goals where each goal is either admissible or non-admissible. If the selected literal A from a goal at a node N is not under a recursive predicate then N is always admissible. The construction of an SLD-AL-tree supposes an access to the collection **R** of *r-literals* that have been considered so far and a collection **L** of *r-lemmas* that have been proved so far. A subgoal in **R** and the node N at which it was selected can become a *producer* for other subgoals. However, by default it is not a producer. Initially, both **R** and **L** are initialized to empty and the root is considered as a producer.

Suppose **D** is a database and G is a goal. Then an SLD-AL-tree for $\mathbf{D} \cup \{G\}$ is constructed as follows:

(1) The root is labelled by G, which is admissible and a producer.

(2) Choose a node N_i labelled with a goal $G_i = \leftarrow A_1 \wedge \cdots \wedge A_p \wedge \cdots A_n$ and suppose A_p is the selected literal in G_i. If A_p is non-admissible then this resolution must be a resolution against a lemma in **L**; otherwise the resolution is against a clause $C = A \leftarrow B_1 \wedge \cdots B_m$ of the database. Add a child N_j of N_i labelled by the goal G_j, where G_j is the resolvent of G_i and C on A_p. If N_j is a proof node for an r-literal B, then add B to **L** if it is not an instance of a lemma already in **L**. If the selected atom A_q from the goal G_j is an instance of a subgoal M in **R**, mark A_q as non-admissible and M as producer; otherwise N_j is admissible and A_q is added to **R**.

Each node of an SLD-AL-tree is either admissible or non-admissible, depending on whether the selected literal is admissible or non-admissible. An admissible literal is always resolved against a clause of the database. The admissibility test prevents a subgoal from being indefinitely solved. The resolution of non-admissible subgoals against previously derived lemmas permits the production of further answers.

As the database has been considered to be function free, any SLD-AL-tree is finite. The restriction to the local selection function is necessary with respect to the completeness of SLD-AL-resolution and the following example illustrates this.

EXAMPLE 11.2

Database:	R1. $P(x, y) \leftarrow Q(x, y) \wedge R(x)$
	R2. $Q(x, y) \leftarrow S(x, y)$
	R3. $Q(x, y) \leftarrow S(x, z) \wedge Q(z, y)$
	F1. $S(b, a)$
	F2. $S(c, b)$
	F3. $R(c)$
Goal:	$\leftarrow P(x, a)$

Without following the local selection function for selecting literals, an SLD-AL-tree for the above program and the goal is shown in Figure 11.3. The choice of $R(x)$ from the goal at node N_2 is not local because $S(x, a)$ has been introduced between the nodes N_0 and N_2. The result of instantiation of x to c prevents the production of the lemma $Q(b, a)$. Because of this the tree does not show an

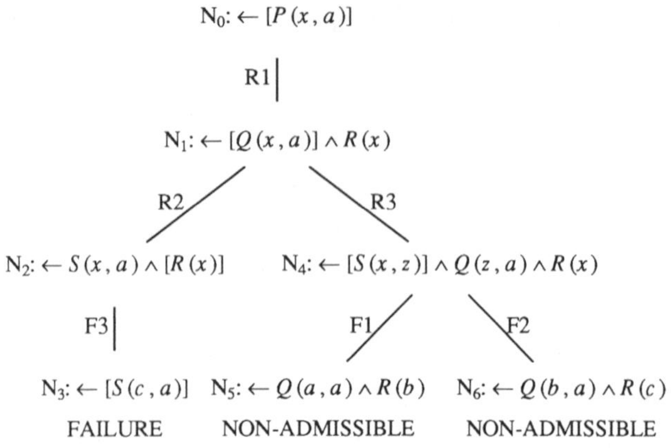

Figure 11.3 An SLD-tree in the case of Example 11.2 (bracketed literals are selected literals).

answer to the top goal through the rightmost branch whereas $P(c, a)$ is an answer to the goal.

EXAMPLE 11.3

Database: R1: $SG(x, y) \leftarrow Equal(x, y)$

R2: $SG(x, y) \leftarrow SG(u, v) \wedge Parent(u, x) \wedge Parent(v, y)$

$Parent(a, b)$

$Parent(a, c)$

$Equal(a, a)$

$Equal(b, b)$

$Equal(c, c)$

Goal: $\leftarrow SG(b, y)$

Obviously, the SLD-tree is infinite with the leftmost literal selection strategy. An SLD-AL-tree for this example is shown in Figure 11.4. The selected literal $SG(u_1, v_1)$ from the goal

$$\leftarrow SG(u_1, v_1) \wedge Parent(u_1, u) \wedge Parent(v_1, v) \wedge Parent(u, b) \wedge Parent(v, y)$$

is not admissible as it is a variant of a previously selected literal $SG(u, v)$. Hence it is resolved against the two lemmas $SG(b, b)$ and $SG(b, c)$. No answer is produced from either branch. For this node the local selection function will not allow either $Parent(u, b)$ or $Parent(v, y)$ to be selected before solving the other

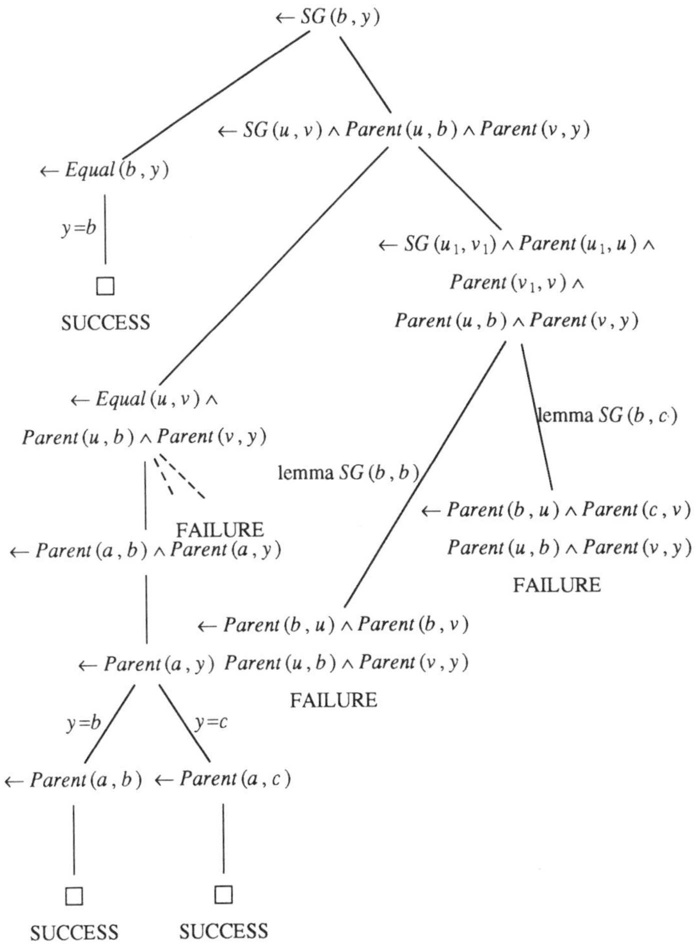

Figure 11.4 A complete SLD-AL-tree in the case of Example 11.3 using the leftmost literal selection strategy.

three recently introduced literals $SG\,(u_1, v_1)$, $Parent\,(u_1, u)$ and $Parent\,(v_1, v)$.

11.3.2 Naive evaluation

The naive evaluation method is a pure evaluation, bottom-up strategy which computes the least model of a datalog program. It is an iterative strategy and at each iteration all rules are applied to the set of tuples produced thus far to generate all implicit tuples. This iterative process continues until no more new tuples can be generated. If the database is range restricted and function free, termination is guaranteed and the method is complete.

The naive evaluation process is similar to the fixpoint computation in the case of definite programs. The fixpoint computation procedure computes the whole model of the database and does not take into account the query patterns. Therefore the fixpoint computation process may generate tuples which are not relevant to the query. For example, tuples may be generated through a rule whose predicate symbol in the head is not connected to predicate symbols occurring in the query via edges of the dependency graph of the underlying program. A better solution is to select a subset of the set of all rules with the help of the dependency graph. An additional step has been incorporated in the following naive computation procedure to do this.

Algorithm 11.1

Input: A function free, range-restricted, definite database $\mathbf{D}$ and a query Q.

Output: The set of answers to the query Q.

Step 1: Select a subset $\mathbf{D}_{rule}$ of the set of rules in $\mathbf{D}$ which helps to derive the answers to the query Q. One way to obtain the set $\mathbf{D}_{rule}$ is by using the dependency graph for $\mathbf{D}$. A rule R will be a member of $\mathbf{D}_{rule}$ if and only if there is a connection in the graph between the node corresponding to the predicate symbol of the head of R and the node corresponding to a predicate symbol occurring in the query.

Step 2: Set $\mathbf{M}$ = All facts of $\mathbf{D}$.

Step 3: Repeat
  Set $\mathbf{M}_{old} = \mathbf{M}$;
  For each rule $H \leftarrow$ B in $\mathbf{D}_{rule}$
    compute every substitution θ to the variables of B
      such that $B\theta$ is true in $\mathbf{M}$;
    for each such θ, if $H\theta$ is not in $\mathbf{M}$ then add $H\theta$ to $\mathbf{M}$;
  Until ($\mathbf{M} = \mathbf{M}_{old}$).

Step 4: Generate every answer substitution θ to the variables of Q such that every fact occurring in Q is a member of $\mathbf{M}$ ($\neg Q\theta$ is true in $\mathbf{M}$).

The following example illustrates the process of deriving answers by means of the naive strategy.

EXAMPLE 11.4

Database **D**: R1: $SG(x, y) \leftarrow Equal(x, y)$

R2: $SG(x, y) \leftarrow Parent(u, x) \wedge SG(u, v) \wedge Parent(v, y)$

R3: $GrandParent(x, y) \leftarrow Parent(x, z) \wedge Parent(z, y)$

$Equal(\alpha, \alpha)$, where $\alpha = a, b, c, d, e, f$

$Parent(a, b)$

$Parent(a, c)$

$Parent(b, d)$

$Parent(c, e)$

$Parent(c, f)$

Query Q: $\leftarrow SG(d, y)$

Suppose $\mathbf{D}_{fact}$ is the set of all facts of the database **D**. The status at each iteration of execution can be traced as follows:

Step 0: $\mathbf{D}_{rule} = \{R1, R2\}$

$\mathbf{M} = \mathbf{D}_{fact}$

Step 1: $\mathbf{M}_{old} = \mathbf{D}_{fact}$

Facts generated by R1 = $\{SG(a, a), SG(b, b), SG(c, c), SG(d, d), SG(e, e), SG(f, f)\}$

Facts generated by R2 = { }

$\mathbf{M} = \mathbf{D}_{fact} \cup \{SG(a, a), SG(b, b), SG(c, c), SG(d, d), SG(e, e), SG(f, f)\}$

Step 2: $\mathbf{M}_{old} = \mathbf{D}_{fact} \cup \{SG(a, a), SG(b, b), SG(c, c), SG(d, d), SG(e, e), SG(f, f)\}$

Facts generated by R1 = $\{SG(a, a), SG(b, b), SG(c, c), SG(d, d), SG(e, e), SG(f, f)\}$

Facts generated by R2 = $\{SG(b, b), SG(c, c), SG(d, d), SG(e, e), SG(f, f), SG(b, c), SG(e, f), SG(c, b), SG(f, e)\}$

$\mathbf{M} = \mathbf{D}_{fact} \cup \{SG(a, a), SG(b, b), SG(c, c), SG(d, d), SG(e, e), SG(f, f)\} \cup \{SG(b, b), SG(c, c), SG(d, d), SG(e, e), SG(f, f), SG(b, c), SG(e, f), SG(c, b), SG(f, e)\}$

Step 3: $\mathbf{M}_{old} = \mathbf{D}_{fact} \cup \{SG(a,a), SG(b,b), SG(c,c), SG(d,d), SG(e,e), SG(f,f), SG(b,c), SG(e,f), SG(c,b), SG(f,e)\}$

Facts generated by R1 $= \{SG(a,a), SG(b,b), SG(c,c), SG(d,d), SG(e,e), SG(f,f)\}$

Facts generated by R2 $= \{SG(b,b), SG(c,c), SG(d,d), SG(e,e), SG(f,f), SG(b,c), SG(e,f), SG(c,b), SG(f,e), SG(d,e), SG(d,f), SG(e,d), SG(f,d)\}$

$\mathbf{M} = \mathbf{D}_{fact} \cup \{SG(a,a), SG(b,b), SG(c,c), SG(d,d), SG(e,e), SG(f,f)\} \cup \{SG(b,b), SG(c,c), SG(d,d), SG(e,e), SG(f,f), SG(b,c), SG(e,f), SG(c,b), SG(f,e), SG(d,e), SG(d,f), SG(e,d), SG(f,d)\}$

Step 4: $\mathbf{M}_{old} = \mathbf{D}_{fact} \cup \{SG(a,a), SG(b,b), SG(c,c), SG(d,d), SG(e,e), SG(f,f), SG(b,c), SG(e,f), SG(c,b), SG(f,e), SG(d,e), SG(d,f), SG(e,d), SG(f,d)\}$

Facts generated by R1 $= \{SG(a,a), SG(b,b), SG(c,c), SG(d,d), SG(e,e), SG(f,f)\}$

Facts generated by R2 $= \{SG(b,b), SG(c,c), SG(d,d), SG(e,e), SG(f,f), SG(b,c), SG(e,f), SG(c,b), SG(f,e), SG(d,e), SG(d,f), SG(e,d), SG(f,d)\}$

$\mathbf{M} = \mathbf{D}_{fact} \cup \{SG(a,a), SG(b,b), SG(c,c), SG(d,d), SG(e,e), SG(f,f)\} \cup \{SG(b,b), SG(c,c), SG(d,d), SG(e,e), SG(f,f), SG(b,c), SG(e,f), SG(c,b), SG(f,e), SG(d,e), SG(d,f), SG(e,d), SG(f,d)\}$

Step 5: $\mathbf{M}_{old}$ is equal to $\mathbf{M}$ and therefore no more new tuples can be generated after this step. By filtering the final status of $\mathbf{M}$ on the basis of the goal, the set of possible values of y which satisfy the query is $\{d, e, f\}$.

Being an evaluation which is based on a bottom-up technique, naive evaluation is inefficient for several reasons:

(1) Naive evaluation does not use the query constants and entire relations are evaluated irrespective of the pattern of queries. For example, generation of the fact $SG(e,f)$ is unnecessary in Example 11.4.

(2) Any inferences performed at one iteration will also be performed at each subsequent iteration. For example, in Example 11.4, the whole computation in step 2 is duplicated in step 3.

11.3.3 Seminaive evaluation

The seminaive method is an improvement over naive evaluation. It uses the same approach as naive evaluation except that at each iteration rules are applied to only the new tuples generated since the previous iteration. Hence at each iteration the seminaive algorithm computes a differential. The iterative process continues until no new tuples are generated. The algorithm for this evaluation method is given below.

Algorithm 11.2

Input: A function free, range-restricted, definite database $\mathbf{D}$ and a query Q.

Output: The set of answers to the query Q.

Step 1: Same as step 1 of Algorithm 11.1.

Step 2: Set $\mathbf{M} =$ All facts of $\mathbf{D}$;
$\mathbf{M}_{diff} = \mathbf{M}$.

Step 3: Repeat
Set $\mathbf{M}_{old} = \mathbf{M}$;
For each rule $H \leftarrow$ B in $\mathbf{D}_{rule}$
compute every substitution θ of the variables of B
such that $B\theta$ is true in $\mathbf{M}$ and
at least one of the facts occurring in Bθ is a member of $\mathbf{M}_{diff}$;
for each such θ, if $H\theta$ is not in $\mathbf{M}$ then add $H\theta$ to $\mathbf{M}$;
Set $\mathbf{M}_{diff} = \mathbf{M} - \mathbf{M}_{old}$;
Until ($\mathbf{M}_{diff} = \varnothing$).

Step 4: Same as step 4 of Algorithm 11.1.

The following trace shows the status at each iteration of execution obtained when the seminaive method is applied to Example 11.4.

Step 0: $\mathbf{D}_{rule} = \{$R1, R2$\}$
$\mathbf{M} = \mathbf{D}_{fact}$
$\mathbf{M}_{diff} = \mathbf{M}$

Step 1: $\mathbf{M}_{old} = \mathbf{D}_{fact}$

Facts generated by R1 (using differential) = $\{SG(a,a), SG(b,b), SG(c,c), SG(d,d), SG(e,e), SG(f,f)\}$

Facts generated by R2 (using differential) = $\{\}$

$\mathbf{M} = \mathbf{D}_{fact} \cup \{SG(a,a), SG(b,b), SG(c,c), SG(d,d), SG(e,e), SG(f,f)\}$

$\mathbf{M}_{diff} = \mathbf{M} - \mathbf{M}_{old} = \{SG(a,a), SG(b,b), SG(c,c), SG(d,d), SG(e,e), SG(f,f)\}$

Step 2: $\mathbf{M}_{old} = \mathbf{D}_{fact} \cup \{SG(a,a), SG(b,b), SG(c,c), SG(d,d), SG(e,e), SG(f,f)\}$

Facts generated by R1 (using differential) = $\{\}$

Facts generated by R2 (using differential) = $\{SG(b,b), SG(c,c), SG(d,d), SG(e,e), SG(f,f), SG(b,c), SG(e,f), SG(c,b), SG(f,e)\}$

$\mathbf{M} = \mathbf{D}_{fact} \cup \{SG(a,a), SG(b,b), SG(c,c), SG(d,d), SG(e,e), SG(f,f)\} \cup \{SG(b,b), SG(c,c), SG(d,d), SG(e,e), SG(f,f), SG(b,c), SG(e,f), SG(c,b), SG(f,e)\}$

$\mathbf{M}_{diff} = \{SG(b,c), SG(e,f), SG(c,b), SG(f,e)\}$

Step 3: $\mathbf{M}_{old} = \mathbf{D}_{fact} \cup \{SG(a,a), SG(b,b), SG(c,c), SG(d,d), SG(e,e), SG(f,f), SG(b,c), SG(e,f), SG(c,b), SG(f,e)\}$

Facts generated by R1 (using differential) = $\{\}$

Facts generated by R2 (using differential) = $\{SG(d,e), SG(d,f), SG(e,d), SG(f,d)\}$

$\mathbf{M} = \mathbf{D}_{fact} \cup \{SG(a,a), SG(b,b), SG(c,c), SG(d,d), SG(e,e), SG(f,f), SG(b,c), SG(e,f), SG(c,b), SG(f,e)\} \cup \{SG(d,e), SG(d,f), SG(e,d), SG(f,d)\}$

$\mathbf{M}_{diff} = \{SG(d,e), SG(d,f), SG(e,d), SG(f,d)\}$

Step 4: $\mathbf{M}_{old} = \mathbf{D}_{fact} \cup \{SG(a,a), SG(b,b), SG(c,c), SG(d,d), SG(e,e), SG(f,f), SG(b,c), SG(e,f), SG(c,b), SG(f,e), SG(d,e), SG(d,f), SG(e,d), SG(f,d)\}$

Facts generated by R1 (using differential) = $\{\}$

Facts generated by R2 (using differential) = $\{\}$

$\mathbf{M} = \mathbf{D}_{fact} \cup \{SG(a,a), SG(b,b), SG(c,c), SG(d,d), SG(e,e), SG(f,f), SG(b,c), SG(e,f), SG(c,b), SG(f,e), SG(d,e), SG(d,f), SG(e,d), SG(f,d)\}$

$\mathbf{M}_{diff} = \{\}$

Step 5: $\mathbf{M}_{diff}$ is empty and therefore no more new tuples can be generated after this step. By filtering the final status of **M** on the basis of the goal, the set of possible values of y which satisfy the query is $\{d, e, f\}$.

The term 'using differential' means that the ground body of a rule which generates a new answer must contain an occurrence of an atom from the differential. This condition has been incorporated in step 3 of Algorithm 11.2. For example, the ground instance

$$Parent(b, d) \wedge SG(b, c) \wedge Parent(c, e)$$

of the body of R2 generates $SG(d, e)$ at step 3 and this ground instance contains $SG(b, c)$ from the differential of step 2.

Although seminaive evaluation is an improvement over naive evaluation it still fails to use the query constants and the entire relations are still evaluated. The magic sets method is an improvement over the seminaive method.

11.3.4 Magic sets

The *magic sets* method (Bancilhon *et al.*, 1986) is a bottom-up query evaluation technique which solves a query with particular *adornments* to the goal predicate. The program is transformed to an equivalent program using its adorned rules and *sideways information passing*. The transformed program models the constant propagation strategy of top-down methods through its *magic subgoals* added to the body of rules in the original program. The concepts of adornments, sideways information passing, and so on, will be introduced before the description of the method itself.

Definition 11.4: An adornment (Ullman, 1985) of an atom A is an assignment either bound or free (abbreviated to b or f respectively) to each argument of A. An adornment of an atom with n arguments is denoted as an n-tuple. An atom $P(t_1, ..., t_n)$ with adornments $<a_1, ..., a_n>$ is denoted as $P^{a_1 \cdots a_n}(t_1, ..., t_n)$, where each a_i is assigned to t_i and is either b or f.

Definition 11.5: Given an adornment of the head of rule R, an argument of a subgoal of R is said to be *distinguished* if either

(1) It is a constant, or

(2) It is a variable occurring in the head of R and the corresponding adornment is b, or

(3) It appears in an EDB subgoal of R which has a distinguished argument.

An EDB subgoal occurring in an adorned rule is said to be distinguished if all of its arguments are distinguished.

Definition 11.6: Given an adornment of the head of a rule R, the *adorned rule* for R is an adornment for all the IDB atoms occurring in R and is obtained by considering all distinguished arguments of each subgoal of R to be b.

If R is a rule, then $\mathcal{Ad}$(R) denotes the set of all adorned rules for R for all possible adornments of the head of R. Given a set of rules $\mathbf{R}$, $\mathcal{Ad}(\mathbf{R})$ is the union of all the sets $\mathcal{Ad}$(R) for R $\in$ $\mathbf{R}$.

EXAMPLE 11.5

For the adornment $<b, f>$ of the head of the rule R which is

$$SG(x, y) \leftarrow Parent(u, x) \wedge SG(u, v) \wedge Parent(v, y)$$

where *Parent* is an EDB predicate, the adorned version of R is given by

$$SG^{bf}(x, y) \leftarrow Parent(u, x) \wedge SG^{bf}(u, v) \wedge Parent(v, y)$$

The first argument of the subgoal $SG^{bf}(u, v)$ is distinguished and the EDB subgoal $Parent(u, x)$ is distinguished while $Parent(v, y)$ is not. The set $\mathcal{Ad}$(R) contains the following four clauses:

$$SG^{bb}(x, y) \leftarrow Parent(x, u) \wedge SG^{bb}(u, v) \wedge Parent(v, y)$$
$$SG^{bf}(x, y) \leftarrow Parent(x, u) \wedge SG^{bf}(u, v) \wedge Parent(v, y)$$
$$SG^{fb}(x, y) \leftarrow Parent(x, u) \wedge SG^{fb}(u, v) \wedge Parent(v, y)$$
$$SG^{ff}(x, y) \leftarrow Parent(x, u) \wedge SG^{ff}(u, v) \wedge Parent(v, y)$$

Definition 11.7: Given a set of adorned rules $\mathbf{S}$ and an adornment for the atom A, the set of all *reachable* rules for A from $\mathbf{S}$ is recursively defined as follows:

(1) An adorned rule $H \leftarrow$ B in $\mathbf{S}$ is reachable for A if both A and H are under the same predicate symbol and have the same adornments.

(2) An adorned rule $H \leftarrow$ B in **S** is reachable for A if there exists a reachable rule for A with a subgoal M such that both H and M are under the same predicate symbol and have the same adornments.

Definition 11.8: Suppose G is a goal and M is one of its subgoals with some bound arguments. Then the bindings for other uninstantiated arguments of another subgoal N of G with variables in common with M can be obtained by solving M, and then N can transmit bindings to other variables. This process of passing information from one subgoal to another is called sideways information passing (Ullman, 1985).

Sideways information passing is normal behaviour in the case of resolution-based methods using a unification strategy. The concept of distinguished arguments also indicates the direction of the sideways information passing. The magic sets method uses the concept of the distinguished argument to achieve sideways information passing.

Definition 11.9: Suppose **D** is a database, G $= \leftarrow B_1 \wedge \cdots \wedge B_m$ a goal and $x_1, ..., x_n$ are all the variables occurring in G. Let **R** be the set of rules of **D** together with the rule $Query(x_1, ..., x_n) \leftarrow B_1 \wedge \cdots \wedge B_m$. The *reachable adorned system* for the goal and the database **D**, denoted as $\mathcal{RAd}(\mathbf{D}, G)$, is the set of reachable rules for $Query^{ff \cdots f}(x_1, ..., x_n)$ from $\mathcal{Ad}(\mathbf{R})$.

EXAMPLE 11.6

In the case of Example 11.4, this reachable adorned system is

$$Query^f(y) \leftarrow SG^{bf}(d, y)$$
$$SG^{bf}(x, y) \leftarrow Equal(x, y)$$
$$SG^{bf}(x, y) \leftarrow Parent(u, x) \wedge SG^{bf}(u, v) \wedge Parent(v, y)$$

Given a database **D** and a query G, the magic sets method for answering the query essentially consists of the following three steps:

(1) Construct the reachable adorned system $\mathcal{RAd}(\mathbf{D}, G)$ for **D** and G.
(2) Apply Algorithm 11.3 to construct an equivalent set of rules $\mathcal{Magic}(\mathcal{RAd}((\mathbf{D}, G)))$.
(3) (Optional) Rewrite the set $\mathcal{Magic}(\mathcal{RAd}((\mathbf{D}, G)))$ in a more convenient and optimized form.

(4) The seminaive generation process can be performed on the transformed set $\mathcal{Magic}(\mathcal{RAd}((\mathbf{D}, G)))$ of rules but only for the tuples marked by magic predicates.

Algorithm 11.3

Input: A set $\mathbf{S}$ of adorned rules.

Output: A new set of adorned rules $\mathcal{Magic}(\mathbf{S})$.

Step 1: Set $\mathcal{Magic}(\mathbf{S}) = \varnothing$

Step 2: *Generation of magic rules*. Perform steps 2.1 to 2.4 for each rule R in $\mathbf{S}$ and for each IDB subgoal $Q^{A'}(y_1, ..., y_q)$ of R, where R has the form

$$P^A(x_1, ..., x_p) \leftarrow B_1 \wedge \cdots \wedge B_i \wedge Q^{A'}(y_1, ..., y_q) \wedge B_{i+1} \wedge \cdots \wedge B_n \quad (11.3)$$

in which A and A' are adornments of $P(x_1, ..., x_p)$ and $Q(y_1, ..., y_q)$ respectively.

Step 2.1: Transform the adorned rule (11.3) to

$$\begin{aligned} P^A(x_1, ..., x_p) \leftarrow B'_1 \wedge \cdots \wedge B'_j \wedge Q^{A'}(y_1, ..., y_q) \wedge \\ B'_{j+1} \wedge \cdots \wedge B'_m \end{aligned} \quad (11.4)$$

where $B'_1, ..., B'_j$ are all distinguished EDB subgoals of $B_1, ..., B_i$ and B'_{j+1}, ..., B'_m are all distinguished EDB subgoals of $B_{i+1}, ..., B_n$.

Step 2.2: Transform rule (11.4) to

$$\begin{aligned} Magic\_P^A(x'_1, ..., x'_{p_1}) \leftarrow B'_1 \wedge \cdots \wedge B'_j \wedge \\ Magic\_Q^{A'}(y'_1, ..., y'_{q_1}) \wedge B'_{j+1} \wedge \cdots \wedge B'_m \end{aligned} \quad (11.5)$$

where the tuple $<x'_1, ..., x'_{p_1}>$ (resp. $<y'_1, ..., y'_{q_1}>$) is obtained from $<x_1, ..., x_p>$ (resp. $<y_1, ..., y_q>$) by deleting all non-distinguished arguments.

Step 2.3: Transform rule (11.5) to

$$\begin{aligned} Magic\_Q^{A'}(y'_1, ..., y'_{q_1}) \leftarrow B'_1 \wedge \cdots \wedge B'_j \wedge \\ Magic\_P^A(x'_1, ..., x'_{p_1}) \wedge B'_{j+1} \wedge \cdots \wedge B'_m \end{aligned} \quad (11.6)$$

Step 2.4: Add rule (11.6) to $\mathcal{Magic}(\mathbf{S})$.

Step 3: *Generation of modified rules.* Perform steps 3.1 to 3.2 for each rule R in **S** and for each IDB subgoal $Q^{A'}(y_1, ..., y_q)$ of R, where R has the form (11.3).

Step 3.1: If $P \neq Q$, then transform (11.3) to R′ as

$$\begin{aligned} P^A(x_1, ..., x_p) \leftarrow B_1 \wedge \cdots \wedge B_i \wedge Magic\_\mathrm{R}\_Q^{A'}(y'_1, ..., y'_{q_1}) \wedge \\ Q^{A'}(y_1, ..., y_q) \wedge B_{i+1} \wedge \cdots \wedge B_n \end{aligned} \tag{11.7}$$

else (that is, $P = Q$) transform (11.3) to R′ as

$$\begin{aligned} P^A(x_1, ..., x_p) \leftarrow Magic\_\mathrm{R}\_Q^{A'}(y'_1, ..., y'_{q_1}) \wedge \\ B_1 \wedge \cdots B_i \wedge \cdots \wedge Q^{A'}(y_1, ..., y_q) \wedge B_{i+1} \wedge \cdots \wedge B_n \end{aligned} \tag{11.8}$$

where the tuple $<y'_1, ..., y'_{q_1}>$ is obtained from $<y_1, ..., y_q>$ by deleting all non-distinguished arguments.

Step 3.2: Add R′ to $\mathcal{Magic}(\mathbf{S})$.

Step 4: *Generation of complementary rules.* For each rule R in **S** and for each IDB subgoal $Q^{A'}(y_1, ..., y_q)$ of R, add the rule

$$Magic\_Q^{A'}(y'_1, ..., y'_{q_1}) \leftarrow Magic\_\mathrm{R}\_Q^{A'}(y'_1, ..., y'_{q_1}) \tag{11.9}$$

to $\mathcal{Magic}(\mathbf{S})$, where the tuple $<y'_1, ..., y'_{q_1}>$ is obtained from $<y_1, ..., y_q>$ by deleting all non-distinguished arguments.

EXAMPLE 11.7

Suppose $\mathrm{R} = P^{bf}(x, y) \leftarrow S(x, y) \wedge U^{bf}(x, u) \wedge V^{bf}(y, v) \wedge T(u)$, where P, U and V are IDB predicates and S and T are EDB predicates. Let $V^{bf}(y, v)$ be the chosen IDB subgoal. Then the equations

$$\begin{aligned} &P^{bf}(x, y) \leftarrow S(x, y) \wedge V^{bf}(y, v) \\ &Magic\_P^{bf}(x) \leftarrow S(x, y) \wedge Magic\_V^{bf}(y) \\ &Magic\_V^{bf}(y) \leftarrow S(x, y) \wedge Magic\_P^{bf}(x) \\ &P^{bf}(x, y) \leftarrow S(x, y) \wedge U^{bf}(x, u) \wedge Magic\_\mathrm{R}\_V^{bf}(y) \wedge V^{bf}(y, v) \wedge T(u) \\ &Magic\_V^{bf}(y) \leftarrow Magic\_\mathrm{R}\_V^{bf}(y) \end{aligned}$$

are generated at steps 2.1, 2.2, 2.3, 3.1 and 4 respectively.

The reachable adorned rules are singled out by using the adornment $<b, f>$ for the goal atom $SG(d, y)$. With the goal $\leftarrow SG(d, y)$, the set of rules in Example 11.4 is transformed using the magic sets method as follows:

Magic rules:	$Magic\_R0\_SG^{bf}(d) \leftarrow Magic\_query^{f}$
	$Magic\_R2\_SG^{bf}(x) \leftarrow Parent(y, x) \wedge Magic\_SG^{bf}(y)$
Modified rules:	$Query^{f}(x) \leftarrow Magic\_R0\_SG^{bf}(d) \wedge SG^{bf}(d, x)$
	$SG^{bf}(x, y) \leftarrow Equal(x, y)$
	$SG^{bf}(x, y) \leftarrow Magic\_R2\_SG^{bf}(u) \wedge$ $Parent(u, x) \wedge SG^{bf}(u, v) \wedge Parent(v, y)$
Complementary rules:	$Magic\_SG^{bf}(d) \leftarrow Magic\_R0\_SG^{bf}(d)$
	$Magic\_SG^{bf}(x) \leftarrow Magic\_R2\_SG^{bf}(x)$

First by adding the fact $Magic\_Query^{f}$ (this kind of fact should always be added) and then by some simple transformations and renaming, the above set of rules can be rewritten as follows:

$$Magic(d)$$
$$Magic(x_1) \leftarrow Magic(x) \wedge Parent(x, x_1)$$
$$Query^{f}(y) \leftarrow SG^{bf}(d, y)$$
$$SG^{bf}(x, y) \leftarrow Equal(x, y)$$
$$SG^{bf}(x, y) \leftarrow Magic(x_1) \wedge Parent(x_1, x) \wedge SG^{bf}(x_1, y_1) \wedge Parent(y_1, y)$$

The seminaive generation process is performed on the transformed set of rules though only for the tuples marked by magic predicates. If there is a tuple $Parent(a', b')$ in the database, the magic predicate will not mark this tuple as $Magic(a')$ is not true in the transformed database.

Exercises

11.1 For each of the following databases and queries:

(a) Draw a complete SLD-AL-tree for each query and the database.

(b) Apply Magic Sets algorithm for each query and the set of rules.

(c) Apply the Seminaive algorithm to the transformed set of rules and the set of tuples to generate answers.

Database: $Mother(x, y) \leftarrow Father(z, y) \wedge Husband(z, x)$

$Parent(x, y) \leftarrow Father(x, y)$

$Parent(x, y) \leftarrow Mother(x, y)$

$AncestorF(x, y) \leftarrow Father(x, y)$

$AncestorF(x, y) \leftarrow Father(x, z) \wedge AncestorF(z, y)$

$AncestorP(x, y) \leftarrow Parent(x, y)$

$AncestorP(x, y) \leftarrow Parent(x, z) \wedge AncestorP(z, y)$

$SamegenF(x, y) \leftarrow Equal(x, y)$

$SamegenF(x, y) \leftarrow Father(u, x) \wedge$
$SamegenF(u, v) \wedge Father(v, y)$

$SamegenP(x, y) \leftarrow Equal(x, y)$

$SamegenP(x, y) \leftarrow Parent(u, x) \wedge$
$SamegenP(u, v) \wedge Parent(v, y)$

$Equal(\alpha, \alpha)$, where $\alpha = a, b, c, d, e, f, g, h$

$Father(a, b)$

$Father(b, c)$

$Father(b, d)$

$Father(a, e)$

$Husband(a, f)$

$Husband(b, g)$

$Husband(d, h)$

Queries: $\leftarrow Parent(f, y)$

$\leftarrow Parent(x, b)$

$\leftarrow Parent(f, b)$

$\leftarrow AncestorF(a, y)$

$\leftarrow AncestorF(x, d)$

$\leftarrow AncestorP(f, y)$

$\leftarrow SamegenF(c, x)$

$\leftarrow SamegenP(h, x)$

Database: $NonComWithdraw(x, y) \leftarrow Account(x, y)$

$ComWithdraw(x, y) \leftarrow Account(x, z) \wedge link(z, y)$

$Withdraw(x, y) \leftarrow NonComWithdraw(x, y)$

$Withdraw(x, y) \leftarrow ComWithdraw(x, y)$

$Link(x, y) \leftarrow DirectLink(x, y)$

$Link(x, z) \leftarrow CentralLink(z, x) \wedge CentralLink(z, y)$

$CentralLink(Group\,1, Bank\,1)$

$CentralLink(Group\,1, Bank\,2)$

$DirectLink(Bank\,1, Bank\,3)$

$Account(a, Bank1)$
$Account(b, Bank2)$
$Account(c, Bank1)$

Queries: $\leftarrow Withdraw(a, y)$
$\leftarrow Withdraw(a, Bank1)$
$\leftarrow Withdraw(x, Bank2)$

11.2 Complete Tables 11.1 and 11.2 to give a summary of the characteristics of the query evaluation methods introduced in this chapter and a few others from logic programming part.

Table 11.1 Characteristics comparison of different methods.

	Characteristics			
Methods	*Application Domain*	*Formalism*	*Technique*	*Approach*
Naive				
Seminaive				
SLD-resolution				
SLI-resolution				
SLDNF-resolution				
SLD-AL-resolution				
Magic sets				

Table 11.2 Extension of Table 11.1.

Characteristics				
Answering technique	*Mode of evaluation*	*Correctness*	*Objective*	*Representation of clauses*

12

Integrity constraints

The chapter is devoted to a systematic study of different aspects of integrity constraints. This includes a detailed classification according to the nature of the constraints, their representation in logical formulae, a discussion of the different views of constraint satisfiability and constraint verification in deductive databases. Several methods for handling integrity constraints in deductive databases will be introduced in Chapter 13.

12.1 What are integrity constraints?

Part of the semantics of a database is expressed as *(integrity) constraints* (Date, 1985; Eswaran and Chamberlin, 1975; Fernandez *et al.*, 1981; Reiter, 1981; Stonebraker, 1989; Ullman, 1984). Constraints are properties that the data of a database is required to satisfy and they are expected to be satisfied after each transaction performed on the database. To illustrate the concept of constraints and their satisfaction in the context of databases, consider the following example.

EXAMPLE 12.1

Database: $Research(x) \leftarrow Student(x) \wedge \neg Graduate(x)$
$Student(Bitu)$
$Graduate(Bitu)$
$Student(Kiti)$
$Supervisor(Robert, Kiti)$

Constraint: $\forall x (Research(x) \rightarrow \exists y\ Supervisor(y, x))$

Transaction: insert $Student(Piklu)$

In this example, the only constraint imposed on the database expresses the fact that every research student should have a supervisor. According to the semantics of the database (for example, consider the completed database semantics), *Bitu* is not a research student and therefore does not need to have any supervisor. Student *Kiti* is a research student and has a supervisor *Robert*. Hence, before the transaction is applied to the database, the database satisfies the constraint. When the transaction is applied to the database, that is, when the fact *Student*(*Piklu*) is inserted into the database, the fact *Research*(*Piklu*) is also implicitly inserted into the database. But in the updated database there is no supervisor for *Piklu* and hence the updated database does not satisfy the constraint.

The verification of constraints in a database is often quite expensive in terms of time as well as being complex. Some important factors related to this issue include the structure of the underlying database upon which the constraints are imposed, the nature of the imposed constraints, and the method adopted for their evaluation. Constraint handling in deductive databases is even more complex and more expensive than in relational databases as a single addition or deletion of tuple from a deductive database may cause a number of implicit additions to and deletions from the database. The discussions and results related to deductive databases are also applicable to relational databases as the former generalizes the concept of the latter. The classification and representation aspects of constraints as discussed in this chapter are independent of the underlying databases.

12.2 Classification

A detailed classification is necessary to understand the nature of imposed constraints. As an initial formal classification of all constraints, the whole class can broadly be divided into two, *immediate* and *deferred.* Constraints that must be satisfied after the completion of a transaction are known as deferred constraints; constraints that must be satisfied after every action are known as immediate constraints. To clarify this distinction consider the constraint which expresses the following:

(A) *The sum of debit and credit in a ledger is equal to the budget amount.*

Suppose a transaction, corresponding to an expense incurred, causes an amount to be subtracted from the credit and an amount is to be added to the debit. The consistency of the database is preserved if the above constraint is treated as a deferred constraint. Consistency is violated if the same constraint is treated as an immediate constraint.

Considering every action in a transaction on a database as a transaction of a single action, the class of immediate constraints can be verified in the same way as for deferred constraints. The set of all deferred constraints can be subdivided into the set of *static* constraints and the set of *transitional* (or *dynamic*) constraints. Static constraints deal with information in a single state of the world. The current state is independent of previous or future states. The following are some examples of static constraints:

(B) *The name of a department belongs to the domain {Fin, Adm, Exe}.*

(C) *An employee's salary must be less than £10,000.*

(D) *Every worker has a manager.*

(E) *Every child has only one father.*

(F) *The total number of employees in a particular department may not exceed 100.*

(G) *The average salary of any department must be less than £10,000.*

(H) *The total salary of all the employees in a department must be less than the budget of the department.*

The static constraints can be subdivided into two categories: *aggregate* (Bernstein *et al.*, 1980) and *non-aggregate*. Static aggregate constraints involve one or more aggregate operations such as counting, summation, average, maximum or minimum. For example, constraint (F) above requires the help of the counting operation on the *Employee* relation and hence this is classified as a *static aggregate count* constraint.

Static non-aggregate constraints are classified into the following major categories:

- *Not null* Can be specified for any attribute and any attempt to introduce null in such an attribute is rejected.
- *Check* Given a relation R (that is a predicate symbol), this constraint can be specified for any attribute or combination of attributes within R, provided not null is also specified for every column involved. Any attempt to introduce a tuple into R that violates the specified constraint, for example, the attribute value is not in the specified *Range* (example C) or does not belong to the specified *Domain* (example B), is rejected.

- *Unique* Given a relation R, this constraint can be specified for any attribute or combination of attributes within R, provided not null is also specified for every attribute involved. Any attempt to introduce a tuple in R with the same value in the specified attribute or combination of attributes as some existing row is rejected. *Primary key* is a special case of unique. The identified attribute or combination of attributes constitutes the primary key for the relation R.
- *Existential* An existential constraint is specified on an attribute or a combination of attributes in one relation whose values are required to match the values of an attribute (the primary key, in the case of *foreign key*) in some relation (example D). A *reference* type constraint is an alternative way of specifying foreign keys. The imposed constraint is called a *referential constraint* (Casanova *et al.*, 1988; Date, 1981).
- *Multivalued dependence* Multivalued dependencies (Fagin and Vardi, 1984) are a generalization of *functional dependencies* (Carlson *et al.*, 1982; Fagin and Vardi, 1984). Given a relation R, attribute Y of R is functionally dependent on attribute X if and only if each X-value in R has associated with it precisely one Y-value in R (example E).

A different classification of constraints concerns whether a constraint is applied to an individual tuple of a base relation or to more than one tuple from different relations. The former class of constraints would be considered as *single-record* (or *single-tuple*) constraints whereas the latter would be denoted as *multiple-record* (or *multiple-tuple*) constraints. This classification has a special implication for the process of constraint checking. When a transaction is encountered all the single-record constraints can be verified by looking at the transaction alone without accessing the database. However, to verify a multiple-record constraint one has to access the database. Examples (B) and (C) fall into the single-record category whereas (D)–(H) fall into the multiple-record category. As an example, constraint (C) is applied only to an individual tuple of the *Employee* relation. On the other hand, constraint (D) is applied to two tuples, one from *Worker* and the other from *Manager*. Likewise constraints (F)–(H) are applied to all the tuples of the relation *Employee* who are working in a particular department.

Unlike static constraints, *transitional constraints* deal with the way in which the world evolves, in other words, an imposed constraint is related to at least two states of the database. Consider the constraint

(I) *Initially, the minimum loan amount is £5,000.*

This means that if a person negotiates a loan then initially the amount of the loan has to be greater than or equal to £10,000. Subsequently, when the person repays the loan amount by instalments, the loan amount outstanding may be less than £10,000. Hence transitional constraints have to be satisfied only at the time the operation occurs.

Here are some more examples of transitional constraints considered in the cases of addition, deletion and updates of tuples to the database:

(J) *Lay-off of employees whose income is less than £10,000 will be prevented.*

(K) *On updating the salary of an employee it should always increase.*

(L) *The maximum loan an employee can have is five times his/her salary unless the employee has been given permission for a special loan.*

(M) *A change in grade must be accompanied by a change in salary.*

Transitional constraints can be subdivided into *addition type*, *deletion type*, *update type* and a mixture of one or more of these. Each of the above types of transitional constraint is divided into two categories. An addition type transitional constraint involving aggregate operations (such as *Count*, *Sum*, *Avg*, *Max*, *Min*) on one or more relations is classified as an *addition type aggregate transitional constraint* whereas an addition type transitional constraint not involving aggregate on any relation is classified as an *addition type non-aggregate transitional constraint.* Similarly, this applies to deletion and update types of transitional constraints. For example, the constraints

(N) *On update of the salary of an employee the difference of salaries should be between £10 and £100.*

(O) *On insertion of a new employee in a department the new average salary of the department must be less than the old average salary of the department.*

are considered as an update type non-aggregate transitional constraint and an addition type aggregate transitional constraint respectively.

Figure 12.1 illustrates the scheme of classification of constraints. The symbol '...' denotes repetition and a 'mixed' type of constraint in a particular level of the hierarchy denotes a constraint of a combination of types in that level.

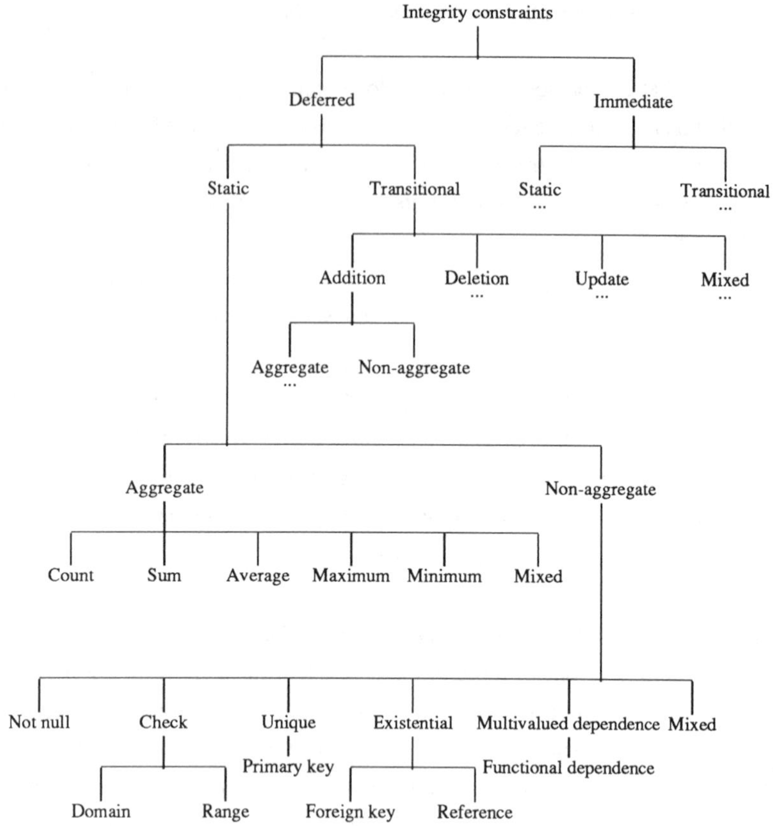

Figure 12.1 Classification of integrity constraints.

12.3 Representation

The idea behind considering logic as a theoretical foundation of database systems is to use logic as a uniform language for data, programs, queries and constraints. In this context, a constraint is a closed formula (first-order as well as aggregate). This kind of formal representation of constraints is important with regard to processing by different strategies.

EXAMPLE 12.2

All the static non-aggregate constraints described in the previous section (except 'not null' type) can be represented by closed first-order formulae. The representation of constraints (B)–(E) in this form can be illustrated as follows:

$$\forall x \forall y \forall z (Employee(x, y, z) \rightarrow y = Fin \vee y = Adm \vee y = Exe) \quad (12.1)$$

$$\forall x \forall y \forall z (Employee(x, y, z) \rightarrow z < 10{,}000) \quad (12.2)$$

$$\forall x (Worker(x) \rightarrow \exists y\ Manager(y, x)) \quad (12.3)$$

$$\forall x \forall y (Father(x, z) \wedge Father(y, z) \rightarrow x = y) \quad (12.4)$$

Checking whether or not a particular argument of a tuple is null requires a special feature of the implementation.

To view the constraint evaluation in the context of a database as query evaluation in the database, static non-aggregate constraints are assumed in the form of range-restricted denials, that is, a range-restricted goal of the form

$$\leftarrow L_1 \wedge \cdots \wedge L_n$$

where each L_i is a literal and variables are assumed to be universally quantified over the whole formula.

EXAMPLE 12.3

Constraints (12.1), (12.2) and (12.4) can directly be represented in denial form as, respectively,

$$\leftarrow Employee(x, y, z) \wedge y \neq Fin \wedge y \neq Adm \wedge y \neq Exe \quad (12.5)$$

$$\leftarrow Employee(x, y, z) \wedge z \geq 10{,}000 \quad (12.6)$$

$$\leftarrow Father(x, z) \wedge Father(y, z) \wedge x \neq y \quad (12.7)$$

Constraint (12.3) can also be represented as a range-restricted denial of the form

$$\leftarrow Worker(x) \wedge \neg P(x) \quad (12.8)$$

by adding the rule $P(x) \leftarrow Manager(y, x)$ to the underlying database, where the predicate symbol P does not occur elsewhere in the database. An even more general form of static non-aggregate constraint can be transformed to denials with the help of the 10 transformations given in Chapter 7. This process, of course, cannot be applied to a constraint of the form $\forall x Q(x)$ which is itself not range restricted.

To represent static aggregate constraints conveniently, some *aggregate predicates* (*Count*, *Sum*, *Max*, *Min*, *Avg*) are allowed (Das and Williams, 1990) in the representation of constraints. *Aggregate formulae* are defined in the same way as first-order formulae. An aggregate formula can contain both first-order literals and *aggregate literals* under these aggregate predicates. There are five different kinds of aggregate atoms corresponding to these five aggregate predicates and they are $Count(W, n)$, $Avg(x, W, r)$, $Sum(x, W, r)$, $Max(x, W, r)$ and $Min(x, W, r)$. A detailed description of these aggregate atoms is provided in Chapter 16. As an example, $Count(W, n)$ is interpreted as counting the number of different answers to the query $\leftarrow W$ which are true in D and returning this value as n; $Avg(x, W, r)$ computes the average of all the values of the variable x obtained from different answers of the query $\leftarrow W$ which are true in D, and returns this value as r; and so on. An *aggregate constraint* is thus defined as a closed aggregate formula. This definition generalizes the definition of first-order constraints.

EXAMPLE 12.4

The example constraints (F) and (G) given in Section 12.2 can be expressed in the form of closed general formulae as follows:

$$\forall x \forall y (Dept(x) \wedge Count(\exists u \exists v \; Employee(u, x, v), y) \rightarrow y \leq 100) \quad (12.9)$$

$$\forall x \forall y (Dept(x) \wedge Avg(v, \exists u \exists v Employee(u, x, v), y) \rightarrow y < 10{,}000) \quad (12.10)$$

To represent a transitional constraint it is necessary to allow some *action relations* (Nicolas and Yazdanian, 1978) within database schema.

EXAMPLE 12.5

Constraints (I), (J) and (K) can be represented, using action relations *Add_Loan*, *Del_Employee*, *Upd_Employee* respectively, as

$$\forall x \forall y (Add\_Loan(x, y) \rightarrow y \geq 5{,}000) \quad (12.11)$$

$$\forall x \forall y \forall z (Del\_Employee(x, y, z) \rightarrow z \geq 10{,}000) \quad (12.12)$$

$$\forall x \forall y \forall y' \forall z \forall z' (Upd\_Employee(x, y, z, x, y', z') \wedge z \neq z' \rightarrow z' > z) \quad (12.13)$$

Similarly, constraint (M) can be represented, using action relations *Upd_Grade* and *Upd_Income*, as

$$\forall x \forall y \forall y' \forall z \forall z' (Upd\_Grade(x, z, x, z') \wedge z \neq z' \rightarrow Upd\_Income(x, y, x, y') \wedge y \neq y') \quad (12.14)$$

A detailed discussion on action relations and transitional constraints is provided in Chapter 16.

12.4 Satisfiability

This section introduces the declarative notion of first-order constraint (that is, closed first-order formulae) satisfiability in normal databases. The concepts of aggregate and transitional constraints satisfiability will be described in Chapter 16.

The standard definition of first-order constraint satisfiability (*the theoremhood view*) in normal databases is as follows. Let **D** be a database such that the completion of **D** (*Comp*(**D**) (Clark, 1978; Lloyd, 1987)) is consistent. Then **D** is said to satisfy W, where W is a first-order constraint, if W is a logical consequence of *Comp*(**D**); otherwise **D** violates W. **D** is said to satisfy **I**, where **I** is a set of constraints, if **D** satisfies each constraint in **I**; otherwise **D** violates **I**. This definition is followed by Bry *et al.* (1988), Das and Williams (1989a), Decker (1986), Ling (1987) and Lloyd and Topor (1985).

An alternative definition of constraint satisfiability (*the consistency view*, adopted by Asirelli *et al.* (1985) and Sadri and Kowalski (1987)) is as follows. A normal database **D** satisfies a set of first-order constraints **I** if and only if the set of formulae comprising the completion of **D** together with the formulae in **I** are consistent.

The above two definitions of constraint satisfiability are equivalent if and only if *Comp*(**D**) is complete. If a constraint W is a theorem of the completion of a database **D** then *Comp*(**D**) together with W is always consistent, but the converse may not be true. Hence the second definition of constraint satisfiability deals with a larger class of databases.

The alternative definition of constraint satisfiability may differ from the standard view in its outcome if either of the following two conditions is met:

(1) The database is recursive, or

(2) A predicate symbol occurs in the constraints but not in the database.

Each of the above points will be clarified with the aid of examples.

EXAMPLE 12.6

To illustrate the problem associated with (1), consider the database **D** = $\{P(a) \leftarrow P(a)\}$ and the constraint set **I** = $\{P(a)\}$. The database is recursive and its completion *Comp*(**D**), apart from the equality axiom, is $P(x) \leftrightarrow x = a \wedge P(a)$.

Therefore, $Comp(\mathbf{D}) \cup \mathbf{I}$ is consistent as $\{P(a)\}$ is a model of $Comp(\mathbf{D}) \cup \mathbf{I}$. On the other hand $P(a)$ is not a theorem of $Comp(\mathbf{D})$.

EXAMPLE 12.7

Considering point (2), consider the database $\mathbf{D} = \{P(a)\}$ and the constraint set $\mathbf{I} = \{Q(a)\}$. The predicate symbol Q does not occur in the database. The completion of $\mathbf{D}$, apart from the equality axiom, is given by $\{P(x) \leftrightarrow x = a\}$. Therefore, $Comp(\mathbf{D}) \cup \mathbf{I}$ has a model $\{P(a), Q(a)\}$ and hence $Comp(\mathbf{D}) \cup \mathbf{I}$ is consistent. But $Q(a)$ cannot be proved as a theorem from $Comp(\mathbf{D})$.

Suppose $\leftarrow$ B is a first-order constraint in denial form and **D** is a normal database such that its completion is consistent. From the soundness result of SLDNF-resolution, the procedural definition of the standard view of constraint satisfiability can be given as follows:

(1) If there exists an SLDNF-refutation of $\mathbf{D} \cup \{\leftarrow \mathrm{B}\}$ then **D** violates $\leftarrow$B.

(2) If $\mathbf{D} \cup \{\leftarrow \mathrm{B}\}$ has a finitely failed SLDNF-tree then **D** satisfies $\leftarrow$B.

The declarative definition of first-order constraint satisfiability in a general database **D** has been given (Das, 1990) in terms of its possible forms of **D**. According to the strict theoremhood view, a database **D** is said to satisfy a constraint C if C is a logical consequence of the completion of each of the possible forms of D. The database **D** is said to satisfy a set of constraints **I** if **D** satisfies each of the constraints of **I**; otherwise **D** violates **I**. According to the relaxed theoremhood view, a database **D** is said to satisfy a set of constraints **I** if there exists at least one possible form $\mathbf{D}'$ of **D** such that each constraint C in **I** is a logical consequence of the completion of $\mathbf{D}'$. To clarify the definition, consider the following example.

EXAMPLE 12.8

Database: $Postgraduate(x) \leftarrow MSc(x)$

$Postgraduate(x) \leftarrow PhD(x)$

$Student(x) \leftarrow Undergraduate(x)$

$MSc(x) \vee PhD(x) \leftarrow Student(x) \wedge \neg\, Undergraduate(x)$

$Student(Pupai)$

$Supervisor(Robert, Pupai)$

$Undergraduate(Piklu) \vee MSc(Piklu)$

Constraint: $\forall x\,(Postgraduate(x) \rightarrow \exists y\; Supervisor(y, x))$

In this case, the strict definition of constraint satisfiability says that the integrity of the database would be violated as *Piklu* can be proved to be a postgraduate student in one of the possible forms (for example, all normal clauses and $MSc(x) \leftarrow Student(x) \wedge \neg Undergraduate(x)$ and $MSc(Piklu)$) of the database without having a supervisor in that possible form. On the other hand, by choosing a suitable possible form (such as all normal clauses and $MSc(x) \vee \leftarrow Student(x) \wedge \neg Undergraduate(x)$ and $Undergraduate(Piklu)$) the database satisfies the constraint if the alternative relaxed view is followed.

Each of the above two definitions generalizes the theoremhood view of constraint satisfiability in normal databases. The consistency view in general databases can be generalized in a similar manner as follows. According to the strict consistency view, a database **D** is said to satisfy a set of constraints **I** if **I** is consistent with the completion of each of the possible forms of **D**; otherwise **D** violates **I**. According to the relaxed consistency view, a database **D** is said to satisfy a set of constraints **I** if there exists at least one possible form **D′** of **D** such that the completion of **D′** is consistent with **I**. Constraint satisfiability in general databases can also be given in terms of the generalized completion introduced in Chapter 8.

12.5 Verification

It is desirable to check (or verify or preserve) the integrity (Bertino and Musto, 1988; Bry and Manthey, 1986; Kobayashi, 1984; Qian and Smith, 1987; Weber *et al.*, 1983) of a database at the end of each transaction which changes the database. The efficiency of integrity checking is largely improved by making one important assumption that the database satisfies constraints prior to its update. The simplest approach to checking integrity in a database involves the evaluation of each constraint whenever the database is updated. However, such an approach is too inefficient, especially for large databases, and does not make use of the assumption stated above. This assumption and the simplification of constraints (Nicolas, 1982) can be clarified using the following example.

EXAMPLE 12.9

Database: $P(x) \leftarrow Q(x)$

$R(a, c)$

$R(b, c)$

$Q(a)$

	$S(a)$
	$T(a)$
Constraints:	$\forall x(P(x) \rightarrow \exists y R(x, y))$
	$\forall x(S(x) \rightarrow T(x))$
Transaction:	insert $Q(b)$

The second constraint is not relevant to the transaction and does not need to be evaluated. Its satisfaction in the updated database is guaranteed from the fact that the database satisfied constraints before the transaction was performed to the database. Also, in the updated database, the simplified form $P(b) \rightarrow \exists y R(b, y)$ of the first constraint rather than the whole constraint has to be verified. To choose a subset of the set of all constraints (that is, affected constraints) and to simplify them, it is important to realize the difference between the models of the two database states, that is, the states before and after the transaction. Some methods realize this difference by computing a set of partially instantiated atoms (Lloyd and Topor, 1985), some by computing a set of ground facts (Decker, 1986), and some by a mixed strategy (Das and Williams, 1989a; Sadri and Kowalski, 1987). These methods are discussed in Chapter 13.

Exercises

12.1 Represent the following constraints in logical formulae assuming the relation schema

Employee (Employee_Id, Department, Salary), and
Manager (Manager_Id, Employee_Id):

(a) An employee's department must be one of {*Fin*, *Admin*, *Exe*} and his/her salary must be less than £10,000.

(b) Every employee's salary and department are unique.

(c) On updating the salary of an employee it should always increase or the department should be changed.

(d) An employee's salary must be less than his/her manager's salary.

12.2 Following the standard view of constraint satisfiability, check whether the integrity of the database is violated or not in each of the following examples:

EXAMPLE A

Database: $P(x) \leftarrow S(x)$

$Q(a, b)$

$Q(a, c)$

$R(b)$

$S(b)$

$S(c)$

Constraint: $\forall x (P(x) \wedge \neg R(x) \rightarrow \exists y Q(y, x))$

EXAMPLE B

Database: $P(x) \leftarrow Q(x)$

$P(x) \leftarrow \neg Q(x)$

$Q(x) \leftarrow Q(x)$

$R(a)$

Constraint: $\forall x (R(x) \rightarrow P(x))$

13

Constraint checking methods

This chapter presents and then compares four different methods for checking static, non-aggregate constraints in normal deductive databases. For ease of presentation all the constraints are assumed to be in the form of range-restricted denials. As has been discussed previously, a general constraint can be transformed to its denial form by applying the set of transformations provided in Chapter 7. Note that a further discussion of aggregate and transitional constraints is given in Chapter 16.

13.1 The methods

Methods are introduced in this section in chronological order. The operation of each of the methods will be expressed with the help of the following example.

EXAMPLE 13.1

Database:

R1. $Mother(x, y) \leftarrow Father(z, y) \wedge Husband(z, x)$

R2. $Parent(x, y) \leftarrow Father(x, y)$

R3. $Parent(x, y) \leftarrow Mother(x, y)$

R4. $Ancestor(x, y) \leftarrow Parent(x, y)$

R5. $Ancestor(x, y) \leftarrow Parent(x, z) \wedge Ancestor(z, y)$

R6. $Samegen(x, x) \leftarrow Person(x)$.

R7. $Samegen(x, y) \leftarrow Parent(u, x) \wedge Samegen(u, v) \wedge Parent(v, y)$

R8. $Wife(x, y) \leftarrow Husband(y, x)$

R9. $Married(x, y) \leftarrow Husband(x, y)$

R10. $Married(x, y) \leftarrow Wife(x, y)$

R11. $Employed(x) \leftarrow Occupation(x, Service)$

R12. $Student(x) \leftarrow Occupation(x, Student)$

R13. $Dependent(x, y) \leftarrow Parent(y, x) \wedge Employed(y) \wedge Student(x)$

R14. $Dependent(x, y) \leftarrow Married(y, x) \wedge Employed(y) \wedge \neg Employed(x)$

R15. $SelfSufficient(x) \leftarrow Married(y, x) \wedge \neg Employed(y)$

R16. $Guardian(x, y) \leftarrow Dependent(y, x)$

F1. *Person (Robert)*

F2. *Person (Madeleine)*

F3. *Person (Christelle)*

F4. *Occupation (Madeleine, Service)*

F5. *Occupation (Christelle, Student)*

F6. *Husband (Robert, Madeleine)*

F7. *Father (Robert, Christelle)*

F8. *Sponsor (Madeleine, Christelle)*

F9. *Sponsor (Madeleine, Robert)*

Constraints: IC1. $\leftarrow Guardian(x, y) \wedge \neg Sponsor(x, y)$

IC2. $\leftarrow Married(x, y) \wedge Student(x)$

Transaction: insertfact *Occupation (Robert, Service)*.

13.1.1 The method of Lloyd et al.

The simplification method of Lloyd *et al.* is based on the standard view of constraint satisfiability and a generalization of the simplification method proposed by Nicolas (1982) for relational databases. The method was first proved to be correct for the class of definite databases by Lloyd and Topor (1985) and later for the class of stratified databases by Lloyd *et al.* (1986). An important task of the method is to capture the difference between a model for $Comp(\mathbf{D}')$ and a model for $Comp(\mathbf{D})$, where $\mathbf{D}$ and $\mathbf{D}'$ are databases and $\mathbf{D}'$ is obtained from $\mathbf{D}$ by the application of a transaction $\mathbf{T}$ to $\mathbf{D}$. Let the transaction $\mathbf{T}$ consist of a sequence of deletions followed by a sequence of additions and let the application of the sequence of deletions to $\mathbf{D}$ produce the intermediate database $\mathbf{D}''$. By using only rules of the database and the transaction, the method computes inductively the four sets of partially instantiated atoms $\mathcal{P}os_{\mathbf{D}'',\mathbf{D}'}$, $\mathcal{N}eg_{\mathbf{D}'',\mathbf{D}'}$, $\mathcal{P}os_{\mathbf{D}'',\mathbf{D}}$ and $\mathcal{N}eg_{\mathbf{D}'',\mathbf{D}}$ by the following formula.

Let $\mathbf{X}$ and $\mathbf{X}'$ be normal databases such that $\mathbf{X} \subseteq \mathbf{X}'$. Then the two sets $\mathcal{P}os_{\mathbf{X},\mathbf{X}'}$ and $\mathcal{N}eg_{\mathbf{X},\mathbf{X}'}$ are inductively defined as follows:

$$\mathcal{P}os^{0}_{\mathbf{X},\mathbf{X}'} = \{A : A \leftarrow \mathrm{B} \in \mathbf{X}' - \mathbf{X}\}$$
$$\mathcal{N}eg^{0}_{\mathbf{X},\mathbf{X}'} = \{\}$$

$$\mathcal{Pos}^{n+1}_{\mathbf{X},\mathbf{X}'} = \{A\theta : A \leftarrow \mathrm{B} \in \mathbf{X}',\ M \text{ is a positive condition of } A \leftarrow \mathrm{B},\ N \in \mathcal{Pos}^{n}_{\mathbf{X},\mathbf{X}'}, \text{ and } \theta \text{ is an mgu of } M \text{ and } N\}$$
$$\cup\ \{A\theta : A \leftarrow \mathrm{B} \in \mathbf{X}',\ \neg M \text{ is a negative condition of } A \leftarrow \mathrm{B},\ N \in \mathcal{Neg}^{n}_{\mathbf{X},\mathbf{X}'}, \text{ and } \theta \text{ is an mgu of } M \text{ and } N\}$$

$$\mathcal{Neg}^{n+1}_{\mathbf{X},\mathbf{X}'} = \{A\theta : A \leftarrow \mathrm{B} \in \mathbf{X}',\ M \text{ is a positive condition of } A \leftarrow \mathrm{B},\ N \in \mathcal{Neg}^{n}_{\mathbf{X},\mathbf{X}'}, \text{ and } \theta \text{ is an mgu of } M \text{ and } N\}$$
$$\cup\ \{A\theta : A \leftarrow \mathrm{B} \in \mathbf{X}',\ \neg M \text{ is a negative condition of } A \leftarrow \mathrm{B},\ N \in \mathcal{Pos}^{n}_{\mathbf{X},\mathbf{X}'}, \text{ and } \theta \text{ is an mgu of } M \text{ and } N\}$$

$$\mathcal{Pos}_{\mathbf{X},\mathbf{X}'} = \bigcup_{n\geq 0} \mathcal{Pos}^{n}_{\mathbf{X},\mathbf{X}'}$$
$$\mathcal{Neg}_{\mathbf{X},\mathbf{X}'} = \bigcup_{n\geq 0} \mathcal{Neg}^{n}_{\mathbf{X},\mathbf{X}'}$$

Now define the two sets $\mathcal{Pos}_{\mathbf{D},\mathbf{D}'}$ and $\mathcal{Neg}_{\mathbf{D},\mathbf{D}'}$ as follows:

$$\mathcal{Pos}_{\mathbf{D},\mathbf{D}'} = \mathcal{Pos}_{\mathbf{D}'',\mathbf{D}'} \cup \mathcal{Neg}_{\mathbf{D}'',\mathbf{D}}$$
$$\mathcal{Neg}_{\mathbf{D},\mathbf{D}'} = \mathcal{Neg}_{\mathbf{D}'',\mathbf{D}'} \cup \mathcal{Pos}_{\mathbf{D}'',\mathbf{D}}$$

These two sets of atoms represent respectively the part that is added to the model for $Comp(\mathbf{D})$ when passing from $\mathbf{D}$ to $\mathbf{D}'$ due to a transaction and the part that is deleted. To preserve the integrity of the updated database, constraints are instantiated and evaluated according to the following theorem which is derived from the simplification theorem for integrity constraint checking (Lloyd, 1987).

Theorem 13.1: Let $\mathbf{D}$ be a database, $\leftarrow \mathrm{B}$ be a constraint in denial form and $\mathbf{D}'$ be obtained from $\mathbf{D}$ by applying the transaction $\mathbf{T}$ to $\mathbf{D}$. Suppose the completion of each of $\mathbf{D}$ and $\mathbf{D}'$ is consistent and $\mathbf{D}$ satisfies $\leftarrow \mathrm{B}$. Define the following two sets:

$$\Theta = \{\theta | \theta \text{ is an mgu of an atom of } \mathcal{Pos}_{\mathbf{D},\mathbf{D}'} \text{ and an atom occurring positively in B}\}$$
$$\Psi = \{\theta | \theta \text{ is an mgu of an atom of } \mathcal{Neg}_{\mathbf{D},\mathbf{D}'} \text{ and an atom occurring negatively in B}\}$$

Then the following properties hold:

(1) $\mathbf{D}'$ satisfies $\leftarrow \mathrm{B}$ iff $\mathbf{D}'$ satisfies $\leftarrow \mathrm{B}\phi$ for all $\phi \in \Theta \cup \Psi$.

(2) If $\mathbf{D}' \cup \{\leftarrow \mathrm{B}\phi\}$ has an SLDNF-refutation for some $\phi \in \Theta \cup \Psi$, then $\mathbf{D}'$ violates $\leftarrow \mathrm{B}$.

(3) If $\mathbf{D}' \cup \{\leftarrow \mathrm{B}\phi\}$ has a finitely failed SLDNF-tree for all $\phi \in \Theta \cup \Psi$, then $\mathbf{D}'$ satisfies $\leftarrow \mathrm{B}$.

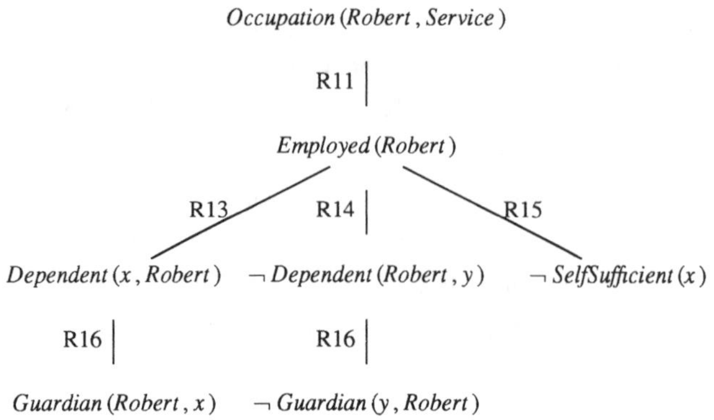

Figure 13.1 Illustration of the process of deriving the two sets of partially instantiated atoms $\mathcal{P}os_{\mathbf{D},\mathbf{D}'}$ and $\mathcal{N}eg_{\mathbf{D},\mathbf{D}'}$ in Lloyd *et al.*'s method.

Proof Consult Lloyd (1987). ■

To apply the method to Example 13.1, the following two sets of atoms $\mathcal{P}os_{\mathbf{D},\mathbf{D}'}$ and $\mathcal{N}eg_{\mathbf{D},\mathbf{D}'}$ are determined.

$$\mathcal{P}os_{\mathbf{D},\mathbf{D}'} = \{Occupation(Robert, Service), Employed(Robert), Dependent(x, Robert), Guardian(Robert, x)\}$$
$$\mathcal{N}eg_{\mathbf{D},\mathbf{D}'} = \{SelfSufficient(x), Dependent(Robert, y)\}.$$

The following shows the different inductive steps of determining the sets $\mathcal{P}os_{\mathbf{D},\mathbf{D}'}$ and $\mathcal{N}eg_{\mathbf{D},\mathbf{D}'}$:

Initial stage: $\mathcal{P}os^0_{\mathbf{D},\mathbf{D}'} = \{Occupation(Robert, Service)\}$
$\mathcal{N}eg^0_{\mathbf{D},\mathbf{D}'} = \{\}$

First stage: $\mathcal{P}os^1_{\mathbf{D},\mathbf{D}'} = \{Employed(Robert)\}$
$\mathcal{N}eg^1_{\mathbf{D},\mathbf{D}'} = \{\}$

Second stage: $\mathcal{P}os^2_{\mathbf{D},\mathbf{D}'} = \{Dependent(x, Robert)\}$
$\mathcal{N}eg^2_{\mathbf{D},\mathbf{D}'} = \{Dependent(Robert, y), SelfSufficient(x)\}$

Third stage: $\mathcal{P}os^3_{\mathbf{D},\mathbf{D}'} = \{Guardian(Robert, x)\}$
$\mathcal{N}eg^3_{\mathbf{D},\mathbf{D}'} = \{Guardian(y, Robert)\}$

Fourth stage: $\mathcal{P}os^4_{\mathbf{D},\mathbf{D}'} = \{\}$
$\mathcal{N}eg^4_{\mathbf{D},\mathbf{D}'} = \{\}$

$\leftarrow Guardian\,(Robert\,,x)\wedge\neg\,Sponsor\,(Robert\,,x)$

R16

$\leftarrow Dependent\,(x\,,Robert\,)\wedge\neg\,Sponsor\,(Robert\,,x)$

R13

R14

$\leftarrow Parent\,(Robert\,,x)\wedge Employed\,(Robert\,)\wedge Student\,(x)\wedge\neg\,Sponsor\,(Robert\,,x)$

R2

R3

$\leftarrow Father\,(Robert\,,x)\wedge Employed\,(Robert\,)\wedge Student\,(x)\wedge\neg\,Sponsor\,(Robert\,,x)$

F7

$\leftarrow Employed\,(Robert\,)\wedge Student\,(Christelle\,)\wedge\neg\,Sponsor\,(Robert\,,Christelle\,)$

R11

$\leftarrow Occupation\,(Robert\,,Service\,)\wedge Student\,(Christelle\,)\wedge\neg\,Sponsor\,(Robert\,,Christelle\,)$

Transaction

$\leftarrow Student\,(Christelle\,)\wedge\neg\,Sponsor\,(Robert\,,Christelle\,)$

R12

$\leftarrow Occupation\,(Christelle\,,Student\,)\wedge\neg\,Sponsor\,(Robert\,,Christelle\,)$

F5

$\leftarrow\neg\,Sponsor\,(Robert\,,Christelle\,)$

NAF

☐

SUCCESS

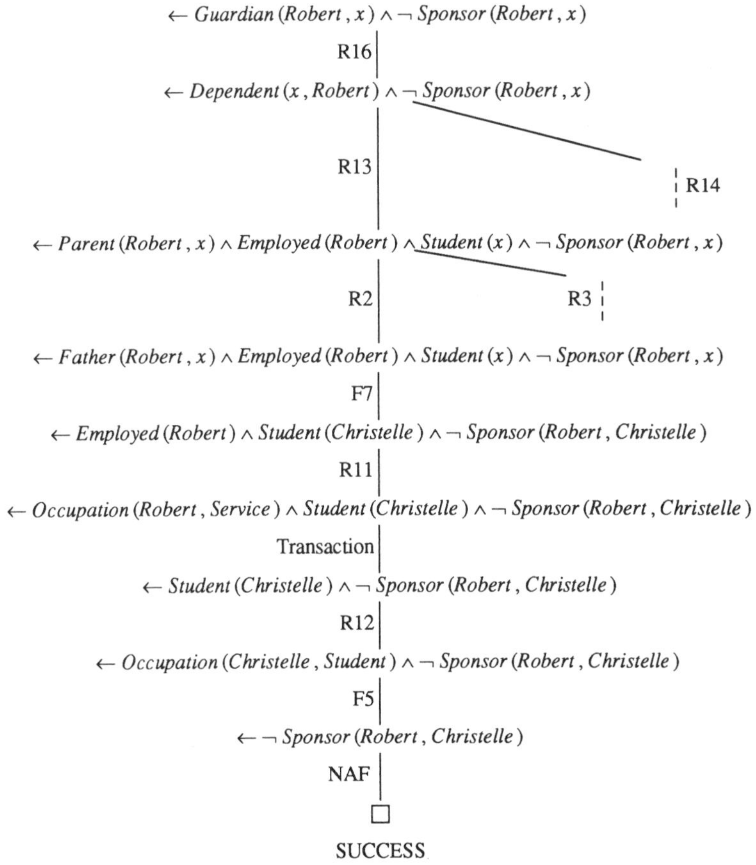

Figure 13.2 Partial search space for evaluating the constraint in Lloyd *et al.*'s method by SLDNF-resolution with the leftmost literal selection strategy through safe selection.

At this point, no more new atoms can be generated. The number of stages for calculating the two sets of atoms is always finite, even in the presence of recursive rules, as at any stage a generated atom is excluded if it is an instance of an atom which has already been generated. In Figure 13.1, the tree diagram illustrates the process of deriving the above two sets of atoms by a depth-first approach. All positive literals belong to the set $\mathcal{P}os_{\mathbf{D},\,\mathbf{D}'}$ and all negative literals belong to the set $\mathcal{N}eg_{\mathbf{D},\,\mathbf{D}'}$.

Using the two sets of atoms $\mathcal{P}os_{\mathbf{D},\,\mathbf{D}'}$ and $\mathcal{N}eg_{\mathbf{D},\,\mathbf{D}'}$, constraints are instantiated appropriately. The only constraint affected is IC1 and an instance of this that has to be evaluated in the database is the denial form

$$\leftarrow Guardian(Robert, x) \wedge \neg Sponsor(Robert, x)$$

This evaluation is carried out using the SLDNF-resolution in the updated database. Figure 13.2 shows the partial search space in which at each step a leftmost literal is selected from a goal under the safe literal selection strategy.

13.1.2 The method of Decker

Just as with the previous method, the method proposed by Decker (1986) is also based on a standard view of constraint satisfiability and a generalization of the simplification method put forward by Nicolas (1982) for relational databases. Decker's method simplifies the constraints with induced updates and only affected constraints are evaluated. Each constraint F is represented in the database as a set $\mathcal{UC}$(F) of *update constraints*, each of which is either an *insert constraint* or a *delete constraint*. An insert constraint has the form

insert *UL* only_if UC

and a delete constraint has the form

delete *UL* only_if UC

where *UL* is an *update literal* and UC is an *update condition* which is in range form. If a constraint F has the form

$$\leftarrow M_1 \wedge \cdots \wedge M_p \wedge \neg N_1 \wedge \cdots \wedge \neg N_q$$

where each M_i and N_j is an atom, then the set $\mathcal{UC}$(F), for $i = 1, ..., p$

insert M_i only_if $\leftarrow M_1 \wedge \cdots \wedge M_{i-1} \wedge M_{i+1} \wedge \cdots \wedge M_p \wedge$
$\neg N_1 \wedge \cdots \wedge \neg N_q$
delete N_j only_if $\leftarrow M_1 \wedge \cdots \wedge M_p \wedge \neg N_1 \wedge \cdots \wedge$
$\neg N_{j-1} \wedge \neg N_{j+1} \wedge \cdots \wedge \neg N_q$

For example, the set of update constraints corresponding to the first constraint in Example 13.1 is given as

$\mathcal{UC}$(IC1) = { insert $Guardian(x, y)$ only_if $\leftarrow \neg Sponsor(x, y)$,
delete $Sponsor(x, y)$ only_if $\leftarrow Guardian(x, y)$ }

When a transaction $\mathbf{T}$ is performed on a database $\mathbf{D}$ the set of all update literals due to $\mathbf{T}$ is divided into two sets of ground atoms, $\mathbf{D}^{\mathbf{T}}$ and $\mathbf{D}_{\mathbf{T}}$, defined as follows. Let $\mathbf{D}'$ denote the set of clauses obtained after execution of the transaction $\mathbf{T}$ on the database $\mathbf{D}$. Then, $\mathbf{D}^{\mathbf{T}} = \mathbf{D}'^{*} - \mathbf{D}^{*}$ and $\mathbf{D}_{\mathbf{T}} = \mathbf{D}^{*} - \mathbf{D}'^{*}$, where $\mathbf{X}^{*}$ denotes the set of facts derivable from $\mathbf{X}$ following completed database semantics. Each element of $\mathbf{D}^{\mathbf{T}}$ is called an *include fact* and each element in $\mathbf{D}_{\mathbf{T}}$ is called a *remove fact*. Intuitively, $\mathbf{D}^{\mathbf{T}}$ (resp. $\mathbf{D}_{\mathbf{T}}$) is the set of facts added to (resp. deleted from) the database due to the transaction.

Decker proposes an algorithm which evaluates all relevant simplified constraints defined above for each fact in $\mathbf{D}^{\mathbf{T}}$ and $\mathbf{D}_{\mathbf{T}}$. The elements of $\mathbf{D}^{\mathbf{T}}$ and $\mathbf{D}_{\mathbf{T}}$ are computed in stages for each operation of $\mathbf{T}$. The algorithm is called with argument *include* (C) (resp. *remove* (C)) for each element insertfact C or insertrule C (resp. deletefact C or deleterule C) in $\mathbf{T}$. The three-step algorithm essentially does the following. In the first step the relevant insert (resp. delete) constraints simplified by each include (resp. remove) fact of $\mathbf{D}^{\mathrm{C}}$ (resp. $\mathbf{D}_{\mathrm{C}}$) are evaluated, where $\mathbf{D}^{\mathrm{C}}$ (resp. $\mathbf{D}_{\mathrm{C}}$) is the set of facts added to (resp. deleted from) the database by the clause C itself. If $\mathrm{C} = H \leftarrow \mathrm{B}$, then $\mathbf{D}^{\mathrm{C}}$ and $\mathbf{D}_{\mathrm{C}}$ are defined as follows:

$$\mathbf{D}^{\mathrm{C}} = \{H\theta \mid H\theta \text{ is ground, B}\theta \text{ is true in } \mathbf{D}' \text{ and } H\theta \text{ is false in } \mathbf{D}\}$$
$$\mathbf{D}_{\mathrm{C}} = \{H\theta \mid H\theta \text{ is ground, B}\theta \text{ is true in } \mathbf{D} \text{ and } H\theta \text{ is false in } \mathbf{D}'\}$$

In fact, the set of all include (resp. remove) facts $\mathbf{D}^{\mathbf{T}}$ (resp. $\mathbf{D}_{\mathbf{T}}$) is the union of all $\mathbf{D}^{\mathrm{C}}$ (resp. $\mathbf{D}_{\mathrm{C}}$), where C is in $\mathbf{D}'$ (resp. $\mathbf{D}$). If a simplified constraint is falsified then an inconsistency occurs and the algorithm stops. In the second and third stages, the algorithm is called recursively with arguments of the form include(R) or remove(R), where R is an instantiated rule in $\mathbf{D}$ which could possibly add to or delete some facts from the database $\mathbf{D}$ due to the facts of $\mathbf{D}^{\mathrm{C}}$ or $\mathbf{D}_{\mathrm{C}}$. The algorithm is formally described below:

Input: include(C)/remove(C)

Step 1: Suppose the input is include(C) (resp. remove(C)) and compute $\mathbf{D}^{\mathrm{C}}$ (resp. $\mathbf{D}_{\mathrm{C}}$). For each L in $\mathbf{D}^{\mathrm{C}}$ (resp. $\mathbf{D}_{\mathrm{C}}$) and each update constraint insert (resp. delete) *UL* only_if UC such that L unifies *UL* with an mgu θ, evaluate UCθ in $\mathbf{D}'$. If the evaluation results false, integrity of the database is violated and the algorithm stops.

Step 2: For each fact A in $\mathbf{D}^{\mathrm{C}}$ (resp. $\mathbf{D}_{\mathrm{C}}$) and for each rule R in $\mathbf{D}$ such that A unifies with an atom A' (with an mgu θ) occurring in the body of R, call the algorithm recursively with the argument include(Rθ) (resp. remove(Rθ)).

Step 3: For each fact A in $\mathbf{D}^{\mathrm{C}}$ (resp. $\mathbf{D}_{\mathrm{C}}$) and for each rule R in $\mathbf{D}$ such that A unifies with an atom A' (with an mgu θ) of the literal $\neg A'$ occurring in the body of R, call the algorithm recursively with the argument remove(Rθ) (resp. include(Rθ)).

To apply the algorithm to Example 13.1, the following two sets of facts are determined:

(1) The facts added to the database as a result of the transaction are

$$\mathbf{D}^{\mathrm{T}} = \{Occupation(Robert, Service), Employed(Robert), Dependent(Christelle, Robert), Guardian(Robert, Christelle)\}$$

(2) The facts deleted from the database as a result of the transaction are

$$\mathbf{D}_{\mathrm{T}} = \{SelfSufficient(Madeleine)\}$$

The following shows the different stages of determining the sets $\mathbf{D}^{\mathrm{T}}$ and $\mathbf{D}_{\mathrm{T}}$. $\mathbf{D}^{\mathrm{T}}$ (resp. $\mathbf{D}_{\mathrm{T}}$) is the union of all $\mathbf{D}^{\mathrm{T}_i}$ (resp. $\mathbf{D}_{\mathrm{T}_i}$).

Initial stage: $\mathbf{D}^{\mathrm{T}_0} = \{Occupation(Robert, Service)\}$
$\mathbf{D}_{\mathrm{T}_0} = \{\}$

No constraint is affected by an atom in $\mathbf{D}^{\mathrm{T}_0}$ or $\mathbf{D}_{\mathrm{T}_0}$, that is, none of the literals in the set $\mathbf{D}^{\mathrm{T}_0}$ (resp. $\mathbf{D}_{\mathrm{T}_0}$) unifies with an update literal of an insert (resp. delete) type constraint.

First stage: $\mathbf{D}^{\mathrm{T}_1} = \{Employed(Robert)\}$
$\mathbf{D}_{\mathrm{T}_1} = \{\}$

No constraint is affected by an atom in $\mathbf{D}^{\mathrm{T}_1}$ or $\mathbf{D}_{\mathrm{T}_1}$.

Second stage: $\mathbf{D}^{\mathrm{T}_2} = \{Dependent(Christelle, Robert)\}$
$\mathbf{D}_{\mathrm{T}_2} = \{SelfSufficient(Madeleine)\}$

No constraint is affected by an atom in $\mathbf{D}^{\mathbf{T}_2}$ or $\mathbf{D}_{\mathbf{T}_2}$.

Third stage: $\mathbf{D}^{\mathbf{T}_3} = \{Guardian\,(Robert, Christelle)\}$

At this stage the fact *Guardian* (*Robert*, *Christelle*) in $\mathbf{D}^{\mathbf{T}_3}$ unifies with the update literal of the insert type constraint

insert *Guardian* (x , y) only_if $\leftarrow \neg$ *Sponsor* (x , y)

Therefore, the update condition $\leftarrow \neg$ *Sponsor* (*Robert*, *Christelle*) has to be true in the updated database. Clearly this is not evaluable in the updated database and hence integrity is violated.

The tree diagram in Figure 13.3 illustrates the process of deriving the above two sets of atoms and evaluation of constraints. All positive literals belong to $\mathbf{D}^{\mathbf{T}}$ and all negative literals belong to the set $\mathbf{D}_{\mathbf{T}}$.

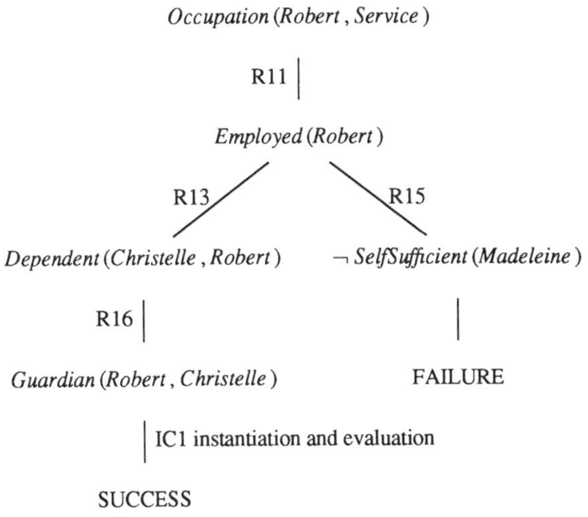

Figure 13.3 The process of deriving the two sets of ground atoms $\mathbf{D}^{\mathbf{T}}$ and $\mathbf{D}_{\mathbf{T}}$ in Decker's method.

13.1.3 The method of Kowalski et al.

The consistency method introduced by Sadri and Kowalski (1987) and later formalized by Kowalski *et al.* (1987) is based on the consistency view of constraint satisfaction. The method is essentially an attempt to construct a *refutation tree* (a search space in which at least one path ends at the empty clause) taking each of the updates in turn as a candidate top clause. If all possible attempts fail then integrity is preserved in the updated database. The method uses a proof procedure which is an extension of the SLDNF-resolution and provides both forward and backward reasoning. In the SLDNF-resolution, the set of formulae which appear in the derivation are either denials or the empty clause. But to reason forward, the new proof procedure allows as top clause any clause, denial or negated atom and the set of formulae appearing in the derivation may be any of these, the empty clause or a formula of the form

$$\neg A \leftarrow L_1 \wedge \cdots \wedge L_n \qquad n \geq 1$$

where A is an atom and the L_i s are literals. The method selects literals through a safe literal selection strategy. The method defines some meta-level rules for reasoning about implicit deletions and a generalized resolution step for reasoning forward from negation as failure.

In the formalization of the proof procedure a relation *REFUTE* (**D**, C) has been defined which means that there is a refutation with **D** as input set and C as top clause. The relation is defined by five different rules. The first three formalize the process of resolution and the negation as failure rule is defined as follows:

MR1: *REFUTE* (**S**, □).

MR2: *REFUTE* (**S**, C) ⇐ *SELECT* (L, C) AND
IN (C′, **S**) AND
RESOLVE (C′, C, L, R) AND
REFUTE (**S**, R).

MR3: *REFUTE* (**S**, $L \leftarrow$ B) ⇐ *SELECT* ($\neg A$, B) AND
NOT *REFUTE* (**S**, $\leftarrow A$) AND
REMOVE (B, $\neg A$, RestB) AND
REFUTE (**S**, $L \leftarrow$ RestB).

The above proof procedures are defined by using a meta-language whose logical symbols are AND, NOT and $\Leftarrow$, predicate symbols are *REFUTE*, *SELECT*, and so on. The relation *SELECT*(L, C) means L is selected from clause C via a safe literal selection strategy; *REMOVE*$(\mathrm{B}, \neg A, \mathrm{RestB})$ means RestB is obtained from the conjunction B by removing the occurrence of $\neg A$; *RESOLVE*$(\mathrm{C}', \mathrm{C}, L, \mathrm{R})$ means R is the resolvent of C′ and C on literal L; *IN*$(\mathrm{C}', \mathbf{S})$ means C′ is a clause in $\mathbf{S}$.

Suppose a transaction consists of a set of additions $\mathbf{T}_{add}$ and a set of deletions $\mathbf{T}_{del}$. This transaction may contain the addition of constraints which are represented in denial form. The transaction when applied to a database $\mathbf{D}$ and a set of constraints $\mathbf{I}$ produces the updated database $\mathbf{D}'$ and updated set of constraints $\mathbf{I}'$.

The following two rules defining the predicate *REFUTE* cater for the cases of implicit deletions resulting from additions and deletions:

$$\text{MR4:}\quad REFUTE(\mathbf{D}' \cup \mathbf{I}', A \leftarrow \mathrm{B}) \Leftarrow \begin{array}{l} IN(A' \leftarrow \mathrm{B}', \mathbf{D}') \text{ AND} \\ ON(\neg A, \mathrm{B}') \text{ AND} \\ DELETED(\mathbf{D}', \mathbf{D}, A') \text{ AND} \\ REFUTE(\mathbf{D}' \cup \mathbf{I}', \neg A' \leftarrow \mathrm{B}). \end{array}$$

$$\text{MR5:}\quad REFUTE(\mathbf{D}' \cup \mathbf{I}', \neg A \leftarrow \mathrm{B}) \Leftarrow \begin{array}{l} SELECT(\neg A, \neg A \leftarrow \mathrm{B}) \text{ AND} \\ IN(A' \leftarrow \mathrm{B}', \mathbf{D}') \text{ AND} \\ ON(A, \mathrm{B}') \text{ AND} \\ DELETED(\mathbf{D}', \mathbf{D}, A') \text{ AND} \\ REFUTE(\mathbf{D}' \cup \mathbf{I}', \neg A' \leftarrow \mathrm{B}). \end{array}$$

where *ON*$(\neg A, \mathrm{B}')$ means literal $\neg A$ occurs in the conjunction B′; *DELETED*$(\mathbf{D}', \mathbf{D}, A')$ means A' is provable in $\mathbf{D}$ but not in $\mathbf{D}'$ and is defined as follows:

$$DELETED(\mathbf{D}', \mathbf{D}, A') \Leftarrow \begin{array}{l} REFUTE(\mathbf{D}, \leftarrow A') \text{ AND} \\ \text{NOT } REFUTE(\mathbf{D}', \leftarrow A'). \end{array}$$

To check whether the updated database $\mathbf{D}'$ satisfies the updated set of constraints $\mathbf{I}'$, one has to determine whether *IC_VIOLATED*$(\mathbf{D}' \cup \mathbf{I}', \mathbf{T}_{add} \cup \mathbf{T}_{del})$ is true in the meta-level formalism. The rules defining the predicate *IC_VIOLATED* are as follows:

$$IC\_VIOLATED(\mathbf{D}' \cup \mathbf{I}', \mathbf{T}_{add} \cup \mathbf{T}_{del}) \Leftarrow \begin{array}{l} ON(\mathrm{C}, \mathbf{T}_{add}) \text{ AND} \\ REFUTE(\mathbf{D}' \cup \mathbf{I}', \mathrm{C}). \end{array}$$

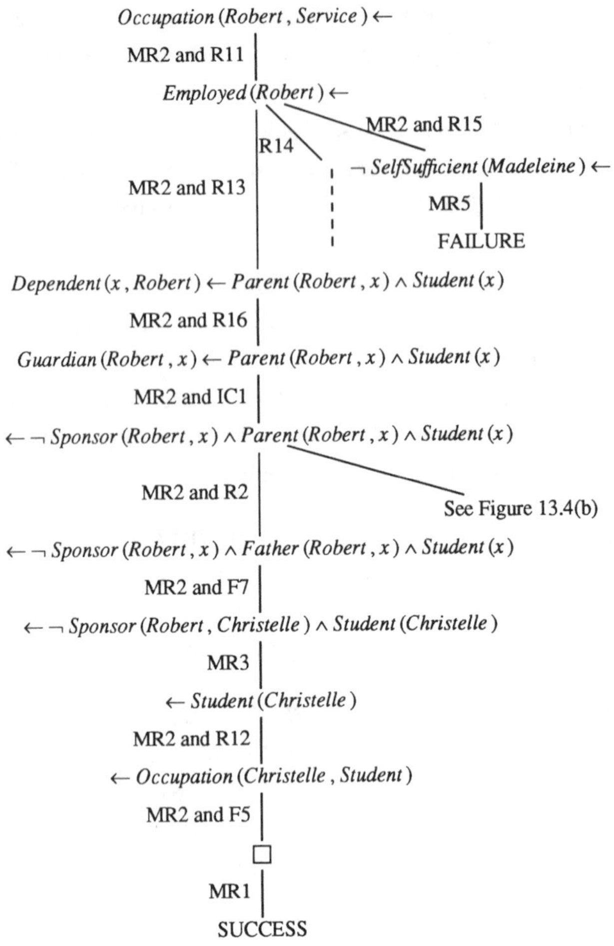

Figure 13.4(a) Partial search space generated by taking the update as the top clause in Kowalski *et al.*'s method.

$$IC\_VIOLATED\,(\mathbf{D'} \cup \mathbf{I'}, \mathbf{T}_{add} \cup \mathbf{T}_{del}) \Leftarrow \quad ON\,(A \leftarrow \mathrm{B}, \mathbf{T}_{del})\ \text{AND}$$
$$DELETED\,(\mathbf{D'}, \mathbf{D}, A)\ \text{AND}$$
$$REFUTE\,(\mathbf{D'} \cup \mathbf{I'}, \neg A).$$

To apply the algorithm to Example 13.1, the update is taken as a candidate top clause and a refutation tree is constructed. Part of the search space for this is shown in Figure 13.4(a) and (b). According to the order of clauses and constraints of database of Example 13.1, only the leftmost branch will be followed. The rightmost branch of the search space shown in the figure implies an implicit

See Figure 13.4(a)

MR2 and R3

$\leftarrow \neg\, Sponsor\,(Robert\,, x) \wedge Mother\,(Robert\,, x) \wedge Student\,(x)$

MR2 and R1

$\leftarrow \neg\, Sponsor\,(Robert\,, x) \wedge Father\,(z\,, x) \wedge Husband\,(z\,, Robert) \wedge Student\,(x)$

MR2 and F7

$\leftarrow \neg\, Sponsor\,(Robert\,, Christelle) \wedge Husband\,(Robert\,, Robert) \wedge Student\,(Christelle)$

MR3

$\leftarrow Husband\,(Robert\,, Robert) \wedge Student\,(Christelle)$

MR2

FAILURE

Figure 13.4(b) Another branch of the tree in Figure 13.4(a).

deletion of the fact *SelfSufficient* (*Madeleine*) from the database. In the example, the method selects the leftmost literal through a safe literal selection strategy. For ground negated atoms, the negation as failure rule has been applied through the rule MR3. A meta-rule number and a clause number (for example MR2 and R11), labelling an arc, are used for resolution purposes with the selected literal.

13.1.4 Path finding method

The path finding method (Das, 1990; Das and Williams, 1989a), is based on the standard view of constraint satisfiability. In this method verification of the constraints in the updated database is reduced to the process of constructing paths from update literals to the heads of constraints. A *path* in a set **D** of normal clauses is defined as a chain of literals

$$L_0 \xrightarrow{R_1} L_1 \xrightarrow{R_2} \cdots \xrightarrow{R_n} L_n$$

where L_0 is called the *source* of the path, L_n its *destination*, *n* its *length* and R_1, ..., R_n are clauses from **D** used to construct the path from L_0 to L_n. If the source L_0 is positive then it is ground. For any two consecutive literals L_i and L_{i+1}, L_{i+1} is the successor of L_i in the path, and is obtained from L_i in one of the following ways:

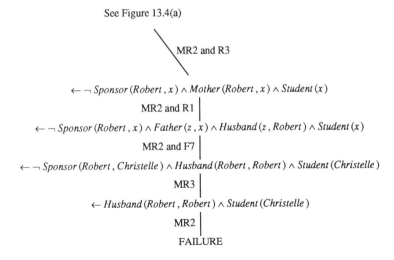

(1) If (a) L_i is positive, and (b) L_i unifies with a positive literal L occurring in the body of the clause $R_i : H \leftarrow B$, and (c) α is an mgu of L_i and L, and (d) G' is a resolvent of $\leftarrow B$ and $L_i \leftarrow$ on L, and (e) θ is a computed answer for $\mathbf{D} \cup \{G'\}$, then L_{i+1} is $H\alpha\theta$.

(2) If (a) L_i is positive, and (b) the negative literal $\neg L$ occurs in the body of the clause $R_i : H \leftarrow B$ such that L_i unifies with L, and (c) α is an mgu of L_i and L, and (d) $\neg H\alpha$ is not an instance of any one of the L_js, where $0 \le j \le i$, then L_{i+1} is $\neg H\alpha$.

(3) If (a) L_i is negative, and (b) L_i unifies with a negative literal L occurring in the body of the clause $R_i : H \leftarrow B$, and (c) α is an mgu of L_i and L, and (d) θ is a computed answer for $\mathbf{D} \cup \{G\}$, where G is the goal $\leftarrow B\alpha$, then L_{i+1} is $H\alpha\theta$.

(4) If (a) L_i is negative and has the form $\neg M$, and (b) M unifies with a positive literal L occurring in the body of the clause $R_i : H \leftarrow B$, and (c) α is an mgu of M and L, and (d) $\neg H\alpha$ is not an instance of any one of the L_js, where $0 \le j \le i$, then L_{i+1} is $\neg H\alpha$.

To check integrity in the updated database $\mathbf{D}'$ due to a transaction $\mathbf{T}$ applied to $\mathbf{D}$ the source is taken as an update literal. An *update literal* of the transaction $\mathbf{T}$ applied to a database $\mathbf{D}$ may be one of the following :

(1) A fact of $\mathbf{T}$ which is to be added to $\mathbf{D}$.

(2) The negation of a fact of $\mathbf{T}$ which is to be deleted from $\mathbf{D}$.

(3) If a rule $H \leftarrow B$ in $\mathbf{T}$ is to be added to $\mathbf{D}$ then for a computed answer θ for $\mathbf{D}' \cup \{\leftarrow B\}$, the corresponding instance of the head of the rule $H \leftarrow B$ is $H\theta$, which is implicitly added to $\mathbf{D}$ due to the transaction.

(4) If a rule $H \leftarrow B$ in $\mathbf{T}$ is to be deleted from $\mathbf{D}$ then the negation of the head of the rule $H \leftarrow B$, is $\neg H$, whose instances are likely to be deleted from $\mathbf{D}$ due to the transaction.

Suppose $\mathbf{I}$ is a set of constraints in denial form. The set $\mathbf{I}_d$ represents the set of clauses of the form

$$IC(No) \leftarrow B$$

where $\leftarrow B$ is a constraint from $\mathbf{I}$ and No is a unique identification of the constraint. $IC(No)$ is the head of the constraint $\leftarrow B$.

A *path space* in $\mathbf{D}' \cup \mathbf{I}_d$ rooted at an update literal L is a tree defined as follows:

(1) Each node of the tree is a literal.

(2) The root node is L.

(3) Let N be a node of the tree. Then the set of all the successors of N in the paths of $\mathbf{S}$ is the only descendants of N in the tree, where $\mathbf{S}$ is the set of all paths with L as the source.

To check integrity in a database when a new constraint is added, the database is queried directly to ensure that the constraint is a logical consequence of the completed database. If a constraint is deleted then this cannot cause any inconsistency. To preserve integrity in the updated database for the rest of the cases the following theorem for integrity checking is followed.

Theorem 13.2: Let $\mathbf{D}$ be a database, $\mathbf{I}$ be a set of constraints and $\mathbf{D}'$ be obtained from $\mathbf{D}$ by applying the transaction $\mathbf{T}$ to $\mathbf{D}$. Suppose the completion of each of $\mathbf{D}$ and $\mathbf{D}'$ is consistent and $\mathbf{D}$ satisfies $\mathbf{I}$. Then the following properties hold:

(1) If there exists a *success path* (a path which ends at $IC(No)$) in $\mathbf{D}' \cup \mathbf{I}_d$ taking the source as one of the update literals, then $\mathbf{D}'$ violates $\mathbf{I}$.

(2) If there exists no success path in $\mathbf{D}' \cup \mathbf{I}_d$ from any one of the update literals, then $\mathbf{D}'$ satisfies $\mathbf{I}$.

Proof See Das (1990). ■

To apply the path finding method to Example 13.1, the update literal $Occupation(Robert, Service)$ is taken as a source. Owing to the insertion of this fact into the database, with the help of R11 one can say that the fact $Employed(Robert)$ is implicitly added to the database and so $Employed(Robert)$ is the next literal of the path. Continuing in this way one can construct the following success path (which ends at the head of a constraint):

$Occupation(Robert, Service) \rightarrow Employed(Robert) \rightarrow$
$Dependent(Christelle, Robert) \rightarrow$
$Guardian(Robert, Christelle) \rightarrow IC(Robert)$

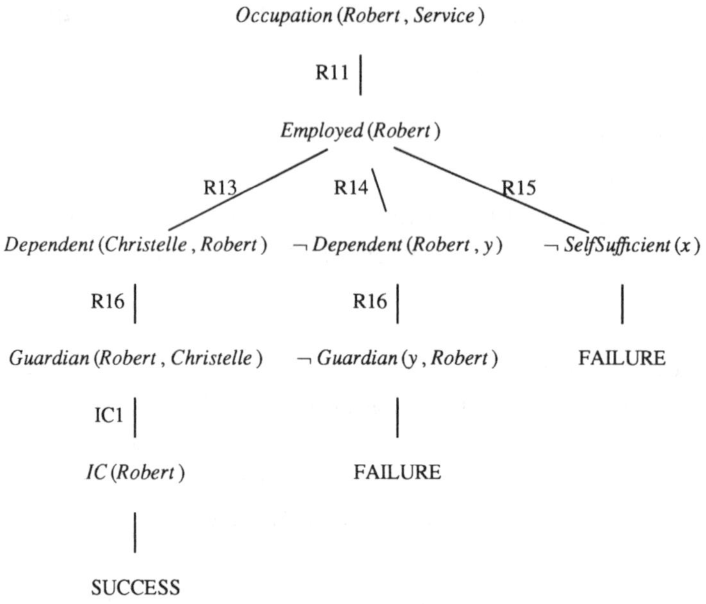

Figure 13.5 The complete path space traversed by the path finding method, taking the update as the source.

and the complete path space generated by the insertion is shown in Figure 13.5. The leftmost branch corresponds to the success path and this is followed according to the order of the clauses. The successor literal of *Employed* (*Robert*) along the second branch of the path space is ¬ *Dependent* (*Robert*, *y*), by rule R14. This shows that instances of *Dependent* (*Robert* ,*y*) are likely to be deleted from the database owing to the the implicit addition of *Employed* (*Robert*) to the database.

13.2 Characteristics comparison of the methods

The four constraint checking methods presented above are compared (Das, 1990; Das and Williams, 1989b) in this section on the basis of a number of characteristics. The definitions of these characteristics are self-explanatory.

13.2.1 Constraint satisfiability

The methods of Lloyd *et al.* and Decker and the path finding method are based on the theoremhood view of constraint satisfiability. On the other hand, the method of Kowalski *et al.* is based on the consistency view of constraint satisfiability.

13.2.2 Application domain

As far as the application domain of the underlying database is concerned, the path finding method, Decker's method and the method of Kowalski *et al.* can handle those recursive rules for which the underlying SLDNF-resolution terminates. The simplification of constraints in Lloyd *et al.*'s method is independent of the evaluation method chosen. The method will work in the presence of recursive rules if the underlying query evaluator handles recursion.

Each of the methods can deal with range-restricted closed first-order formulae as constraints. The method of Lloyd *et al.* can handle any closed first-order formulae as constraints if the underlying query evaluator can.

The size of the database size also affects each of the methods. In a natural way, as the database size increases, the times taken by some operations (such as search or unification) employed with constraint checking increase accordingly. In this kind of situation the time taken by each of the methods to check consistency can vary with the the number of relevant clauses present in the database.

13.2.3 Constraint representation

The representations of a particular constraint by the four methods may differ. Constraints are not distinguished from rules in their representation in both Kowalski *et al.*'s method and the path finding method. In Decker's method a constraint has been converted to a set of update constraints and each update constraint is stored under the predicate *update_cons*. In Lloyd *et al.*'s method each constraint can be kept in its original form as long as the underlying query evaluator can cope.

13.2.4 Overall strategy

As was pointed out earlier, the simplest way of maintaining consistency is by evaluating every constraint for each update; however, this is very inefficient since it ignores the assumption that the database satisfies the constraints prior to the update. All the methods presented do take advantage of this assumption.

The major difference in strategy between the path finding approach and the approach by Decker on the one hand and that of Lloyd *et al.* on the other is as follows. In the first kind of approach instantiation and evaluation of constraints and the derivation of implicitly added or deleted facts is done simultaneously. In Lloyd *et al.*'s approach instantiation and evaluation of constraints are performed after the derivation of the two sets of partially instantiated atoms.

The literal selection strategy in Kowalski *et al.*'s method can play an important role in determining the efficiency of the method. An example of a literal selection strategy is to select (under safe selection) a literal from the condition part of the top clause until no such literal remains. Another example of a literal selection strategy is to select a literal from the conclusion part first, if there is a conclusion. Decker's method and the method of Lloyd *et al.* can be approximated by considering respectively the previous two literal selection strategies.

In the path finding method finding a path from an update to the head of a constraint is similar to the problem of finding a refutation with an update literal as a top clause in Kowalski's method. In the latter method finding a refutation means arriving at an empty head of the denial form of a constraint from an update literal. In the path finding method constructing a success path means reaching the head of a constraint from an update literal. The difference lies in the way in which this is achieved: in the method of Kowalski *et al.* the computation of positive induced updates can be deferred by a proper literal selection strategy but the computation of negative induced updates is essential; in the path finding method the computation of positive induced updates is essential and the computation of negative induced updates is deferred.

13.2.5 Implementation performance

A typical way of implementing a constraint evaluator is through a meta-interpreter on its own or built on top of the underlying query evaluator of the system. A meta-interpreter is characterized by its *granularity* (Sterling and Shapiro, 1986), that is, the size of the computation made accessible to the programmers. A disadvantage of Kowalski *et al.*'s method is that the degree of granularity required for the meta-interpreter is much finer than that required for the other methods. This is because the former models the literal selection strategy. This should result in a loss of efficiency. On the other hand the other three methods can rely on the strategy built into the underlying query evaluator.

13.2.6 Strategy for induced update computation

When a transaction is performed on the database the path finding method derives in stages a set of fully instantiated atoms which are added to the database and a set of partially instantiated atoms whose instances are likely to be deleted from the database. By contrast Decker's method derives two sets of fully instantiated atoms. The first set is the set of atoms implicitly added to the database and the second set is the set of atoms deleted from the database. The method of Lloyd *et al.* derives two sets of partially instantiated atoms. These represent the set of atoms likely to be added to the database and the set of atoms likely to be deleted from the database.

The approach taken by the path finding method to compute induced updates is identical to that of Decker when there is no implicit deletion in the database. When an implicit deletion occurs in a stage, the method follows a similar approach to that of Lloyd *et al.* It can be observed from Figure 13.5 that the rightmost two paths starting from the literal *Employed*(*Robert*) are similar to the paths in the same position in Figure 13.1. This is because these two paths do not show any implicit addition to the database. It is also observed from Figure 13.5 that starting from the root the leftmost branch is similar to the branch in the same position in Figure 13.3. This is because this path does not show any implicit deletion from the database.

Decker's method could be inefficient for a complex transaction which requires reasoning with two database states (before and after update) to calculate the two sets of atoms mentioned earlier. For each induced update, that is, each fact which is implicitly added or deleted, the method checks whether it is provable in the database before update or not. The method may show better performance than the other methods when constraints are relevant to the induced updates, but some of the induced updates are already provable in the database before update.

13.2.7 Redundant evaluation of constraints

In Lloyd *et al.*'s approach two sets of partially instantiated atoms are always derived even if no ground instance of these atoms is true in the updated database and hence may cause redundant evaluation of the constraints. Consider the following example.

EXAMPLE 13.2

Database: Rules from Example 13.1.
Some facts under the predicates *Father*, *Husband*, *Occupation* and *Sponsor* not involving constants *Robert* and *Madeleine*.
Occupation (*Robert*, *Service*)
Occupation (*Madeleine*, *Service*)

Constraints: $\leftarrow$ *Guardian* $(x, y) \wedge \neg$ *Sponsor* (x, y)
$\leftarrow$ *Sponsor* $(x, y) \wedge$ *Guardian* $(z, y) \wedge \neg$ *parent* (x, y)

Transaction: insertfact *Husband* (*Robert*, *Madeleine*)

In the above example, the database satisfies the constraints. Now if one wants to insert the fact *Husband* (*Robert*, *Madeleine*) to the database, Lloyd *et al.*'s method will derive the two sets of atoms

{*Husband* (*Robert*, *Madeleine*), *Mother* (*Madeleine*, y),
Parent (*Madeleine*, y), *Ancestor* (x, y), *Samegen* (x, y),
Dependent (y, *Madeleine*), *Guardian* (*Madeleine*, y),
Wife (*Madeleine*, *Robert*), *Married* (*Madeleine*, *Robert*),
SelfSufficient (*Robert*), *Married* (*Robert*, *Madeleine*),
Dependent (*Madeleine*, *Robert*), *Guardian* (*Robert*, *Madeleine*),
SelfSufficient (*Madeleine*)} and { }

Derivation of these two sets of atoms is highly redundant as no ground instance of these atoms under the predicate *Guardian*, which simplify the constraints, is true in the updated database and hence cause redundant evaluations of the instantiated constraints corresponding to the atoms *Guardian* (*Madeleine*, y) and *Guardian* (*Robert*, *Madeleine*). As no fact is implicitly added to the database corresponding to the insertion of *Married* (*Robert*, *Madeleine*), in both the approach by Decker and the path finding method, no constraint is evaluated.

13.2.8 Evaluation of unsimplified constraints

Lloyd *et al.*'s approach may sometimes evaluate unsimplified constraints which may cause inefficiency. For example, if one wants to delete (resp. insert) a ground instance of *Occupation* (y, *Service*) from (to) a database **D** containing rules described in Example 13.1, then *SelfSufficient* (x) would be a member of $\mathcal{Pos}_{\mathbf{D},\mathbf{D}'}$ (resp. $\mathcal{Neg}_{\mathbf{D},\mathbf{D}'}$). In that case if there is a constraint C relevant to the atom

SelfSufficient (x) (resp. $\neg$ *SelfSufficient* (x)), no simplification for C is possible before its evaluation. In Decker's method constraints are always simplified before evaluation as the method always calculates two sets of ground atoms implicitly added to or deleted from the database. In the case of addition, the path finding method follows Decker's approach and hence C is simplified accordingly. But, in the case of deletion, the method follows the approach of Lloyd *et al.* and hence causes the evaluation of unsimplified C.

13.2.9 Redundant computation of induced updates

Both the path finding method and Decker's method suffer from the drawback that all induced updates are computed, including those for which no constraints are relevant. The method of Kowalski *et al.* can avoid this by a proper literal selection strategy while the method of Lloyd *et al.* does not suffer from this drawback as it computes only potential updates that represent possible ground induced updates. Consider the following example.

EXAMPLE 13.3

Database:	Rules from Example 13.1.
	Some facts under the predicates *Father*, *Husband*, *Occupation*, *Person* and *Sponsor* not involving constants *Robert* and *Christelle*.
	Some facts under the predicate *Father* with 1 as the first argument.
	Occupation (*Madeleine*, *Service*)
	Occupation (*Christelle*, *Student*)
	Father (*Robert*, *Christelle*)
Constraints:	$\leftarrow Father(x, z) \wedge Father(y, z) \wedge x \neq y$
Transaction:	insertfact *Husband* (*Robert*, *Madeleine*)

In this example, the database satisfies the constraints. Now if one wants to insert the fact *Husband* (*Robert*, *Madeleine*) in to the database, the path finding method and Decker's method will derive in stages the following set of atoms:

{*Wife* (*Robert*, *Madeleine*), *Married* (*Robert*, *Madeleine*),
Married (*Madeleine*, *Robert*), *Mother* (*Madeleine*, x_c),
Parent (*Madeleine*, x_c), *Ancestor* (*Madeleine*, x_c),
Dependent (x_c, *Madeleine*), *SelfSufficient* (*Madeleine*),
Guardian (*Madeleine*, x_c)}

x_c is a constant and *Father* (*Robert*, x_c) is true in the updated database}

and, possibly, some more under the predicates *Ancestor* and *Samegen*. It is clear that no constraint of Example 13.3 is relevant to the above set of atoms and hence causes redundant evaluation. The evaluation time in this case depends mainly on the number of facts present in the database under the predicate *Father* whose first argument is the constant *Robert*. In the case of deletion of the fact *Husband* (*Robert*, *Madeleine*) from the updated database, Decker's method calculates all the facts implicitly deleted from the database due to the deletion of *Husband* (*Robert*, *Madeleine*). These are precisely those which were implicitly added to the database of Example 13.3 by the addition of the fact *Husband* (*Robert*, *Madeleine*). This calculation is redundant and the path finding method avoids this by following Lloyd *et al.*'s approach.

In this approach, an instance of a literal from any one of the two sets of partially instantiated atoms may be evaluated more than once if that particular literal simplifies more than one constraint. This causes inefficiency. The path finding method also has a similar drawback but only when a negative literal simplifies a constraint. On the other hand Decker's method does not have this drawback at all as the literal which simplifies the constraint is always true in the database and hence it is removed from the unified constraint.

Table 13.1 Characteristics comparison of constraint checking methods.

Methods	*Constraint satisfiability*	*Constraint representation*	*Application domain of database*
Lloyd *et al.*	Theoremhood view	Closed first-order	Extended database
Decker	Theoremhood view	Update constraints	Range-restricted normal database
Kowalski *et al.*	Consistency view	Range-restricted denial	Range-restricted normal database
Path finding	Theoremhood view	Range-restricted denial with head	Range-restricted normal database

Table 13.1(contd) Characteristics comparison of constraint checking methods.

Induced update computation	*Implementation*
Two sets of partially instantiated atoms	Meta-interpretor for computing partially instantiated atoms and a query evaluator implementing SLDNF-resolution for extended databases to verify instantiated constraints
Two sets of fully instantiated atoms	Meta-interpretor for computing fully instantiated atoms and a query evaluator implementing SLDNF-resolution to verify instantiated constraints
Depends on literal selection strategy	Meta-interpretor for computing instantiated atoms as well as for implementing an extended SLDNF-resolution scheme
One set of partially instantiated atoms and another set of fully instantiated atoms	Meta-interpretor for computing fully instantiated atoms and and a query evaluator implementing SLDNF-resolution to verify instantiated constraints

13.2.10 Characteristics comparison table

Table 13.1 summarizes the characteristics comparison among the four methods. Some of the entries in the table have been completed from the original proposals (Das 1990; Decker, 1986; Kowalski *et al.*, 1987; Lloyd *et al.*, 1986) rather than their limited forms considered this chapter.

Exercises

13.1 A few example databases, associated sets of constraints and some transactions to be performed on them are given below. By applying each of the four methods discussed in this chapter determine whether the integrity of the database is violated or not in each case. Discuss also the advantages or disadvantages of each method over the rest in terms of the total number of added or deleted facts, computation due to the transaction, amount of reasoning, and so on.

EXAMPLE A

Database: $Worker(x) \leftarrow Employee(x) \wedge \neg Officer(x)$
$Employee(a)$
$Employee(b)$
$Manager(c, b)$
$Officer(b)$

Constraints: $\forall x(Worker(x) \rightarrow \exists y Manager(y, x))$

Transactions: {insertfact $Employee(d)$}
{deletefact $Superior(c, b)$}
{insertfact $Employee(d)$, insertfact $Superior(c, d)$}
{deletefact $Superior(c, b)$, insertfact $Superior(f, b)$}

EXAMPLE B

Database: $Group(Sc, Phy)$
$Group(Sc, Che)$
$Group(Sc, Math)$
$Group(Com, Acc)$
$Group(Com, BK)$
$Student(a, Sc)$
$Student(b, Com)$
$Marks(a, Phy, 50)$
$Marks(a, Chem, 70)$
$Marks(b, Acc, 50)$

Constraints: $\forall x \forall y \forall z_1 \forall z_2(Marks(x, y, z_1) \wedge Marks(x, y, z_2) \rightarrow z_1 = z_2)$
$\forall x \forall y \forall z(Marks(x, y, z) \rightarrow z \geq 0 \wedge z \leq 100)$
$\forall x \forall y \forall z \exists t(Marks(x, y, z) \rightarrow Group(t, y) \wedge Student(x, t))$
$\forall x \forall y_1 \forall y_2(Student(x, y_1) \wedge Student(x, y_2) \rightarrow y_1 = y_2)$

Transactions: {insertfact $Marks(a, Math, 110)$,
insertfact $Marks(b, BK, 75)$}
{insertfact $Marks(a, Phy, 50)$}
{insertfact $Marks(a, Chem, 75)$}
{deletefact $Group(Sc, Phy)$}
{deletefact $Student(b, Com)$, insertfact $Student(b, Sc)$}

EXAMPLE C

Database: $P(x, y) \leftarrow Q(x, y) \wedge \neg R(x, y)$

$R(x, y) \leftarrow S(x, z) \wedge R(z, y)$

$R(x, y) \leftarrow S(x, y)$

$S(x, y) \leftarrow T(x) \wedge U(y)$

$Q(a, d)$

$Q(a, c)$

$S(b, c)$

$T(a)$

$U(b)$

$V(d, f)$

Constraints: $\forall x \forall y (P(x, y) \rightarrow \exists z V(y, z))$

Transactions: {deletefact $T(a)$}

{deletefact $U(b)$}

{insertfact $Q(a, c)$}

EXAMPLE D

Database: $ValidAccOpen(x, y) \leftarrow ValidAppl(x, y) \wedge \neg Account(x, y)$

$ValidAppl(x, y) \leftarrow Applied(x, y) \wedge Recommend(z, x) \wedge \neg Related(z, x) \wedge Account(z, y) \wedge \neg BadRecord(z, y)$

$BadRecord(x, y) \leftarrow OverWithdraw(x, y, z) \wedge z > 1000$

Constraints: $\forall x \forall y \forall z (Account(x, y) \wedge Account(x, z) \rightarrow y = z)$

$\forall x \forall y (Applied(x, y) \rightarrow \exists z_1 Recommend(x, z_1) \wedge \exists z_2 Deposit(x, z_2))$

Transactions: {insertfact *Applied* (*a*, *Bank* 1)}

{insertfact *Applied* (*a*, *Bank* 1),
insertfact *Recommend* (*b*, *a*),
insertfact *deposit* (*a*, 200)}

14

A prototype deductive database system

This chapter discusses a number of possible architectures for deductive database systems. By adopting one of these architectures, a prototype deductive database system is developed on top of a Prolog interpreter. The Prolog code which implements the prototype is presented in Appendix A.

14.1 Deductive database system architectures

The two most fundamental requirements of a deductive database system are that

(1) It should be efficient for manipulating large amount of data, and
(2) It should have a powerful logical inference mechanism.

The techniques for managing large volumes of data in relational database systems are particularly useful in achieving the former whereas logic programming systems are ideal for the latter. Hence constructing deductive database systems by combining relational database and logic programming systems would be highly desirable. This argument can further be strengthened by the fact that relational tuples are a special form of clauses with empty bodies. *Coupling architectures* are based on this idea and integrate the functionalities of logic programming and conventional (for example, relational) database systems (Berghel, 1985; Bocca, 1986; Brodie and Jarke, 1989; Chang and Walker, 1985; Futo *et al.*, 1978; Ramamohanarao *et al.*, 1988; Schwind, 1984) to achieve a flavour of deductive database systems.

Coupling (Ceri *et al.*, 1990; Shao *et al.*, 1990; Gardarin and Valduriez, 1989) is the interfacing of a logic programming system (such as a Prolog interpreter) and a conventional database system. Three different levels of coupling are possible in a system:

(1) *Logical level coupling* which is at the top level of the system and brings together a logic programming language and a relational data manipulation language (Naqvi and Tsur, 1989) to enhance the expressive power of data manipulation languages (see Exercise 14.4).

(2) *Function level coupling* which brings together the logical inference mechanisms of a logic programming system and database management functions of a relational database management systems so as to retrieve or deduce information efficiently.

(3) *Physical level coupling* which deals with the physical organizations of tuples of relational database management systems and the rules of deductive database management systems.

A particular level (either logical or functional or physical) is *loosely coupled* if the two components co-exist independently; otherwise it is *tightly coupled.*

As opposed to coupling, *integration* produces a single system which provides a number of the facilities of conventional database systems plus efficient management of rules, and a recursive query processor (which could be based on any method in Chapter 11). In other words, an integrated architecture is specially designed to use a logic programming system as a deductive database system.

14.2 The prototype

The prototype developed in Prolog in this chapter is largely based on the idea of integration and its architecture is displayed in Figure 14.1. The following are the major functions of the prototype developed:

(1) Clause management,

(2) Bottom-up compiled query evaluation using the magic sets method,

(3) Top-down interpreted query evaluation using SLDNF-resolution,

(4) Integrity maintenance using the path finding method.

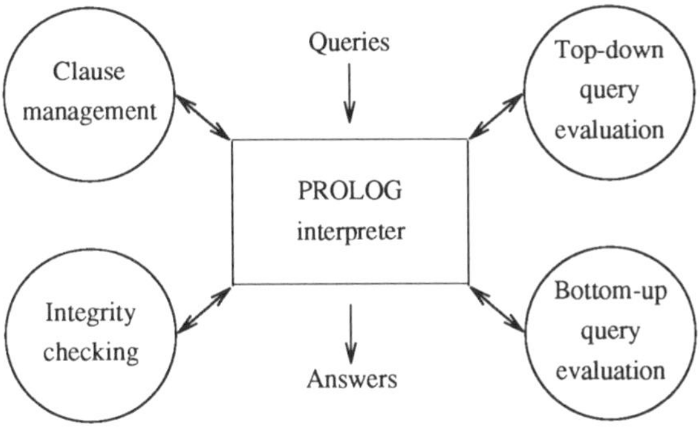

Figure 14.1 Architecture of the prototype.

The application domain of the prototype is that of separate range-restricted normal programs and goals except when using the magic sets method. When the query evaluation is done by choosing the magic sets method option, the input rules and goals have to be definite.

Every command to the interpreter has to be terminated by '.'. The following is the BNF syntax for the input rules, goals and constraints:

<rule> ::= <head> :- <body>
<fact> ::= <pred>[(<constants>)]
<constraint> ::= forall(<variable>, <constraint>) |
exists(<variable>, <constraint>) |
imply(<constraint>, <constraint>) |
and(<constraint>, <constraint>) |
or(<constraint>, <constraint>) |
not <constraint> | <literal>
<head> ::= <atom>
<body> ::= <literal> | <literal>, <body>
<literal> ::= not <atom> | <atom>
<atom> ::= <pred>[(<variables>)]
<variables> ::= <variable> | <variable>, <variables>
<constants> ::= <constant> | <constant>, <constants>

The code of the prototype has been provided in Appendix A. The code is self-explanatory although comments have been added in several places to enhance readability.

Example 14.1 demonstrates how to create a database schema and also shows how facts, rules and constraints are maintained.

EXAMPLE 14.1

Database: $P(x) \leftarrow U(x)$

$S(x,y) \leftarrow V(x,y) \wedge \neg W(x)$

$Q(b)$

$Q(c)$

$V(a,b)$

$V(a,c)$

$R(b,d)$

$U(b)$

Constraint: $\forall x \forall y (\exists z R(x,z) \leftarrow (P(x) \leftarrow Q(x)) \wedge S(y,x))$

The relations of the database are created by the following set of `createrel` commands:

```
|: createrel(p,1,idb).
|: createrel(q,1,edb).
|: createrel(r,2,edb).
|: createrel(s,2,idb).
|: createrel(u,1,edb).
|: createrel(v,2,edb).
|: createrel(w,1,edb).
```

The rules, constraints and facts can be inserted by using the following set of commands:

```
|: insertrule((p(X):-u(X))).
|: insertrule((s(X,Y):-v(X,Y),not w(X))).
|: insertic(imply(exists([Z],r(X,Z)),
        and(imply(p(X),q(X)),s(Y,X))), 'IC 1').
|: insertfact(q(b)).
|: insertfact(q(c)).
|: transaction([insertfact(v(a,b)),
        insertfact(v(a,c))]).
|: insertfact(r(b,d)).
|: insertfact(u(b)).
```

The constraint is represented internally as the following set of rules:

```
$ic_1(1):-(p(X),s(Y,X)),not $ic_3(1,1,[X])
$ic_1(1):-(not q(X),s(Y,X)),not $ic_3(1,2,[X])
$ic_3(1,1,[X]):-r(X,Y)
$ic_3(1,2,[X]):-r(X,Y)
```

Note that if an attempt is made to insert the fact `u(c)`, the integrity of the database is reported as having been violated. The procedures for implementing the path finding method internally construct the success path

```
u(c) -> p(c) -> $ic_1(1)
```

from `u(c)` to the head `$ic_1(1)` of a constraint.

Exercises

14.1 Extend the prototype to deal with arithmetic.

14.2 Extend the prototype by introducing type.

14.3 Extend the prototype to cope with operations on rules or integrity constraints in a transaction.

14.4 The function of the database query language SQL (Date, 1989) is to support the definition, manipulation and control of data in relational databases. Imposing integrity constraints on a database is one of the ways of controlling the data of the database. A BNF-syntax for an SQL-like language (SQL-DDDB) has been provided at the end of this exercise for defining, manipulating and controlling data in deductive databases (Waugh *et al.*, 1990) whose clauses are similar to ones in extended normal deductive databases (see Chapter 7 for extended normal programs). Database clauses, queries and integrity constraints expressed in SQL-DDDB can be transformed to first-order formulae. By using the transformations of Chapter 7, formulae representing database clauses can be stored as normal clauses and formulae representing queries and integrity constraints can be expressed as denial forms. Improve the prototype in the following ways:

(a) Build a Prolog module on top of the prototype to translate the input database clauses and integrity constraints expressed in SQL-DDDB to their equivalent first-order formulae. Also the module should be able to store these formulae by transforming them into normal clauses and normal goals.

(b) Confine the input databases clauses, queries and integrity constraints expressed in SQL-DDDB so that they can always be transformed to clauses and goals which can be handled by the prototype. In such a situation, carry out query evaluation and integrity checking in the prototype by translating each SQL-DDDB statement into one of the available commands of the prototype.

BNF syntax for SQL-DDDB

Schema definition in SQL-DDDB

<relation-schema> ::= CREATE SCHEMA <relation-schema-element>
<relation-schema-element> ::= <relation> (<column-def-commalist>)
<column-def> ::= <column> <data-type>

Clause manipulation in SQL-DDDB

<transaction> ::= <operation> | BEGIN <operation-commalist> END
<operation> ::= <insert-statement> | <delete-statement>
<insert-statement> ::= INSERT INTO <relation> VALUE <data>
<delete-statement> ::= DELETE FROM <relation> VALUE <data>
<data> ::= <tuple> | <rule-definition>
<tuple> ::= (<constant-commalist>)
<rule-definition> ::= (<semantical-query>)

Query evaluation in SQL-DDDB

<query> ::= <syntactical-query> | <semantical-query>
<syntactical-query> ::= SELECT <clause> <relation-exp>
<semantical-query> ::= SELECT <selection> <relation-exp>
<clause> ::= FACT | RULE | CLAUSE
<selection> ::=<scalar-exp-commalist> | *
<relation-exp> ::= <from-clause> [<where-clause>]
[<group-by-clause>] [<having-clause>]

<from-clause> ::= FROM <relation-ref-commalist>

<where-clause> ::= WHERE <search-condition>

<group-by-clause> ::= GROUP BY <column-ref-commalist>

<having-clause> ::= HAVING <search-condition>

<relation-ref> ::= <relation> [<range-variable>]
    [ON INSERT | ON DELETE | ON UPDATE <column-ref>]

<search-condition> ::= <boolean-term> |
    <search-condition> OR <boolean-term>

<column-ref> ::= [OLD | NEW] [<column-qualifier> .] <column>

<column-qualifier> ::= <relation> | <range-variable>

<boolean-term> ::= <boolean-factor> |
    <boolean-term> AND <boolean-factor>

<boolean-factor> ::= [NOT] <boolean-primary>

<boolean-primary> ::= <predicate> | (<search-condition>)

<predicate> ::= <comparison-predicate> |
    <in-predicate> | <existence-test>

<comparison-predicate> ::= <scalar-exp> <comparison>
    { <scalar-exp> | <subquery> }

<comparison> ::= = | <> | < | > | <= | >=

<in-predicate> ::= <scalar-exp> [NOT] IN <semantical-subquery>

<existence-test> ::= EXISTS <semantical-subquery>

<semantical-subquery> ::= (<semantical-query>)

<scalar-exp> ::= <term> | <scalar-exp> { + | - } <term>

<term> ::= <factor> | <term> { * | / } <factor>

<factor> ::= [+ | -] <primary>

<primary> ::= <column-ref> | (<scalar-exp>) | <function-ref>

<function-ref> ::= { AVG | MAX | MIN | SUM | COUNT }

Constraint manipulation in SQL-DDDB

An integrity constraint is inserted into, deleted from and viewed into a system using the following syntax:

<constraint-manipulation-statement> ::=
    IMPOSE CONSTRAINT <constraint-id> AS
        <constraint-specification>
    | RELEASE CONSTRAINT <constraint-id>
    | DISPLAY CONSTRAINT <constraint-id>

A constraint can be specified as an equality or containment relationship between the results of two queries. Since a query in SQL-DDDB represents a set of tuples, a constraint has been expressed by a set inclusion relationship between the results of two SQL-DDDB queries.

<constraint-specification> ::=
<semantical-query> IS IN <semantical-query>
| <semantical-query> IS EMPTY

Intuitively, in the above constraint specification, the second alternative covers the constraints which are already in denial form. For the sake of users' convenience, the first alternative has been specified to cover constraints which are more general forms than denials. Such a constraint can always be converted to its equivalent denial form by using the transformations in Chapter 7.

Consider the following example to show how schema creation, facts, rules and constraints manipulation and query evaluation are done through SQL-DDDB:

EXAMPLE A

Database: $Superior(x, y) \leftarrow Manager(x, y)$
$Superior(x, y) \leftarrow Manager(x, z) \wedge Superior(z, y)$
$Employee(skd, admin, 9000)$
$Employee(jd, fin, 9500)$
$Department(admin)$
$Department(fin)$
$Manager(rc, jd)$

Constraints: $\forall x \forall y \forall z (Employee(x, y, z) \rightarrow y < 20\,000)$
$\forall x \forall y \forall z (Employee(x, y, z) \rightarrow \exists t\ Manager(t, x))$
$\forall x \forall y \forall z (Manager(x, z) \wedge Manager(y, z) \rightarrow x = y)$
$\forall x \forall y \forall z (Add\_Employee(x, y, z) \rightarrow y < 10\,000)$
$\forall x \forall y \forall z \forall y' \forall z' (Upd\_Employee(x, y, z, x, y', z') \wedge$
$z \neq z' \rightarrow z' > z)$
$\forall x \forall y (Department(x) \wedge Avr(v, \exists u \exists v\ Employee(u, x, v), y)$
$\rightarrow y < 10\,000)$

Queries: $\leftarrow Employee(x, y, z) \wedge z > 9000$

$\leftarrow Manager(x_1, x_2) \wedge Employee(x_1, y_1, z_1) \wedge Employee(x_2, y_2, z_2) \wedge y_1 \neq y_2$

SQL-DDDB statements for schema definition

```
CREATE SCHEMA Employee ( name string,
                         department string, salary integer )
CREATE SCHEMA Manager ( manager string, employee string )
CREATE SCHEMA Superior ( superior string, subordinate string )
```

SQL-DDDB statements for clause manipulation

```
INSERT INTO Superior VALUE
    (   SELECT   *
        FROM     Manager
    )
INSERT INTO Superior VALUE
    (   SELECT   M.manager, S.subordinate
        FROM     Manager M, Superior S
        WHERE    M.employee = S.superior
    )
BEGIN
    INSERT INTO Employee VALUE ( 'skd', 'admin', 9000 ),
    INSERT INTO Employee VALUE ( 'jd', 'fin', 9500 )
END
BEGIN
    INSERT INTO Department VALUE ( 'admin' ),
    INSERT INTO Department VALUE ( 'fin' )
END
INSERT INTO Manager VALUE ( 'rc', 'jd' )
```

SQL-DDDB statements for constraint manipulation

```
IMPOSE CONSTRAINT ic1 AS
    (   SELECT   *
        FROM     Employee E
        WHERE    E.salary >= 20000
    ) IS EMPTY
IMPOSE CONSTRAINT ic2 AS
    (   SELECT   E.name
```

```
            FROM     Employee E
        ) IS IN
        (   SELECT   M.employee
            FROM     Manager M
        )
    IMPOSE CONSTRAINT ic3 AS
        (   SELECT   M1.manager, M2.manager
            FROM     Manager M1, Manager M2
            WHERE    M1.employee = M2.employee
            AND NOT M1.manager = M2.manager
        ) IS EMPTY
    IMPOSE CONSTRAINT ic4 AS
        (   SELECT   *
            FROM     Employee E ON INSERT
            WHERE    E.salary >= 10000
        ) IS EMPTY
    IMPOSE CONSTRAINT ic5 AS
        (   SELECT   *
            FROM     EMPLOYEE E ON UPDATE E.salary
            WHERE    OLD E.salary >= NEW E.salary
        ) IS EMPTY
    IMPOSE CONSTRAINT ic6 AS
        (   SELECT   E.department
            FROM     Employee
            GROUP    BY E.department
            HAVING   AVG(E.salary) >= 10000
        ) IS EMPTY
```

SQL-DDDB statements for query evaluation

```
    SELECT   *
    FROM     Employee E
    WHERE    E.salary > 9000

    SELECT   *
    FROM     Manager M, Employee E1, Employee E2
    WHERE    M.manager = E1.employee
    AND M.employee = E2.employee
    AND NOT E1.department = E2.department
```

15

Parallel deductive databases

This chapter describes several possible parallel computer architectures for implementing deductive database systems. An algorithm is described in detail for processing queries in deductive databases implemented on the shared nothing architecture. The queries are considered to be definite and the databases definite as well as separated and function free. The chapter ends with a discussion of the parallel evaluation of integrity constraints.

15.1 Parallel systems architectures

An obvious way to enhance the performance of a query processing method is to implement it in a parallel fashion as opposed to a sequential one. Sequential computer architectures are based on the von Neumann principle and have a single sequential flow of computation. Such systems have a single processor and associated memory. A *parallel computer architecture* (Treleaven, 1990) assumes more than one processor with each either having its own memory or sharing memory with others. A *processing element* (PE) (Figure 15.1) consists of a processor, a local main-memory and an optional secondary storage device. The whole computation load on a parallel computer is distributed across its processing elements.

Parallel computer architectures are classified according to the organization of their processors and memory units, the style of computation, and so on. In a *switched system* a separate unit connects together a number of processors and memory units. In a *networked system* a number of processing elements are connected together in some identifiable topology (such as *mesh*, *cube* or *hypercube*). In a *reconfigurable network* the interconnection pattern between

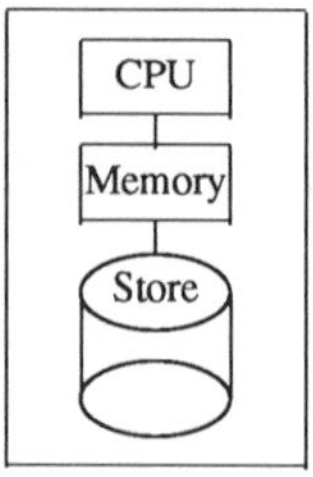

Figure 15.1 Processing element (PE).

processing elements can be changed. This means that any kind of topology can be constructed in a reconfigurable network system. Two major popular architectures are of special interest in this discussion.

15.1.1 Shared nothing architecture

A *shared nothing architecture* consists of a set of PEs and a message passing network to interconnect these PEs. Hence it could either be a switched (Figure 15.2) or a networked (Figure 15.3) system. For database applications, each processing element owns a portion of the database, in other words, the database is partitioned amongst the multiple processing elements.

15.1.2 Shared disk architecture

In a *shared disk architecture*, the disks containing the database are shared amongst the multiple processing elements. Each processing element has an instance of the database in its own buffer space. A global control mechanism is required in this approach to maintain the buffer coherency. Figure 15.4 shows a shared disk system.

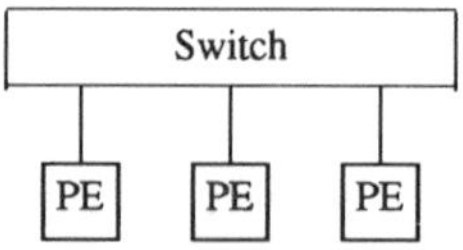

Figure 15.2 Shared nothing (switched) architecture.

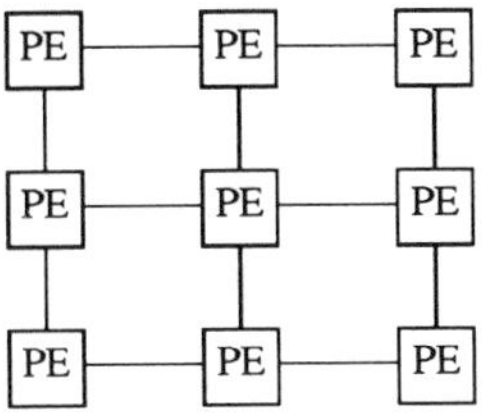

Figure 15.3 Shared nothing (network-mesh) architecture.

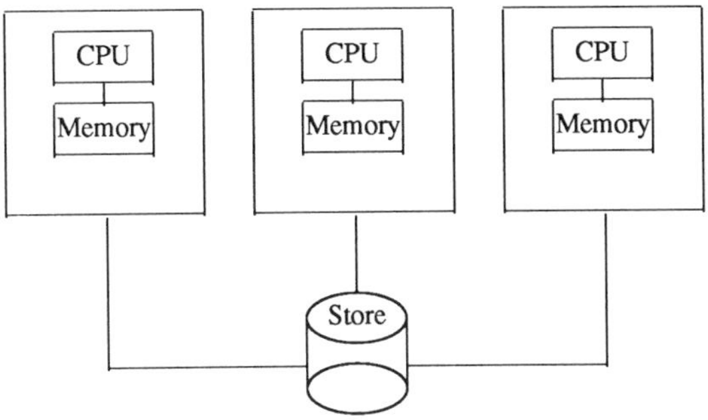

Figure 15.4 Shared disk architecture.

15.1.3 Shared everything architecture

In the *shared everything* approach, in addition to disks, memory is also shared across the processors. Figure 15.5 shows a shared everything system.

Each system architecture has its own advantages and disadvantages. For example, several messages are passed across several processing elements in a shared nothing environment during the execution of a program. Naturally, the performance of any program executing in this environment is highly dependent on how quickly the messages are getting across other processors. On the other hand, in a shared memory environment two processing elements can communicate with each other through common buffer space residing in the shared memory. Partitioning the data is also a problem for shared nothing system.

A shared everything system has scalability problems. The number of nodes for a shared disk or shared nothing system can be reduced by incorporating shared everything systems within processing elements.

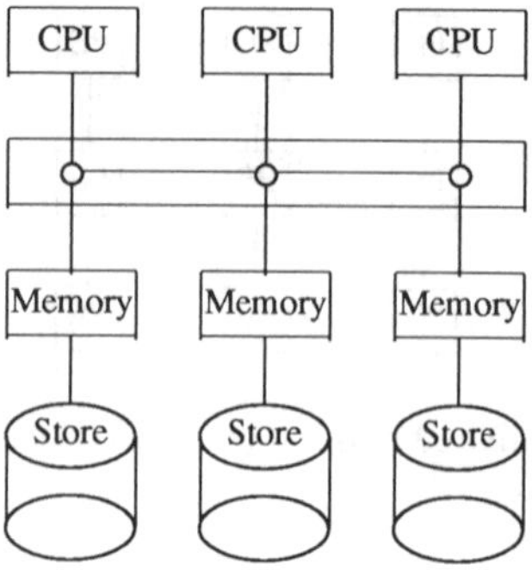

Figure 15.5 Shared everything (switched) architecture.

When main memory is limited and secondary storage is provided in either a sequential or a parallel environment, two factors are important for performance reasons:

(1) Swap area for a particular base/derived relation, and

(2) Time to bring a tuple from secondary storage to main memory.

When there is no secondary storage neither factor is relevant, of course.

15.2 Query processing in parallel

The SLD-resolution mechanism is a sequential computational model of logic programs or deductive databases. Two kinds of parallelism can be introduced into this computational model and each has emerged due to non-determinism within the definition of the SLD-resolution:

(1) The first arises because a subgoal of a goal can unify the heads of different clauses and one of them can be selected non-deterministically for reduction. SLD-resolution selects arbitrarily one after another and reduces sequentially. A logic programming system incorporating *or-parallelism* selects all clauses at the same time to reduce in parallel.

(2) The second is because the order of execution of the subgoals of a goal is arbitrary. In the case of SLD resolution, the selection function decides the order. It selects one goal at a time and executes sequentially. A logic programming system incorporating *and-parallelism* selects several goals to reduce concurrently.

The query evaluation algorithm (Hulin, 1989) presented is suitable for shared nothing architectures and incorporates or-parallelism and a kind of and-parallelism called *stream and-parallelism* or *pipelining*. Query evaluation by this algorithm is divided into two phases, the *compilation phase* and the *dynamic phase*. The compilation phase statically constructs a *derivation tree* with the help of the query scheme and the rules of the system. The definition of a derivation tree is provided below.

Definition 15.1: A *query scheme* under a predicate P is an atom $P(x_1, ..., x_n)$, where some of the variables $x_1, ..., x_n$ are marked as *entry variables*. A variable x marked as an entry variable is denoted by x^*. Variables other than entry variables in a query scheme are *exit* variables. Two query schemes under the same predicates are same if their entry variable positions are same; otherwise they are different.

Definition 15.2: Suppose Q is a query scheme and **R** is a set of rules. Then a derivation tree for Q and **R** is recursively defined as follows:

(1) The root node is labelled by Q.

(2) Suppose the query scheme A labels a node N and there is a rule $A' \leftarrow B_1 \wedge \cdots B_n$ such that A and A' unify with an mgu θ. Then N is connected by a bundle of directed arcs to nodes labelled by $B_1\theta, ..., B_n\theta$. A variable in $B_i\theta$ $(1 \le i \le n)$ is marked as an entry variable if it occurs in A as an entry variable or occurs in one of $B_1\theta, ..., B_{i-1}\theta$.

EXAMPLE 15.1

Database: R1. $Mother(x, y) \leftarrow Father(z, y) \wedge Husband(z, x)$

R2. $Parent(x, y) \leftarrow Father(x, y)$

R3. $Parent(x, y) \leftarrow Mother(x, y)$

R4. $SameGenP(x, y) \leftarrow Equal(x, x)$

R5. $SameGenP(x, y) \leftarrow Parent(u, x) \wedge SameGenP(u, v) \wedge Parent(v, y)$

$Equal(a, a)$	$Father(a, c)$	$Husband(a, b)$	$Mother(b, e)$
$Equal(b, b)$	$Father(c, d)$		
$Equal(c, c)$			
$Equal(d, d)$			

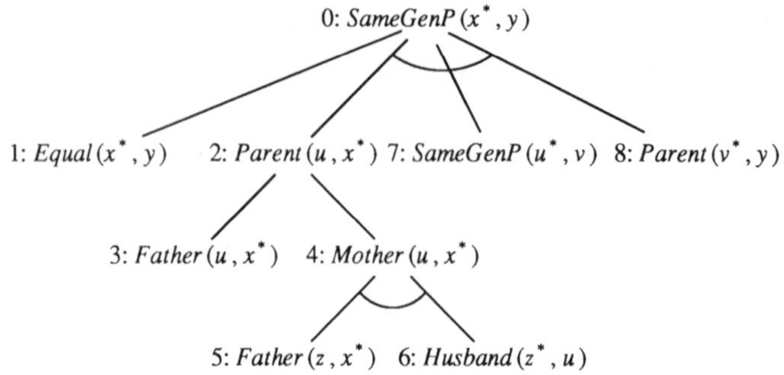

Figure 15.6 The derivation tree for Example 15.1.

Query: $\leftarrow SameGenP(c, y)$

The derivation tree for the query and rules is shown in Figure 15.6, where $SameGenP(x^*, y)$ is the query scheme corresponding to the query $SameGenP(c, y)$. In this tree, the query schemes $SameGenP(x^*, y)$ and $SameGenP(u^*, v)$ are same whereas query schemes $Parent(x^*, u)$ and $Parent(y, v^*)$ are different.

Definition 15.3: The derivation tree is also a kind of *hypertree* where *hyperarcs* connect a parent node to an ordered list of successor nodes.

EXAMPLE 15.2

A hyperarc in the context of the tree in Figure 15.6 is the one which connects $SameGenP(x, y)$ to its list $[Parent(u, x), SameGenP(u, v), Parent(v, y)]$ of ordered children.

Definition 15.4: A node N of the derivation tree precedes a node N' (or N' follows N) if they both appear in the ordered list of same hyperarc and N appears before N' in the list. A node without a predecessor is called an *initial node* and a node without a successor is called a *terminal node*.

EXAMPLE 15.3

In the derivation tree of Figure 15.6, node 2 precedes node 8, node 6 follows node 5, and so on. Also, nodes 1, 2, 3, and so on are initial nodes and nodes 6, 8, and so on are terminal nodes.

Definition 15.5: When several nodes are labelled with equivalent query schemes (that is, if they are identical up to the renaming of their variables), the first one encountered during depth-first traversal of the tree is called the *archetype node*. An archetype node whose query scheme is under an IDB (resp. EDB) predicate is called a *virtual archetype* (resp. *base archetype*) *node*. Nodes other than archetype are called *non-archetype*.

EXAMPLE 15.4

In Figure 15.6, nodes 0, 2 and 4 are virtual archetype, nodes 1, 3 and 6 are base archetype, and nodes 5, 7, and 8 are non-archetype.

The nodes of the tree in Figure 15.6 are ordered according to the depth-first traversal. The following is another type of ordering which is based on depth-first traversal and is useful for detecting the termination of queries.

Definition 15.6: The following four steps are performed to obtain an *extended depth-first traversal* of a derivation tree:

(1) Generate the sequence S_1 by traversing the tree in a depth-first manner.

(2) Generate the sequence S_2 from S_1 by inserting parent nodes immediately after every terminal node.

(3) Generate the sequence S_3 from S_2 by replacing all of its non-archetype nodes by their corresponding archetype ones.

(4) Finally, generate the sequence S from S_3 by deleting every node which is followed by itself.

EXAMPLE 15.5

Consider the tree in Figure 15.6.

S_1 is 0 1 2 3 4 5 6 7 8

S_2 is 0 1 0 2 3 2 4 5 6 4 2 7 8 0

S_3 is 0 1 0 2 3 2 4 3 6 4 2 0 2 0

$S = S_3$

Unlike depth-first ordering of nodes, in extended depth-first ordering there may be more than one node next to a given node. However, when two consecutive nodes are given in an extended depth-first ordering, a unique node can be identified which occurs next to the given pair of nodes.

EXAMPLE 15.6

Both nodes 3 and 4 are next to 2 in the tree in Figure 15.6. Given two consecutive occurrences of nodes 2 and 3 in extended depth-first ordering of the tree in Figure 15.6, the next node is 2 again.

Definition 15.7: An *entry substitution* (resp. *exit substitution*) for a query scheme is a substitution for its entry (resp. exit) variables.

The algorithm combines the work of several nodes of the derivation tree into one. The dynamic phase associates cooperative processes with each node of the derivation tree. Processes communicate with each other by message passing without sharing memory. Given the extended depth-first ordering $N_0, N_1, ..., N_p$ of a derivation tree, messages can only be sent from node N_i to node N_{i+1} with $0 \leq i < p$ but not from N_i to N_j where $j \neq i + 1$. Each process executes in a dynamic *context*, where a context of invocation of a process at a particular node contains an entry value inherited from its parent and a relevant value at that particular node. The structure of a context is a 3-ary tuple of the form <Node, Relevant_Subst_Node, Entry_Subst_Parent_Node>. To describe this structure in detail, suppose Parent_Node is the parent of Node and Node belongs to the hyperarc $[N_1, ..., N_i$, Node, $N_{i+1}, ..., N_k]$. The field Entry_Subst_Parent_Node is an entry substitution of Parent_Node. The field Relevant_Subst_Node is the substitution defined by the following two conditions:

(1) If an entry variable x of one of $N_{i+1}, ..., N_k$ is also an entry variable of Parent_Node or an exit variable of one of $N_1, ..., N_i$, then x is also a variable of Relevant_Subst_Node.

(2) If an exit variable x of Parent_Node is also an exit variable of one of $N_1, ..., N_i$, then x is also a variable of Relevant_Subst_Node.

Definition 15.8: The set of variables of Relevant_Subst_Node defined above is called *relevant variables* at the Node.

Hence, the Relevant_Subst_Node field in a context remembers the values of variables that are known before evaluating the current query at the node and will still be needed after its evaluation.

EXAMPLE 15.7

Consider the derivation tree in Figure 15.6. The set of relevant variables at each node is empty. Consider the derivation tree in Figure 15.7. The set of relevant variables is empty at node 1 is $\{x\}$ at node 2 and 3 is $\{x, y, z\}$ and at node 4 is $\{y, z\}$. An entry value at a node N is a set of values of its entry variables. The exit variable of node 2, (u) becomes an entry variable of node 3.

In the implementation of query evaluation on a shared nothing system, each node of the derivation tree in question corresponds to a processing element of the system. A node is then associated with the following major items:

(1) A process EVALUATE to compute answers to queries and communicate with other nodes through message passing.

(2) A message queue MESSAGE_QUEUE for the incoming messages to be processed at the node.

(3) A local memory ACTIVE_QUERY_SET to store a set of active queries.

(4) The variable TERMINATION_FLAG which is either true or false and is set to false at the start of the execution.

A message has the form <Message_Type, Message> where the two fields represent respectively the type of the message and the value of the message. A message has four different forms depending on the type of message.

- *Request* A message of this type is called a *request message* and the value of the message is a pair of entry substitution and *context*. A context remembers the minimal part of the computation state necessary to carry on with the computation.
- *Answer* A message of this type is called an *answer message* and the value of the message is a substitution for the variables of the node.
- *Termination token* A message of this type is called termination token and there is only one of this type of message in the entire system at any time during the execution of a query. The value of the message has the form

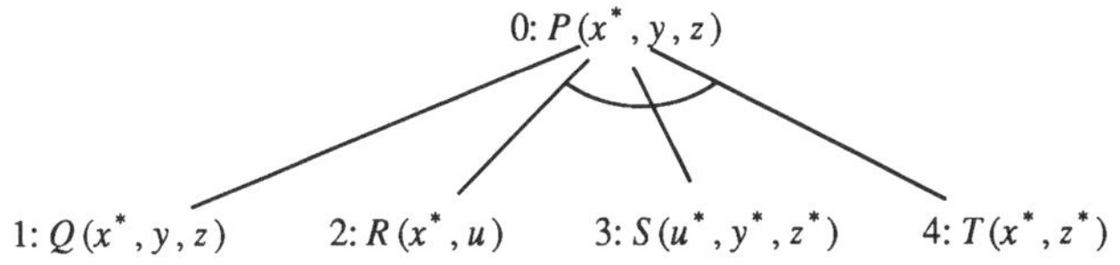

Figure 15.7 A derivation tree.

<Source_Node, Previous_Node>. The first field denotes the node where the terminal token originates and the second field is the node that sends this terminal token message. If the terminal token returns to its source node after travelling through the other nodes in the extended depth-first order and without changing any TERMINATION_FLAG field from true to false, the whole execution terminates. This successful travelling ensures that buffers are empty and there is no message currently being travelling or processed.

The computation is initiated by sending a request message to node 0, that is, the root node and that is followed by another termination token message. The message contains the binding information of the query and other relevant information. The process at node 0 adds the request to the memory of active queries. The query is solved by parallel decomposition along each hyperarc issuing from node 0. Each decomposition corresponds to a rule defining the predicate of node 0 and contributes some answers to the query. The decomposition necessarily sends requests to the first node of each hyperarc. A request at each of these nodes is decomposed further amongst their respective hyperarcs. Answer messages are processed in parallel with request messages. Termination occurs when the request and answer buffers are empty and there is no message currently being processed. The answer to the query can be obtained by accumulating the relevant answers (which match the initial query binding) at node 0.

An algorithm for implementing the EVALUATE process will now be described. First a few function symbols used in this algorithm are introduced below:

- *Rename_Subst(Subst, Node_1, Node_2)* The query schemes at Node_1 and Node_2 are equivalent. The first argument Subst of this function is a substitution for the query scheme at Node_1 and the value of the function is the corresponding substitution at Node_2. In the derivation tree of Figure 15.6, query schemes at nodes 0 and 7 are equivalent. If $\{u/a,\ v/b\}$ is a substitution of variables at node 7, then the value Rename_Subst($\{u/a,\ v/b\}$, 7, 0) is $\{x/a, y/b\}$.
- *Relevant_Subst(Subst, Node)* Given a substitution Subst, the function computes the relevant substitution for Node.
- *Entry_Subst(Subst, Node)* Given a substitution Subst, the function computes the entry substitution for Node.

Algorithm EVALUATE

```
Input: Node
Step 1: Instantiate the following global parameters for this node:
            MEMORY = { };
            NODE = Node;
            TERMINATION_FLAG = False;
        Repeatedly execute the following two steps.
Step 2: If the queue is empty then wait until a message arrives;
        else take a message <Message_Type, Message> out of the message queue.
Step 3: If Message_Type is
        "Request":
            set TERMINATON_FLAG = False;
            call algorithm PROCESS_REQUEST with the parameter Message.
        "Answer":
            set TERMINATON_FLAG = False;
            call algorithm PROCESS_ANSWER with the parameter Message.
        "Termination Token":
            set Message = <Source_Node, Previous_Node>;
            if TERMINATON_FLAG = True then
                if Source_Node = NODE then
                    send termination signal  to all other nodes and stop;
                else
                    set Next_NODE to the node next to Previous_Node and NODE
                        (according to the extended depth-first ordering);
                    send the message <"Termination Token",<Source_Node, NODE>>
                        to Next_NODE;
            else
                set TERMINATION_FLAG = True;
                set Next_NODE to the node next to Previous_Node and NODE
                    (according to the extended depth-first ordering);
                send the message
                    <"Termination Token", <NODE, NODE>> to Next_NODE.
```

Algorithm PROCESS_REQUEST

```
Input: Message
Step 1: set Message = <Entry_Subst_Node, Context>, where
            Context = <Node, Relevant_Subst_Node, Entry_Subst_Parent_Node>;
        set Entry_Subst_NODE = Rename_Subst(Entry_Subst_Node, Node, NODE).
```

```
Step 2: type of NODE is
    "Virtual Arche":
        if there exists a Query =
                <Entry_Subst_NODE, SOLUTION_SET, CONTEXT_SET>
                in ACTIVE_QUERY_SET then
            if Context is not in CONTEXT_SET then
                add Context to CONTEXT_SET;
                for each Exit_Subst_NODE in SOLUTION_SET,
                  call algorithm PROPAGATE with parameters
                        Rename_Subst(Exit_Subst_NODE, NODE, Node)
                        and Context.
        else
            set New_Query = <Entry_Subst_NODE, { }, {Context}>;
            add New_Query to ACTIVE_QUERY_SET;
            for each hyperarc H issuing from NODE
                set Origin_H to the origin of H;
                set Entry_Subst_Origin_H =
                      Entry_Subst(Entry_Subst_NODE, Origin_H);
                set Relevant_Subst_Origin_H =
                  Relevant_Subst(Entry_Subst_NODE, Origin_H);
                set Context_Origin = <Origin_H,
                  Relevant_Subst_Origin_H, Entry_Subst_NODE>;
                set Origin_H_A to the archetype of Origin_H;
                send <"Request", <Entry_Subst_Origin_H,
                      Context_Origin>> to Origin_H_A.
    "Base Arche":
        Same as the above case of "Virtual Arche" except
                the steps in the else block are replaced by the following:
            set New_Query = <Entry_Subst_NODE, { }, {Context}>;
            add New_Query to ACTIVE_QUERY_SET;
            compute SOLUTION_SET corresponding to Entry_Subst_NODE;
            replace the empty set of solution set
                in New_Query by SOLUTION_SET;
            for each SOLUTION in SOLUTION_SET
                call the algorithm PROPAGATE with parameters
                      Rename_Subst(SOLUTION, NODE, Node) and Context
```

Algorithm PROCESS_ANSWER

```
Input: Message
Step 1: set Solution_Subst_NODE = Rename_Subst(Message, NODE).
Step 2: if there is an element <Entry_Subst_NODE, SOLUTION_SET, CONTEXT_SET>
                in ACTIVE_QUERY_SET such that
                Entry_Subst_NODE ⊆ Solution_Subst_NODE and
                Exit_Subst_NODE is not in SOLUTION_SET, where
                Exit_Subst_NODE =
                    Solution_Subst_NODE - Entry_Subst_NODE, then
            add Exit_Subst_NODE to SOLUTION_SET;
            for each Context = <Node, Relevant_Subst_Node,
                    Entry_Subst_Parent_Node> in CONTEXT_SET,
                call the algorithm PROPAGATE with parameters
                    Rename_Subst(Exit_Subst_NODE, NODE, Node)
                    and Context.
```

Algorithm PROPAGATE

```
Input: Exit_Subst_Node, Context
Step 1: set Context = <Node, Relevant_Subst_Node, Entry_Subst_Parent_Node>.
Step 2: if Node is a terminal node then
            if Node has a parent Parent_Node then
                send the message <"Answer", Entry_Subst_Parent_Node∪
                Relevant_Subst_Node∪Exit_Subst_Node>
                to Parent_Node;
        else
            set Succ_Node to the successor of Node;
            set Entry_Subst_Succ_Node = Entry_Subst(Relevant_Subst_Node∪
                Exit_Subst_Node, Succ_Node);
            set Relevant_Subst_Succ_Node = Relevant_Subst
                (Relevant_Subst_Node∪Exit_Subst_Node, Succ_Node);
            set Context_Succ = <Succ_Node,
                Relevant_Subst_Succ_Node, Entry_Subst_Parent_Node>;
            set Succ_NODE_A to the archetype of Succ_NODE;
            send <"Request", <Entry_Subst_Succ_Node, Context_Succ>>
                to Succ_Node_A.
```

EXAMPLE 15.8

In Example 15.1, the computation starts by sending the message <"Request", <{x/c}, <0, {}, {}>>> to the node 0. A part of the whole execution is displayed in the following. This part is divided into the following units of execution. Each unit corresponds to the processing of a particular message and has been executed at a particular node.

Unit:	1
Processing node:	0
Message processed:	<"Request", <{x/c}, <0, {}, {}>>>
Messages sent:	<"Request", <{x/c}, <1, {}, {x/c}>>> to node 1
	<"Request", <{x/c}, <2, {}, {x/c}>>> to node 2
Active query buffer:	{<{x/c}, {}, {<0, {}, {}>}>}

Unit:	2
Processing node:	1
Message processed:	<"Request", <{x/c}, <1, {}, {x/c}>>>
Messages sent:	<"Answer", {x/c, y/c}> to node 0
Active query buffer:	{<{x/c}, {{y/c}}, {<1, {}, {x/c}>}>}

Unit:	3
Processing node:	2
Message processed:	<"Request", <{x/c}, <2, {}, {x/c}>>>
Messages sent:	<"Request", <{x/c}, <3, {}, {x/c}>>> to node 3
	<"Request", <{x/c}, <4, {}, {x/c}>>> to node 4
Active query buffer:	{<{x/c}, {}, {<2, {}, {x/c}>}>}

Unit:	4
Processing node:	0
Message processed:	<"Answer", {x/c, y/c}>
Messages sent:	{x/c, y/c} to the user as an answer.
Active query buffer:	{<{x/c}, {{y/c}}, {<0, {}, {}>}>}

Unit:	5
Processing node:	4
Message processed:	<"Request", <{x/c}, <4, {}, {x/c}>>>
Messages sent:	<"Request", <{x/c}, <5, {}, {x/c}>>> to node 3
Active query buffer:	{<{x/c}, {}, {<4, {}, {x/c}>}>}

Unit:	6
Processing node:	3
Message processed:	<"Request", <{x/c}, <3, {}, {x/c}>>>
Messages sent:	<"Answer", {x/c, u/a}> to node 2
Active query buffer:	{<{x/c}, {{u/a}}, {<3, {}, {x/c}>}>}

Unit:	7
Processing node:	2
Message processed:	<"Answer", {x/c, u/a}>
Messages sent:	<"Request", <{u/a}, <7, {}, {x/c}>>> to node 7
Active query buffer:	{<{x/c}, {{u/a}}, {<2, {}, {x/c}>}>}

Unit:	8
Processing node:	3
Message processed:	<"Request", <{x/c}, <5, {}, {x/c}>>>
Messages sent:	<"Request", <{z/a}, <6, {}, {x/c}>>> to node 6
Active query buffer:	{<{x/c}, {{u/a}}, {<3, {}, {x/c}>, <5, {}, {x/c}>}}

Unit:	9
Processing node:	6
Message processed:	<"Request", <{z/a}, <6, {}, {x/c}>>>
Messages sent:	<"Answer", {u/b, x/c}> to node 4
Active query buffer:	{<{z/a}, {{u/b}}, {<6, {}, {x/c}>}>}

Unit:	10
Processing node:	4
Message processed:	<"Answer", {u/b, x/c}>
Messages sent:	<"Answer", {u/b, x/c}> to node 2
Active query buffer:	{<{x/c}, {{u/b}}, {<4, {}, {x/c}>}>}

Some units have been executed concurrently. For example, processing of unit 1 and unit 2 can be carried out concurrently and similarly units 5 and 6. There is no processing involved for request and answer type messages at a non-archetype node (for example, node 5). In the above example, termination type messages have not been considered. But as an example consider the case when node 2 receives the message <"Termination Token", <6, 0>>. If the termination flag is set to true then node 2 will send the message <"Termination Token", <6, 2>> to node 3. If the termination flag is set to false then node 2 will set the flag to true and send the message <"Termination Token", <2, 2>> to node 3. If node 2 receives a message <"Termination Token", <2, 0>> and the termination flag is set to true then the termination signal is sent to the rest of the nodes and the execution at node 2 stops. It is also important to remember that this kind of halting algorithm works only when messages arrive at a particular node in the order they were sent from another node. A message of the terminal token type should be processed at every node with the lowest priority.

The two algorithms PROCESS_REQUESTS and PROCESS_ANSWERS at a virtual archetype node can be split into two parallel processes separately processing request type and answer type messages respectively. These two processes share the memory allocated for the ACTIVE_QUERY_SET. This gives an idea for incorporating a two-node shared everything system within a processing element of the shared nothing system on which the algorithm is implemented.

15.3 Constraint checking in parallel

A typical implementation of a constraint checking program in a database system exploits the underlying query evaluation system of the database. The constraint checking program takes the form of a meta-interpreter which calculates implicitly added or deleted facts, simplifies the constraints, and so on. For example, the meta-interpreter developed in Chapter 14 checks integrity in normal databases by the path finding method. In a database system implemented on a conventional type of machine each constraint is instantiated and evaluated in turn. Here this has been done with the help of the backtracking mechanism built into a Prolog system. When a set of constraints is imposed on a database system and the system follows the standard view of constraint satisfiability, the properties of the imposed constraints are independent of each other. Hence the evaluation of an instantiated set of constraints can be made simultaneously. In such cases efficiency is considerably higher.

In a shared nothing parallel machine, this concept of simultaneous evaluation of constraints can be described by considering the following example of hierarchical definite database (rules only) and a set of static constraints imposed on it.

EXAMPLE 15.9

Database rules: $S(x) \leftarrow P(x) \wedge \neg Q(x)$

$P(x) \leftarrow R(x)$

$U(x, y) \leftarrow V(x, y) \wedge \neg W(x)$

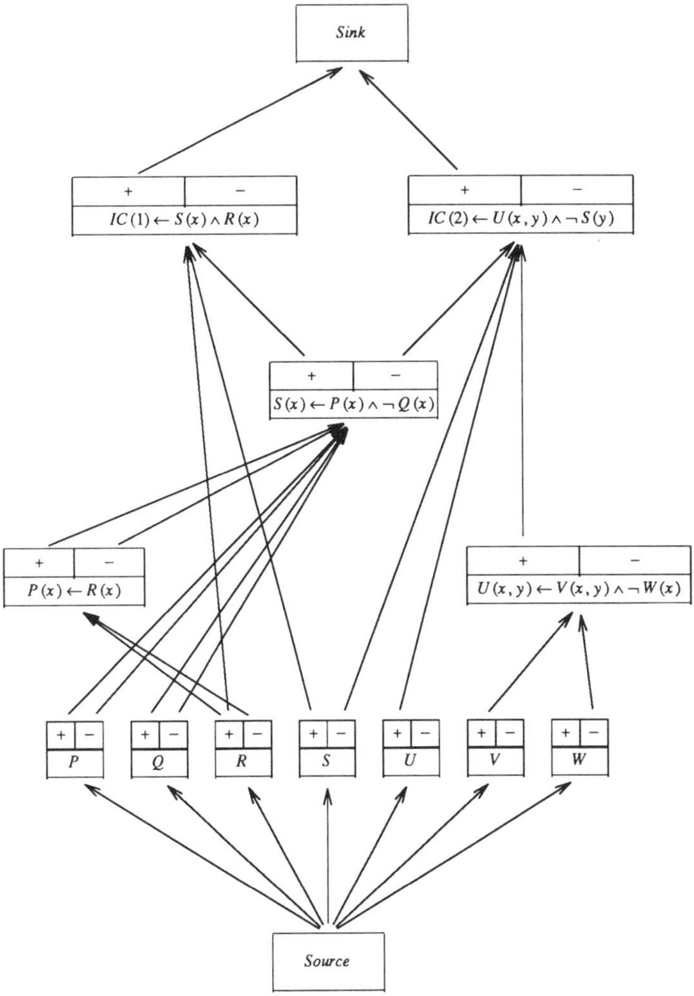

Figure 15.8 The network for constraint evaluation for Example 15.9.

Constraints in denial form: $IC(1) \leftarrow S(x) \wedge R(x)$

$$IC(2) \leftarrow U(x, y) \wedge \neg S(y)$$

A *constraint evaluation network*, given in Figure 15.8, is established with the help of the rules and constraints above. The network has a *source node* (the node in the bottom layer), a *sink node* (the node in the top layer), seven *predicate nodes* (nodes in the last but bottom layer), two *constraint nodes* (nodes in the next to top layer) and three *rule nodes* (the nodes in the third and the fourth layers). There are as many predicate nodes as the number of relations in the database, as many constraint nodes as the number of constraints and as many rule nodes as the number of rules.

The source node distributes the set of facts, either (implicitly or explicitly) added to and deleted from the database due to the transaction, to the appropriate predicate nodes. The predicate node supplies a literal (positive, if it is an added fact, and negative, if it is a deleted fact) to the appropriate rule or constraint nodes. For example, the set of all added facts under the predicate V is sent to the rule node representing the rule $U(x,y) \leftarrow V(x,y) \wedge \neg W(x)$, as this may implicitly add some facts under the predicate U and they, in turn, may violate constraints with the help of the constraint identified by 2. The set of all deleted facts under the predicate V is not sent to the same rule node, although these facts may delete implicitly some facts under the predicate U and eventually will not cause any constraint violation. The constraint violation is reported when the control of execution reaches the sink node.

In the actual implementation each node of the network can be considered as a processing element. Each rule node is capable of evaluating an instantiated body of a rule and each constraint node is capable of evaluating an instantiated body of a constraint. The produced literals (ground, in the case of implicit additions) are streamed to the appropriate processing elements.

Exercise

15.1 Perform the following for each example in Exercise 6.1:

(a) Draw the derivation tree.

(b) Show the state of each processing node in terms of message flow, buffer status, and so on, by applying the parallel algorithm provided in this chapter.

16

Formalizing aggregate and transitional constraints

The methods proposed for integrity checking in Chapter 13 dealt only with the class of static non-aggregate constraints in normal databases. This chapter formalizes both aggregate and transitional constraints so that these methods can deal with such constraints by means of suitable extensions. The first half of this chapter deals with the formalization of aggregate constraints in normal databases and the second half does the same by considering transitional constraints. Most of the results of this chapter are due to Das (1990). Unless otherwise stated, a database is taken as a normal database.

16.1 Aggregate constraints

This section extends the concept of constraint satisfiability to cover aggregate constraints and generalizes Lloyd *et al.*'s simplification method. Before formally representing aggregate constraints, remember that aggregate constraints are constraints, for example, of the form

The total number of employees in a particular department
may not exceed 100, or
A student obtaining an average mark greater than or equal to 50,
passes the exam.

16.1.1 Representation

The five aggregate predicates *Count*, *Sum*, *Avg*, *Max* and *Min* have been chosen as an initial set in extending the first-order representation of constraint. This set can clearly be enlarged to include other such functions.

Definition 16.1: An *aggregate atom* is one of the following forms:

$Count(\mathrm{W}, n)$
$Avg(x, \mathrm{W}, r)$
$Sum(x, \mathrm{W}, r)$
$Max(x, \mathrm{W}, r)$
$Min(x, \mathrm{W}, r)$

where W is a conjunction of literals (a goal written without ←) in which some of the variables are free and the remaining variables are assumed to be existentially quantified in front of W. The variable x is one of the bound variables of W, and variables n and r represent the result of the function (as an integer or real number, respectively). The variable x can be replaced by an identifier (for example, an integer) which identifies uniquely the occurrence of x in W. For the sake of readability, it is considered to be a variable.

The atom $Count(W, n)$ is interpreted as counting the number of different instances of W obtained from all answers to the query ← W which are true in **D**: returning this value as n; $Avg(x, \mathrm{W}, r)$ computes the average of all the values of the variable x obtained from different answers of the query ← W which are true in **D**, and return this value as r; and so on. In each case the query ← W is assumed to be allowed.

Definition 16.2: An aggregate literal is either an aggregate atom or the negation of an aggregate atom. In each of the above aggregate atoms the formula W is called the *key formula*.

An aggregate formula is defined in the usual manner by using connectives, quantifiers, literals and aggregate literals. An aggregate formula not containing any occurrence of aggregate literals is reduced to an ordinary first-order formula.

Definition 16.3: Let γ be an aggregate literal. Then all the bound variables of the key formula W of γ are said to be *local* to the aggregate literal γ. Any other variables occurring in γ are said to be *global*. All global variables of the literals occurring in an aggregate formula A are called *global variables* of A.

The definition of a closed aggregate formula is generalized accordingly with respect to its global variables only.

Definition 16.4: An aggregate formula A is *closed* if each of its global variables is under the scope of some quantifier.

Definition 16.5: An *aggregate constraint* is a closed aggregate formula.

EXAMPLE 16.1

The two constraints given at the beginning of this section can be expressed using this notation as follows:

$$\forall x \forall t (Dept(x) \wedge Count(\exists y \exists z Employee(y, x, z), t) \rightarrow t \leq 100)$$
$$\forall x \forall y \forall z \forall t (Student(x, y, z) \wedge$$
$$Avg(v, \exists u \exists v Marks(x, u, v), t) \wedge t \geq 50 \rightarrow Pass(x))$$

Note that the definition of an aggregate constraint generalizes the definition of a first-order constraint, that is, an aggregate constraint not containing any occurrences of aggregate literals is reduced to a first-order constraint. Also, all the definitions and results introduced in this chapter in the context of aggregate constraints are equally applicable in the presence of first-order constraints only.

Definition 16.6: An *aggregate denial* is an aggregate formula of the form

$$\leftarrow \gamma_1 \vee \cdots \vee \gamma_n$$

where each γ_i is a either a literal or an aggregate literal and global variables are assumed to be universally quantified over the whole denial.

For uniformity of presentation, an aggregate constraint will be considered as aggregate denial which is range-restricted with respect to its global variables. The two constraints given at the beginning can be expressed using this notation as follows:

$\leftarrow Dept(x) \wedge Count(\exists y \exists z Employee(y, x, z), t) \wedge t > 100$

$\leftarrow Student(x, y, z) \wedge Avg(v, \exists u \exists v Marks(x, u, v), t) \wedge t \geq 50 \wedge \neg Pass(x)$

In the following two subsections, the only aggregate predicate considered is the predicate *Count*. Later this will be generalized to other aggregate predicates from the initial set.

16.1.2 Satisfiability

Let **D** be a database and $\mathbf{Q_D}$ be the set of all queries. Consider the function $\chi_D : \mathbf{Q_D} \rightarrow$ N, where N is the set of all non-negative integers, defined in the following way:

$$\text{For} \leftarrow W \in \mathbf{Q_D}, \chi_D(\leftarrow W) = card\ (\{W\theta : Comp(\mathbf{D}) \not\vdash W\theta\})$$

where *card* (X) denotes the cardinality of the set X. Clearly the mapping is well defined, that is, every query $\leftarrow$ W is mapped into a unique integer which is equal to the number of instances of W which can be derived from $Comp(\mathbf{D})$. This asserts that the number of different instances of W which are true in **D** is $\chi_D(\leftarrow W)$. Thus if a constraint contains the aggregate atom $Count(W, n)$ and all global variables occurring in W are instantiated, $\chi_D(\leftarrow W)$ represents n. In other words, $\chi_D(\leftarrow W)$ is the number of different computed answers of the SLDNF-derivation of $\mathbf{D} \cup \{\leftarrow W\}$, provided that it is capable of returning all answers without going into an infinite loop.

Lemma 16.1: Let **D** be a database and $\leftarrow$ W be a member of $\mathbf{Q_D}$. Let $x_1, ..., x_n$ be all the variables of W and $\mathbf{D}_t$ be $\mathbf{D} \cup \{\forall x_1 \cdots \forall x_n (P(x_1, ..., x_n) \leftarrow W)\}$, where P is a predicate symbol not occurring elsewhere in the database **D**. If $\chi_D : \mathbf{Q_D} \rightarrow$ N and $\chi_{\mathbf{D}_t} : Q_{\mathbf{D}_t} \rightarrow$ N are the two mappings defined as above, then $\chi_D(\leftarrow W) = \chi_{\mathbf{D}_t}(\leftarrow P(x_1, ..., x_n))$.

Proof This follows from the fact that $Comp(\mathbf{D}) \not\vdash W\theta$ if and only if $Comp(\mathbf{D}_t) \not\vdash P(x_1, ..., x_n)\theta$. ■

In view of the above lemma, the key formula of an aggregate atom under the predicate *Count* occurring in a constraint will be assumed to be an atom.

Definition 16.7: The *first-order equivalent of an aggregate atom* $Count(A, n)$ is the atom $Count_A(n, y_1, ..., y_g)$ (or simply $Count(n, y_1, ..., y_g)$ if A is clear from the context), where n is a variable and $y_1, ..., y_g$ are the arguments of A other than its local variables. The *first-order equivalent form of an aggregate denial* $\leftarrow \Gamma$, is obtained from $\leftarrow \Gamma$ by replacing its aggregate atoms with their first-order equivalent form.

Definition 16.8: Let **D** be a database and $Count(A, n)$ be an aggregate atom. Suppose, $z_1, ..., z_l$ are the local variables of A and $y_1, ..., y_g$ are the other arguments of A (some of which may be constants). One can always assume that A has the form $P(z_1, ..., z_l, y_1, ..., y_g)$, where P is a first-order predicate. Suppose there is a finite number of constant terms $a_1, ..., a_m$ in the language underlying the database (observe this restriction). In the context of database **D**, the *expansion* of $Count(A, n)$ defining its first-order equivalent, denoted by $Exp_{\mathbf{D}}(Count(A, n))$ (or simply $\mathcal{Exp}(Count(A, n))$, when **D** is clear from the context), is the following set of

$$m^g + m^l + \frac{m^l(m^l-1)}{2} + \frac{m^l(m^l-1)(m^l-2)}{3.2} + ... + 1$$

first-order clauses:

- m^g clauses:

  $$Count(0, y_1, ..., y_g) \leftarrow y_1 = a_1^1 \wedge \cdots \wedge y_g = a_g^1 \wedge$$
  $$\neg Count(1, y_1, ..., y_g) \wedge \cdots \wedge \neg Count(m^l, y_1, ..., y_g)$$

  where each a_i^1 is equal to a_p, for some p.

- m^l clauses:

  $$Count(1, y_1, ..., y_g) \leftarrow P(a_1^1, ..., a_l^1, y_1, ..., y_g) \wedge$$
  $$\neg Count(2, y_1, ..., y_g) \wedge \cdots \wedge \neg Count(m^l, y_1, ..., y_g)$$

  where each a_i^1 is equal to a_p, for some p.

- $\frac{m^l(m^l-1)}{2}$ clauses:

  $$Count(2, y_1, ..., y_g) \leftarrow P(a_1^1, ..., a_l^1, y_1, ..., y_g) \wedge$$
  $$P(a_1^2, ..., a_l^2, y_1, ..., y_g) \wedge$$
  $$\neg Count(3, y_1, ..., y_g) \wedge \cdots \wedge \neg Count(m^l, y_1, ..., y_g)$$

where each a_i^k $(k = 1, 2)$ is equal to a_p, for some p, and for $k \neq k'$, $1 \leq k, k' \leq 2$, there exists p such that $a_p^k \neq a_p^{k'}$.

- $\dfrac{m^l(m^l-1)(m^l-2)}{3.2}$ clauses:

$$\begin{aligned} & Count(3, y_1, ..., y_g) \leftarrow P(a_1^1, ..., a_l^1, y_1, ..., y_g) \wedge \cdots \wedge \\ & \qquad P(a_1^3, ..., a_l^3, y_1, ..., y_g) \wedge \\ & \neg Count(4, y_1, ..., y_g) \wedge \cdots \wedge \neg Count(m^l, y_1, ..., y_g) \end{aligned}$$

where each a_i^k $(k = 1, 2, 3)$ is equal to a_p, for some p, and for $k \neq k'$, $1 \leq k, k' \leq 3$, there exists p such that $a_p^k \neq a_p^{k'}$.

.

.

.

- 1 clause:

$$\begin{aligned} & Count(m^l, y_1, ..., y_g) \leftarrow P(a_1^1, ..., a_l^1, y_1, ..., y_g) \wedge \cdots \wedge \\ & \qquad P(a_1^{m^l}, ..., a_l^{m^l}, y_1, ..., y_g) \end{aligned}$$

where each a_i^k $(k = 1, 2, ..., m^l)$ is equal to a_p, for some p, and for $k \neq k'$, $1 \leq k, k' \leq m^l$, there exists p such that $a_p^k \neq a_p^{k'}$.

When the above set of clauses is added to the database, it is said that the *database is expanded wrt the aggregate literal* $Count(A, n)$ and the expanded database is denoted as $\mathcal{Exp}(\mathbf{D}, Count(A, n))$.

Lemma 16.2: For all ground substitutions θ of the variables in $\{y_1, ..., y_g\}$, at most one of $Count(1, y_1, ..., y_g)\theta$, ..., $Count(m^l, y_1, ..., y_g)\theta$ can be derived at a time from $Comp(\mathcal{Exp}(\mathbf{D}, Count(A, n)))$.

Proof Assume that both $Count(n_1, y_1, .., y_g)\theta$ and $Count(n_2, y_1, ..., y_g)\theta$ can be derived from $Comp(\mathcal{Exp}(\mathbf{D}, Count(A, n)))$, for $n_1 \neq n_2$. Without any loss of generality one can assume $0 \leq n_1 < n_2 \leq m^l$. Since $Count(n_1, y_1, ..., y_g)\theta$ is derivable from $Comp(\mathcal{Exp}(\mathbf{D}, Count(A, n)))$, from the clauses defining $Count(n_1, y_1, ..., y_g)$ one can say that none of $Count(n_1+1, y_1, ..., y_g)\theta$, ..., $Count(n_2, y_1, ..., y_g)\theta$, ..., $Count(m^l, y_1, ..., y_g)\theta$ is derivable from $Comp(\mathcal{Exp}(\mathbf{D}, Count(A, n)))$. This contradicts the initial assumption. Hence the lemma. ■

Lemma 16.3: For all ground substitutions θ of the variables in $\{y_1, ..., y_g\}$, $\chi_D(\leftarrow A\,\theta) = m$, if $Count(m, y_1, ..., y_g)\theta$ is derivable from $Comp(\mathcal{Exp}(\mathbf{D}, Count(A, n)))$.

Proof Suppose that only m' different instances of $A\,\theta$ are derivable from $Comp(\mathbf{D})$ (that is, $\chi_D(\leftarrow A\,\theta) = m'$). The instances of $A\,\theta$ which are derivable from $Comp(\mathbf{D})$, occur in the body of Cθ, where C is a clause in $\mathcal{Exp}(\mathbf{D}, Count(A, n))$. The head of C is $Count(m', y_1, ..., y_g)$ and $Count(m', y_1, ..., y_g)\theta$ is derivable from $Comp(\mathcal{Exp}(\mathbf{D}, Count(A, n)))$. Hence, by Lemma 16.2, $m = m'$.

Definition 16.9: Let $\mathbf{D}$ be a database and $\leftarrow\Gamma$ be an aggregate constraint, and suppose that $Count(A_1, n_1)$, ..., $Count(A_p, n_p)$ $(p \geq 0)$ are the only aggregate literals occurring in $\leftarrow\Gamma$. The *expansion of* $\mathbf{D}$ wrt $\leftarrow\Gamma$, denoted by $\mathcal{Exp}(\mathbf{D}, \leftarrow\Gamma)$, is the set $\mathbf{D} \cup \mathcal{Exp}(Count(A_1, n_1)) \cup \cdots \cup \mathcal{Exp}(Count(A_p, n_p))$. If $p = 0$ then $\mathcal{Exp}(\mathbf{D}, \leftarrow\Gamma)$ is $\mathbf{D}$. Let $\mathbf{I}$ be a set $\leftarrow\Gamma_1$, ..., $\leftarrow\Gamma_p$ of constraints. The *expansion of* $\mathbf{D}$ wrt $\mathbf{I}$, denoted by $\mathcal{Exp}(\mathbf{D}, \mathbf{I})$, is the set $\mathbf{D} \cup \mathcal{Exp}(\mathbf{D}, \leftarrow\Gamma_1) \cup \cdots \cup \mathcal{Exp}(\mathbf{D}, \leftarrow\Gamma_p)$.

Lemma 16.4: Let $\mathbf{D}$ be a database and $\mathbf{I}$ be a set of constraints with occurrences of aggregate literals $Count(A_1, n_1)$, ..., $Count(A_p, n_p)$. If $Comp(\mathbf{D})$ is consistent then $Comp(\mathcal{Exp}(\mathbf{D}, \mathbf{I}))$ is also consistent.

Proof For each integer n, suppose that $Count(n, y_1, ..., y_g)$ corresponding to $Count(P_i, n_i)$ for some $i = 1, ..., p$, is replaced by another atom $Countn_i(y_1, ..., y_g)$, where $Countn_i$ does not appear elsewhere in the database. Then the clauses added to $\mathbf{D}$ to obtain $Comp(\mathcal{Exp}(\mathbf{D}, \mathbf{I}))$ can be taken as satisfying the hierarchical constraint. Because of the hierarchical nature of the clauses added to $\mathbf{D}$ and the fact that the added clauses define predicates which are not already defined in $\mathbf{D}$, $Comp(\mathcal{Exp}(\mathbf{D}, \mathbf{I}))$ is consistent. ■

Definition 16.10: Suppose $\leftarrow\Gamma$ is an aggregate constraint and $\leftarrow\Gamma_d$ is its first-order equivalent denial. In view of Lemma 16.3, $\mathbf{D}$ can be said to satisfy $\leftarrow\Gamma$ if $\leftarrow\Gamma_d$ is a logical consequence of $Comp(\mathcal{Exp}(\mathbf{D}, \leftarrow\Gamma))$; otherwise $\mathbf{D}$ violates $\leftarrow\Gamma$. $\mathbf{D}$ is said to satisfy $\mathbf{I}$, where $\mathbf{I}$ is a set of constraints, if $\mathbf{D}$ satisfies each constraint in $\mathbf{I}$; otherwise $\mathbf{D}$ violates $\mathbf{I}$.

When a first-order constraint $\leftarrow W$ is considered, the standard method of determining whether a database satisfies or violates the constraint is by evaluating the query $\leftarrow W$ in the context of the database. If there is an SLDNF-refutation of $\mathbf{D} \cup \{\leftarrow W\}$ then $\mathbf{D}$ violates $\leftarrow W$. If $\mathbf{D} \cup \{\leftarrow W\}$ has a finitely failed SLDNF-tree, then $\mathbf{D}$ satisfies $\leftarrow W$. When an aggregate constraint $\leftarrow \Gamma$ is considered, it is transformed to its equivalent first-order denial form $\leftarrow \Gamma_d$ by transforming the database $\mathbf{D}$ to $\mathcal{Exp}(\mathbf{D}, \leftarrow \Gamma)$. Then one can have the following syntactic definition of aggregate constraint satisfiability.

Lemma 16.5: Let $\mathbf{D}$ be a database and $\leftarrow \Gamma$ be an aggregate constraint. The terms $\mathcal{Exp}(\mathbf{D}, \leftarrow \Gamma)$ and $\leftarrow \Gamma_d$ are defined as above. Suppose $Comp(\mathbf{D})$ is consistent. If there is an SLDNF-refutation of $\mathcal{Exp}(\mathbf{D}, \leftarrow \Gamma) \cup \{\leftarrow \Gamma_d\}$ then $\mathbf{D}$ violates $\leftarrow \Gamma$. If $\mathcal{Exp}(\mathbf{D} \leftarrow \Gamma) \cup \{\leftarrow \Gamma_d\}$ has a finitely failed SLDNF-tree, then $\mathbf{D}$ satisfies $\leftarrow \Gamma$.

Proof Similar to the case of a first-order constraint. ■

16.1.3 Simplification theorem

Lloyd *et al.*'s simplification method for checking integrity in definite databases was described in Chapter 13 and the two sets of partially instantiated atoms $\mathcal{Pos}_{\mathbf{D},\mathbf{D}'}$ and $\mathcal{Neg}_{\mathbf{D},\mathbf{D}'}$ were defined there. The generalized simplification theorem to handle the case for an aggregate constraint is as follows.

Theorem 16.1: Let $\mathbf{D}$ be a database, $\leftarrow \Gamma$ be an aggregate constraint and $\mathbf{D}'$ be obtained from $\mathbf{D}$ by applying the transaction $\mathbf{T}$ to $\mathbf{D}$. Suppose that the completion of each of $\mathbf{D}$ and $\mathbf{D}'$ are consistent. If $x_1, ..., x_m$ are the global variables of $\leftarrow \Gamma$, the following three sets can be defined:

- $\Theta = \{\theta | \theta$ is the restriction on $x_1, ..., x_m$ of an mgu of the atom A, where $Count(A, n)$ is an aggregate atom occurring either positively or negatively in Γ, and an atom in $\mathcal{Pos}_{\mathbf{D},\mathbf{D}'} \cup \mathcal{Neg}_{\mathbf{D},\mathbf{D}'}\}$,
- $\Phi = \{\phi | \phi$ is the restriction on $x_1, ..., x_m$ of an mgu of an atom occurring positively in Γ and an atom in $\mathcal{Pos}_{\mathbf{D},\mathbf{D}'}\}$, and
- $\Psi = \{\psi | \psi$ is the restriction to $x_1, ..., x_m$ of an mgu of an atom occurring negatively in Γ and an atom in $\mathcal{Neg}_{\mathbf{D},\mathbf{D}'}\}$.

Then **D**′ satisfies $\leftarrow \Gamma$ if and only if **D**′ satisfies $\leftarrow \Gamma\mu$, for all $\mu \in \Theta \cup \Phi \cup \Psi$.

Proof Let **E** denote $\mathcal{Exp}(\mathbf{D}, \leftarrow \Gamma)$. If $\mathcal{Comp}(\mathbf{D})$ is consistent, then by Lemma 16.4, $\mathcal{Comp}(\mathbf{E})$ is also consistent. Suppose that the transaction **T** produces **E**′ when it is applied to **E**. Recall that $Count(n, y_1, ..., y_g)$ is the first-order equivalent of an aggregate atom $Count(A, n)$, where $y_1, ..., y_g$ are the arguments other than the bound variables of A. Suppose $\leftarrow$ G is the first-order equivalent of $\leftarrow \Gamma$. Consider the following two sets:

- $\Omega_1 = \{\omega |\ \omega$ is the restriction on $y_1, ..., y_g$ of an mgu of an atom $Count(n, y_1, ..., y_g)$ occurring in G and an atom in $\mathcal{Pos}_{\mathbf{E}, \mathbf{E}'}\}$, and
- $\Omega_2 = \{\omega |\ \omega$ is the restriction on $y_1, ..., y_g$ of an mgu of an atom $Count(n, y_1, ..., y_g)$ occurring negatively in G and an atom in $\mathcal{Neg}_{\mathbf{E}, \mathbf{E}'}\}$.

Suppose $\theta \in \Theta$ and $A' \in \mathcal{Pos}_{\mathbf{D}, \mathbf{D}'}$ (the case when $A' \in \mathcal{Neg}_{\mathbf{D}, \mathbf{D}'}$ is similar) such that A' unifies with A, where A has the form $P(z_1, ..., z_l, y_1, ..., y_g)$. Each y_j is equal to x_k, for some k, $1 \le k \le m$. Whatever the bindings to the variables $z_1, ..., z_l$ corresponding to θ, $Count(1, y_1, ..., y_g)\theta$, ..., $Count(m, y_1, ..., y_g)\theta$ are members of $\mathcal{Pos}_{\mathbf{E}, \mathbf{E}'}$, and $Count(0, y_1, ..., y_g)\theta$, ..., $Count(m-1, y_1, ..., y_g)\theta$ are members of $\mathcal{Neg}_{E, E'}$.

Again, suppose $\omega \in \Omega_1$. This implies that $P(a_1^i, ..., a_l^i, y_1, ..., y_g)\omega$ is a member of $\mathcal{Pos}_{\mathbf{E}, \mathbf{E}'}$, that is, $P(a_1^i, ..., a_l^i, y_1, ..., y_g)\omega$ is a member of $\mathcal{Pos}_{\mathbf{D}, \mathbf{D}'}$.

The above two paragraphs prove that the satisfiability of $\leftarrow \Gamma\theta$ ($\theta \in \Theta$) in **D**′ is equivalent to the satisfiability of $\leftarrow$ Gω ($\omega \in \Omega_1 \cup \Omega_2$) in **E**′. Again, for all $\theta \in \Theta \cup \Phi \cup \Psi$, **D**′ satisfies $\leftarrow \Gamma\theta$ if and only if **E**′ satisfies $\leftarrow$ Gθ. Hence, **E**′ satisfies $\leftarrow$ Gθ, for all $\theta \in \Theta \cup \Phi \cup \Psi$ if and only if **E**′ satisfies $\leftarrow$ Gω, for all $\omega \in \Omega_1 \cup \Omega_2 \cup \Phi \cup \Psi$.

Again,

	D′ satisfies $\leftarrow \Gamma$	
iff	**E**′ satisfies $\leftarrow$ G	By definition.
iff	**E**′ satisfies $\leftarrow$ Gω for all $\omega \in \Omega_1 \cup \Omega_2 \cup \Phi \cup \Psi$	By the simplification theorem for first-order constraints.
iff	**E**′ satisfies $\leftarrow$ Gθ, for all $\theta \in \Theta \cup \Phi \cup \Psi$	Established above.
iff	**D**′ satisfies $\leftarrow \Gamma\theta$, for all $\theta \in \Theta \cup \Phi \cup \Psi$. ■	

16.1.4 Generalization of other aggregate predicates

If an aggregate atom under the predicate *Sum* occurs in a constraint then the Lemmas 16.1–16.4 as well as the above simplification theorem still hold. This is true since an occurrence of an aggregate atom of the form $Sum(z, A, r)$ in a constraint can be replaced by $Sum(r, y_1, ..., y_g)$ by adding the following clauses to the database (assuming that A has the form $P(z_1, ..., z_l, y_1, ..., y_g)$ and without any loss of generality z is taken as z_1):

- 1 clause:

  $$Sum(x, y_1, ..., y_g) \leftarrow Sum(\_, x, y_1, ..., y_g)$$

- $\dfrac{m^l(m^l-1) \cdots (m^l-k+1)}{k\ (k-1) \cdots 2\,1}$ clauses, for each $k = 1, ..., m^l$:

  $$\begin{gathered} Sum(k, x, y_1, ..., y_g) \leftarrow \\ P(a_1^1, ..., a_l^1, y_1, ..., y_g) \wedge \cdots \wedge P(a_1^k, ..., a_l^k, y_1, ..., y_g) \wedge \\ x = a_1^1 + \cdots + a_1^k \wedge \\ \neg Sum(k+1, \_, y_1, ..., y_g) \wedge \cdots \wedge \neg Sum(m^l, \_, y_1, ..., y_g) \end{gathered}$$

  where each a_i^p, $p = 1, ..., k$, is equal to a_q, for some q, and for $q \neq q'$, $1 \leq q, q' \leq k$, there exists an i such that $a_i^q \neq a_i^{q'}$ T}

For an occurrence of the aggregate predicate *Max*, the set of clauses added is the following:

- 1 clause:

  $$Max(x, y_1, ..., y_g) \leftarrow Max(\_, x, y_1, ..., y_g)$$

- For each k=1, ..., m^l, $k \times \dfrac{m^l \cdots (m^l-k+1)}{k\ (k-1) \cdots 2\,1}$ clauses:

  $$\begin{gathered} Max(k, a_1^j, y_1, ..., y_g) \leftarrow \\ P(a_1^1, ..., a_l^1, y_1, ..., y_g) \wedge \cdots \wedge P(a_1^k, ..., a_l^k, y_1, ..., y_g) \wedge \\ a_1^j > a_1^1 \wedge \cdots \wedge a_1^j > a_1^{j-1} \wedge a_1^j > a_1^{j+1} \wedge \cdots \wedge a_1^j > a_l^k \wedge \\ \neg Max(k+1, \_, y_1, ..., y_g) \wedge \cdots \wedge \neg Max(m^l, \_, y_1, ..., y_g) \end{gathered}$$

where each a_i^p, $p = 1, ..., k$, is equal to a_q, for some q, and for $q \neq q'$, $1 \leq q, q' \leq k$, there exists an i such that $a_i^q \neq a_i^{q'}$. T}

An aggregate atom involving the predicate *Min* is similar to the case for *Max*. The aggregate predicate *Avg* can be defined as an extension of the predicate *Sum*.

16.2 Transitional constraints

This section deals with transitional (or dynamic) constraints in normal databases. Static constraints are concerned with a particular state of a database; by contrast, an imposed transitional constraint relates to different states of a database. Integrity can be verified for transitional constraints in the same way as for static constraints, if the underlying language of the database is extended with some *action relations* (Nicolas and Yazdanian, 1978) (or *action predicates*) to represent transitional constraints. The representable class of constraints using this extended language covers static as well as transitional constraints. Remember that transitional constraints are, for example, of the form

Initially, the maximum salary is £10,000.
On updating the salary of an employee it should always increase.

16.2.1 Implicit update

In a deductive database the addition or deletion of a fact may cause a number of implicit additions or deletions of facts while an update may cause a number of *implicit updates* as well as implicit additions and deletions. So far, an update in a deductive database has been taken as a deletion followed by an addition for the purposes of integrity checking. However, this approach cannot detect any implicit updates. Before introducing formally the definition of an implicit update, its concept is illustrated through the following examples.

EXAMPLE 16.2

Database:	$Employee(x, y, z) \leftarrow EmpDept(x, y) \wedge EmpSal(x, z)$
	$EmpSal(a, 10{,}000)$
	$EmpDept(a, 50)$
Constraint:	$\forall x \forall y \forall z (Upd\_Employee(x, y, z, x, y', z') \wedge z \neq z' \rightarrow z' > z)$
Transaction:	update $EmpSal(a, 10{,}000)$ by $EmpSal(a, 12{,}000)$

The update type transitional constraint imposed on the database involves an IDB relation *Employee*. Before the transaction is applied, the fact *Employee* $(a, 50, 10{,}000)$ is true in the database but *Employee* $(a, 50, 12{,}000)$ is not. When the transaction is completed, *Employee* $(a, 50, 12{,}000)$ will be true in the database but *Employee* $(a, 50, 10{,}000)$ will no longer be so. This behaviour can be interpreted as an update of the fact *Employee* $(a, 50, 10{,}000)$ by *Employee* $(a, 50, 12{,}000)$. Since this update is on an IDB relation, it is called an implicit update and *Upd_Employee* $(a, 50, 10{,}000, a, 50, 12{,}000)$ is taken as true for constraint verification purposes in the updated database.

The following is another example of an implicit update involving an addition type transitional constraint.

EXAMPLE 16.3

Database: $Employee(x, y, z) \leftarrow EmpDept(x, y) \wedge EmpSal(x, z)$

$EmpDept(a, 50)$

$EmpDept(b, 60)$

$EmpSal(a, 10{,}000)$

Constraints: $\forall x \forall y \forall z\, (Upd\_Employee(x, y, z, x, y', z') \wedge z \neq z' \rightarrow z' > z)$

$\forall x \forall y \forall z\, (Add\_Employee(x, y, z) \rightarrow z \leq 10{,}000)$

Transaction: {update *EmpSal* $(a, 10{,}000)$ by *EmpSal* $(a, 12{,}000)$,
insert *EmpSal* $(b, 9000)$}

Before the transaction is applied to the database, neither *Employee* $(a, 50, 12{,}000)$ nor *Employee* $(b, 60, 9000)$ is true and they become derived facts of the updated database. Only *Add_Employee* $(b, 60, 9000)$ is taken as true under the addition type action relation *Add_Employee* and not the fact *Add_Employee* $(a, 50, 12{,}000)$ as it comes from an update.

Capturing all implicit updates as well as all implicit additions and deletions (not through updates) due to a transaction in deductive databases is an important issue for constraint checking in the presence of transitional constraints. This issue will be resolved in this chapter for the class of normal databases.

Definition 16.11: Let **D** be a database, M be a ground literal and A be a ground atom. Then M is said to be required to prove A by a rule R:$H \leftarrow$ B in **D** (and a literal L occurring in B) if there exists a substitution θ such that the following conditions hold:

(1) $R\theta$ is ground, and

(2) A is $H\theta$, and

(3) $B\theta$ is true in **D** and M is $L\theta$.

The variables common to both L and H are called *contributory variables* of L to the rule R. The following example clarifies this definition.

EXAMPLE 16.4

Database: $P(x, y) \leftarrow Q(x, y, z) \wedge \neg R(y, z)$
$Q(a, b, d)$
$Q(a, c, d)$
$R(c, d)$

In this example, $Q(a, b, d)$ is required to prove $P(a, b)$ by the first rule and the literal $Q(x, y, z)$. Also, $\neg R(b, d)$ is required to prove $P(a, b)$ by the first rule and the literal $\neg R(y, z)$. In the former case, the variables x and y are the contributory variables and in the latter the contributory variable is y only.

The concept of facts implicitly or explicitly added to or deleted from a database can formally be defined as follows.

Definition 16.12: Let **D** be a database and **T** be a transaction whose application to **D** produces the updated database **D′**:

(1) If an operation of **T** is an addition of a fact A to **D** and A is not true in **D**, then A is said to be a fact explicitly added to **D** due to the transaction **T**.

(2) If an operation of **T** is a deletion of a fact A from **D** and A is present in **D**, then A is said to be a fact explicitly deleted from **D** due to the transaction **T** if A is not true in **D′**.

(3) A fact A is said to be implicitly added to **D** due to the transaction **T** if the following conditions hold:

   (a) A is not provable in **D** but provable in **D′**, and

   (b) A is a not explicitly added to **D**.

(4) A fact A is said to be implicitly deleted from **D** due to the transaction **T** if the following conditions hold:

(a) A is provable in **D** but not provable in **D**$'$, and

(b) A is a not explicitly deleted from **D**.

(5) The set of all facts which are either explicitly or implicitly added to **D** are said to be added to **D** due to the transaction **T** and are denoted as $\mathcal{Add}_{\mathbf{D},\mathbf{D}'}$.

(6) The set of all facts which are either explicitly or implicitly deleted from **D** are said to be deleted from **D** due to the transaction **T** and are denoted as $\mathcal{Del}_{\mathbf{D},\mathbf{D}'}$.

Definition 16.13: Let **D** be a database and **T** be a transaction whose application to **D** produces the database **D**$'$:

(1) A fact A has been updated explicitly by another fact A' in **D** due to the transaction **T** if **T** contains an operation which is an update of A by A' and A and A' are facts under the same predicate.

(2) A fact F has been *updated positive-implicitly* by another fact F' in **D** due to the transaction **T** if the following conditions are met:

(a) F' is a fact which is added to **D** and F is a fact deleted from **D** due to the transaction, and

(b) A fact A has been updated either explicitly or implicitly by A', and

(c) A is required to prove F by a rule R:$H \leftarrow$ B in **D** and a literal L occurring in B, and

(d) A' is required to prove F' by a rule R$'$:$H' \leftarrow$ B$'$ in **D**$'$ and a literal L' occurring in B$'$, and

(e) F' unifies with $H\{x_{i_1}/a_{i_1}, ..., x_{i_l}/a_{i_l}\}$, where $i_1, ..., i_l$ are the only argument positions of A such that the value at each position i_j of A and A' are equal and also each variable x_{i_j} is a contributory variable of the literal L to the rule R. In other words, the unchanged contributory variables in an update are also unchanged in all implicit updates caused by the update.

(3) A fact F has been *updated negative-implicitly* by another fact F' in **D** due to the transaction **T** if the following conditions are met:

(a) F' is a fact which is added to **D** and F is a fact deleted from **D** due to the transaction, and

(b) A fact A' has been updated either explicitly or implicitly by A, and

(c) $\neg A$ is required to prove F by a rule R:$H \leftarrow$ B in **D** and a literal L occurring in B, and

(d) $\neg A'$ is required to prove F' by a rule R$'$:$H' \leftarrow$ B$'$ in **D$'$** and a literal L' occurring in B$'$, and

(e) F unifies with $H'\{x_{i_1}/a_{i_1}, ..., x_{i_l}/a_{i_l}\}$, where $i_1, ..., i_l$ are the only attribute positions of A' such that the attribute value at each position i_j of A' and A are equal and also each variable x_{i_j} is a contributory variable of the literal L' to the rule R$'$.

(4) The set of all positive-implicit or negative-implicit updates due to a transaction is called the set of implicit updates.

(5) The set of all implicit or explicit updates due to a transaction is called the set of updates and is denoted by $\mathcal{U}pd_{\mathbf{D},\mathbf{D}'}$. Each element of $\mathcal{U}pd_{\mathbf{D},\mathbf{D}'}$ is of the form $<R(s_1, ..., s_n), R(t_1, ..., t_n)>$ and is read as '$R(s_1, ..., s_n)$ has been updated by $R(t_1, ..., t_n)$'.

The above definition of implicit updates is illustrated in the following examples.

EXAMPLE 16.5

Consider Example 16.2. The fact *EmpSal* $(a, 10{,}000)$ (resp. *EmpSal* $(a, 12{,}000)$) is required to prove *Employee* $(a, 50, 10{,}000)$ (resp. *Employee* $(a, 50, 12{,}000)$) in the database (resp. in the updated database) by the only rule of the database, and the binding of the contributory variable x is $\{x/a\}$. The value at the attribute position x is a in both *EmpSal* $(a, 10{,}000)$ and *EmpSal* $(a, 12{,}000)$. Since *Employee* $(a, 50, 12{,}000)$ unifies with *Employee* $(x, y, z)\{x/a\}$, it can be said that *Employee* $(a, 50, 10{,}000)$ has been updated implicitly by *Employee* $(a, 50, 12{,}000)$ which is due to the explicit update of *EmpSal* $(a, 10{,}000)$ by *EmpSal* $(a, 12{,}000)$.

EXAMPLE 16.6

Database:
$P(x, y) \leftarrow Q(x, y) \wedge R(x, y)$
$P(x_1, y_1) \leftarrow Q(x_1, y_1) \wedge S(y_1)$
$P(x_2, y_2) \leftarrow T(x_2, y_2) \wedge Q(z_2, x_2)$
$Q(a, b)$
$R(a, b)$
$S(c)$

	$T(c, d)$
Transaction:	update $Q(a, b)$ by $Q(a, c)$

Before the transaction is applied to the database, $P(a, b)$ is provable from the database but $P(a, c)$ and $P(c, d)$ are not. Also, $Q(a, b)$ is required to prove $P(a, b)$ in the database by the first rule and $Q(a, c)$ is required to prove $P(a, c)$ in the updated database by the second rule. In the first case, the binding to the contributory variable x is $\{x/a\}$, and the arguments of the update candidates $Q(a, b)$ and $Q(a, c)$ match only at the position of the contributory variable x of the literal $Q(x, y)$. Since $P(a, c)$ unifies $P(x, y)\{x/a\}$, $P(a, b)$ has been implicitly updated by $P(a, c)$. Although $Q(a, c)$ is required to prove $P(c, d)$ by the third rule in the updated database, $P(a, b)$ has not been updated implicitly by $P(c, d)$ as $P(c, d)$ fails to unify with $P(x, y)\{x/a\}$.

The above example is a case of positive-implicit update. The following example demonstrates a case of negative-implicit update.

EXAMPLE 16.7

Database:	$Married(x, y) \leftarrow Husband(x, y) \wedge \neg Divorced(x, y)$
	$Husband(a, b)$
	$Husband(a, c)$
	$Divorced(a, b)$
Transaction:	update $Divorced(a, b)$ by $Divorced(a, c)$

Before the update is applied to the database, $Married(a, c)$ is provable from the database but $Married(a, b)$ is not. In the updated database, $Married(a, b)$ is provable but $Married(a, c)$ is not. All the conditions for $Married(a, c)$ implicitly updated by $Married(a, b)$ can be proved to be satisfied. Therefore, $Married(a, c)$ is implicitly updated by $Married(a, b)$ due to the explicit update of $Divorced(a, b)$ by $Divorced(a, c)$.

In certain circumstances two different explicit updates may cause the same implicit update. Consider the following example.

EXAMPLE 16.8

Database:	$P(x, y) \leftarrow Q(x) \wedge R(y)$
	$Q(a)$
	$R(b)$
Transaction:	update $Q(a)$ by $Q(a')$ and

update $R(b)$ by $R(b')$

Each of the updates in the transaction causes an implicit update of $P(a, b)$ by $P(a', b')$. Note that in each of the updates there is no contributory variable position which carries the same values before and after the transaction.

Definition 16.14: Let **D** be a database and **T** be a transaction whose application to **D** produces the updated database **D'**. Consider the following four sets:

$$\mathit{UpdAdd}_{\mathbf{D},\mathbf{D}'} = \{R(t_1, \ldots, t_n) | \langle R(s_1, \ldots, s_n), R(t_1, \ldots, t_n)\rangle \in \mathit{Upd}_{\mathbf{D},\mathbf{D}'}\}$$
$$\mathit{UpdDel}_{\mathbf{D},\mathbf{D}'} = \{R(s_1, \ldots, s_n) | \langle R(s_1, \ldots, s_n), R(t_1, \ldots, t_n)\rangle \in \mathit{Upd}_{\mathbf{D},\mathbf{D}'}\}$$
$$\mathit{NonUpdAdd}_{\mathbf{D},\mathbf{D}'} = \mathit{Add}_{\mathbf{D},\mathbf{D}'} - \mathit{UpdAdd}_{\mathbf{D},\mathbf{D}'}$$
$$\mathit{NonUpdDel}_{\mathbf{D},\mathbf{D}'} = \mathit{Del}_{\mathbf{D},\mathbf{D}'} - \mathit{UpdDel}_{\mathbf{D},\mathbf{D}'}$$

or, in other words

$$\mathit{Add}_{\mathbf{D},\mathbf{D}'} = \mathit{UpdAdd}_{\mathbf{D},\mathbf{D}'} \cup \mathit{NonUpdAdd}_{\mathbf{D},\mathbf{D}'}$$
$$\mathit{Del}_{\mathbf{D},\mathbf{D}'} = \mathit{UpdDel}_{\mathbf{D},\mathbf{D}'} \cup \mathit{NonUpdDel}_{\mathbf{D},\mathbf{D}'}$$

Each element of $\mathit{UpdAdd}_{\mathbf{D},\mathbf{D}'}$ is a fact added due to update and each element of $\mathit{UpdDel}_{\mathbf{D},\mathbf{D}'}$ is a fact deleted due to update. Also, each element of $\mathit{NonUpdAdd}_{\mathbf{D},\mathbf{D}'}$ is a fact added not due to update and each element of $\mathit{NonUpdDel}_{\mathbf{D},\mathbf{D}'}$ is a fact deleted not due to update.

EXAMPLE 16.9

In the case of Example 16.3

$$\mathit{Add}_{\mathbf{D},\mathbf{D}'} = \{\mathit{EmpSal}(a, 12{,}000), \mathit{EmpSal}(b, 9000)\}$$
$$\mathit{Del}_{\mathbf{D},\mathbf{D}'} = \{\mathit{EmpSal}(a, 10{,}000)\}$$
$$\mathit{Upd}_{\mathbf{D},\mathbf{D}'} = \{\langle \mathit{EmpSal}(a, 10{,}000), \mathit{EmpSal}(a, 12{,}000)\rangle\}$$
$$\mathit{UpdAdd}_{\mathbf{D},\mathbf{D}'} = \{\mathit{EmpSal}(a, 10{,}000)\}$$
$$\mathit{UpdDel}_{\mathbf{D},\mathbf{D}'} = \{\mathit{EmpSal}(a, 12{,}000)\}$$
$$\mathit{NonUpdAdd}_{\mathbf{D},\mathbf{D}'} = \{\mathit{EmpSal}(b, 9000)\}$$
$$\mathit{NonUpdDel}_{\mathbf{D},\mathbf{D}'} = \{\}$$

The facts in $\mathit{NonUpdAdd}_{\mathbf{D},\mathbf{D}'}$ (resp. $\mathit{NonUpdDel}_{\mathbf{D},\mathbf{D}'}$) are the set of all facts under all addition (resp. deletion) type action relations defined below, for the current transaction.

16.2.2 Action relations

Let **D** be a database and **T** be a transaction whose application to **D** produces the updated database **D′**. Corresponding to each n-ary relation R in **D** add another three relation names, *Add_R* (n-ary), *Del_R* (n-ary) and *Upd_R* (2n-ary), into the language of the database **D**. The relation name *Add_R* is an *addition type action relation* corresponding to R, *Del_R* is a *deletion type action relation*, and *Upd_R* is an *update type action relation* corresponding to R.

When a transaction **T** is performed on **D** to produce the updated database **D′**, for constraint verification purposes the updated database is assumed to be extended with facts under the action relations given in the three sets:

$$\mathcal{NonUpdAdd}_{\mathbf{D},\mathbf{D}'},\ \mathcal{NonUpdDel}_{\mathbf{D},\mathbf{D}'} \text{ and}$$
$$\{Upd\_R(s_1, ..., s_n, t_1, ..., t_n) | \langle R(s_1, ..., s_n), R(t_1, ..., t_n)\rangle \in \mathcal{Upd}_{\mathbf{D},\mathbf{D}'}\}$$

Transitional constraints are then verified in the same way as for static constraints. A formal description of how to compute the action relations corresponding to a transaction is as follows:

(1) A tuple $\langle t_1, ..., t_n\rangle$ belongs to an addition type action relation *Add_R* if and only if $R(t_1, ..., t_n)$ is added to the database not due to update. In other words, $Add\_R(t_1, ..., t_n)$ is true if and only if $R(t_1, ..., t_n) \in \mathcal{NonUpdAdd}_{\mathbf{D},\mathbf{D}'}$.

(2) A tuple $\langle t_1, ..., t_n\rangle$ belongs to an action relation *Del_R* if $R(t_1, ..., t_n)$ is deleted from the database not due to update. In other words, $Add\_R(t_1, ..., t_n)$ is true if and only if $R(t_1, ..., t_n) \in \mathcal{NonUpdDel}_{\mathbf{D},\mathbf{D}'}$.

(3) A tuple $\langle s_1, ..., s_n, t_1, ..., t_n\rangle$ belongs to an update type action relation *Upd_R* if and only if $R(s_1, ..., s_n)$ is updated by $R(t_1, ..., t_n)$. In other words, $Upd\_R(s_1, ..., s_n, t_1, ..., t_n)$ is true if and only if $\langle R(s_1, ..., s_n), R(t_1, ..., t_n)\rangle \in \mathcal{Upd}_{\mathbf{D},\mathbf{D}'}$.

EXAMPLE 16.10

Consider Example 16.2. Owing to the nature of the transaction applied to the database, the fact *Upd_Employee* (a, 50, 10,000, a, 50, 12,000) under the action relation *Upd_Employee* is taken as true temporarily to evaluate the transitional constraints imposed on the database. As in the case of static non-aggregate constraints evaluation, this fact affects the constraint and eventually the integrity of the database is maintained.

Exercises

16.1 Generalize the path finding method to handle aggregate and transitional constraints.

16.2 Let **D** be a database and $\leftarrow \Gamma$ be an aggregate constraint. Lemma 16.5 and Theorem 16.1 state that the simplified first-order equivalent denial form of $\leftarrow \Gamma$ would have to be evaluated in the updated database **E**′ to preserve consistency, where **E**′ is obtained by applying the transaction to **E** (=$\mathcal{E}xp$(**D**, $\leftarrow \Gamma$). However, in a Prolog implementation, the effect of resolution in **E**′ with a selected literal $Count(n, y_1, ..., y_g)$ (which is the first-order equivalent of an aggregate literal $Count(P(z_1, ..., z_l, y_1, ..., y_g), n))$ can be achieved by evaluating the Prolog subgoal `setof((Z1,...,Zl), p(Z1,...,Zl,Y1,...,Yg), L)` in **D**′ and then by counting the number of elements in the list `L`. Hence, the underlying database **D** does not have to be expanded to **E**. To obtain the correct intended meaning of an aggregate constraint $\leftarrow \Gamma$, it is necessary to follow a generalized computation rule, called *aggregate safe*, which selects

(a) a first-order negative literal, only when it is ground, and

(b) an aggregate positive literal, only when its key formula is ground wrt to its free global variables, and

(c) an aggregate negative literal, only when it is ground wrt its global variables.

To achieve the effect of an aggregate safe computation rule in Prolog's leftmost literal selection strategy, an aggregate literal λ (resp. negative literal L) can be placed after all the positive literals containing all the occurrences of global variables of λ (resp. variables of L). The other aggregate predicates can be implemented using a similar mechanism.

By following the above guidelines for the implementation of 'Count' and other aggregate predicates, expand the prototype of Chapter 14 to handle aggregate constraints.

16.3 Extend the prototype of Chapter 14 to incorporate the facility of computing action relations to handle transitional constraints.

PART V

Conclusion

17

Extensions and additional references

This chapter provides brief introductions to some important areas of research in the fields of logic programming and deductive databases. These areas include typed, meta-level and higher-order extensions of logic programming and deductive databases. The chapter also provides references to several additional techniques and issues beyond the scope of this text.

17.1 Typed logic programs and deductive databases

Some of the advantages of having types in logic programs (Hill and Lloyd, 1991) or in deductive databases are as follows:

(1) Intended interpretations of logic programming applications are typed.

(2) Type provides a natural way of expressing domain concepts which are already there in conventional databases.

(3) Correctly typing a formula ensures that important kinds of semantic integrity constraints are automatically maintained.

Type in first-order logic is called *many sorted logic* and it generalizes ordinary one-sorted first-order logic. Many sorted logic has sort declarations for the variables, constants, functions and predicates. Formulae in many sorted logic are typed formulae. A typed formula can be transformed into a type-free formula with the aid of the following two transformations (Lloyd, 1987):

Replace $\forall x/\tau W$ by $\forall x\,(W \leftarrow \tau(x))$
Replace $\exists x/\tau W$ by $\exists x\,(W \wedge \tau(x))$

where τ is the type predicate symbol corresponding to the type of the variable x. The evaluation of goals in a typed system can be done equivalently in its corresponding transformed type-free system.

Discussions on many sorted first-order logic can be found in Enderton (1972), Gallier (1987) and Lloyd (1987). A special discussion on typed deductive databases and their transformation to equivalent type-free systems can be found in Lloyd (1987).

17.2 Higher order logic programs and deductive databases

The logic-related discussions in the text so far have been confined to propositional (zero-order) and first-order logic. However, greater consideration is being given (Chen *et al.*, 1989; Miller and Nadathur, 1986; Nadathur and Miller, 1988) to exploiting higher-order logics (Andrew, 1986; Kaplan and Montague, 1965; Robinson, 1969) to obtain higher-order logic programming and deductive databases. *Second-order logic* (Hilbert and Ackerman, 1950) permits quantifiers on predicate, propositional and functional variables as well as individual variables. For example, the transitive closure of an arbitrary relation R is defined in HiLog (Chen *et al.*, 1989) by the following pair of second-order formulae:

```
trans_closure(R)(X,Y)  :- R(X,Y).
trans_closure(R)(X,Y)  :-
    R(X,Z), trans_closure(R)(Z,Y).
```

Third-order logic allows higher type predicate and function variables to denote predicates and functions whose arguments may be predicates and functions of individuals as well as individuals. *Fourth-order logic* permits quantification wrt these new variables. Continuing this way, a system of logics can be obtained which includes logics of all orders, called *type theory* (Andrews, 1986; Church, 1940; Henkin, 1950, 1963). *Finite type theory* or ω-*order logic* includes all finite-order logics and an arbitrary formula from a finite type theory is called a ω-*order formula*. The most popular and effective formalization of type theory is through λ-*calculus* (Barendregt, 1984; Hindley and Seldin, 1990) which treats every relation or function symbol as a set of monadic functions in the following manner.

First, either functions or relations are considered without losing any expressive power because for every n-ary function f there corresponds an $(n+1)$-ary relation R such that for all $x_1, ..., x_n$ and y with appropriate types

$$R(x_1, ..., x_n, y) \text{ if and only if } f(x_1, ..., x_n) = y$$

Now the n-ary function symbol f can be considered equivalently as a set of monadic function symbols $\{f^i_{a_1 \cdots a_i}\}$ such that $f^i_{a_1 \cdots a_i}(a) = f^{i+1}_{a_1 \cdots a_i a}$, $i = 0, 1, ..., n-1$, where a_i runs over the domain of the ith argument position of f. As an example, consider f as a 2-ary function symbol and $\mathbf{D}_1$ and $\mathbf{D}_2$ as the domains of the first and second arguments of f. Then for each $a \in \mathbf{D}_1$, $f^0(a)$ is a function f^1_a which maps each $b \in \mathbf{D}_2$ to f_{ab}, that is, $f^1_a(b) = f^1_{ab} = f(a, b)$.

A monadic function whose value on any argument x_α of type α is A_β of type β is written in type theory as $\lambda x_\alpha . A_\beta$, where λ is an *abstraction operator* and $\lambda x_\alpha . A_\beta$ is an *abstraction.* Thus, for example, $\lambda n.(n+1)$ is the successor function whose value on any natural number is its successor. This abstraction can be used to represent a set of type α by just taking the type β as truth value type. Thus, for example, the abstraction $\lambda n.(n < 5)$ represents the set $\{1, 2, 3, 4\}$. The value of the function on each member of this set is $\mathbf{T}$, whereas the value on any other natural number is $\mathbf{F}$. This usage of abstraction as a set has an important effect on database formulae representation and is discussed in the following section.

17.3 Specifying deductive databases in meta-logic

In Chapter 16, the inclusion of five aggregate predicates within the language helped to represent constraints of the form

The total number of employees in a particular department may not exceed 100 (17.1)

as an aggregate formula

$$\forall x \forall t (Dept(x) \wedge Count(\exists y \exists z Employee(y, x, z), t) \wedge \rightarrow t \leq 100) \quad (17.2)$$

This, of course, does not include constraints of the form

No more than two tests may have an average mark of less than 50 (17.3)

and one possible representation of the above constraints in a further general class of formulae might be

$$\begin{array}{c}\forall x\, \forall u\, \forall v\, (Student\,(x) \wedge Count\,(\exists y\ (ExamType\,(y) \wedge \\ Avg\,(t, \exists t\ ExamMarks\,(x, y, z, t), u), u < 50), v) \wedge v \leq 2)\end{array} \tag{17.4}$$

This approach may continue indefinitely and one requires a further general class of formulae. Hence, for the sake of total generalization, both deductive database statements and integrity constraints (particularly those involving aggregate operations) are required to be represented using a syntax which is more general than first order.

Dealing with a database system which is beyond first order raises the question of how far the extension should be stretched from first order. Unlike the first-order case, the unification in higher order logic is undecidable (Snyder and Gallier, 1989). Furthermore, implementing a database system on a general-purpose higher order theorem prover would not be useful for practical purposes because of its inefficiency. Hence it is impractical to deal with the whole higher order logic in a database.

An extension of first-order logic, called a *meta-logic*, is proposed by Das (1991a) to include many important database statements and integrity constraints which cannot otherwise be represented conveniently in first-order logic. A formal study of logic within the domain of these statements is regarded as a meta-logic. It has been shown that theoretical issues regarding the formal study of the proposed meta-logic can be dealt with by a subsystem of typed λ-calculus.

The syntax of meta-logic allows abstraction of a function (that is, higher order λ-calculus terms) as arguments of predicates representing relations to the database. Using the syntax of meta-logic, constraint (17.1) can be converted to

$$\forall x_{str}\, \forall y_{int} (Dept\,(x_{str}) \wedge Count\,(\lambda z_{id}\ Emp\,(z_{id}, x_{str}), y_{int}) \rightarrow y_{int} \leq 100 \tag{17.5}$$

Since there is an equivalence in the representations of functions and relations, the predicate symbols appearing in (17.5) can be replaced by their equivalent function representation. Hence, by treating ∀, ∧ and → as functions with appropriate domains and ranges, (17.5) can be replaced by its equivalent λ-term of the form

$$\begin{array}{c}\forall_{(\alpha o)o}(\lambda x_{\alpha}(\forall_{(\beta o)o}(\lambda y_{\beta}((\rightarrow_{ooo}(((\wedge_{ooo}(DEPT_{\alpha o}\, x_{\alpha})) \\ ((COUNT_{(\gamma o)\beta o}\, (\lambda z_{\gamma}(EMP_{\gamma\alpha o}\, z_{\gamma})\, x_{\alpha}))\, y_{\beta})))) ((\leq_{\beta\beta o}\, y_{\beta})\, 100)))))\end{array} \tag{17.6}$$

where the suffix of a symbol denotes its type and $\alpha = str$, $\beta = int$, $\gamma = id$. For the sake of readability, the initial level of a λ-term has been expanded to a first-order predicate calculus-like syntax such as (17.5) which can be thought of as an abbreviation of the λ-term (17.6).

By keeping the syntax within the typed first-order logic, another way constraint (17.1) could be represented is by replacing the abstraction $\lambda z_{id}\ Emp(z_{id}, x_{str})$ by the variable x_{str} itself and rewriting (17.5) as

$$\forall x_{str} \forall y_{int}(Dept(x_{str}) \wedge Count(x_{str}, y_{int}) \rightarrow y_{int} \leq 100) \quad (17.7)$$

One obvious disadvantage is that the predicate *Count* now relates an integer to a department name of the *Employee* relation only. If one wants to impose a similar constraint on the number of students in a particular class then either an extra procedure for the *Count* relation has to be added to the database or the predicate *Count* has to be broken up into two predicates, *Count_Emp* and *Count_Stud*. This process of modifying the database state and schema continues whenever a similar sort of aggregate operation is needed on an attribute domain of a new relation. Since the first argument position of *Count* in (17.2) can have any abstraction of a function whose domain is the set of *id*s and whose range is the set of truth values, constraint (17.1) in the case of students can be represented in the form of (17.1) as

$$\forall x_{str} \forall y_{int}(Class(x_{str}) \wedge Count(\lambda z_{id}\ Stud(z_{id}, x_{str}), y_{int}) \rightarrow y_{int} \leq 100) \quad (17.8)$$

Formulae in propositional calculus are considered as meta-logic statements of zero order and formulae in first-order predicate calculus are meta-logic statements of first order. Formulae (17.5) and (17.8) are meta-logic statements (Hill and Lloyd, 1989; Subrahmanian, 1989) of second order. A meta-logic statement can occur within another meta-logic statement. To represent a constraint like (17.3) one requires a meta-logic statement of third order as

$$\begin{gathered}\forall x_{id} \forall y_{int} \forall z_{int}(Stud(x_{id}) \wedge Count(\\ \lambda p_{str}\ (Avg\ (\lambda q_{int}\ Mark(x_{id}, p_{str}, q_{int}), y_{int}) \wedge y_{int} < 50), z_{int}) \rightarrow z_{int} \leq 2)\end{gathered} \quad (17.9)$$

Even after a simplification process, verification of the above kinds of constraints is sometimes expensive as they are evaluated as a query over the whole domain. For example, the arrival of a new employee in a particular department means counting the total number of employees in that department by fetching each employee record. This is also the case when there are frequent queries to the database relating to the counting of a domain or calculating an average on a domain. Efficiency in these cases can be increased by storing facts as λ-terms, for example

$$Count(\lambda y_{id}\ Stud(y_{id}, Math), 95) \quad (17.10)$$

which stores the present number of students in the mathematics (Math) department (which is 95). These kinds of facts, of course, may have to be updated after each transaction to the database.

This discussion suggests the use of higher order facts in a database. Rules of this kind are also necessary as is evident from the following example which counts the total number of students in the science faculty (*SF*), which consists of, say, mathematics (*Math*) and computer science (*CS*).

$$\begin{aligned} &\forall x_{int}\forall y_{int}\forall z_{int}(Count(\lambda p_{id}\ Stud(p_{id}, SF), x_{int}) \leftarrow \\ &\quad Count(\lambda q_{id}\ Student(q_{id}, Math), y_{int}) \wedge \\ &Count(\lambda r_{id}\ Employee(r_{id}, CS), z_{int}) \wedge x_{int} = y_{int} + z_{int}) \end{aligned} \tag{17.11}$$

The approach adopted by Das (1991a) is to consider meta-logic statements as database statements and some closed meta-logic statements as integrity constraints. This generalizes first-order database statements and first-order static constraints. Although this approach increases flexibility for representing problems, some complexities arise regarding unification, efficient answering of queries and simplification of constraints. Unification has been tackled as a subsystem of typed ω-order λ-calculus and Huet's unification procedure (Huet, 1975) is decidable in this subsystem. A resolution based theorem proving scheme has also been devised for such logic.

17.4 Additional references

Further discussions on the semantics of deductive databases and logic programming are largely accumulated in Falaschi *et al.* (1988), Gelfond and Przymusinski (1986), Naqvi (1986b), Przymusinski (1989), Przymusinska and Przymusinski (1988), Raatz and Gallier (1988), Ross (1989) and Seki and Itoh (1988) for declarative and procedural semantics. Discussions on circumscription related to logic programming and deductive databases can be found in Lifschitz (1985a), Lifschitz (1985b), Minker and Perlis (1985) and Moinard (1988).

A number of additional strategies for query evaluation are available for processing queries in definite databases. These include generalized differential (Balbin and Ramamohanrao, 1987), APEX (Lozinskii, 1985), counting (Bancilhon *et al.*, 1986), generalized counting (Sacca and Zaniolo, 1986), magic counting (Sacca and Zaniolo, 1987), static filtering (Kifer and Lozinski, 1986), Alexander (Rohmer *et al.*, 1986), QRGT (Ullman, 1989), magic functions (Gardarin, 1987), query/subquery (Vieille, 1986, 1988), the RQA/FQI strategy (Nejdi, 1987) and compilation of separable recursion (Naughton, 1988). Some of these methods have been extended to be applicable in larger application domains (Abiteboul and Hull, 1988).

Another strategy for parallel evaluation of queries in definite databases has been proposed by Das (1991c). The strategy resembles the one described in Chapter 15 but evaluates queries using networks and exploits more parallelism.

A number of methods (Das and Williams, 1989b) available for dealing with the static non-aggregate type of constraints in either definite or normal databases were not mentioned in Chapter 13. These methods include a generalized simplification methods by Bry *et al.* (1988), using the Prolog not-predicate by Ling (1987), the consistency proof method and a modified program method by Asirelli *et al.* (1985), a top-down method by Griefahn and Luttringhans (1990) and a unifying approach by Moerkotte and Karl (1988).

Repeated costly global computations of the `setof` predicate for implementing aggregate constraints verification, demonstrated in Exercise 16.2, can be replaced by more efficient incremental modifications as described by Bernstein *et al.* (1980) and Koenig and Paige (1981).

A generalization of the path finding method to check integrity constraints in general databases in the presence of range-restricted static constraints is described by Das (1990). There is a close relationship between the definition of constraint satisfiability adopted for general databases and the semantics of general databases given by the negation by all possible failure rule. The query evaluator required for constraint evaluation operates on possible and definite resolutions.

A few more papers discussing different theoretical as well as practical issues pertinent to integrity constraints in conventional and deductive databases are Cosmadakis and Kanellakis (1985), Cremers and Domann (1983), Eswaran and Chamberlin (1975), Goebel *et al.* (1986), Mazumdar *et al.* (1988), Motro (1989) and Paredaens (1980).

Prolog is mainly confined to untyped normal programs and normal goals. An extension of Prolog is in progress in different directions to handle full first-order formulae (Loveland, 1987; Smith and Loveland, 1988), to replace the concept of unification by the concept of constraint solving (Colmerauer, 1990), to incorporate types and facilitate meta-programming (Hill and Lloyd, 1991; Staples *et al.*, 1989) and also to deal with higher order formulae (Nadathur and Miller, 1988).

APPENDIX A

Listing of the prototype

```
%
%    A PROTOTYPE DEDUCTIVE DATABASE
%

%
%    REPEATEDLY EXECUTE COMMANDS
%

ddb :-
    write('--------- Deductive Database ---------'),nl,
    repeat,
        read(Cmd),
        T1 is cputime,
        execute(Cmd),
        T2 is cputime,
        T is T2-T1,
        write('CPU Time :'),
        write(T), nl,
        Cmd = quit, !.

%
%    AVAILABLE COMMANDS
%

execute(createrel(Name,Arity,Type)):-!,
    createrel(Name, Arity, Type).
execute(destroyrel(Name)):-!,
    destroyrel(Name).
execute(dumprels):-!,
    dumprels(user).
execute((dumprels>FileName)):-!,
    dumprels(FileName).

execute(insertfact(Fact)):-!,
    insertfact(Fact).
execute(deletefact(Fact)):-!,
```

```
    deletefact(Fact).
execute(insertfacts(FileName)):-!,
    consult(FileName).
execute(transaction(Tran)):-!,
    transaction(Tran).
execute(dumpfacts(RelName)):-!,
    dumpfacts(RelName, user).
execute(dumpfacts):-!,
    dumpfacts(user).
execute(dumpallfacts(RelName)):-!,
    dumpallfacts(RelName, user).
execute(dumpallfacts):-!,
    dumpallfacts(user).
execute((dumpfacts(RelName)>FileName)):-!,
    dumpfacts(RelName, FileName).
execute((dumpfacts>FileName)):-!,
    dumpfacts(FileName).
execute((dumpallfacts(RelName)>FileName)):-!,
    dumpallfacts(RelName, FileName).
execute((dumpallfacts>FileName)):-!,
    dumpallfacts(FileName).

execute(insertrule(Rule)):-!, insertrule(Rule).
execute(deleterule(Id)):-!, deleterule(Id).
execute(dumprules(RelName)):-!, dumprules(RelName, user).
execute(dumprules):-!, dumprules(user).
execute((dumprules(RelName)>FileName)):-!,
    dumprules(RelName, FileName).
execute((dumprules>FileName)):-!,
    dumprules(FileName).

execute(insertic(IC,Mes)):-!,
    insertic(IC,Mes).
execute(deleteic(ICId)):-!,
    deleteic(ICId).
execute(dumpics):-!,
    dumpics(user).
execute((dumpics>FileName)):-!,
    dumpics(FileName).

execute(cmdfile(FileName)):-!,
    cmdfile(FileName).
execute(savedb(DataBase)):-!,
    savedb(DataBase).
execute(loaddb(DataBase)):-!,
    loaddb(DataBase).
execute(purgedb):-!,
    purgedb.
execute(dumpall):-!,
    dumpall(user).
```

```
execute((dumpall>FileName)):-!,
    dumpall(FileName).

execute(query(Method,Query)):-!,
    query(Method, Query).

execute(help):-!, help.
execute(quit):-!.
execute(Cmd):-
    write('**** Inavlid Command: '),
    write(Cmd), nl, fail.

%
%   HELP DISPLAY
%

help:-
write('
COMMAND: createrel(<relname>, <arity>, <type>).
     EXAMPLE: createrel(employee, 3, edb).
     EXAMPLE: createrel(ancestor, 2, idb).
COMMAND: destroyrel(<relname>).
COMMAND: dumprels.
COMMAND: dumprels > <filename>.'),
write('
COMMAND: insertfact(<fact>).
     EXAMPLE: insertfact(employee(das,30,computer)).
COMMAND: deletefact(<fact>).
COMMAND: insertfacts(<filename>).'),
write('
COMMAND: transaction(<transaction>).
     EXAMPLE: transaction([insertfact(...),
            deletefact(...), ...])'),
write('
COMMAND: dumpfacts.
COMMAND: dumpfacts > <filename>.
COMMAND: dumpfacts(<relname>).
COMMAND: dumpfacts(<relname>) > <filename>.'),
write('
COMMAND: dumpallfacts.
COMMAND: dumpallfacts > <filename>.
COMMAND: dumpallfacts(<relname>).
COMMAND: dumpallfacts(<relname>) > <filename>.'),
write('
COMMAND: insertrule(<rule>).
     EXAMPLE: insertrule((ancestor(X,Y):-
            parent(X,Z), ancestor(Z,Y))).
COMMAND: deleterule(<ruleid>).'),
write('
COMMAND: dumprules.
```

```
COMMAND: dumprules > <filename>).
COMMAND: dumprules(<relname>).
COMMAND: dumprules(<relName>) > <filename>).'),
write('
COMMAND: insertic(<ic>,<message>).
     EXAMPLE: insertic(imply(exists([Y],manager(Y,X)),
                 employee(X)),''XXXX'').
COMMAND: deleteic(<icid>).
COMMAND: dumpics.
COMMAND: dumpics > <filename>.'),
write('
COMMAND: savedb(<dbname>).
COMMAND: loaddb(<dbname>).
COMMAND: purgedb.'),
write('
COMMAND: dumpall.
COMMAND: dumpall > <filename>.'),
write('
COMMAND: query(<methodname>,<query).
     EXAMPLE: query(magic,ancestor(das,X)).
COMMAND: cmdfile(<filename>).
COMMAND: quit.'), nl.

%
%   PROCEDURES FOR MANAGING RELATIONS
%

createrel(Name, Arity, Type):-
    valid_rel_name(Name, Arity),
    valid_rel_arity(Arity),
    valid_rel_type(Type),
    assert($relation(Name,Arity,Type)).

destroyrel(Name):-
    rel_exists(Name), !,
    rel_scheme(Name, RelScheme),
    clause(RelScheme, _), !,
    write('**** facts/rules exist under the relation: '),
    write(Name), nl,
    fail.
destroyrel(Name):-
    retract(Name, _, _).

dumprels(FileName):-
    tell(FileName),
    $relation(Name, Arity, Type),
    write((Name, Arity, Type)), nl,
    fail.
dumprels(_):-told.
```

```
valid_rel_name(Name, _):-
    not atom(Name), !,
    write('**** relation name is not an atom: '),
    write(Name), nl,
    fail.
valid_rel_name(Name, _):-
    $relation(Name, _, _), !,
    write('**** duplicate relation name: '),
    write(Name), nl,
    fail.
valid_rel_name(Name, Arity):-
    rel_scheme(Name, Arity, [], RelScheme),
    clause(RelScheme, _), !,
    write('**** a program clause is already defined by:'),
    write(Name), nl,
    fail.
valid_rel_name(_, _).

valid_rel_type(edb):-!.
valid_rel_type(idb):-!.
valid_rel_type(Type):-
    write('**** invalid relation type: '),
    write(Type), nl,
    fail.

valid_rel_arity(Arity):-
    integer(Arity),
    Arity >= 0, !.
valid_rel_arity(Arity):-
    write('**** invalid arity: '),
    write(Arity),nl,
    fail.

rel_scheme(Name, RelScheme):-
    $relation(Name, Arity, _),
    rel_scheme(Name, Arity, [], RelScheme).
rel_scheme(Name, 0, L, RelScheme):-!,
    RelScheme =.. [Name|L].
rel_scheme(Name, N, L, RelScheme):-
    N1 is N-1,
    rel_scheme(Name, N1, [_|L], RelScheme).

rel_exists(Name):-
    not $relation(Name, _, _), !,
    write('**** relation does not exist:'),
    write(Name), nl,
    fail.
rel_exists(_).

%
```

```
%   PROCEDURES FOR MANAGING FACTS
%

insertfact(Fact):-
    transaction([insertfact(Fact)]).

deletefact(Fact):-
    transaction([deletefact(Fact)]).

dumpfacts(FileName):-
    $relation(RelName, _, _),
    dumpfacts(RelName, FileName),
    fail.
dumpfacts(_).

dumpfacts(RelName, FileName):-
    rel_exists(RelName),
    tell(FileName),
    rel_scheme(RelName, RelScheme),
    dumpexfacts(RelScheme),
    told.

dumpallfacts(FileName):-
    $relation(RelName, _, _),
    dumpallfacts(RelName, FileName),
    fail.
dumpallfacts(_).

dumpallfacts(RelName, FileName):-
    rel_exists(RelName),
    tell(FileName),
    rel_scheme(RelName, RelScheme),
    dumpexfacts(RelScheme),
    dumpimfacts(RelScheme),
    told.

dumpexfacts(RelScheme):-
    clause(RelScheme, true),
    write(RelScheme), nl,
    fail.
dumpexfacts(_).

dumpimfacts(RelScheme):-
    RelScheme,
    not clause(RelScheme, true),
    write(RelScheme),
    write('*'), nl,
    fail.
dumpimfacts(_).
```

```
%
%   PROCEDURES FOR MANAGING TRANSACTIONS
%   (only insertion and deletion of facts are allowed
%       in a transaction).
%

transaction(T):-
    valid_trans(T),
    execute_trans(T),
    ic_violated(T), !,
    roll_back_trans(T),
    fail.
transaction(_).

%
%   Check the validity of a transaction.
%

valid_trans([]):-!.
valid_trans([T|Ts]):-!,
    valid_trans(T),
    valid_trans(Ts).
valid_trans(insertfact(A)):-
    valid_fact(A).
valid_trans(deletefact(A)):-
    clause(A, true), !.
valid_trans(deletefact(A)):-
    write('**** fact not found: '),
    write(A), nl,
    fail.

valid_fact(Fact):-
    valid_atom(Fact, edb),
    ground(Fact).

valid_atom(Atom, Type):-
    Atom =.. [Name|Vs],
    $relation(Name, Arity, Type), !.
valid_atom(Atom, Type):-
    write('**** edb/idb relation undefined: '),
    write(Atom), nl,
    fail.

%
%   Perform and roll back a transaction.
%

execute_trans([]).
execute_trans([insertfact(A)|Ts]):-
    assert(A),
```

```
    execute_trans(Ts).
execute_trans([deletefact(A)|Ts]):-
    retract(A),
    execute_trans(Ts).

roll_back_trans([]).
roll_back_trans([insertfact(A)|Ts]):-
    retract(A),
    roll_back_trans(Ts).
roll_back_trans([deletefact(A)|Ts]):-
    assert(A),
    roll_back_trans(Ts).

%
%   PROCEDURES FOR MANAGING RULES
%

insertrule((H:-B)):-
    valid_rule((H:-B)),
    insertrule_info(Id, (H:-B)),
    call(B),
    ic_violated([insertfact(H)]), !,
    deleterule_info(Id), fail.
insertrule(_).

deleterule(Id):-
    $rule(Id, H, B),
    deleterule_info(Id),
    ic_violated([deletefact(H)]), !,
    insertrule_info(_, (H:-B)),
    fail.
deleterule(_).

dumprules(RelName, FileName):-
    rel_exists(RelName),
    tell(FileName),
    rel_scheme(RelName, RelScheme),
    $rule(Id, RelScheme, B),
    write((Id,' ')),
    write(RelScheme),
    write((':-')), write(B), nl,
    fail.
dumprules(_, _):-told.

dumprules(FileName):-
    $relation(RelName, _, idb),
    dumprules(RelName, FileName),
    fail.
dumprules(_):-told.
```

```
valid_rule((H:-B)):-!,
    valid_head(H),
    valid_body(B).

valid_head(Head):-
    valid_atom(Head, idb).

valid_body((L,Ls)):-!,
    valid_body(L),
    valid_body(Ls).
valid_body(L):-
    valid_lit(L).

valid_lit((not Atom)):-!,
    valid_atom(Atom, _).
valid_lit(Atom):-
    valid_atom(Atom, _).

insertrule_info(Id, (H:-B)):-
    id($rule, Id),
    assert($rule(Id,H,B)),
    assert((H:-B), Ref),
    assert($internal_ref(Id,Ref)),
    generate_depend_clauses(Ref, H, B).

deleterule_info(Id):-
    not $rule(Id, $ic_1(_), _),
    not $rule(Id, $ic_3(_,_,_), _),
    retract($rule(Id,H,B)), !,
    retract($internal_ref(Id,Ref)),
    erase(Ref),
    retractall($depend(Ref,_,_)).
deleterule_info(Id):-
    write( '**** rule not found: '),
    write(Id), nl,
    fail.

generate_depend_clauses(Ref, H, B):-
    in_conj(BLit, B),
    assertz($depend(Ref,H,BLit)),
    not H=$ic_1(_),
    complement(BLit, NBLit),
    assertz($depend(Ref,not H,NBLit)),
    fail.
generate_depend_clauses(_, _, _).

complement(not A,A):-!.
complement(A,not A).

id(_, Id):-nonvar(Id), !.
```

```
id(Type, Id):-
    retract($maxid(Type, OldId)), !,
    Id is OldId+1,
    assert($maxid(Type, Id)).
id(Type, 1):-
    assert($maxid(Type, 1)).

%
%   PROCEDURES FOR MANAGING INTEGRITY CONSTRAINTS
%

insertic(IC, Mes):-
    insertic_info(Id, IC, Mes),
    (call($ic_1(Id)) ->
        deleteic_info(Id),
        write( '**** imposed ic violated'), nl; true).

deleteic(Id):-
    not $ic(Id,_,_), !,
    write( '**** ic not found: '), write(Id), nl,
    fail.
deleteic(Id):-
    deleteic_info(Id), !.

dumpics(FileName):-
    tell(FileName),
    $ic(Id, IC, Mes),
    write((Id,IC,Mes)), nl,
    fail.
dumpics(_):-
    $ic(Id, _, _),
    clause($ic_1(Id), B),
       write($ic_1(Id)),
    write((':-')), write(B), nl,
    fail.
dumpics(_):-
    $ic(Id, _, _),
    clause($ic_3(Id,PredId,X), B),
       write($ic_3(Id,PredId,X)),
       write((':-')), write(B), nl,
    fail.
dumpics(_):-told.

insertic_info(Id, IC, Mes):-
    id($ic, Id),
    assert($ic(Id,IC,Mes)),
    denial(Id, IC, RList),
    insertrule_list(RList).

deleteic_info(Id):-
```

```
    $ic(Id, _, _),
    $rule(Id1, $ic_1(Id), _),
    deleterule_info(Id1),
    fail.
deleteic_info(Id):-
    $ic(Id, _, _),
    $rule(Id2, $ic_3(Id,_,_), _),
    deleterule_info(Id2),
    fail.
deleteic_info(Id):-
    retract($ic(Id,_,_)).

insertrule_list([]).
insertrule_list([R|Rs]):-
    insertrule_info(_, R),
    insertrule_list(Rs).

%
%   PROCEDURES CONCERNING SOME GLOBAL COMMANDS
%

cmdfile(FileName):-
    file_exists(FileName), !,
    see(FileName),
    repeat,
        read(Cmd),
        (Cmd = end_of_file -> !, seen;
            execute(Cmd), fail).

savedb(FileName):-
    tell(FileName),
    $relation(Name, Arity, Type),
    writeq($relation(Name,Arity,Type)),
    write('.'), nl,
    fail.
savedb(_):-
    $rule(Id, Head, Body),
    writeq($rule(Id,Head,Body)),
    write('.'), nl,
    fail.
savedb(_):-
    $ic(Id, IC, Mes),
    writeq($ic(Id,IC,Mes)),
    write('.'), nl,
    fail.
savedb(FileName):-
    $relation(Name, Arity, edb),
    rel_scheme(Name, RelScheme),
    RelScheme,
    writeq(RelScheme),
```

```
     write('.'), nl,
     fail.
savedb(_):-told.

loaddb(FileName):-
     file_exists(FileName), !,
     see(FileName),
     repeat,
          read(Item),
          loaditem(Item),
          Item = end_of_file, !,
          seen.

purgedb:-
     retractall($maxid(_,_)),
     retract($relation(Name,Arity,_)),
     abolish(Name, Arity),
     fail.
purgedb:-
     $rule(Id, _, _),
     deleterule_info(Id),
     fail.
purgedb:-
     $ic(Id, _, _),
     deleteic_info(Id),
     fail.
purgedb.

dumpall(FileName):-
     dumprels(FileName),
     dumprules(FileName),
     dumpfacts(FileName),
     dumpics(FileName).

file_exists(FileName):-
     exists(FileName), !.
file_exists(FileName):-
     write('**** file does not exist: '),
     write(FileName),nl.

loaditem(end_of_file):-!.
loaditem($rule(_,H,B)):-!,
     insertrule_info(_, (H:-B)).
loaditem(Item):-
     assert(Item).

%
%    PROCEDURES CONCERNING INTEGRITY CHECKING
%
```

```
ic_violated([]):-!, fail.
ic_violated([Op|_]):-
    ( Op = insertfact(A), S = A;
        Op = deletefact(A), S = (not A) ),
    path($ic_1(Id), S, []), !,
    write('**** ic violated and transaction cancelled:'),
    $ic(Id, _, Mes),
    write(Mes), nl,
    write('      operation addition/deletion- '),
    write(A), nl.
ic_violated([_|Ops]):-
    ic_violated(Ops).

%
%   Procedures to implement the path finding method.
%

path(D, S, _):-
    $depend(Ref, D, S),
    clause(D, B, Ref),
    simplify(B, S, SB),
    call(SB).

path(D, S, NegList):-
    $depend(_, Via, S),
    Via=(not A),
    not instance1(A, NegList),
    path(D, Via, [A|NegList]).

path(D, S, NegList):-
    $depend(Ref, Via, S),
    not Via=(not _),
    clause(Via, B, Ref),
    simplify(B, S, SB),
    call(SB),
    path(D, Via, NegList).

simplify((L,Ls), L1, (SL,Ls)):-
    simplify(L, L1, SL).
simplify((L,Ls), L1, (L,SLs)):-!,
    simplify(Ls, L1, SLs).
simplify(L, L1, SL):-
    simplify1(L, L1, SL).
simplify1(not A, not A, not A):-!.
simplify1(A, A, true).

instance1(A, []):-!, fail.
instance1(A, [H|T]):-!,
    (instance1(A, H), !;instance1(A, T)).
instance1(A, H):-
```

```
    A=..[P|VA],
    H=..[P|VH],
    instance2(VA, VH).
instance2([], []).
instance2([H1|T1], [H2|T2]):-
    ((nonvar(H1) -> H1=H2);var(H2)), !,
        instance2(T1, T2).

%
%   PROCEDURES TO CONVERT ICs INTO DENIAL FORMS
%
%   See Chapter 7 for the transformation rules (a)-(j).
%   The set of rules generated corresponding to a
%   constraint are stored in the list 'RList'.

denial( Id, IC, RList ) :-
    normal( Id, imply($ic_1(Id),not IC), RList ).

normal( Id, imply(A,B), NC ) :-        %% Rule (a) %%
    pattern( not and(V,W), B ), !,
    replace( not and(V,W), not V, B, RBV ),
    replace( not and(V,W), not W, B, RBW ),
    normal( Id, imply(A,RBV), NRBV ),
    normal( Id, imply(A,RBW), NRBW ),
    append( NRBV, NRBW, NC ).

normal( Id, imply(A,B), NC ) :-        %%% Rule (b) %%
    pattern( forall(X,W), B ), !,
    replace( forall(X,W), not exists(X,not W), B, RB ),
    normal( Id, imply(A,RB), NC ).

normal( Id, imply(A,B), NC ) :-        %%% Rule (c) %%
    pattern( not forall(X,W), B ), !,
    replace( forall(X,W), exists(X,not W), B, RB ),
    normal( Id, imply(A,RB), NC ).

normal( Id, imply(A,B), NC ) :-        %%% Rule (d) %%
    pattern( imply(V,W), B ), !,
    replace( imply(V,W), V, B, RBV ),
    replace( imply(V,W), not W, B, RBW ),
    normal( Id, imply(A,RBV), NRBV ),
    normal( Id, imply(A,RBW), NRBW ),
    append( NRBV, NRBW, NC ).

normal( Id, imply(A,B), NC ) :-        %%% Rule (e) %%
    pattern( not imply(V,W), B ), !,
    replace( not imply(V,W), and(W,not V), B, RB ),
    normal( Id, imply(A,RB), NC ).

normal( Id, imply(A,B), NC ) :-        %%% Rule (f) %%
```

```
    pattern( or(V,W), B ), !,
    replace( or(V,W), V, B, RBV ),
    replace( or(V,W), W, B, RBW ),
    normal( Id, imply(A,RBV), NRBV ),
    normal( Id, imply(A,RBW), NRBW ),
    append( NRBV, NRBW, NC ).

normal( Id, imply(A,B), NC ) :-        %%% Rule (g) %%
    pattern( not or(V,W), B ), !,
    replace( not or(V,W), and(not V,not W), B, RB ),
    normal( Id, imply(A,RB), NC ).

normal( Id, imply(A,B), NC ) :-        %%% Rule (h) %%
    pattern( not not W, B ), !,
    replace( not not W, W, B, RB ),
    normal( Id, imply(A,RB), NC ).

normal( Id, imply(A,B), NC ) :-        %%% Rule (i) %%
    pattern( exists(X,W), B ), !,
    replace( exists(X,W), W, B, RB ),
    normal( Id, imply(A,RB), NC ).

normal( Id, imply(A,B), NC ) :-        %%% Rule (j) %%
    pattern( not exists(X,W), B ),
    ( setof( M, (var_in( M, W ), not member( M, X )), Y ) ;
    Y = [] ), !,
    id($ic_3, PredId),
    P = $ic_3(Id,PredId,Y),
    replace( not exists(X,W), not P, B, RB ),
    normal( Id, imply(P,exists(X,W)), NP ),
    normal( Id, imply(A,RB), NRB ),
    append( NRB, NP, NC ).

normal( _, W, [InfW] ):-      %%% Normal case %%
    infix(W, InfW).

%
%   Convert the rules generated by the above
%   procedure to the Prolog rules.
%

infix( imply(H,B), (IH:-IB) ):-!,
    infix( H, IH ),
    infix( B, IB ).
infix( and(H,B), (IH,IB) ):-!,
    infix( H, IH ),
    infix( B, IB ).
infix( X, X ).

%
```

```
%   Find a pattern and replace its occurrences.
%

pattern( X, X ).
pattern( X, and(U,V) ) :-
    pattern( X, U );
    pattern( X, V ).

replace( X, Y, U, Y ):-
    X == U, !.
replace( X, Y, and(U,V), and(RU,RV)) :- !,
    replace( X, Y, U, RU),
    replace( X, Y, V, RV).
replace( _, _, U, U ).

%
%   Find all free variables in a clause.
%

free_vars( X, W, Y ) :-
    setof(M, (var_in(M, W),not member(M, X)), Y), !.
free_vars( _, _, [] ).

var_in( X, (H:-B) ):-!,
    ( var_in( X, H ) ; var_in( X, B ) ).
var_in( X, (H,B) ):-!,
    ( var_in( X, H ) ; var_in( X, B ) ).
var_in( X, (H,B) ):-!,
    ( var_in( X, H ) ; var_in( X, B ) ).
var_in( X, exists(H) ):-!,
    var_in( X, H ).
var_in( X, forall(H) ):-!,
    var_in( X, H ).
var_in( X, not H ):-!,
    var_in( X, H ).
var_in( X, H ):-
    H =.. [_|Vs],
    in_list( X, Vs ).

in_list( _, [] ):-fail.
in_list( X, [X|_] ).
in_list( X, [_|Ys] ) :-
    in_list( X, Ys ).

member( X, [H|_] ):-X == H, !.
member( X, [_|T] ):-member( X, T ).

concatenate([], '').
concatenate([H|T], C):-
    concatenate(T, C1),
```

```
    concatenate(H, C1, C).

concatenate( A1, A2, C ):-
        name( A1, StrA1 ),
        name( A2, StrA2 ),
        append( StrA1, StrA2, StrA1A2 ),
        name( C, StrA1A2 ).

append( [], L, L ).
append( [X|L1], L2, [X|L3] ):-append( L1, L2, L3 ).

%
%   QUERY EVALUATION BY MAGIC SETS METHOD
%   (for definite databases)
%

query( magic, Query ):-
    valid_query( Query ),
    assert($query(Query)),
    generate_standard_query,
    magic_algorithm,
    generate_answers,
    detect_answers,
    retract($query(_)),
    clear.

%
%   Generate the standard query, e.g. 'query(X)' is
%   generated corresponding to the query 'ancestor(a,X)'
%   and the rule 'query(X):-ancestor(a,X)'
%   is inserted to the database.
%

generate_standard_query:-
    $query(Query),
    Query =.. [Pred|Args],
    collect_vars_in_list( Args, SArgs ),
    SQuery =.. [query|SArgs],
    insertrule_info(0, (SQuery:-Query)).

%
%   Apply magic sets transformation on the query and
%   the rules in the database.
%

magic_algorithm:-
    write( 'magic sets transformation ...' ), nl,
    generate_variable_rules,
    generate_adorned_rules,
    generate_magic_rules,
```

```
    generate_modified_rules,
    generate_complementary_rules,
    generate_transformed_rules.

%
%   Variable rules generation
%   i.e. to transform clauses into an internal structure.
%

generate_variable_rules:-
    $rule(Id, H, B),
    transform( H, HT ),
    bagof( X, in_conj( X, B ), BList ),
    transform( BList, BT ),
    assertz( $variable_rule(Id,HT,BT) ),
    fail.
generate_variable_rules.

transform( [], [] ):-!.
transform( [H|Hs], [HT|HTs] ):-!,
    transform( H, HT ),
    transform( Hs, HTs ).
transform( H, (Pred,Args,Ads) ):-
    H =.. [Pred|Args],
    var_adornment( Args, Ads ).

var_adornment( [], [] ).
var_adornment( [Arg|Args], [_|Ads] ):-
    var_adornment( Args, Ads ).

%
%   Adorned rules generation.
%

generate_adorned_rules:-
    $query(Query),
    Query =.. [_|Args],
    collect_vars_in_list( Args, VArgs ),
    query_adornment( VArgs, VAds ),
    generate_adorned_rules( [(query,VArgs,VAds)] ).

query_adornment( [], [] ).
query_adornment( [Arg|Args], [f|Ads] ):-
    var( Arg ),
    query_adornment( Args, Ads ).
query_adornment( [Arg|Args], [b|Ads] ):-
    nonvar( Arg ),
    query_adornment( Args, Ads ).

generate_adorned_rules( [] ).
```

```
generate_adorned_rules( [(Pred,_,_)|T] ):-
    edb( Pred ), !,
    generate_adorned_rules( T ).
generate_adorned_rules( [(Pred,_,Ads1)|T] ):-
    $adorned_rule( _, (Pred,_,Ads2), B ),
    Ads1 == Ads2, !,
    generate_adorned_rules( T ).
generate_adorned_rules( [H1|T] ):-
    H1 = (Pred,Args1,Ads),
    $variable_rule( N, (Pred,Args2,Ads), B ),
    H2 = (Pred,Args2,Ads),
    body_adornment( H2, B ),
    assertz( $adorned_rule(N,H2,B) ),
    generate_adorned_rules( B ),
    generate_adorned_rules( T ).


%
%   Compute the adornment of the body of a rule.
%

body_adornment( H, B ):-
    body_adornment( H, B, B ).

body_adornment( _, [], _ ).
body_adornment( H, [B|Bs], DupB ):-
    body_adornment( H, B, DupB ),
    body_adornment( H, Bs, DupB ).
body_adornment( _, (_,[],[]), _ ).
body_adornment( H, (Pred,[BArg|BArgs],[b|BAds]), DupB ):-
    nonvar(BArg), !,
    body_adornment( H, (Pred,BArgs,BAds), DupB ).
body_adornment( H, (Pred,[BArg|BArgs],[b|BAds]), DupB ):-
    H = (_,HArgs,HAds),
    bound_var_member( BArg, HAds, HArgs ), !,
    body_adornment( H, (Pred,BArgs,BAds), DupB ).
body_adornment( H, (Pred,[BArg|BArgs],[BAd|BAds]), DupB ):-
    var_in_distinguished_edb_pred( BArg, H, DupB ), !,
    BAd = b, body_adornment( H, (Pred,BArgs,BAds), DupB ).
body_adornment( H, (Pred,[_|BArgs],[f|BAds]), DupB ):-
    body_adornment( H, (Pred,BArgs,BAds), DupB ).

in_conj( X, (B,Bs) ):-!,
    ( in_conj( X, Bs ) ; in_conj( X, B ) ).
in_conj( X, X ).

bound_var_member( X, [Ad|_], [Arg|_] ):-
    Ad == b, X == Arg, !.
bound_var_member( X, [_|Ads], [_|Args] ):-
    bound_var_member( X, Ads, Args ).
```

```
var_in_distinguished_edb_pred( X, _, [(Pred,Args,Ads)|_] ):-
    member( X, Args ),
    distinguished( (Pred,Args,Ads) ), !.
var_in_distinguished_edb_pred( X, (_,HArgs,HAds),
                    [(BPred,BArgs,_)|_] ):-
    edb( BPred ),
    member( X, BArgs ),
    bound_var_list_intersection( BArgs, HAds, HArgs ), !.
var_in_distinguished_edb_pred( X, H, [_|Bs] ):-
    var_in_distinguished_edb_pred( X, H, Bs ).

bound_var_list_intersection( [BArg|_], HAds, HArgs ):-
    bound_var_member( BArg, HAds, HArgs ), !.
bound_var_list_intersection( [_|BArgs], HAds, HArgs ):-
    bound_var_list_intersection( BArgs, HAds, HArgs ).

collect_vars_in_list( [], [] ).
collect_vars_in_list( [H|T], [H|T1] ):-
    var( H ), !, collect_vars_in_list( T, T1 ).
collect_vars_in_list( [_|T], T1 ):-
    collect_vars_in_list( T, T1 ).

distinguished( (Pred,[Arg|_],_) ):-
    edb( Pred ), nonvar( Arg ), !.
distinguished( (Pred,_,[Ad|_]) ):-
    edb( Pred ), Ad == b, !.
distinguished( (Pred,[_|Args],[_|Ads]) ):-
    distinguished( (Pred,Args,Ads) ).

magic( Pred ):-
    name( Pred, [A,B,C,D,E|_] ),
    name( magic, [A,B,C,D,E] ).
idb( Pred ):-$variable_rule( _, (Pred,_,_), _ ), !.
edb( Pred ):-( idb( Pred ) ; magic( Pred ) ), !, fail.
edb( _ ).

%
%   Magic rules generation.
%

generate_magic_rules:-
    $adorned_rule( N, H, B ),
    idb_pred_occurrence( B, P ),
    del_idb_nd_edb_preds( B, P, NB ),
    repl_bpred_name_del_nd_vars( N, NB, NNB ),
    repl_hpred_name_del_nd_vars( H, NH ),
    exchange( NH, NNB, NNH, NNNB ),
    assertz( $magic_rule( N, NNH, NNNB ) ),
    fail.
generate_magic_rules.
```

```
idb_pred_occurrence( [], _ ):-fail.
idb_pred_occurrence( [B|_], B ):-
    B = (Pred,_,_),
    idb( Pred ).
idb_pred_occurrence( [_|Bs], B ):-
    idb_pred_occurrence( Bs, B ).

del_idb_nd_edb_preds( [], _, [] ).
del_idb_nd_edb_preds( [B|Bs], P, [B|NBs] ):-
    ( B == P ; distinguished( B ) ),!,
    del_idb_nd_edb_preds( Bs, P, NBs ).
del_idb_nd_edb_preds( [_|Bs], P, NBs ):-
    del_idb_nd_edb_preds( Bs, P, NBs ).

repl_bpred_name_del_nd_vars( _, [], [] ).
repl_bpred_name_del_nd_vars( N, [B|Bs],
                [(NPred,NArgs,Ads)|NBs] ):-
    B = (Pred,Args,Ads),
    idb( Pred ),!,
    concatenate([magic,'_','R',N,'_',Pred], NPred),
    del_nd_vars( Ads, Args, NArgs ),
    repl_bpred_name_del_nd_vars( N, Bs, NBs ).
repl_bpred_name_del_nd_vars( N, [B|Bs], [B|NBs] ):-
    repl_bpred_name_del_nd_vars( N, Bs, NBs ).

repl_hpred_name_del_nd_vars( (Pred,Args,Ads),
                (NPred,NArgs,Ads) ):-
    concatenate([magic,'_',Pred], NPred),
    del_nd_vars( Ads, Args, NArgs ).

del_nd_vars( [], [], [] ).
del_nd_vars( [f|Ads], [_|Args], NArgs ):-
    del_nd_vars( Ads, Args, NArgs ).
del_nd_vars( [b|Ads], [Arg|Args], [Arg|NArgs] ):-
    del_nd_vars( Ads, Args, NArgs ).

exchange( _, [], _, [] ).
exchange( H, [B|Bs], NH, [B|NBs] ):-
    B = (Pred,_,_),
    edb( Pred ),!,
    exchange( H, Bs, NH, NBs ).
exchange( H, [B|Bs], B, [H|NBs] ):-
    exchange( H, Bs, B, NBs ).

%
%   Modified rules generation.
%

generate_modified_rules:-
    $adorned_rule( N, H, B ),
```

```
    idb_pred_occurrence( B, P ),
    P = (Pred,Args,Ads),
    del_nd_vars( Ads, Args, NArgs ),
    concatenate([magic,'_','R',N,'_',Pred], NPred),
    MPred = (NPred,NArgs,Ads),
    H = (HPred,_,_),
    ( Pred == HPred -> NB = [MPred|B];
          insert_just_before( MPred, P, B, NB ) ),
    assertz( $modified_rule( N, H, NB ) ),
    fail.
generate_modified_rules.

%
%   Complementary rules generation.
%

generate_complementary_rules:-
    $adorned_rule( N, H, B ),
    idb_pred_occurrence( B, (Pred,Args,Ads) ),
    concatenate([magic,'_','R',N,'_',Pred], NBPred),
    del_nd_vars( Ads, Args, NArgs ),
    concatenate([magic,'_',Pred], NHPred),
    assertz( $complementary_rule(N,(NHPred,NArgs,Ads),
                   [(NBPred,NArgs,Ads)]) ),
    fail.
generate_complementary_rules.

insert_just_before( _, _, [], [] ).
insert_just_before( MPred, P, [B|Bs], [MPred|[B|NBs]] ):-
    P == B,!,
    insert_just_before( MPred, P, Bs, NBs ).
insert_just_before( MPred, P, [B|Bs], [B|NBs] ):-
    insert_just_before( MPred, P, Bs, NBs ).

%
%   Convert the internal form of adorned, modified, etc.
%   rules to the standard format.
%

generate_transformed_rules:-
    tell('magic.rule'),
    get_rule( H, B ),
    standard_atom(H, SH),
    standard_conj(B, SB),
    write((SH:-SB)),
    write('.'), nl,
    assertz( $transformed_rule( SH, SB ) ),
    fail.
generate_transformed_rules:-told.
```

```
get_rule( H, B ):-
    $magic_rule( _, H, B ) ;
    $adorned_rule( N, H, B ),
        not $modified_rule( N, H, _ ) ;
    $modified_rule( _, H, B );
    $complementary_rule( _, H, B ).

standard_atom( (Pred,Args,_), Atom ):-
    edb( Pred ), !,
    Atom =.. [Pred|Args].
standard_atom( (Pred,Args,Ads), Atom ):-
    name( Pred, StrPred ),
    name_ads( Ads, StrAds ),
    append( StrPred, [95], T1 ),
    append( T1, StrAds, T2 ),
    name( NPred, T2 ),
    Atom =.. [NPred|Args].

standard_conj( [H], SH ):-!,
    standard_atom( H, SH ).
standard_conj( [H|T], (SH,ST) ):-
    standard_atom( H, SH ),
    standard_conj( T, ST ).

name_ads( [], [] ).
name_ads( [b|Ads], [98|NAds] ):-name_ads( Ads, NAds ).
name_ads( [f|Ads], [102|NAds] ):-name_ads( Ads, NAds ).

%
%   Generate answers by bottom-up on the transformed
%   set of rules.
%

generate_answers:-
    write('executing ...'),nl,
    generate_initial_magic_fact(MFact),
    assert(MFact),
    generate_initial_answers,
    generate_subsequent_answers,
    retract(MFact).

generate_initial_magic_fact( MFact ):-
    $query( Query ),
    Query =.. [Pred|Args],
    collect_vars_in_list( Args, NArgs ),
    query_adornment( NArgs, Ads ),
    name_ads( Ads, StrAds ),
    name(NameAds, StrAds),
    concatenate( [magic_query, '_', NameAds], MFact ).
```

```
generate_initial_answers:-
    $transformed_rule( H, B ),
    call( B ),
    not H,
    assert( $new(1,H) ),
    fail.
generate_initial_answers:-
    accumulate_answers( 1 ).

generate_subsequent_answers:-
    generate_subsequent_answers( 1 ).
generate_subsequent_answers( Step ):-
    generate_new_answers( Step ),
    NewStep is Step+1,
    $new( NewStep, _ ),
    accumulate_answers( NewStep ),
    retractall( $new(Step,_) ),!,
    generate_subsequent_answers( NewStep ).
generate_subsequent_answers( _ ).

generate_new_answers( Step ):-
    NewStep is Step+1,
    $transformed_rule( H, B ),
    instantiate_by_new( Step, B ),
    solve( magic, B ),
    not H,
    not $new( NewStep, H ),
    assert( $new(NewStep,H) ),
    fail.
generate_new_answers( _ ).

accumulate_answers( NewStep ):-
    $new( NewStep, H ),
    asserta( H ),
    fail.
accumulate_answers( _ ).

instantiate_by_new( Step, (B1,B2) ):-
    instantiate_by_new( Step, B1 ) ;
    instantiate_by_new( Step, B2 ).
instantiate_by_new( Step, B ):-
    $new( Step, B ).

%
%   Detect the answers from tuples generated above.
%

detect_answers:-
    standard_adorned_query( AQuery ),
    clause( AQuery, true ),
```

```
    write( AQuery ),nl,
    fail.
detect_answers( _ ).

standard_adorned_query( AQuery ):-
    $query( Query ),
    Query =.. [Pred|Args],
    collect_vars_in_list( Args, NArgs ),
    query_adornment( NArgs, Ads ),
    name_ads( Ads, StrAds ),
    name(NameAds, StrAds),
    concatenate( [query, '_', NameAds], NPred ),
    AQuery =.. [NPred|NArgs].

%
%   Clear the intermediate rules generated during
%   magic sets transformation.
%

clear:-
    abolish( $variable_rule, 3 ),
    abolish( $adorned_rule, 3 ),
    abolish( $magic_rule, 3 ),
    abolish( $modified_rule, 3 ),
    abolish( $complementary_rule, 3 ),
    abolish( $transformed_rule, 2 ),
    deleterule_info(0).

%
%   QUERY EVALUATION BY THE SLDNF PROOF PROCEDURE
%   (a special literal selection rule has been adopted)
%

query( sldnf, Query ):-
    valid_query( Query ),
    solve( sldnf, Query ),
    write(Query), nl,
    fail.
query( _, _ ).

valid_query( Query ):-
    valid_body( Query ).

solve( _, not A ):-!,
    not A.
solve( _, A ):-
    not A = (_,_),
    clause( A, true ).
solve( sldnf, A ):-
    not A = (_,_), !,
```

```
    $rule( _, A, B ),
    solve( sldnf, B ).
solve( X, B ):-
    select_literal( L, B ),
    rest_conj( L, B, RestB ),
    solve( X, L ),
    solve( X, RestB ).

select_literal( L, B ):-
    in_conj( L, B ),
    ( L = (not A), ground( A );
        instantiated_edb_atom( L ) ), !.
select_literal( L, (L,_) ):-!.

rest_conj( L, (M,B), B ):-L==M, !.
rest_conj( L, (B,M), B ):-L==M, !.
rest_conj( L, (M,B), (M,RB) ):-
    rest_conj( L, B, RB ).

instantiated_edb_atom( A ):-
    A =.. [Pred|[]], !,
    $relation( Pred, _, edb ).
instantiated_edb_atom( A ):-
    A =.. [Pred|Vars],
    $relation( Pred, _, edb ),
    instantiated_var( Vars ).

instantiated_var( [H|_] ):-
    nonvar( H ),!.
instantiated_var( [_|T] ):-
    instantiated_var( T ).

%
%   END OF CODE
%
```

References

Abiteboul, S. and Hull, R. (1988). 'Data functions, datalog and negation'. In *Proceedings of the ACM SIGMOD International Conference on Management of Data* (Chicago, Illinois, June), pp. 143–153.

Abramson, H. and Rogers, M. H. (eds.) (1989). *Meta-programming in Logic Programming*. Cambridge, MA: MIT Press.

Agrawal, R. and Jagadish, H. V. (1987). 'Direct algorithms for the transitive closure and database relations'. In *Proceedings of the 13th International Conference on Very Large Data Bases* (Brighton, England, September), pp. 255–266.

Agrawal, R. and Jagadish, H. V. (1988). 'Multiprocessor transitive closure algorithms'. In *Proceedings of International Symposium on Databases in Parallel and Distributed Systems*, pp. 56–66.

Andrews, P. B. (1986). *An Introduction to Mathematical Logic and Type Theory: To Truth Through Proof.* Orlando, Florida: Academic Press.

Apt, K. R., Blair, H. A. and Walker, A. (1988). 'Towards a theory of declarative knowledge'. In *Foundation of Deductive Databases and Logic Programming*, J. Minker (ed.), Los Altos, CA: Morgan Kaufman, pp. 89–148.

Apt, K. R. and Van Emden, M. H. (1982). 'Contributions to the theory of logic programming'. *Journal of the Association for Computing Machinery*, **29**, pp. 841–862.

Asirelli, P., Santis, M. D. and Martelli, M. (1985). 'Integrity constraint in logic databases'. *Journal of Logic Programming*, **3**, pp. 221–232.

Balbin, I. and Ramamohanarao, K. (1987). 'A generalization of the differential approach to recursive query evaluation'. *Journal of Logic Programming*, **4**, pp. 259–262.

Bancilhon, F., Maier, D., Sagiv, Y. and Ullman, J. D. (1986). 'Magic sets and other strange ways to implement logic programs'. In *Proceedings of the 5th ACM SIGMOD-SIGACT Symposium on Principles of Database Systems* (Cambridge, MA, March), pp. 1–15.

Bancilhon, F. and Ramakrishnan, R. (1989). 'An amateur's introduction to recursive query processing strategies'. In *Readings in Artificial Intelligence and Databases*, J. Mylopoulos and M. L. Brodie (eds.), Los Altos, CA:

Morgan Kaufmann, pp. 376–430.

Bancilhon, F. and Spyratos, N. (1981). 'Update semantics of relational views'. *ACM Transactions on Database Systems*, **6**(4), pp. 557–575.

Baratella, S. and File, G. (1988). 'A completeness result for SLDNF-resolution'. In *Bulletin of the European Association for Theoretical Computer Science 46*, pp. 97–105.

Barbuti, R. and Martelli, M. (1986). 'Completeness of the SLDNF-resolution for a class of logic programs'. In *Proceedings of the 3rd International Conference on Logic Programming* (London, July), pp. 600–614.

Barendregt, H. P. (1984). *The Lambda Calculus: Its Syntax and Semantics*. Amsterdam: North-Holland.

Beeri, C. and Ramakrishnan, R. (1987). 'On the power of Magic', In *Proceedings of the 6th ACM SIGMOD-SIGACT Symposium on Principles of Database Systems* (San Diego, CA, March), pp. 269–283.

Berghel, H. L. (1985). 'Simplified integration of Prolog with RDBMS'. *DATA BASE*, **16**(3), pp. 3–12.

Bernstein, P. A., Blaustein, B. T. and Clarke, E. M. (1980). 'Fast maintenance of semantic integrity assertions using redundant aggregate data'. In *Proceedings of the 6th International Conference on Very Large Data Bases* (Montreal, Canada, October), pp. 126–136.

Bertino, E. and Musto, D. (1988). 'Correctness of semantic integrity checking database management systems'. *Acta Informatica*, **26**, pp. 25–57.

Blausius, K., Eisinger, N., Siekmann, J., Smolka, G., Herold, A. and Walther, C. (1981). 'The Markgraf Karl refutation procedure'. In *Proceedings of the 7th International Joint Conference on Artificial Intelligence* (Vancouver, Canada), pp. 511–518.

Blyth, T. S. and Robertson, E. F. (1986). *Abstract Algebra*. London: Chapman and Hill.

Bocca, J. (1986). 'EDUCE: A marriage of convenience – Prolog and relational DBMS'. In *Proceedings of the Symposium on Logic Programming* (Salt Lake City, Utah, USA, September), pp. 36–45.

Bondy, J. A. and Murty, U. S. R. (1976). *Graph Theory with Applications*. London: Macmillan.

Boole, G. (1948). *The Mathematical Analysis of Logic: Being an Essay Towards a Calculus of Deductive Reasoning*. Oxford, England: Basil Blackwell.

Boolos, G. S. and Jeffrey, R. C. (1988). *Computability and Logic*. Cambridge, England: Cambridge University Press.

Bratko, I. (1990). *Prolog Programming for Artificial Intelligence*, 2nd Edition. Wokingham, England: Addison-Wesley.

Brodie, M. L. and Jarke, M. (1989). 'On integrating logic programming and databases'. In *Expert Database Systems*, L. Kerschberg (ed.), pp. 191–205.

Brodie, M. L. and Manola, F. (1989). 'Database management: A survey'. In *Readings in Artificial Intelligence and Databases*, I. Mylopoulos and M. L. Brodie (eds.), Los Altos, CA: Morgan Kaufmann, pp. 10–34.

Bry, F., Decker, H. and Manthey, R. (1988). 'A uniform approach to constraint satisfaction and constraint satisfiability in deductive databases'. In *Proceedings of International Conference on Extending Database Technology* (Venice, Italy, March), pp. 488–505.

Bry, F. and Manthey, R. (1986). 'Checking consistency of database constraints: A logical basis'. In *Proceedings of the 12th International Conference on Very Large Data Bases* (Kyoto, Japan, August), pp. 25–28.

Carlson, C. R., Arora, A. K. and Carlson, M. M. (1982). 'The application of functional dependency theory to relational databases'. *The Computer Journal*, **25**(1), pp. 68–73.

Casanova, M. A., Tucherman, L. and Furtado, A. L. (1988). 'Enforcing inclusion dependencies and referential integrity'. In *Proceedings of the 14th International Conference on Very Large Data Bases* (Los Angeles, CA, August), pp. 38–49.

Cavedon, L. and Lloyd, J. W. (1989). 'A Completeness theorem for SLDNF-resolution'. *Journal of Logic Programming*, **7**, pp. 177–191.

Ceri, S., Gottlob, G. and Tanca, L. (1990). *Logic Programming and Databases*. Berlin, Germany: Springer-Verlag.

Chan, D. (1988). 'Constructive negation based on the completed database'. In *Proceedings of the 5th International Conference and Symposium on Logic Programming* (Seattle, USA, August), pp. 111–125.

Chandra, A. K. (1988). 'Theory of database queries'. In *Proceedings of the 7th ACM SIGACT-SIGMOD-SIGART Symposium on Principles of Database Systems* (Austin, Texas, March), pp. 1–9.

Chandra, A. and Harel, D. (1985). 'Horn clause queries and generalizations'. *Journal of Logic Programming*, **1**, pp. 1–15.

Chang, C. L. (1970). 'The unit proof and the input proof in theorem proving'. *Journal of the Association for Computing Machinery*, **17**(4), pp. 698–707.

Chang, C. L. (1981). 'On evaluation of queries containing derived relations in a relational databases'. In *Advances in Database Theory 1*, H. Gallaire, J. Minker and J. M. Nicolas (eds.), New York: Plenum Press, pp. 235–260.

Chang, C. L. and Lee, R. C. T. (1973). *Symbolic Logic and Mechanical Theorem Proving*. New York: Academic Press.

Chang, C. L. and Walker, A. (1986). 'PROSQL: a prolog programming interface with SQL/DS'. In *Proceedings of the 1st International Conference on Expert Database Systems* (Charleston, South Carolina, April), pp. 233–246.

Chen, W., Kifer, M. and Warren, D. S. (1989). 'HiLog: a first-order semantics of higher-order logic programming constructs'. In *Proceedings of the North American Conference on Logic Programming* (October), pp. 1090–1114.

Church, A. (1940). 'A formulation of the simple theory of types'. *Journal of Symbolic Logic*, **5**, pp. 56–68.

Church, A. (1952). *Introduction to Mathematical Logic*. Princeton, New Jersey: Princeton University Press.

Church, A. and others (1978). 'Logic: Applied, Formal, History and Philosophy'. In *Encyclopedia Britannica*, **15**, pp. 28–77.

Clark, K. L. (1978). 'Negation as failure'. In *Logic and Databases*, H. Gallaire and J. Minker (eds.), New York: Plenum Press, pp. 293–322.

Clark, K. L. (1979). 'Predicate logic as a computational formalism'. *Research Report DOC 79/59*, Department of Computer Science, Imperial College, London.

Clocksin, W. F. and Mellish, C. S. (1984). *Programming in Prolog*. Berlin, Germany: Springer-Verlag.

Codd, E. F. (1970). 'A relational model for large shared data banks'. *Communications of the ACM*, **13**(6), pp. 377–387.

Cohen, D. E. (1989). *Computability and Logic*. England: Ellis Horwood.

Colmerauer, A. (1990). 'An introduction to Prolog III'. In *Computational Logic*, J. Lloyd (ed.), Berlin, Germany: Springer-Verlag, pp. 37–79.

Colmerauer, A., Kanoui, A. H., Roussel, P. and Pasero, R. (1973). 'Un Systeme de Communication Homme-Machine en Francais'. Marseille, France: Groupe de Recherche en Intelligence Artificielle, Universite d'Aix-Marseille.

Copi, I. M. (1979). *Symbolic Logic*. New York: Macmillan.

Cosmadakis, S. S. and Kanellakis, P. C. (1985). 'Equational theories and database constraints'. In *Proceedings of the ACM SIGACT-SIGMOD-SIGART Symposium on Principles of Database Systems.*

Cremers, A. B. and Domann, G. (1983). 'AIM: An integrity monitor for the database system INGRES'. In *Proceedings of the 9th International Conference on Very Large Data Bases* (Florence, Italy, October-November), pp. 167–170.

Das, S. K. (1990). 'Integrity constraints in deductive databases'. *PhD Thesis*, Department of Computer Science, Heriot-Watt University, Edinburgh, Scotland.

Das, S. K. (1991a). 'Specifying deductive database and integrity constraints in typed lambda-calculus'. In *Proceeding of the International Workshop on Specifications of Database Systems* (Glasgow, Scotland, January), London: Springer-Verlag, pp. 64–87.

Das, S. K. (1991b). 'Query processing strategies in deductive databases: characteristics establishment and performance evaluation'. *Research Report*, Department of Computer Science, Heriot-Watt University, Edinburgh, Scotland.

Das, S. K. (1991c). 'Network evaluation of recursive queries'. *Research Report*, Department of Computer Science, Heriot-Watt University, Edinburgh, Scotland.

Das, S. K. and Williams, M. H. (1989a). 'A path finding method for checking integrity in deductive databases'. *Data & Knowledge Engineering*, **4**, Amsterdam: Elsevier Science (North-Holland), pp. 223–244.

Das, S. K. and Williams, M. H. (1989b). 'Integrity checking methods in deductive databases: A comparative evaluation'. In *Proceedings of the 7th British National Conference on Databases* (Edinburgh, Scotland, July), Cambridge, England: Cambridge University Press, pp. 85–116.

Das, S. K. and Williams, M. H. (1990). 'Extending integrity maintenance capability in deductive databases'. In *Proceedings of the UK ALP-90 Conference* (Bristol, England, January), Oxford, England: Intellect, pp. 75–111.

Date, C. J. (1981). 'Referential integrity'. In *Proceedings of the 7th International Conference on Very Large Data Bases* (Cannes, France, September), pp. 2–12.

Date, C. J. (1985). *An Introduction to Database Systems*, Volume 2. Reading, MA: Addison-Wesley.

Date, C. J. (1986). *An Introduction to Database Systems*, Volume 1, 4th edition. Reading, MA: Addison-Wesley.

Date, C. J. (1989). *A Guide to SQL Standard.* Reading, MA: Addison-Wesley.

Davey, B. A. and Priestley, H. A. (1990). *Introduction to Lattices and Order.* Cambridge, England: Cambridge University Press.

Davis, M. (1980). 'The mathematics of non-monotonic reasoning'. *Artificial Intelligence*, **13**, pp. 73–80.

Davis, M. and Putnam, H. (1960). 'A computing procedure for quantification theory'. *Journal of the Association for Computing Machinery*, **7**, pp. 201–215.

Dayal, U. and Bernstein, P. A. (1978). 'On the updatability of relational views'. In *Proceedings of the 4th VLDB Conference* (West Berlin, September).

Decker, H. (1986). 'Integrity enforcements on deductive databases'. In *Proceedings of the 1st International Conference on Expert Database Systems* (Charleston, South Carolina, April), pp. 271–285.

Decker, H. (1991). 'On generalized cover axioms'. In *Proceedings of the 8th International Conference on Logic Programming* (Paris, June), pp. 693–707.

Delong, H. (1970). *A Profile of Mathematical Logic.* Reading, MA: Addison-Wesley.

Deo, N. (1974). *Graph Theory with Applications to Engineering and Computer Science*, Prentice-Hall.

Deville, Y. (1991). *Logic Peogramming: Systematic Program Development*, Wokingham, England: Addison-Wesley.

Elcock, E. W. (1988). 'Absys: The first logic programming language - A retrospective and a commentary'. *Technical Report No. 210* (July), Department of Computer Science, The University of Western Ontario, Canada.

Enderton, H. B. (1972). *A Mathematical Introduction to Logic.* New York: Academic Press.

Eswaran, K. P. and Chamberlin, D. D. (1975). 'Functional specification of a subsystem for database integrity'. In *Proceedings of the 1st International Conference on Very Large Data Bases* (Framingham, Massachusetts, September).

Fagin, R., Kuper, G. M., Ullman, J. D. and Vardi, M. Y. (1986). 'Updating logical databases'. *Advances in Computing Research*, **3**, JAI Press, pp. 1–18.

Fagin, R. and Vardi, M. Y. (1984). 'The theory of data dependencies: a survey'. *Research Report RJ 4321 (47149)*, IBM Research Laboratory, San Jose, California.

Falaschi, M., Levi, G., Martelli, M. and Palamidessi, C. (1988). 'A new declarative semantics for logic languages'. In *Proceedings of the 5th International Conference and Symposium on Logic Programming* (Seattle, USA, August), pp. 993–1005.

Fernandez, E. B., Summers, R. C. and Wood, C. (1981). *Database Security and Integrity*, Reading, MA: Addison-Wesley.

Fitting, M. (1985). 'A deterministics Prolog fixpoint semantics'. *Journal of Logic Programming*, **2**, pp. 111–118.

Fitting, M. C. (1986). 'A Kripke-Kleene semantics for logic programs'. *Journal of Logic Programming*, **3**, pp. 93–114.

Fitting, M. and Ben-Jacob, M. (1988). 'Stratified and three-valued logic programming semantics'. In *Proceedings of the 5th International Conference and Symposium on Logic Programming* (Seattle, USA, August), pp. 1054–1069.

Fraenkel, A. A. and Bar-Hillel, Y. (1984). *Foundations of Set Theory*, Amsterdam: North-Holland.

Futo, I., Darvas, F., and Szeredi, P. (1978). 'The application of Prolog to the development of QA and DBM systems'. In *Logic and Databases*, H. Gallaire and J. Minker (eds.), New York: Plenum Press.

Gabby, D. M. and Sergot, M. J. (1986). 'Negation as inconsistency'. *Journal of Logic Programming*, **1**, pp. 1–35.

Gallaire, H. (1983). 'Logic databases vs deductive databases'. In *Proceedings of Logic Programming Workshop* (Algarve, Portugal, June-July), pp. 608–622.

Gallaire, H. (1986). 'Boosting logic programming', *Technical Report 86*, ECRC, Munich, Germany.

Gallaire, H., Minker, J. and Nicolas, J. M. (1978). 'An overview and introduction to logic and databases'. In *Logic and Databases*, H. Gallaire and J. Minker (eds.), New York: Plenum Press, pp. 3–30.

Gallaire, H. and Minker, J. (eds.) (1978). *Logic and Databases*, New York: Plenum Press.

Gallaire, H., Minker, J. and Nicolas, J. M. (eds.) (1981a). *Advances in Database Theory 1*, Plenum Press, New York.

Gallaire, H., Minker, J. and Nicolas, J. M. (1981b). 'Background for advances in database theory'. In *Advances in Database Theory 1*, H. Gallaire, J. Minker and J. M. Nicolas (eds.), New York: Plenum Press, pp. 3–21.

Gallaire, H., Minker, J. and Nicolas, J. M. (eds.) (1983). *Advances in Database Theory 2*, New York: Plenum Press.

Gallaire, H., Minker, J. and Nicolas, J. M. (1984). 'Logic and databases: a deductive approach', *ACM Computing Surveys*, **16**(2), pp. 153–185.

Gallier, J. H. (1987). *Logic for Computer Science*, New York: John Wiley & Sons.

Ganguly, S., Silberschatz, A. and Tsur, S. (1990). 'A framework for the parallel processing of Datalog queries'. In *Proceedings of the ACM SIGMOD International Conference on Management of Data* (Atlantic City, NJ, May), pp. 143–152.

Gardarin, G. (1987). 'Magic Functions: a technique to optimize extended datalog recursive programs'. In *Proceedings of the 13th International Conference on Very Large Data Bases* (Brighton, England, September), pp. 21–30.

Gardarin, G. and Valduriez, P. (1989). *Relational Databases and Knowledge Bases*. Reading, MA: Addison-Wesley.

Gelfond, M. and Lifschitz, V. (1988). 'The stable model semantics for logic programming'. In *Proceedings of the 5th International Conference and Symposium on Logic Programming* (Seattle, USA, August), pp. 1070–1080.

Gelfond, M. and Przymusinska, H. (1986). 'Negation as failure: Careful closure procedure'. *Artificial Intelligence*, **30**, pp. 273–287, Amsterdam: North-Holland.

Gilmore, P. C. (1960). 'A proof method for quantification theory'. *IBM Journal of Research and Development*, **4**, pp. 28–35.

Ginsberg, M. L. (ed.) (1987). *Readings in Nonmonotonic Reasoning*, Los Altos, CA: Morgan Kaufmann.

Goebel, R., Furukawa, K. and Poole, D. (1986). 'Using definite clauses and integrity constraints as the basis for a theory formation approach to diagnostic reasoning'. In *Proceedings of the 3rd International Conference on Logic Programming* (London, July), pp. 211–222.

Goodstein, R. L. (1971). *Development of Mathematical Logic*. London: Logos Press.

Grant, J. and Minker, J. (1989). 'Deductive database theories'. *Knowledge Engineering Review*, **4**, pp. 267–304.

Gray, P. and Lucas, R. (eds.) (1988). *Prolog and Databases: Implementations and New Directions*. England: Ellis Horwood.

Green, C. (1969a). 'Theorem-proving by resolution as a basis for question-answering'. *Machine Intelligence 4*, B. Meltzer and D. Michie (eds.), Edinburgh, Scotland: Edinburgh University Press, pp. 183–205.

Green, C. (1969b). 'Applications of theorem proving to problem solving'. In *Proceedings of the International Joint Conference on Artificial Intelligence (Washington, D. C.), pp. 219–239.*

Griefahn, U. and Luttringhans, S. (1990). 'Top-down integrity constraint checking for deductive databases'. In *Proceedings of the 7th International Conference on Logic Programming* (Jerusalem, Israel).

Guessoum, A. and Lloyd, J. W. (1990). 'Updating knowledge bases'. *New Generation Computing*, **8**, pp. 71–89.

Guessoum, A. and Lloyd, J. W. (1991). 'Updating knowledge bases II'. *New Generation Computing*, **10**, pp. 73–100.

Halmos, P. R. (1974). *Naive Set Theory*. New York: Springer-Verlag.

Han, J., Qadah, G. and Chaou, C. (1988). 'The processing of the transitive closure queries'. In *Proceedings of International Conference on Extending Database Technology* (Venice, Italy).

Harary, F. (1969). *Graph Theory*. Reading, MA: Addison-Wesley.

Henkin, L. (1950). 'Completeness in the theory of types'. *Journal of Symbolic Logic*, **15**, pp. 81–91.

Henkin, L. (1963). 'A theory of propositional types'. *Fundamental Mathematics*, **52**, pp. 323–344.

Henschen, L. J. and Naqvi, S. A. (1984). 'On compiling queries in recursive first order databases'. *Journal of the Association for Computing Machinery*, **31**(1), pp. 47–85.

Herbrand, J. (1930). 'Investigations in proof theory: the properties of the propositions'. In *From Frege to Gödel: A Source Book in Mathematical Logic*, J. Van Heijenoort (ed.), Cambridge, MA: Harvard University Press.

Herstein, I. N. (1964). *Topics in Algebra*. London: John Wiley & Sons.

Hilbert, D. and Ackermann, W. (1950). *Principles of Mathematical Logic*. New York: Chelsea Publishing Company.

Hill, R. (1974). 'LUSH-resolution and its Completeness'. *DCL Memo 78*, Department of Artificial Intelligence, University of Edinburgh.

Hill, P. M. and Lloyd, J. W. (1989). 'Analysis of meta-programs'. In *Meta-programming in Logic Programming*, H. Abramson and M. H. Rogers (eds.), Cambridge, MA: MIT Press, pp. 23–51.

Hill, P. M. and Lloyd, J. W. (1991). 'The Gödel Report'. *Technical Report 91-02*, University of Bristol, Bristol.

Hindley, J. R. and Seldin, J. P. (1990). *Introduction to Combinators and Lambda-calculus*. Cambridge, England: Cambridge University Press.

Hodges, W. (1988). *Logic: An Introduction to Elementary Logic*. London: Penguin Books.

Hogger, C. J. (1984). *Introduction to Logic Programming*. London: Academic Press.

Hudak, P. (1989). 'Conception, evolution, and application of functional programming'. *ACM Computing Surveys*, **21**, pp. 359–411.

Huet, G. P. (1975). 'A unification algorithm for typed lambda-calculus'. *Theoretical Computer Science*, **1**, pp. 27–57.

Hulin, G. (1989). 'Parallel processing of recursive queries in distributed architecture'. In *Proceedings of the 15th International Conference on Very Large Data Bases* (Amsterdam, Netherlands, August), pp. 87–96.

Ioannidis, Y. E. and Ramakrishnan, R. (1988). 'Efficient transitive closure algorithms'. In *Proceedings of the 14th International Conference on Very Large Data Bases* (Los Angeles, CA, August), pp. 382–394.

Jaffar, J., Lassez, J. L. and Lloyd, J. (1983). 'Completeness of the negation as failure rule'. In *Proceedings of the 8th International Joint Conference on Artificial Intelligence* (Karlsruhe, Germany, August), pp. 500–506.

J. Jaffar, J. L. Lassez and M. J. Maher (1986). 'Some issues and trends in the semantics of logic programming'. In *Proceedings of the 3rd International Conference on Logic Programming* (London, July), pp. 223–241.

Jorgensen, J. (1931). *A Treatise of Mathematical Logic*, 1, 2 & 3. London: Humpherey, Milford, Oxford University Press.

Kanellakis, P. C. (1986). 'Logic programming and parallel complexity'. In *Proceedings of the International Conference on Database Theory* (Rome, Italy, September), pp. 1–29.

Kaplan, D. and Montague, R. (1965). 'Foundations of higher-order logic'. In *Logic, Methodology and Philosophy of Science: Proceeding of the 1964 International Congress*, Y. Bar-Hillel (ed.), Amsterdam: North-Holland, pp. 101–109.

Keynes, J. N. (1928). *Studies and Exercises in Formal Logic.* London: McMillan and Co.

Kifer, M. and Lozinskii, E. L. (1986). 'Filtering dataflow in deductive databases'. In *Proceedings of the International Conference on Database Theory* (Rome, Italy, September), pp. 186–202.

Kleene, S. C. (1967). *Introduction to Metamathematics.* Amsterdam: North-Holland.

Knight, K. (1989). 'Unification: A multidisciplinary survey'. *ACM Computing Surveys*, **21**(1), pp. 93–124.

Kobayashi, I. (1984). 'Validating database updates'. *Information Systems*, **9**, Oxford, England: Pergamon Press, pp. 1–17.

Koenig, S. and Paige, R. (1981). 'A transformational framework for the automatic control of derived data'. In *Proceedings of the 7th International Conference on Very Large Data Bases* (Cannes, France, September), pp. 306–318.

Kolaitis, P. G. and Papadimitriou, C. H. (1988). 'Why not negation by fixpoint?'. *Proceedings of the 7th ACM SIGACT-SIGMOD-SIGART Symposium on Principles of Database Systems* (Austin, Texas, March), pp. 231–239.

R. A. Kowalski, R. A. (1974). 'Predicate logic as a programming language'. In *Proceeding of 4th IFIP World Congress*, Amsterdam: North-Holland, pp. 569–574.

R. A. Kowalski, R. A. (1975). 'A proof procedure using connection graphs'. *Journal of the Association for Computing Machinery*, **22**(4), pp. 572–595.

Kowalski, R. A. (1979a). *Logic for Problem Solving*, New York: North-Holland.

Kowalski, R. A. (1979b). 'Algorithm = Logic + Control'. *Communications of the ACM*, **22**(7), pp. 424–435.

Kowalski, R. A. (1985). 'Directions for logic programming'. In *Proceedings of the 1985 Symposium on Logic Programming* (Salt Lake City, Utah, USA, July), IEEE Computer Society Press, pp. 2–7.

Kowalski, R. A. and Kuehner, D. (1971). 'Linear resolution with selection function'. *Artificial Intelligence*, **2**, pp. 227–260.

Kowalski, R. A., Sadri, F. and Soper, P. (1987). 'Integrity checking in deductive databases'. In *Proceedings of the 13th International Conference on Very Large Data Bases* (Brighton, England, September), pp. 61–69.

Kunen, K. (1988). 'Some remarks on the completed database'. In *Proceedings of the 5th International Conference and Symposium on Logic Programming* (Seattle, USA, August), pp. 978–992.

Kunen, K. (1991). 'Declarative semantics of logic programming'. In *Bulletin of the European Association for Theoretical Computer Science 44*, pp. 147–167.

Lassez, J. L., Nguyen, V. L. and Sonenberg, E. A. (1982). 'Fixed point theorems and semantics: A folk tale'. *Information Processing Letters*, **14**(3), pp. 112–116.

Lemmon, E. J. (1988). *Beginning Logic*, Surrey, England: Thomas Nelson and Sons.

Leung, Y. Y. and Lee, D. L. (1988). 'Logic approaches for deductive databases'. *IEEE Expert* (Winter), pp. 64–75.

Lifschitz, V. (1985a). 'Closed-world databases and circumscription'. *Artificial Intelligence*, **27**, pp. 229–235.

Lifschitz, V. (1985b). 'Computing circumscription'. In *Proceedings of the 9th International Joint Conference on Artificial Intelligence* (Los Angeles, USA, August), pp. 121–127.

Ling, T. W. (1987). 'Integrity constraint checking in deductive databases using the Prolog not-predicate'. *Data & Knowledge Engineering*, **2**, pp. 145–168.

Lloyd, J. W. (1983). 'An introduction to deductive database systems'. *The Australian Computer Journal*, **15**(2), pp. 52–57.

Lloyd, J. W. (1987). *Foundations of Logic Programming*, 2nd Edition, Berlin, Germany: Springer Verlag.

Lloyd, J. W. and Topor, R. W. (1984). 'Making Prolog more expressive'. *Journal of Logic Programming*, **1**(3), pp. 225–240.

Lloyd, J. W. and Topor, R. W. (1985). 'A basis for deductive database systems'. *Journal of Logic Programming*, **2**(2), pp. 93–109.

Lloyd, J. W., Sonenberg, E. A. and Topor, R. W. (1986). 'Integrity constraint checking in stratified databases'. *Technical Report 86/5*, Department of Computer Science, University of Melbourne, Melbourne, Australia.

Lobo, A., Minker, J. and Rajasekar, A. (1988). 'Weak completion theory for non-Horn logic programs'. In *Proceedings of the 5th International Conference and Symposium on Logic Programming* (Seattle, USA, August), pp. 828–842.

Loveland, D. W. (1969). 'Theorem-provers combining model elimination and resolution'. *Machine Intelligence 4*, B. Meltzer and D. Michie (eds.), Edinburgh, Scotland: Edinburgh University Press, pp. 73–86.

Loveland, D. W. (1978). *Automated Theorem Proving*, Amsterdam: North-Holland.

Loveland, D. W. (1987). 'Near-Horn Prolog'. In *Proceedings of the 4th International Conference on Logic Programming* (Tokyo, Japan, July), pp. 456–469.

Lozinskii, E. L. (1985). 'Evaluating queries in deductive databases by generating'. In *Proceedings of the 9th International Joint Conference on Artificial Intelligence* (Los Angeles, USA, August), pp. 173–177.

Maher, M. J. (1986). 'Equivalence of logic programs'. In *Proceedings of the 3rd International Conference on Logic Programming* (London July), pp. 410–424.

Maier, D. and Warren, D. S. (1988). *Computing with Logic: Logic Programming with Prolog*. Menlo Park, California: Benjamin/Cummings.

Mancarella, P., Martini, S. and Pedreschi, D. (1988). 'Complete logic programs with domain-closure axiom'. *Journal of Logic Programming*, **5**, pp. 263–276.

Mancarella, P. and Pedreschi, D. (1988). 'An algebra of logic programs'. In *Proceedings of the 5th International Conference and Symposium on Logic Programming* (Seattle, USA, August), R. A. Kowalski and K. A. Bowen (eds.), pp. 1006–1023.

Martelli, A. and Montanari, U. (1982). 'An efficient unification algorithm'. *ACM Transactions on Programming Languages and Systems*, **4**(2), pp. 258–282.

Matilal, B. K. (1985). *Logic, Language & Reality: An Introduction to Indian Philosophical Studies*, New Delhi, India: Motilal Banarsidass.

Mazumdar, S., Stemple, D. and Sheard, T. (1988). 'Resolving the tension between integrity and security using a theorem prover'. In *Proceedings of the ACM SIGMOD International Conference on Management of Data* (Chicago, Illinois, June), pp. 233–242.

McCarthy, J. (1980). 'Circumscription: A form of non-monotonic reasoning'. *Artificial Intelligence*, **13**, pp. 27–39.

McCarthy, J. (1984). 'Applications of circumscription to formalizing common sense knowledge'. In *Proceeding of AAI workshop on non-monotonic reasoning* (October), pp. 295–323.

McDermott, D. and Doyle, J. (1988). 'Non-monotonic logic I'. In *Readings in Nonmonotonic Reasoning*, M. Ginsberg (ed.), Los Altos, CA: Morgan Kaufmann, pp. 111–126.

Mendelson, E. (1987). *Introduction to Mathematical Logic*. California, USA: *Wadsworth & Brooks/Cole Advanced Books and Software.*

Miller, D. A. and Nadathur, G. (1986). 'Higher-order logic programming'. In *Proceedings of the 3rd International Conference on Logic Programming* (London, July), pp. 448–462.

Minker, J. (1988a). 'On indefinite databases and closed world assumption'. In *Readings for Nonmonotonic Reasoning*, M. Ginsberg (ed.), Los Altos, CA: Morgan Kaufmann.

Minker, J. (1988b). 'Perspectives in deductive databases'. *Journal of Logic Programming*, **5**, pp. 33–60.

Minker, J. and Nicolas, J. M. (1983). 'On recursive axioms in deductive databases'. *Information Systems*, **8**(1), Oxford, England: Pergamon Press, pp. 1–13.

Minker, J. and Rajasekar, A. (1988). 'Procedural interpretation of non-Horn logic programs'. In *Proceedings of the 9th International Conference in Automated Deduction* (May), pp. 278–293.

Minker, J. and Rajasekar, A. (1989). 'A fixpoint semantics for non-Horn logic programs'. *Journal of Logic Programming*.

Moerkotte, G. and Karl, S. (1988). 'Efficient consistency control in deductive databases'. In *Proceedings of the International Conference on Database Theory*, pp. 118–128.

Moinard, Y. (1988). 'Pointwise circumscription is equivalent to predicate completion (sometimes)'. In *Proceedings of the 5th International Conference and Symposium on Logic Programming* (Seattle, USA, August), pp. 1097–1105.

Motro, A. (1989). 'Using integrity constraints to provide intensional answers to relational queries'. In *Proceedings of the 15th International Conference on Very Large Data Bases* (Amsterdam, Netherlands, August), pp. 237–246.

Nadathur, G. and Miller, A. (1988). 'An overview of Lambda-Prolog'. In *Proceedings of the 5th International Conference and Symposium on Logic Programming* (Seattle, USA, August), pp. 810–827.

Naqvi, S. A. (1986b). 'Some extensions to the closed world assumption in databases', *Proceedings of the International Conference on Database Theory* (Rome, Italy, September), pp. 341–348.

Naqvi, S. A. and Krishnamurthy, R. (1988). 'Database updates in logic programming'. In *Proceeding of the 7th Annual ACM Symposium on Principles of Database Systems* (Austin, Texas).

Naqvi, S. and Tsur, S. (1989). *A Logical Language for Data and Knowledge Bases*, New York: Computer Science Press.

Naughton, J. F. (1988). 'Compiling separable recursions'. In *Proceedings of the ACM SIGMOD International Conference on Management of Data* (Chicago, Illinois, June), pp. 312–319.

Nejdi, W. (1987). 'Recursive strategy for answering recursive queries: The RQA/FQI strategy'. In *Proceedings of the 13th International Conference on Very Large Data Bases* (Brighton, England, Brighton), pp. 43–50.

Newton-Smith, W. H. (1985). *Logic: An Introductory Course*. London: Routledge & Kegan Paul.

Nicolas, J. M. (1982). 'Logic for improving integrity checking in relational databases'. *Acta Informatica*, **18**, pp. 227–253.

Nicolas, J. M. and Gallaire, H. (1978). 'Database: Theory vs. interpretation'. In *Logic and Databases*, H. Gallaire and J. Minker (eds.), New York: Plenum Press, pp. 33–54.

Nicolas, J. M. and Yazdanian, K. (1978). 'Integrity checking in deductive databases'. In *Logic and Databases*, H. Gallaire and J. Minker (eds.), New York: Plenum Press, pp. 325–344.

Nidditch, P. H. (1962). *The Development of Mathematical Logic*. New York: Routledge & Kegan Paul.

O'Keefe, R. A. (1990). *Craft of Prolog*. Cambridge, MA: MIT Press.

Paredaens, J.(1980). 'The interaction of integrity constraints in an information system'. *Journal of Computer and System Sciences*, **20**(3), pp. 310–329.

Paterson, M. S.(1978). 'Linear unification'. *Journal of Computer and Systems Sciences*, **16**, pp. 158–167.

Prawitz, D. (1969). 'Advances and problems in mechanical proof procedures'. In *Machine Intelligence 4*, B. Meltzer and D. Michie (eds.), Edinburgh, Scotland: Edinburgh University Press, pp. 59–72.

Przymusinska, H. and Przymusinski, T. C. (1988). 'Weakly perfect model semantics for logic programs'. In *Proceedings of the 5th International Conference and Symposium on Logic Programming* (Seattle, USA, August), pp. 1106–1120.

Przymusinski, T. C. (1988a). 'On the declarative semantics of deductive databases and logic programs'. In *Foundation of Deductive Databases and Logic Programming*, J. Minker (ed.), Los Altos, CA: Morgan Kaufman, pp. 193–216.

Przymusinski, T. C. (1988b). 'Perfect model semantics'. In *Proceedings of the fifth International Conference and Symposium on Logic Programming* (Seattle, USA, August), pp. 1081–1096.

Przymusinski, T. C. (1989). 'Every logic program has a natural stratification and an iterated least fixed point model'. In *Proceedings of the 8th ACM SIGACT-SIGMOD-SIGART Symposium on Principles of Database Systems*, pp. 11–21.

Qian. X. and Smith, D. R. (1987). 'Integrity constraint reformulation for efficient validation'. In *Proceedings of the 13th International Conference on Very Large Data Bases* (Brighton, England, September), pp. 417–425.

Quine, W. V. O. (1980). *Elementary Logic*. Cambridge, MA: Harvard University Press.

Raatz, S. and Gallier, J. (1988). 'A relational semantics for logic programming'. In *Proceedings of the 5th International Conference and Symposium on Logic Programming* (Seattle, USA, August), pp. 1024–1035.

Ramamohanarao, K. *et al.* (1988). 'The NU-Prolog deductive database systems'. In *Prolog and Databases: Implementations and New Directions*, England: Ellis Horwood, pp. 212–250.

Reiter, R. (1978b). 'On closed world databases'. In *Logic and Databases*, H. Gallaire and J. Minker (eds.), New York: Plenum Press, pp. 55–76.

Reiter, R. (1981). 'On the integrity of typed first order databases'. In *Advances in Database Theory 1*, H. Gallaire, J. Minker and J. M. Nicolas (eds.), New York: Plenum Press, pp. 137–157.

Robinson, J. A. (1965a). 'Automatic deduction with hyper-resolution'. *International Journal of Computational Mathematics*, **1**, pp. 227–234.

Robinson, J. A. (1965b). 'A machine-oriented logic based on the resolution principle'. *Journal of the Association for Computing Machinery*, **12**, pp. 23–41.

Robinson, J. A. (1969). 'Mechanizing higher-order logic'. In *Machine Intelligence 4 & 5*, B. Meltzer and D. Michie (eds.), Edinburgh, Scotland: Edinburgh University Press.

Robinson, J. A. (1971). 'Computational logic: The unification computation'. In Machine Intelligence 6, B. Meltzer and D. Michie (eds.), Edinburgh, Scotland: Edinburgh University Press, pp. 63–72.

Robinson, J. A. (1979). *Logic: Form and Function*. Elsevier Science (North-Holland).

Robinson, J. A. and Wos, L. (1969). 'Paramodulation and theorem-proving in first-order theories with equality'. In *Machine Intelligence 4*, B. Meltzer and D. Michie (eds.), Edinburgh, Scotland: Edinburgh University Press, pp. 135–150.

Rohmer, J., Lescoeur, R. and Kerisit, J. M. (1986). 'The Alexander method: A technique for the processing of recursive axioms in deductive databases'. *New Generation Computing*, **4**, OHMSHA and Springer-Verlag, pp. 273–285.

Ross, K. A. (1989). 'A procedural semantics for well-founded negation in logic programs'. In *Proceedings of the 8th ACM SIGACT-SIGMOD-SIGART Symposium on Principles of Database Systems.*

Ross, K. A. and Topor, R. W. (1988). 'Inferring negative information from disjunctive databases'. *Journal of Automated Reasoning*, **4**, pp. 397–424.

Roussel, P. (1975). 'PROLOG: Manuel de Reference et d'Utilization'. Marseille, France: Groupe de Recherche en Intelligence Artificielle, Universite d'Aix-Marseille.

Russell, B. (1948). *Introduction to Mathematical Philosophy*, London: George Allen & Unwin.

Sacca, D. and Zaniolo, C. (1986). 'The generalized Counting method for recursive logic queries'. In *Proceedings of the International Conference on Database Theory* (Rome, September), pp. 31–53.

Sacca, D. and Zaniolo, C. (1987). 'Magic counting methods'. In *Proceedings of the ACM SIGMOD Conference* (San Francisco, CA, May).

Sadri, F. and Kowalski, R. A. (1987). 'An theorem-proving approach to database integrity'. In *Foundation of Deductive Databases and Logic Programming*, J. Minker (ed.), Los Altos, CA: Morgan Kaufman, pp. 313–362.

Schwind, C. B. (1984). 'Embedding deductive capabilities in relational database systems'. *International Journal of Computer and Information Sciences*, **13**(5), pp. 327–338.

Seki, H. and Itoh, H. (1988). 'A query evaluation method for stratified programs under the extended CWA'. In *Proceedings of the 5th International Conference and Symposium on Logic Programming* (Seattle, USA, August), pp. 195–211.

Shao, J., Bell D. A. and Hull, M. E. C. (1990). 'An experimental performance study of a pipelined recursive query processing strategy'. In *Proceeding of the 2nd International Symposium on Databases in Parallel and Distributed Systems* (Trinity College, Dublin, Ireland, July), pp. 30–43.

Shepherdson, J. C. (1984). 'Negation as failure: A comparison of Clerk's completed database and Reiter's closed world assumption'. *Journal of Logic Programming*, **1**, pp. 51–79.

Sinclair, W. A. (1937). *The Traditional Formal Logic*. London: Methuen.

Smith, B. T. and Loveland, D. W. (1988). 'A simple near-Horn Prolog interpreter'. In *Proceedings of the 5th International Conference and Symposium on Logic Programming* (Seattle, USA, August), pp. 794–809.

Snyder, W. and Gallier, J. (1989). 'Higher-order unification revisited: Complete sets of transformations'. *Journal of Symbolic Computation*, **8**, pp. 101–140.

Staples, J., Robinson, P. J., Paterson, R. A., Hagen, R. A., Craddock, A. J. and Wallis, P. C. (1989). 'Qu-Prolog: an extended Prolog for meta level programming'. In *Meta-programming in Logic Programming*, H. Abramson and M. H. Rogers (eds.), Cambridge, MA: MIT Press, pp. 435–452.

Sterling, A. and Lakhotia, A. (1988). 'Composing Prolog meta-interpreters'. In *Proceedings of the 5th International Conference and Symposium on Logic Programming* (Seattle, USA, August), pp. 386–403.

Sterling, L. and Shapiro, E. (1986). *The Art of Prolog*. Cambridge, MA: MIT Press.

Stickel, M. E. (1988). 'Resolution theorem proving'. *Annual Review: Computer Science*, **3**, pp. 285–316.

Stoll, R. R. (1963). *Set Theory and Logic*, New York: W. H. Freeman and Company.

Stonebraker, M. (1989). 'Implementation of integrity constraints and views by query modification'. In *Readings in Artificial Intelligence and Databases*, I. Mylopoulos and M. L. Brodie (eds.), Los Altos, CA: Morgan Kaufmann, pp. 533–546.

Subrahmanian, V. S. (1989). 'A simple formulation of the theory of metalogic programming'. In *Meta-programming in Logic Programming*, H. Abramson and M. H. Rogers (eds.), Cambridge, MA: MIT Press, pp. 65–101.

Tarnlund, S. A. (1986). 'Logic Programming: from logic point of view'. In *Proceedings of the Symposium on Logic Programming* (Salt Lake City, Utah, September), IEEE Computer Society Press, pp. 96–103.

Tarski, A. (1965). *Introduction to Logic and to the Methodology of Deductive Sciences*. Oxford, England: Oxford University Press.

Thayse, A. (ed.) (1988). *From Standard Logic to Logic Programming*. Chichester, England: John Wiley & Sons.

Thayse, A. (ed.) (1989). *From Modal Logic to Deductive Databases.* Chichester, England: John Wiley & Sons.

Topor, R. W., Keddis, T. and Wright, D. W. (1984). 'Deductive database tools'. *Technical Report 84/7*, Department of Computer Science, University of Melbourne, Australia.

Treleaven, P. C. (ed.) (1990). *Parallel Computers.* Chichester, England: John Wiley & Sons.

Ullman, J. D. (1984). *Principles of Database Systems*, 2nd edition. Maryland, USA: Computer Science Press.

Ullman, J. D. (1985). 'Implementation of logical query languages for databases'. *ACM Transactions on Database Systems*, **10**(3), 289–321.

Ullman, J. D. (1989). 'Bottom-up beats top-down for Datalog'. In *Proceedings of the 8th ACM SIGACT-SIGMOD-SIGART Symposium on Principles of Database Systems*, pp. 140–149.

Valduriez, P. and Khoshafian, S. (1988). 'Parallel evaluation of the transitive closure of a database relation'. *International Journal of Parallel Programming*, **17**.

Van Emden, M. H. and Kowalski, R. A. (1976). 'The semantics of predicate logic as a programming language'. *Journal of the Association for Computing Machinery*, **23**(4), pp. 733–742.

Van Gelder, A. (1986). 'A message passing framework for logic query evaluation'. *Proceeding of ACM SIGMOD International Conference on Management of Data* (Washington, D.C., May), pp. 155–165.

Van Gelder, A. (1989). 'The alternating fixpoint of logic programs with negation'. In *Proceedings of the 8th ACM SIGACT-SIGMOD-SIGART Symposium on Principles of Database Systems.*

Van Gelder, A., Ross, K. and Schlipf, J. S. (1988). 'Unfounded sets and well-founded semantics for general logic programs'. In *Proceedings of the 7th ACM SIGACT-SIGMOD-SIGART Symposium on Principles of Database Systems* (Austin, Texas, March), pp. 221–230.

Vieille, L. (1986). 'Recursive axioms in deductive databases: The query/subquery approach'. In *Proceedings of the 1st International Conference on Expert Database Systems* (Charleston, South Carolina, April), pp. 179–194.

Vieille, L. (1988). 'From QSQ to QoSaQ: global optimization of recursive queries'. In *Proceedings of the 2nd International Conference on Expert Database Systems* (Virginia, USA), pp. 421–434.

Vieille, L. (1989). 'Recursive query processing: the power of logic'. *Theoretical Computer Science*, **69**(1), pp. 1–53.

Waugh, K. G., Williams, M. H., Kong, Q., Salvini, S. and Chen, G. (1990). 'Designing SQIRREL: an extended SQL for a dedcutive database system'. *The Computer Journal*, **33**(6).

Weber, W., Stucky, W. and Karszt, J. (1983). 'Integrity checking in database systems'. *Information Systems*, Oxford, England: Pergamon Press, **8**(2), pp. 125–136.

Whitehead, A. N. and Russell, B. (1925–1927). *Principia Mathematica*, 1, 2 & 3, 2nd Edition. Cambridge, England: Cambridge University Press.

Wolfson, O. and Ozeri, A. (1990). 'A new paradigm for parallel and distributed rule-processing'. In *Proceedings of the ACM SIGMOD International Conference on Management of Data* (Atlantic City, NJ, May), pp. 133–142.

Wolfson, O. and Silberschatz, A. (1988). 'Distributed processing of logic programs'. In *Proceedings of the ACM SIGMOD International Conference on Management of Data* (Chicago, Illinois, June), pp. 329–336.

Wos, L., Robinson, G. A. and Carson, D. F. (1968). 'Efficiency and completeness of the set of support strategy in theorem proving'. *Journal of the Association for Computing Machinery*, **12**, pp. 536–541.

Yahya, A. and Henschen, L. J. (1985). 'Deduction in non-Horn databases'. *Journal of Automated Reasoning*, **1**, pp. 141–160.

Symbol index

Subject index